While thoroughly aware of conventional New Testament scholarship, this author brings a challenging and intensely interesting Muslim perspective to the Apostle Paul's claim that Christ brings freedom from religious law. Skilfully drawing out themes that unite and divide members of three monotheistic religions, this commentary is remarkable, provocative, and essential reading.

Paul S. Fiddes, *Professor of Systematic Theology, University of Oxford*

THE NEW TESTAMENT IN MUSLIM EYES

This book explores Christian origins by examining a key New Testament epistle, Paul's letter to the Galatian churches, seen by Christians as the charter of Christian liberty from the inherited Jewish law.

The New Testament in Muslim Eyes provides a close textual commentary on perhaps the earliest declaration of Paul's apostleship and of his undying commitment to the risen Christ. It notes the subtleties of the Greek original against the backdrop of an exciting glimpse of Quranic Arabic parallels and differences. It asks: Does Paul qualify as a prophet of Allah (God)? The thoughts of Paul are assessed by examining his claims against the background of Islam's rival views of Abraham and his legacy. The Arabic Quran framed and inspired the life of the Arab Apostle, Muhammad, who was sent, according to Islam, to all humanity, Jewish and Gentile alike. Pauline themes are set in dialectical tension with the claims of the Quran. Akhtar compares and contrasts the two rival faiths with regard to: the resources of human nature, the salvation of the sinner, and the status of the works of the law. Both Christians and Muslims concur on the need for God's grace, an essential condition of success in the life of faith. The core Pauline Christian doctrine of justification by faith alone is scrutinised and assessed from a variety of non-Christian, especially Islamic, stances.

Providing an Islamic view of Christian origins, this book helps to build bridges between the two religions. It will be a valuable resource to students and scholars of Biblical Studies, Islamic Studies, and the Philosophy of Religion.

Shabbir Akhtar is a research fellow at the Centre for Muslim-Christian Studies and a member of the Faculty of Theology and Religions at the University of Oxford, UK. He is author of *The Quran and the Secular Mind* (Routledge, 2007) and *Islam as Political Religion* (Routledge, 2010).

Routledge Reading the Bible in Islamic Context Series

Series editors: Ida Glaser and Shabbir Akhtar

This series represents an urgent theological initiative for the third millennium: A purposeful interpretation of the Bible in contexts provided by Islam, especially the Quran. Biblical interpretation has affected the development of Western society and continues to be a key determinant of Christian and Jewish action worldwide; and Muslim views of the Bible and of how Jews and Christians interpret it are key determinants of Muslim views of non-Muslims. We therefore expect the series to produce novel perspectives on the continuing religious, political and ideological rivalries which divide the contemporary world as well as fresh insights into biblical texts.

The opening volume features scholarly work from a conference held in Oxford in September 2015 to explore the parameters of this innovative venture. Subsequent monographs explore a range of methodologies and deal with historical and cultural, as well as intertextual, dimensions of the interpretative task. Topics range from an Islamic commentary on a key New Testament epistle, through Christian readings of biblical themes 'in conversation with' the Quran and its interpretations, to historical studies of Muslim engagement with the Bible.

1. Reading the Bible in Islamic Context
Quranic Conversations
Edited by Daniel J. Crowther, Shirin Shafaie, Ida Glaser and Shabbir Akhtar

2. The New Testament in Muslim Eyes
Paul's Letter to the Galatians
Shabbir Akhtar

THE NEW TESTAMENT IN MUSLIM EYES

Paul's Letter to the Galatians

Shabbir Akhtar

Routledge
Taylor & Francis Group
LONDON AND NEW YORK

First published 2018
by Routledge
2 Park Square, Milton Park, Abingdon, Oxon OX14 4RN

and by Routledge
711 Third Avenue, New York, NY 10017

Routledge is an imprint of the Taylor & Francis Group, an informa business

British Library Cataloguing-in-Publication Data
A catalogue record for this book is available from the British Library

Library of Congress Cataloging-in-Publication Data
Names: Akhtar, Shabbir, 1960- author.
Title: The New Testament in Muslim eyes: Paul's letter to the Galatians/
Shabbir Akhtar.
Description: 1 [edition]. | New York: Routledge, 2018. |
Series: Routledge reading the Bible in Islamic context series 2 |
Includes bibliographical references and index.
Identifiers: LCCN 2018000814 | ISBN 9781138213487 (hbk) |
ISBN 9781138213494 (pbk) | ISBN 9781315448282 (ebk)
Subjects: LCSH: Bible. Galatians–Commentaries. | Bible. Galatians–Islamic interpretations.
Classification: LCC BS2685.53.A34 2018 | DDC 227/.406088297–dc23
LC record available at https://lccn.loc.gov/2018000814

ISBN: 978-1-138-21348-7 (hbk)
ISBN: 978-1-138-21349-4 (pbk)
ISBN: 978-1-315-44828-2 (ebk)

Typeset in Bembo
by Sunrise Setting Ltd., Brixham, UK

CONTENTS

INTRODUCTION

Exegesis of a rival scripture can be a concealed form of polemic. Our aim, however, is to enter into St. Paul's mind and present fairly his vision to the Muslim (Gentile) reader. Our exegesis of the Apostle's letter to the Galatians is, therefore, rooted in a critical inquiry into the largest issues at stake: the status, purpose, intentions and alleged limitations of sacred law, the nature of sin and of grace, as understood variously by Jews, Christians and Muslims. It is also an effort in comparative interfaith intellectual encounter, a task with crucial links to the political and diplomatic enterprise of building bridges between the two religious superpowers of our increasingly polarised planet which, for all our talk of globalisation, is ideologically moving further apart as 'ignorant armies clash by night', to apply to our nuclear age Matthew Arnold's prediction about the darkening shadows of the post-Victorian world.

To ask about the place of the law is really and immediately to ask: what final form did Judaism assume in its Christian variant? This agonising struggle to reach its normative climax produced a faith devastatingly pure in motivation, a faith in the all-sufficient grace of Israel's messiah, Jesus Christ. Only such a sincere faith could suit the devastating holiness of a jealous God. This exacting demand inspires an apparently inveterate Christian fascination with Jesus, that unique and comprehensive emblem of a final and incomparable – therefore exclusive – messianic fulfilment. This attachment to Christ Jesus – the reversal is revealing – puzzles and annoys both Jews and Muslims alike, perhaps even for similar reasons.

A Muslim should ask here: what is the cause of the Christian fascination with Muhammad? Answer: the man himself and his Semitic audacity bordering on a psychopathic level of self-assertion and certainty. How many Western Christians are seriously interested primarily in his book, the Quran, which claims to fulfil, Islamic-style, the promise of Abraham, the 'Muslim' iconoclast? Muhammad came with an Arabic Quran which judged as perverse enough core elements of Judaism and

Christianity for most followers of those faiths to reject him. True, the Quran generously concedes and even lauds the divinely guided missions of the prophets who founded those faiths. What does it say of their followers? The Islamic scripture ambiguously compliments Christians: they are morally good people who are doctrinally confused. Its notice of Jews is less ambiguous and much less flattering.

Many Christians retort: Muslims are often good and sincere people whose dogmas are grievously attenuated. Why do they prefer inadequate works of the law to Christ's completely efficacious saving grace? Christian apologists such as the late Bishop Kenneth Cragg (1913–2012) argued strenuously that Muslims wrongly restricted divine action to a *lex divina* delivered by human prophets. Why do Muslims, no doubt unwittingly, deny God's greatness? They shout often enough that indispensable dogma of all monotheisms: 'God is greater!' A truly great God can, if he wills, send his only begotten Son instead of yet another prophet who will be rejected and taunted by sinners.[1]

Two can and have played such games endlessly – and with fatal consequences. Muslims mock Jews and Christians with an analogous rebuke: God's grace is not restricted by or to the envious People of the Book. Why do they not acknowledge that God has favoured a third community, the children of Ishmael (see Q57.29)? Such are the ways of competitive pieties locked in a deadlock – a religious form of rigor mortis.

I

Let me explain my choice of an appropriately ambiguous title for this book. In the New Testament, the 'new testament' refers not to the canonical scripture of Christianity but rather to the new covenant sealed in the blood of Jesus (Luke 22.20). In Paul's letters, this expression means the new (or renewed, that is, post-legal) covenant of Christ's grace. Paul calls himself a minister of this 'new testament' (2 Cor.3.6). Thus, my main title refers both to my assessment of the Christian scripture and of the covenant of grace expounded by Paul. The sub-title, focusing on Paul's Galatian letter, simultaneously exploits and restricts the scope of this fruitful ambiguity. Incidentally, no such ambiguity exists in the word 'Quran' as used in the Quran: in the adjectivally qualified indefinite singular ('an Arabic Quran') or with the definite article, 'the/this Quran', it can only mean the revelation of what subsequently became the Islamic scripture (see Q12.2, 3 respectively).

My commentary on Paul's epistle to the Galatian congregations is a commentary in the Quranic sense of *tafsīr* (see Q25.33) – a defensive or didactic explanation. It is odd to call my effort by this word since it is not a commentary on the Quran but rather on a rival if partly revered scripture that offers competitive claims about human nature and salvation. *Tafsīr* is normally used only of commentary on the Quran although Ibn Rushd (Averroës) used it, somewhat irreverently, to refer to his long commentaries on Aristotle.

The versatile identity of this short letter to the Galatians is as evident in recent academic scholarship as in past exegetical history. Galatians is a manual for Christian witness in a modern pluralist and multi-religious world which is not necessarily more sceptical or more eclectic and varied in thought than the world of the first century Galatian congregations. Admittedly, however, that was a world that did not have to reckon with the virile monotheism of Quranic Islam and its formidable prophet. Nonetheless, Galatians calls for an embrace of persecution for the sake of the Gospel, a call to move beyond the comforts of belonging to a tolerated Judaism within the violent Roman imperium. Paul's indomitable courage, for Christ's sake, is not a disputed thesis even among his many and varied detractors.

Leaving aside Philippians and Philemon, Galatians is Paul's most personal epistle. It answers key questions about his identity while being reticent about some intriguing matters. If we had only this epistle – no material from the Acts of the Apostles, none from Paul's other 'authentic' letters, and no supplements from the deutero-Pauline writings – we would still obtain a profile of this Christian saint. Like the much later epistle to the Philippians, Galatians reflects the unchanging aspects of Paul's volatile personality which endured across his dramatic 'conversion' from Pharisee to follower of Christ: enthusiastic, impulsive, sincere, affectionate, vulnerable, spontaneous, dogmatic and stubbornly pugilistic. For me, Paul resembles Isaiah, Ezekiel and Jeremiah before him: he remained a man of masochistic integrity whose character never essentially altered during his entire active pastoral ministry that ended only with his death.

More of Paul's personal life and religious biography can be extracted from this one short letter than, in the case of Muhammad, from the entire Quran, if we exclude, for the sake of this comparison, Surah 33. Moreover, unlike Galatians, the Quran never offers any chronology, not even a brief one, of Muhammad's life or apostolic career. Muslims sense the Quran's marked indifference to Muhammad's personal life and tragedies and see it as partial evidence of its divine provenance. Some Christians could say that this already betrays something revealingly damaging about the character of his god: a god who rules as sovereign legislator rather than a Lord who seeks loving fellowship with his creatures. As a Maori proverb has it, 'you do not know a man until you know his god.'

Galatians is normative Christianity. Reading it helps modern Christians to understand how Christianity developed the resources to persist as a religious movement – especially when its core values opposed both the outlook of the Roman Empire and some of the key beliefs and practices of its parent faith. Christian apologetics starts earlier than Acts: it begins in Galatians when Paul confronts the senior apostles and argues his case. From this internal dialectic will spring the continuous motivation to argue for the Christian hope and hypothesis in a world not minded to hear the Messiah's message. If we assume that the current slide towards secularism in the West is not so advanced as to be inevitable and irreversible, the volatile intellectual environment and predicament of contemporary Western believers is not dissimilar to that of the Galatian pagans encircled by varied opponents of varied enthusiasms.

II

Paul's letter to the Galatian congregations is too emotional and yet too intellectual for many a modern reader. It is a turbulent epistle, troubling and troubled, dealing with confrontations and agitators galore. This is to be expected: it is probably Paul's earliest letter and one which provided a charter whose directives deracinated the nascent Jesus movement from its parent faith. Whether or not that was Paul's intention is hard to determine. In his later epistle to the Romans, a congregation he did not found, Paul softened his approach to Judaism. Galatians is his most revolutionary epistle, an impulsive and spontaneous manifesto for a radical messianic sect that eventually achieved near-universal expansion. Paul is, I believe, at his most anti-Jewish in Galatians and at his most pro-Jewish in Romans: most anti-Semitic and the most philo-Semitic, respectively, if we smuggle anachronistic vocabulary into Christian origins.

Just as the sudden challenge of the heretic Marcion (c.85–c.160) of Sinope eventually led to the canonisation of the New Testament, a practical crisis in Galatia resulted in the birth of Christianity. It was a crisis, in the Greek sense of a turning point, since Paul decided to take a stance in favour of the gospel of grace only. Like a Henry Newman or G.K. Chesterton, Paul as Christian journalist rather than 'scholarly' theologian, was dealing merely with a concrete crisis: the circumcision of the ethnic Christians. In some Arabian wilderness, on some dark but clear starry night, Paul the nomad saw two roads. Galatians ensured that the Jesus movement would turn decisively outwards in the *ekklēsia* inclusive of the Gentiles. The Galatian crisis of 49 CE, rather than the catastrophe of 66–70 – the destruction of the Jerusalem Temple – ensured the bitter rupture between Judaism and its Christian offspring.

Paul's epistle to the Galatians contains the earliest explicit declaration of his apostleship. This relatively short letter gives us a glimpse of Paul's initial and subsequent mission in Galatia, then a Roman province and now a part of secularised Muslim Turkey. Turkish Christians celebrate him as Aziz Paulus – beloved or exalted Paul. Tarsus lovingly honours his memory with a much-visited church and museum.

On his first journey, using Luke's way of ordering and narrating Paul's Christian life, Paul established assemblies of Gentile Christians who were not obliged to follow Jewish ritual and ceremonial laws. Perhaps owing to changes in policy by the Jerusalem apostles, especially Peter and James, other missionaries from the mother church of Jerusalem visited the Galatian neophytes and caused confusion. Paul felt that they were diluting and adulterating, even contaminating, the pure message of God's free grace in Christ Jesus. Justification is effected through faith alone and the justifier is the risen Christ alone. Christ suffices the Christian.

Paul wrote his seminal letter to rectify a falsely restricted understanding of the scope of the good news. The false teachers, the agitators in Galatia (Gal.1.7), encouraged Gentile believers there to be circumcised as the first step to becoming subject to the whole law. Now, these allegedly sham teachers, armed with their alternative gospel, were also self-professed Christians but not Galatians. Paul writes that he forewarned his Galatian flock about the possibility of such intruders (1.9). There was perhaps one particular false teacher of whom Paul had heard without knowing his name or full identity (5.10).

The false teachers who tried to discredit Paul were claiming to bring Paul's converts to spiritual perfection by making them submit to the Law: the reception and activity of the spirit depended on the converts' conformity to the demands of the Law.

Faith in Christ is insufficient for salvation without supplementary obedience to the whole law. Paul mocks the Galatians when he asks them if they can perfect in the flesh what they started in the spirit (3.3) while exposing the real motive of the sham teachers – namely, to make the Galatians subservient to them (4.17; 6.13).

Paul and probably his opponents both warned the Galatians that circumcision obliges a man to obey the whole law. (Female Galatian converts would be unaffected by the circumcision controversy but the more basic point about the salvific efficacy of the Law was relevant to them too.) Having infiltrated the Galatian assemblies, the agitators nearly convinced the neophytes that they cannot, despite whatever Paul's apparently more lenient version of the gospel promises them, be declared righteous, in God's estimate, without obedience to the whole law. Paul's retort is that the condition of obedience to the whole law is impossible to fulfil since it entails perfect obedience to the whole of a strict, comprehensive and demanding law. Apart from Christ in his human capacity, no one had ever fulfilled that tyrannical and unreasonable condition. The choice reduces to two mutually exclusive ways of being declared righteous: obedience to the Law of Moses or accepting as a gift the grace of Christ. And the former option is not a practicable option, if only the Galatian converts knew. And Paul, the former Pharisee zealous for the Law, knew it all too well. The false teachers were, thundered Paul, misleading the Galatians – and these were foolish enough to believe them.

Never forget that it was Paul, not Peter or the other apostles, who first argued explicitly for the rejection of the single most significant inherited ritual of Judaism, namely circumcision, an emblem of the Law and its works. Paul preached Christ crucified, not Christ circumcised. Sinners crave salvation, not only the gift of divine guidance. Sinners need Christ the Saviour, not another law-bearing messenger from God, since virtue is beyond laws and commandments. This surprises the Muslim reader. But the internal debate, as Christian commentators such as E. P. Sanders famously pointed out, was originally about the distinction between entering into salvation by grace through Jesus and its alternative – staying in the grace of God through obedience to God's law. Both groups concurred that the whole world could enter into the membership of the people of God through the sacrifice of Jesus on the cross – but disagreed concerning how to stay in after the initial entry.[2]

III

In the battle of the baptised versus the circumcised, Paul is the greatest knight of faith. Imagine a Petrine or Jamesian Christianity triumphing instead of the Pauline version. Whether or not one can harmonise these strands of primitive Christianity, their emphasis and tenor undeniably vary. Would a more Judaic Christianity, rooted in James or Peter, have survived the onslaught and intellectual appeal of a confident imperial Islam? The Pauline elements in Christianity distinguished it most sharply from its parent faith. Indeed, it is these distinctive features which safeguarded it against Islam, a faith whose appearance marked the beginning of the end of its greatest rival's tenure in its birthplace in historic Palestine.

Countless Christians see John as the greatest theologian-evangelist. I regard Paul as the first and greatest Christian theologian. If his views are reconstructed and his letters reinterpreted, he disturbs two orthodoxies: that of his inherited Judaism, naturally, but also the Abrahamic faith of the Arabian Apostle to the Gentiles. I explore this competitive role for Paul whose labours were destined to puncture the seventh century Muslim hope of converting the entire globe to Islam. More broadly, inside Christianity, Paul, not Jesus, has been the stimulus for religious revival and reform – although devout Christians and a proportion of scholarly Christians regard Paul as a faithful representative of Jesus Christ's message and teaching. More epistles by Paul than by any other apostle have been chosen for the honour of canonisation, despite the criterion of apostolicity being in reasonable doubt regarding a man who was not an apostle in the standard sense. There could be no more eloquent testimony to Paul's decisive influence on the early church.

Let us suppose you knew Paul and he asked you for a confidential job reference or for a security clearance for a royal visit to his place of work. For vividness, I combine present and narrative past tenses. Paul is not a Jew from the holy land but rather from the diaspora. He was born in Asia Minor, born among Gentiles, perhaps a mystic hint about his later destiny. He was educated in Jerusalem as an interpreter and strict observer of the Torah as understood by the Pharisaic tradition of his zealous forefathers.

Paul does not see his Damascus road experience as a *conversion*, a total or even partial self-conscious rejection of his Jewish past. He calls it a *continuation* of God's action in his life, through the divine *commission* to preach Christ to the Gentiles. His letters hint at this reality; chances are that he would probably dismiss 'conversion' as conveying a rather glamorous and flamboyant impression that many might derive from reading the Acts of the Apostles. Paul was not converted to but rather integrated into messianic Christianity. He feels called to be a Christian missionary but views his previous Jewish lifestyle as blameless under the Law, as would suit someone who was descended of Benjamin, the tribe that gave Israel her first king.

If some enthusiastic journalist were writing a newspaper article or a news bulletin, he or she might write that Paul of Tarsus has today boldly declared that Torah observance was the root obstacle to the spread of a potentially universal Jewish monotheism that was Abraham's legacy to the nations. The Apostle argues that the Mosaic law (Torah) was temporary – limited to its time and purpose. Now, reaching the climax of sacred history, it is finally fulfilled through Christ and thereby transcended and therefore redundant. Judaism has at last become an international and cosmopolitan monotheism centred on belief in a Jewish messiah whose advent works the marvel of salvation for all humanity, including the hitherto excluded Gentiles.

Let me broaden our perspective, away from the vistas of ephemeral journalism. Among founders of universal faiths, only two men have lived and acted under the full light of contemporaneous history: Paul, whose dates of birth and death are not wholly certain, and then Muhammad whose dates of birth and death are not in reasonable dispute. It would be absurd to claim that these two men never existed! They lived and their lives transformed the lives of billions. We do not know enough about Abraham, Moses and Jesus, to assess the extent of their real influence on world history. Although we have four canonical accounts of Jesus' life, much controversy surrounds the end of his life. We know little about the Buddha, the founder of the earliest potentially universal religion. Like Jesus, the dates of his birth and death are disputed, even among Buddhists.

Assuming the veracity of Acts, Paul founded communities: perhaps at least four foundations. Understandably therefore, normative Christian decisions about the scope, purpose and final status of Jewish law within the divine economy, seek Paul's detailed imprimatur rather than merely Jesus' dominical authorisation. Unlike Jesus who wrote nothing, Paul and Muhammad left us literature that can be reliably associated with them. The Apostle left us a corpus of at least seven genuine epistles whose influence is absurdly out of proportion to their length. The Prophet of Islam bequeathed to us a book which, in its original language of incidence, ranks as the world's most recited and liturgically rehearsed scripture. It framed Muhammad's life and inspired him to establish a community, a village-state within Medina, which rapidly expanded into a sizeable empire. The influence of both canons is increasing in today's world. As for Paul's letter to the Galatians, I judge it to be the founding document, 'the Quran' of Christianity and the death warrant for the Torah and Judaism.

IV

If we exclude the Russian land mass, Europe is geographically the least among the traditionally delineated continents. Yet it colonised and evangelised virtually the entire globe. And Paul is, for better or for worse, in my considered judgement, the most influential European. Neither Constantine nor Charlemagne, neither Aristotle nor his pupil Alexander, can compete with the enduringly potent legacy of Paul's life and actions. The Apostle Paul of Tarsus made the Semitic temperament *in religion* part of the European temperament *in general*. Pauline Christianity is the nursery of the European character for some one and a half millennia, the entire lifespan of Muhammadan Islam. Even secularised post-Christian Europeans, especially Marxists and secular liberals, are messianic in outlook: they zealously spread their message to the whole world though many mistake a fashionable Eurocentric cosmopolitanism for an authentic universality, confusing their own local affluence and good fortune for a global condition.

European colonialism owes as much to the Romans as it does to Paul, the first Christian 'colonialist', a description intended to be neutral. I permit the reader to choose to stress either the noun or the adjective. To call Paul a colonialist is not to suggest that he arrived as a conquistador in Philippi, a representative of a colonial Christ. That would be a slanderous absurdity. 'Colonialist' is, nonetheless, not an inappropriate word for a man who plants something, admittedly good and virtuous, but on ideologically foreign soil – even if he does so in humility and meekness and does so merely with his own two hands. Paul would boast only in the Lord. Among his famous admirers, however, the proudly Christian imperialist Rudyard Kipling, proud both of the adjective and of the noun thus qualified, openly boasted in the flesh as he marvelled at the size of Christian Great Britain's universal holdings and dominions on each and every continent.

As for the Arab Apostle, he exerted greater influence on Europe than is ever admitted by virtually any European scholar. Islam was born as a reformed and 'modern' faith. The modernity – the secular practicality and empirical basis – of much of Muhammad's faith is, in my view, the single greatest unacknowledged influence on the formation of modern Europe. Europeans were, typically, at least until the recent past, spared the obligation to cite their intellectual sources – as though the Greeks and Romans owed nothing to the Africans, especially the Egyptians. Islam ended Europe's age of ignorance (*al-jāhiliyya*), its Dark Ages, as Islamic learning provided the major catalyst for the European Renaissance. Muslims preserved and transmitted much of the classical learning of Europe even though they also destroyed parts of this heritage and, in effect, annihilated the North African church. Although Muslim polymaths contributed decisively if informally to the Renaissance, the institutionalisation of science and learning, in the medieval European universities, was largely an indigenous European achievement.

The religion of the Arab Apostle indirectly facilitated European secular modernity – although Muslims see that as a catastrophe for the whole world. Be that as it may, Muhammad remains, in my view, the only non-European who decisively shaped the history of the world's smallest continent with the largest worldwide expansion. I believe that it is mainly prejudice which prevents Europeans from recognising classical Arabic as a European language, albeit one less foundational than Latin and Greek. Since I am not an Arab and indeed reject Arab linguistic imperialism often operating clandestinely inside the universal Islamic *umma*, I offer this judgement, only in the interests of fairness, rather than out of some ulterior race-related motives such as the desire for Arab supremacy and triumphalism.

V

Christianity would not be the world's most widely distributed faith were it not for the dynamic powerhouse of universal European colonialism. Equally, however, had it not been for the trauma of the early Islamic conquests, Eastern Christianity would not have been pulverised – and therefore the Nestorian and other missions would almost certainly have continued to spread the Gospel, peacefully and much more widely. And all this would have happened almost a millennium before the European missionary movements began in earnest! I cannot comment further on this hypothetical claim but, in the meantime, it remains entirely incontestable that Europe was first colonised, for Christianity, by Paul, not by Jesus. Paul has had the greatest influence on the history of Europe, a continent that is by far the mightiest in terms of universal and enduring reach and influence, partly courtesy of colonialism, evangelisation and the efforts of Christian explorers such as Columbus. Equally, were it not for Islam's imperial origins, it would never have become prevalent enough to seriously challenge Christianity. These faiths have competing colonial histories. Muslims concede the need for power as part of the origins of their faith while Christians typically feel religiously obliged to deny the secular truism that all faiths, certainly missionary and imperial ones, survive courtesy of physical and military, rather than only spiritual, power and appeal.

The triumph of Christianity, as a universal faith, has meant that everyone in the modern world, whatever their faith, would have to go west – no matter where they go. Paul is largely responsible for the enduring paradox of an oriental faith's strikingly 'occidental orientation', at least in the early centuries. Some scholars do not use Acts to establish the course of Paul's life since they see Luke as a secondary source. Assuming the veracity of Acts, however, we note that Paul's endeavours were westward ho from Jerusalem to Rome, via Macedonia (Acts 16.6–10). At any rate, globalisation effectively means the Westernisation (and allied Christianization) of the entire globe – while few, Westerners or non-Westerners, even notice this occidental drift. It is the equivalent of a prevalent if not ubiquitous white privilege that is evident in the occidental monopoly, equally unnoticed by Westerners, of major characters in novels and films for universal consumption.

The Galatian churches were the furthest east of any of Paul's foundations, assuming that Paul did not establish churches in Antioch, Arabia and Damascus. This orientation – literally, eastward inclination – is significant for the political history of Europe. Islam's turn from Damascus towards Baghdad, as the caliphate shifted in 762 CE, was a decisive orientation, geographically and politically: Islam would remain oriental and thus inherit none of the republican spirit of classical Greece and Rome. Muslims would be ruled by absolutist caliphs and rulers whose mission would remain essentially eastward ho! Does this perhaps explain the fact that Muslims failed to 'discover' the Americas, a remarkable shortcoming for such a strikingly ambitious imperial faith.

VI

In this section, I shall start to shunt my train of thought onto a different rail as I begin to explore some salient issues of method and analytical technique. In section VII, I explore what it means to write any commentary on scripture. In the final section, I return to the Galatians and state my purpose, intentions and ambitions in writing this particular commentary.

The Bible is read from many and increasingly varied angles. Millions of fundamentalist, evangelical, confessed conservative Christians read it as scripture. Many so-called agnostic and openly non-Christian scholars, academics, professional literary critics and sceptics read its verses with a measure of detachment and historical objectivity, seeing the Bible only as influential literature whose day is past. Countless millions of simple and devout churchgoers, in the global ecumene of their catholic fellowship, proudly sing, in the words of one Southern Bible Belt spiritual, 'Sugar is sweet and my redeemer liveth'. There are yet other believing readers too, the sophisticated believers, rationally alert children of the Enlightenment, too embarrassed even to say grace in a restaurant.

I read the Bible as a Sunni (orthodox) male, as to law a Hanafi, born and raised in Pakistan and then, from the age of ten, raised in the United Kingdom. As to education, I am a philosophically trained scholar of comparative philosophies of religions. While these secular factors may subliminally affect my outlook, my Sunni commitment is certainly decisive. Thus, for example, only Shi'ite (and most mainstream Sufi) perspectives can be expected to evince sympathy, albeit vaguely, for characteristically Christian dimensions of messianic expectation, redemptive suffering, marginalisation and political powerlessness.[3]

Since we all inevitably carry the burden of some presupposition(s) to our reading, there are no agnostic readers of any text, sacred or secular. However, active and sustained awareness of this fact can counteract some prejudices. In any case, a reading nourished by the minimal number of postulates and axioms differs from, and in academic contexts is preferable to, one wholly sustained by some single avowed, intensely felt and robust religious commitment. It is acceptable to make an initial admission of an openly confessional approach so long as this does not compromise the sustained intellectual honesty of the subsequent inquiry. But it is unclear whether anyone can perform this task.

Interpretation is inevitably guided by our prior moral commitments, by the totality of scripture, shared common sense and by the accumulated pressures of contemporary experience. While all interpretation presupposes some assumptions, not all assumptions are arbitrarily made or even arbitrary in their content. Take, for example, the Reformation doctrine of *sola scriptura*, to be discussed in Chapter 2, section X. It is easy enough for Catholics and other hostile critics to dismiss it as an illusion. All scriptures, it is claimed, are interpreted within and by the implicit authority of an existing community and its traditions. But matters are made complex though not intractable when we note the emergence of such an idea inside ecclesiastical history. The setting is political since reverence for an inherited religious context is at best a religious virtue, not a scholarly one.

As a philosopher working in the analytical Cartesian tradition, I would castigate Descartes for his secularised version of *sola scriptura*. His magisterial ambition was to establish Western science solely on the autonomy of individual reason liberated from ecclesiastical strictures. He assumed, incorrectly, that whatever is immediately present to the senses needs no external authority. He forgot that one must still trust in the authority of memory and sense perception – the two sources of experience – and, moreover, in the stability of language as the shared means of communication and therefore an axiomatic social truth. Even the two sources of direct experience are not unmediated or always self-authenticating since deception and self-deception can both subvert them. Nor is scientific inquiry actually grounded in the autonomy of personal reason: it is mediated through the testimony of collaborators. Indeed scientific rationality relies on expert opinion and historical accounts. Social authority is inescapable and fundamental to individual experience, a truth that escaped Descartes as he meditated in the cosy liberal atmosphere of Holland.

VII

Among Christians, though not among Muslims, writing a commentary is usually a veiled way of doing theology or at least of penning a preface to it. A commentary can be simply didactic. One may use a commentary to argue against heresy and to commend orthodoxy. I see exegesis as a branch of the analytical philosophy of revealed religion, as a form of textual dialectic and interrogation. We should distinguish themes from questions. The author's purpose and intention, his or her meaning and implied significance, like that of the law, goes beyond the letter or literal intent of his or her words. For believers, a commentary is a means of making God's word eternally relevant: revealed to one community in history, as it inevitably is, it must be made available to each and every succeeding generation. Whether the correct meaning of the text is to be found solely in the initial authorial intent or in the minds and interpretations of the first audience or in the minds of particular groups of subsequent readers – this matter cannot be settled *ab initio* but rather remains as a standing item that needs to receive attention in varied localised settings.

Writing a commentary on a work must imply some respect for it or its author or both. No sincerely written commentary can be wholly hostile. Many orthodox Muslims were suspicious of the way that Muslim philosophers, especially Avicenna and Averroës, wrote commentaries on human, moreover pagan, authors such as Plato and Aristotle: such an undertaking implied reverence for the superior wisdom of the authors discussed. Now, virtually all commentators on a biblical text are themselves Christian (or Jewish) believers. They regard the text as divine scripture. To respect another faith, however, does not entail endorsing its ideals.

In interfaith inquiry, a non-confessional reading of a scripture, held sacred by one of the two parties, can enable theological insights for both parties. For this, I need not contribute much to the minutiae of existing scholarship on the New Testament but I must be articulate in the tradition. I must locate myself in it to challenge it when appropriate rather than uniformly accommodate myself to it, in the kind of falsely courteous scholarly diffidence and deference that manipulates scholarship into effectively serving some existing, invariably conservative, function while pretending to make novel contributions.

Treating Christianity autonomously means that I accept as valid, in the first instance, the Christian meanings of Christian scripture – for Christians. Moreover, I do not deal with lower biblical criticism (textual studies) but rather with higher biblical criticism which deals with interpretation by encompassing varied dimensions, including historical, literary, source, form and redaction. Form criticism was originally developed for the Hebrew Bible but, in its later application to the New Testament, its aim was to identify authentic Jesus traditions by isolating them from the evangelists' redaction.[4] I regard the New Testament as self-consistent literature supporting Christian faith and conduct. I assume its textual integrity since I work in biblical interpretation, not textual criticism. When noting the few textual variants in manuscripts of Galatians, I merely record the labours of Christian scholars.

In dealing with the New Testament, I restrict myself to higher (interpretive) criticism rather than offer verdicts on lower (textual) criticism. By choosing to study Galatians, I chose a text considered authentic and canonical, and also one not in translation but in the language used by the Apostle. Why? This enables me to shelve the Islamic accusation of *taḥrīf* (distortion) of the Bible. More generally, I also shelve here the Quranic accusation of interpolation (*taḥrīf*), alteration (*tabdīl*) and concealment (*kitmān*), the accusation that Jews and Christians changed and hid parts of their revelations in order to avoid conceding Muhammad's claim to be the last prophet. I shall return to this matter of method in Chapter 9, the epilogue.[5]

VIII

One might call Galatians the *Magna Carta* of Christian liberty, the very constitution of Christianity. It offers freedom from the law, rather than under the law (of the land), to pursue the comparison with the English charter. The Pauline choice between justification by gracious and free faith alone or through works of the law is not addressed in the Islamic scripture. Early Christian history is marked by anxiety about how to enter salvation as opposed to how to stay in that state of grace through continuing discipleship. Virtually all Muslims, no matter how erudite or sympathetic to Christianity, dismiss such issues as Christian over-refinement, at best unnecessary sophistication and at worst convoluted reasoning, similar to other Christian dogmas such as the Trinity. I see it as a complexity arising from a serious attempt to understand God's relationship to humanity and more broadly to understand our common human, all too human, struggle to do good effectively. Naturally, however, I reject the Christian solution to this acknowledged conundrum since I do not think it resolves it.

In the interests of improving Christian-Muslim relations, Muslim readers should seek to understand the subtlety and nuance of Paul's teaching in Galatians and in his other epistles. Otherwise, it is easy to misinterpret complex doctrines and even to slander Christians about ethically relevant matters of the law versus grace debate. It is as easy to deal in caricatures in such matters as in more esoteric matters such as the sophisticated doctrines of Christology, Trinity and the Incarnation. The difference is that the Quran is silent on the law and grace debate and never accuses Christians of being guilty of permissive antinomianism, of exercising excessive Christian liberty in the spirit that the marked 'pneumatic libertarianism' found in some later Pauline charismatic congregations such as the Corinthians. Such charges, unlike the doctrinal ones, are post-Quranic though compatible with the general outlook of the Islamic scripture.

Muslims slander Paul when they assert that he wanted Christians to behave as libertines – literally to do in Rome as the Romans do. In Paul's epistles, we regularly find an appendix containing an ethical epilogue. It furnishes proof of his concern that grace should never deteriorate into licence lest Christ become, God forbid, a minister (*diakonos*) of sin (Gal. 2.17). Christianity introduced high standards of humility and chastity that were novel in the classical world. Paul the pastor helped his flock, especially the former pagans among them, to steer between Jewish legalism and Greek licence.

I want to write with charity and clarity, not evasion and malice. Vilified as Paul the Liar by Muslim apologists, he would regard being vilified for Christ's sake as a privilege and honour (see 1 Pet. 4.12–19). Paul taught that justification is ours solely through the grace of Christ. The believer is called upon to exercise nothing except an effortless, childlike trust in God's promise of salvation and deliverance. This attitude of total trust in God's gracious provision was taught by Jesus too (Matt. 6.25–34). In this regard, at least, Paul was following closely in the footsteps of his Lord.

While distinguishing too sharply between Jesus and Paul betrays an anti-Christian bias, simply identifying the message of the two men is a Christian faith-position.

For nearly one millennium, from the Mu'tazilite judge Abd al-Jabbar (d.1025) and the Andalusian polemicist Ibn Hazm (d.1064) to the martyr-exegete Sayyid Qutb (executed in 1966), Muslim critics of Christian origins have explicitly condemned Paul as the plotter who destroyed monotheism. The two medieval Muslim writers, to use a Western time frame, cursed the Apostle for introducing the deity of Jesus into an otherwise acceptable Christianity while the modern Egyptian activist condemned the zealous ex-Pharisee for inventing the doctrine that Jesus Christ was the Son of God. These are simplistic views, at best caricatures of Christian origins and possibly character assassinations of Paul. These views are not only uncharitable but also lack historical depth: these Islamic thinkers do not even attempt to explain how Christianity, as final consummation of Jewish hopes, was not simply an alien grafting onto some foreign base but rather an organic growth and development of a domestic given. To be fair to the Muslim antagonists, however, it is hard to avoid such accusations if one reads the New Testament evidence solely as a committed Muslim tutored by the Quran – especially if one does not have the joint privilege of proficiency in Hebrew and Greek as languages of Christian genesis.

As a Muslim thinker writing in the twenty-first Christian century, I reassess the Jewish background to Christian origins, in contexts supplied, albeit anachronistically, by Islam and by modern secularism. It is an unparalleled ambition. Its product, if successful, will be an unprecedented new initiative in Pauline studies as we move into Christianity's third and perhaps most precarious millennium in a world defined increasingly by a universal juridical monotheism that rejects the vital essentials of Christian morality, soteriology and ecclesiology as false and misguided.

Notes

1 For a critique of Cragg's view of Islam, see my *Islam as Political Religion* (London: Routledge, 2010) where I give references to Cragg's writings. For a favourable but not uncritical assessment of the Anglican bishop's lifelong achievement, see Christopher Lamb's *A Policy of Hope: Kenneth Cragg and Islam* (London: Melisende, 2014).

2 See E.P. Sanders, *Paul and Palestinian Judaism* (Philadelphia: Fortress, 1977), N.T. Wright, *Paul: In Fresh Perspective* (Minneapolis: Fortress, 2005), and J. Dunn, *The New Perspective on Paul* (Grand Rapids: Eerdmans, 2007).

3 On the final pair of issues, the Shi'ites are not concerned about the theologically original notion of God's voluntary decision to renounce sovereign power for a brief episode nor about the persecution and powerlessness of a faith in its early stages, such as the career of pre-Constantine Christianity. Rather the Shi'ites complain about the forcible Sunni imposition of powerlessness on the Shi'ite minority, an historical imbalance that Shi'ites are currently redressing with remarkable success. But this is hardly a theme with any Christian analogue. For more, see my *Islam as Political Religion* (London: Routledge, 2010).

4 It was applied to the Gospels principally by Karl Ludwig Schmidt, Martin Dibelius and Rudolf Bultmann. See S. Harris, *The New Testament*, 2nd ed. (Mountain View: Mayfield, 1995), p. 70–6.

5 The relevant verses (Q2.41–2, 75; 5.41) employ the verbs associated with the verbal nouns but not the nouns themselves.

1

PREFACE TO THE COMMENTARY

In each chapter of the textual commentary a brief general introduction opens the way to a short commentary on each verse (or a few related verses) of our chosen part of the letter. Sometimes, I merely paraphrase the material under consideration if no commentary is needed. A topic-oriented longer commentary is offered on themes emerging from the *pericopae* being studied. The short commentary consists of aphorisms and brief observations from several perspectives: Christian exegetical, Islamic, agnostic, philosophical and secular humanist. A single verse rarely requires all these perspectives or in this order; I indicate the perspective but it is often self-evident, especially as we proceed further in this inquiry. These somewhat desultory reflections are my *pensées* in the style of Blaise Pascal.[1]

Through these dual commentaries, then, we scrutinise the text while identifying its larger themes of doctrine and ethics and their broader interfaith significance. At the end of each chapter, and especially in Chapter 8, we note the largest issues, many packed with contemporary value. Major themes with modern relevance, mined from the commentary, are initially noted and explored in the textual commentary itself but then run to earth, at the end of each chapter, as we note the contemporary ramifications of these themes. The commentary on Paul's epistle to his disciples in Galatia is sandwiched between the formulation, at one level and the resolution, at another level, of key questions that continue to intrigue us some two millennia after Paul. The very form of this procedure is a tribute to the topicality and enduring relevance of the Apostle's thought.

This is not a typical commentary on Galatians, few of which can any longer lay claim to much originality at this late hour in Christian scholarship. (How much more can we today hope to discover about Paul's letters and life?) My commentary is *sui generis* in terms of omission of themes, choice of themes and format of presentation. I do not systematically survey the views of other commentators although I do refer to the views of some, from Augustine to Luther to Dunn. The bibliography lists some of the commentaries on Galatians and on Acts. Surveying the extensive literature on the New Testament and Galatians and so on enables one to know the state of New Testament scholarship. But an assessment would require one to record and summarise a vast body of literature before assessing it. Instead I have opted to read Galatians, in the broader context supplied by the New Testament, and make direct contact with themes that unite and divide members of the three Near Eastern monotheisms, all of which are potentially universal but in fact respectively ethnic, ethical and juridical, if we define them by dominant emphasis.

The translation of Galatians is my own and it is a wholly literal one. In this way seminal Christian themes are made to confront the text of the Quran, through the human lens of a Muslim thinker. I have also translated the Quran myself and, moreover, endorsed only accepted Sunni interpretations of its claims. For this is the voice of the majority, the inherited normative and orthodox stance of a global community. This is the voice of the mainstream with whom outsiders should seek to engage. The increasingly proliferating views of countless dissident minorities give a distorted and unrepresentative view of original and current Islam. It can be no business of the outsider to encourage or patronise these minority understandings, let alone attempt to make them central.

I

For understanding the message of Paul's letter to the Galatians, one can endorse the conventional tripartite arrangement: roughly two chapters apiece in the sequence these appear in the epistle-sermon itself. I avoid denaturing Paul's thought while presenting and commenting on his letter. Only twice in my commentary do I rearrange the text itself – only to attain greater clarity of presentation. One could alter the arrangement of the entire letter in order to highlight themes with an Islamic dimension. This would be unnecessarily invasive and intrusive. To cite a partial parallel, Muslims resent non-Muslim scholars who rearrange the Quran to suit their own speculative chronology. Like the surahs of the Islamic scripture, Paul's epistles are not arranged chronologically but rather, roughly, in order of decreasing length. Some Muslims even dislike the notion of non-Muslims summarising the Quran and selecting passages for thematic assessment – though I see nothing wrong or malicious in such a procedure.[2]

Chapters 2 and 3 of my commentary cover Gal. 1.1–12 and 1.13–3:5 respectively. The first two chapters of Galatians contain a confessional autobiography. I separate 1.1–12 and read these as an exordium, providing a written preface to key doctrinal concerns of the epistle. I take Paul's apostolic apologia to begin at 1.13 and end at the close of Gal. 2. In Chapter 3 of my commentary, I include my commentary on Gal. 3.1–5, a semi-autobiographical postscript to the apologia, providing Paul's pastoral appendix about the implications of the gospel of grace for the Galatians minded to defect from their initial grace-only stance.

In Chapter 4 (covering Gal. 3.6–4.7), I investigate and assess Paul's arguments, especially his use of scriptural evidence. He juxtaposes the present experience of the spirit's activities among the Galatians with the inherited authority of father Abraham – the believer whose commitment to God demonstrated that faith and its promises precede law and its attendant works.

I perform the first surgery at Chapter 5 of my work where I remove two essentially pastoral portions of the epistle. I scrutinise this pair of pastoral interludes (Gal. 4.8–20 and 5.2–12) in the larger context of a wide-ranging Islamic appraisal of pastoral and practical beliefs and practices that sometimes unite and sometimes divide the trio of Abrahamic monotheisms.

The second rearrangement occurs in Chapter 6 where I treat the concentrated ethical exhortations of Gal. 5.13–26 while discerning the enduring significance of a regrettably influential allegory offered somewhat casually by Paul. It involves some involved scriptural reasoning about Abraham's two sons (Gal. 4.21–31). The allegory highlights the way the spirit-based ethical programme of grace and freedom transcends the ancient covenant based on slavery to the law. The motivation behind the allegory is revealed in Gal. 5.1, a verse best explored here in Chapter 6 where I explain and defend my decision to unite this allegorical material with the preface to the ethical substance of Galatians.

In Chapter 7, I comment on Gal. 6 which contains miscellaneous materials – ethical and pastoral, catechistic and doxological – of course, but also a culminating eschatological and polemical postscript. In the penultimate chapter (8), in an epilogue to the textual commentary, I run to earth the cornucopia of Galatian themes.

Finally, in Chapter 9, I extract lessons from both the letter and the wider spirit of this epistle as I relate my Islamic commentary to the core message of the entire New Testament and 'the new testament' it proclaims. In this panoramic epilogue, I offer a reflection on Paul and Galatians in view of Christian-Muslim relations, the latter captured in a retrospective bifocal glance on their divergent doctrinal origins and their shared future.

II

Students of Paul's epistles are enmeshed in various disputes. There is, for example, no consensus regarding the authorship of Ephesians, its intended recipients, date of composition or even its provenance. Galatians is, however, mysterious for an unusual reason. Though inspired by a known historical occasion, it remains the only authentic epistle for which two specific but competing geographical regions are proposed – making the debate over date of authorship dependent on a decision about the letter's intended geographical destination.

The letter to the Galatians was probably penned some six hundred years before the Caliph Umar walked barefoot into Christian Byzantine Jerusalem to declare it a city under Muslim protection. Nearer its own day, it was written roughly half a dozen years after the start of the Roman conquest of Britain which can be securely dated to 43 CE. I have a special reason for my interest in the precise dating of Galatians. If it is indeed an early work – perhaps completed by the end of 48 or the beginning of 49 CE – this would make it the manifesto of the new Jesus movement.

It is therefore an ideal candidate for an Islamic commentary. Now, Muslims reject Paul's challenging assessment of Jesus but few know that the New Testament is unique among the world's scriptures in being an excellent documentation of the birth of a new world faith. The problem is that we know reliably little or nothing about the central historical figure in this new faith: we know about the movement but not about the man. The scenario for Islam is the opposite. We know a great deal about the life and activities of Muhammad, some facts being even attested in contemporary non-Muslim sources, but the scripture of Islam is, despite being fully contemporaneous with the man who first received it, largely silent about its recipient and his Arab context. The Quran is neither a biography of the Prophet nor an historical account of the emergence and evolution of the new juridical monotheism of the Arab tribes as these engaged in a civil war during Muhammad's lifetime.

Nor is this, incidentally, to endorse a *sceptical* view of Christian origins while opting for a *faith-based* view of the emergence of historical Islam. I believe that an *agnostic* historian would concur with my outlook – though I am here only stating my view rather than arguing for it. I acknowledge that many non-Muslims would challenge if not reject my view that we know reliably little about Jesus but much about Muhammad. They would seek to challenge me on some religious and historical basis. But while I can see motives for their challenge, I see no grounds for it.

Leaving aside such larger Christian-Muslim concerns, we note one crucial point of interest to Muslims who engage with Christian concerns. The text of Galatians is authentic – indeed authentic enough to provide the yardstick for assessing the canonicity of other candidates for Pauline authorship. Apostolicity of authorship, an automatic basis for the grant of canonicity, was the chief criterion for acceptance but, in practice, the ultimate decision involved the reception history of the document. A letter's capacity to instruct and edify supplied a relevant auxiliary consideration. Now, Muslims regard the entire Quran as by definition canonical, there being no apocrypha or disputed surahs and verses, despite the presence of a few occasional but traditionally authorised variant readings – to be found inevitably in any defective pre-vocalised text with only rudimentary consonantal markings. A reliable accompanying oral tradition fixed the correct normative pronunciation while authorising some minor variations. Therefore such readings never substantially alter the sense – although some Shi'ites occasionally point the text differently and dispute the orthodox vocalisation and thus meaning of a few select verses that might have been originally about Ali even though these had, from the start, general application too. Among orthodox Muslims, only the Prophet's traditions are assessed for authenticity in ways resembling Christian judgements about scriptural canonicity.

Paul was the sole author of Galatians though he mentions, as a courtesy, 'all the brothers with me' (1.2). His unnamed amanuensis was a skilled scribe, judging by his small and neat (cursive) letters which contrast with Paul's large and awkward ones (6.11). Paul dictated this letter. Unlike classical poets who, albeit only as a literary convention, formally shared the honour of authorship with the muse, Paul no doubt saw his amanuensis as a scribe with no input into the composition. According to reliable but piously amplified Islamic tradition, Muhammad's amanuenses merely took dictation from his illiterate prophet who repeated divine speech conveyed by Gabriel.

Given the New Testament data, various reconstructions of Paul's life are possible. Apart from Paul's letters, we may use other material, particularly Acts, to organise and reconstruct Paul's life and mission. The second part of Luke's letter to Theophilus, written in about 62–64 CE, is not a history in the post-Enlightenment Western sense of a critical assessment of events but rather a theologised history in which Luke selected, recorded and emphasised certain events, mostly no doubt for ulterior confessional motives. Thus, for all we know, there might have been, say, a dozen missionary journeys! Perhaps Luke did not have the time and space to record all of them. It would be wrong, then, to read Luke as supplying the sole authentic historical setting for Galatians while relegating other materials – such as the two letters to Timothy – to the status of unreliably partisan history. Nonetheless, much in Acts, especially the three accounts of Paul's miraculous conversion and fervent subsequent missionary activity, complements elements of his confessional autobiography first found in Galatians, later confirmed and augmented in the Corinthian correspondence and finally run to earth in Philippians.

Galatians is likely to be one of the peripatetic (travel) epistles written before Paul's first Roman incarceration. It was written from Antioch, destined to become the city of the indomitable martyr-bishop Ignatius of the early second century. Galatians may responsibly be dated to c.49 CE, at the latest, making it Paul's earliest letter. Just before departing on his first missionary journey, Paul (along with Barnabas) went to Jerusalem to bring money for famine relief for the churches in Judaea (Gal. 2.1–2, confirmed at Acts 11.27–30). Galatians was probably written and sent after the visit to Jerusalem to bring money for famine relief and after Paul's return from his first missionary journey. The alternative dating, to 54, would place it far too late in Paul's career as Apostle to the Gentiles. If it were so late, the letter would have been dispatched probably from Ephesus, shortly before Paul wrote his letter to the Romans.

Judging from internal Pauline evidence and from Luke's account, the Galatians were Gentiles. All the Galatian churches, whatever their number, were probably founded at more or less the same time during Paul's first missionary journey. Were these people converts of Galatian ethnic extraction or simply Gentiles who lived in the Roman province of Galatia, regardless of their ethnic identity?

Ultimately, I would judge the southern (provincial) Galatian hypothesis to be true, though not demonstrably so. Fortunately, I am not required to take a stance on this intra-Christian dispute. The epistle then was not written to the ethnic Galatians of the central and northern regions but rather to the Gentile neophytes who inhabited the southern cities located in the Roman province of Galatia. This province was absorbed into Roman dominion in 25 BCE, under Augustus, some 75 years before Paul wrote this epistle. Typically, Paul uses Roman provincial titles when identifying the locations of his foundations. However, he occasionally uses more vague and apolitical designations such as Arabia (Gal. 1.17) and the regions of Syria and Cilicia (1.21).

Two further considerations support the southern Galatian hypothesis. Barnabas, mentioned three times in Galatians, travelled with Paul only during his first missionary journey. Secondly, Timothy is mentioned in all of Paul's genuine letters, except in Galatians. This furnishes strong circumstantial evidence that Paul wrote Galatians before his second missionary journey during which, very early on, he met Timothy who became his protégé. Timothy is mentioned in Acts (16.1–3).

III

Acts records that Barnabas introduced Paul to the apostles in Jerusalem partly because the believers, including those in Damascus, were afraid of this former persecutor of the church. We can correlate key events in Gal. 1–2 with the chronology of Paul's life as given in Acts. Gal. 1.17–19 correlates with Acts 9.23–36. Luke explains that a plot against Paul's life forced him to leave Damascus. Acts 11.27–30 claims that a prophet called Agabus came to Antioch from Jerusalem and predicted a famine that would spread to the whole Roman world. The church in Antioch dispatched Paul and Barnabas to Jerusalem with some charitable donations for famine relief. Paul seems to refer to this event, calling it a revelation (Gal. 2.2), presumably of Jesus, even though it was probably a prophecy of Agabus. Paul and Barnabas go to Jerusalem but, unlike the Apostle himself (see Gal. 2.1), Luke does not mention Titus (see Acts 11.30). Paul and his companions returned to Antioch where Peter later visited them (Gal. 2.11–14).

Gal. 1–2 covers events preceding Paul's inaugural missionary journey, recorded in Acts 13–14. The last event in his own account of his life, which is also mentioned in Acts, is his famine relief visit to Jerusalem, his second visit there – as a follower of Christ Jesus. Paul never calls himself a 'Christian'.

Since the Galatians are the fruit of the Apostle's first journey, he has no reason to mention this journey in a letter to them. I conclude that Paul wrote his epistle to his Galatian disciples after his first missionary journey but before his third visit to Jerusalem to attend the Jerusalem Council (Acts 15). Peter's visit to (Syrian) Antioch probably occurred after Paul's return, to this same Antioch, from his first missionary journey and before he went to Jerusalem for the second time, the aim being to deliver money for famine relief. It is, incidentally, an open question whether or not Peter's visit to Antioch in fact predates the foundation of the Galatian churches. Fortunately, it does not affect any important issues raised in this commentary.

Paul travelled to Pisidian Antioch during his inaugural evangelistic journey (Acts 13.14). Luke records a speech Paul delivered on a Sabbath to a mixed audience of Jews and God-fearing Gentiles in a local synagogue there (Acts 13.15–41). This is Paul's first recorded sermon. He was invited to speak again the following Sabbath but encountered Jewish resistance and therefore vowed to turn to the Gentiles only (Acts 13.44–49). Owing to growing Jewish opposition, Paul and Barnabas left Antioch to go to Iconium (Acts 13.50–52) where Paul preached in the synagogue; his message was confirmed by signs and wonders. We do not know whether this was the occasion when Paul founded the Galatian churches but we do know that many Jews and Gentiles believed (Acts 14.1–4, 15.12).

The threat of persecution soon forced them to leave Iconium, the modern city of Konya now famous for being the burial place of the Muslim mystical poet Jalaluddin

'Rumi' ('The Roman'). Paul and Barnabas travelled on to nearby Lystra and Derbe (Acts 14.5–7) and, in Lystra, Paul healed a man only to find that people wanted to sacrifice to him – thinking he was the god Hermes. Barnabas was mistaken for Zeus (Acts 14.8–18).

This incident, whatever its historical status, sounds like a light touch from Luke and cheers us up temporarily – but trouble was in store for the two missionaries. Jewish opponents from Antioch and Iconium instigated the crowd against Paul and Barnabas. Paul was stoned and dragged out of the city (Acts 14.19–20a). From Lystra, they travelled to Derbe where they preached successfully (Acts 14.20b–21a). On their way back to Syrian Antioch, Paul and his companion passed through Lystra, Iconium and Pisidian Antioch, strengthening the churches in these cities and appointing elders (Acts 14.21b –24). In a deutero-Pauline epistle (2 Tim. 3.11), 'Paul' specifies that he was persecuted in Antioch, Iconium and Lystra.

On his second missionary journey, Luke records that Paul revisited Derbe and Lystra (Acts 16.1a). In Lystra, Paul met Timothy who then travelled with him (Acts 16.1b–5). Paul once cites the Galatians as contributors to his collection project (1 Cor.16.1). Perhaps, Paul visited the Galatian churches even during his third missionary journey to ask for their cooperation (Acts 19.1).

IV

Nothing in Acts prevents us from concluding that Galatians is Paul's earliest epistle, being written in roughly 49 CE, at about the time of the (Syrian) Antioch incident. One senses that this incident is fresh in Paul's mind as he pens this angry epistle. The impending Galatian crisis is a painful reminder of recent events at Antioch. The practical matter of the relationship between Jewish and Gentile Christians, raised in Antioch, has not been resolved. Galatians is the earliest documented attempt to record this friction and to resolve it.

When Paul wrote to the Galatians, he did not mention the decision of the Jerusalem Council because it had not yet convened. If it had, Paul would have quoted its decree since it supported his stance against the false Christian teachers who opposed him in Galatia. Paul and Barnabas were entrusted with a letter to convey the Council's pro-Gentile edict (see Acts 15.22–23, 30–31, 16.4). If the Jerusalem Council had taken place and Paul had omitted this fact in his deliberately comprehensive account of his life thus far – including his visits to Jerusalem as a follower of the risen Christ – then that itself could have been interpreted as a major, if not incriminating, omission. His opponents would have used it to further undermine his already disputed apostolic credentials. This is the most plausible reconstruction of events that may have transpired in a different sequence.

Paul does cite an earlier unofficial decision concerning Gentile converts. It was made by 'those who seemed important' during Paul's second visit to Jerusalem (Gal. 2.1–10). This edict imposes no restrictions on Gentile converts and contrasts starkly with the later and explicit restraints found in the official decree (Acts 15.28–29). The Jerusalem leadership changed its policy and imposed restrictions on Gentile converts more perhaps for the sake of expediency rather than principle – although these two considerations may, for once, have cheerfully coincided.

Peter's hypocrisy regarding table separation in (Syrian) Antioch (Gal. 2.11–14) also occurred before the Jerusalem Council convened. (This confrontation between Paul and Peter is not mentioned in Acts.) Peter's indecision makes sense since the problem of the relationship of Gentile converts to the Law of Moses had not been formally resolved as yet. Perhaps, Peter's visit to Antioch even predated Paul's second Jerusalem visit: even the informal decision had not yet been taken (see Gal. 2.1–10). For our purposes, little hinges on this eventuality, either way.

V

To comprehend the significance of this breach of fellowship between the premier and the last apostles, we must establish provisionally the identity of Paul's opponents and reconstruct the outer parameters of their views. These opponents are dismissed as Judaisers. In the deutero-Pauline writings, Paul's detractors are the Gnostics. Did some belong to both these camps? The only initial caution I must require of the reader is: please do not equate the proponents of the Law in Paul's letter with only Jews or all Jews in general. This is one of the lessons we learn from sympathetic Jewish readings of Paul's letters and indeed from those who uphold the New Perspective on the Apostle. Paul claimed authorisation from the Jewish-Christian leaders, albeit in an ambivalent way. The Apostle's conflicts with other Jewish-Christian missionaries are not always tantamount to conflicts with Jews in general.

Let me comment provisionally here on Paul's general attitude towards his opponents, including Peter. What can we say about Paul's temperament as exhibited in his letter to his Galatian disciples? The letter was written in a combative spirit – controversial and confrontational. To call it 'polemical' is pejorative although Christian origins, like Islamic origins, are reactionary and therefore confrontational, at least in a neutral sense. More charitably, Muslims should salute Paul's uncompromising truthfulness and sincerity. His intention was not to reject or destroy his opponents but rather to save them. Paul respected Peter and the other senior pillar-apostles but he rejected and fought against some of their ideas concerning salvation. This pattern of discerning compassion in Paul's letters resembles and perhaps reflects the concern and care implicit in the teachings of his master, Jesus. One need not be a Christian to notice and applaud such attitudes.

The writings of Paul, Peter and James, though not of the Judaisers, are all canonised in the New Testament. This provides testimony for the ongoing internal disagreements, indeed schisms, within the 'catholic' *ekklēsia*. It is a tribute to the scrupulous honesty of those who recorded the messy details of Christian origins. Christians usually see the canonical inclusion of divergent voices as an attempt to reconcile seminal figures and to recognise varied views as complementary. While this is, in general, true and salutary, it cannot be so in regard to the kind of particularly crucial teaching concerning which Paul confronted Peter.

In any case, it is remarkable that neither Peter nor Paul's teaching on this issue is found in the two letters by (or attributed to) Peter. Presumably, Peter either eventually agreed with Paul and accepted his rebuke and repented of his error. Or, as liberal critical scholars would contend, redactors who compiled (and later canonised) various New Testament writings edited out and reduced the tension between the two apostles, just as the tension between Jesus and John the Baptist seems to have been expertly toned down by the Gospel writers (or redactors).

Let me turn now to Paul's unnamed 'Christian' opponents. According to Acts (15.1, 5, 24), some Jewish Christians in the Jerusalem church, a zealous sub-organisation within the ranks, pontificated that the entire law must be obeyed by both Jews and Gentile converts as a necessary prerequisite for obtaining the eschatological deliverance made available by Christ's death. In the early church, more generally, some believing Pharisees, in sharp contrast to Paul, insisted that all Gentile converts be immediately circumcised and then commanded to observe the whole law as a condition of salvation. Like the pre-Christian Paul, the persecutor who travelled to synagogues in various cities, these law-observant Pharisees travelled to Antioch and tried to persuade the Gentile converts there to adopt their position (see Acts 15.24). The false teachers who infiltrated the Galatian assemblies probably belonged to this group of Jewish Christians. Luke reports that some Jewish-Christian believers were zealous for the Law (Acts 21.20) and were sceptical of Paul's apostolic authority precisely because they had heard reports that he taught Jews, outside of Palestine, to reject obedience to the Law of Moses (Acts 21.20–21).

Paul and the Judaisers concurred that *entry* into the salvation of God was through grace, in the power of the spirit. Paul, however, also saw this as being the sole and sufficient requirement for *maintaining* that state of salvific grace. The Judaisers argued that enduring in the state of salvation required a commitment to legal obedience, a contractual fidelity to the covenant of law. This claim was familiar and dear to Jews.

Why was Paul compelled to seek the approval of the Jerusalem notables, 'those who seemed important' (Gal. 2.2, 6), the pillars (Gal. 2.9)? One reason must be that 'the false brothers' (Gal. 2.4) were undermining his authority by claiming that they truly represented the kerygma of the mother church in the holy city. These sham Christians could have been Paul's opponents inside Jerusalem or perhaps those who plagued his labours later in Galatia, the so-called Judaisers. We shall explore this uncertainty further in the commentary but here note only that Paul did extract from the Jerusalem apostles' an approval of his demand that Gentile believers should not be required to obey the Law of Moses. Thus, Titus, a Gentile, was not forced to have himself circumcised. Since Titus never appears in Acts, we have no independent verification of Paul's claim.

Fairly late in the letter (Gal. 5.2–7), Paul implies that the false teachers were still failing to convince the Galatians to submit to the Abrahamic rite of circumcision. Paul is, however, righteously indignant to hear that even the Galatians had been persuaded to observe those parts of the Jewish law that dictated observance of the festivals punctuating the Jewish religious calendar: Sabbath days, new moon celebrations and perhaps the annual Passover, *Shavuoth* (Pentecost) and *Sukkoth* (Tabernacles). He is angry since this is still seen as a condition of salvation despite the gift of Christ Jesus. Paul sees such observance as honouring Judaic identity markers which symbolise and legitimise Jewish imperialism. In effect, Gentiles must still be Judaized in order to be saved – and that despite Christ. So what was the point of the cross? Did Jesus die in vain? 'May it never be!' We can hear the Apostle's anguished cry across two millennia.

VI

We must read between the lines of Paul's letters to reconstruct his opponents' views. The Apostle's situation differs sharply from Muhammad's encounters with his detractors. The Quran records, albeit laconically, the opponents' views and often registers the strongest versions of the pagan and Jewish reservations about Islamic claims, including mockery of the new faith, before revealing to Muhammad the gravamen of God's rebuttal. The most pungent and caustic exchanges take place between Muhammad and the Arab pagans on the question of the resurrection from the dead and, secondly, between Medinan Jews and Muslims in respect of Jewish claims to have privileged or even wholly exclusive access to God's revelations. We can reconstruct accurately the gossip and slander, spread by the Medinan hypocrites, about Muhammad's sexual conduct. The Quran itself acknowledges it, in its most strident form (Q24.11–23; 33.37; 66.1–5). This material about the Prophet's private life is likely to be based on known facts but in danger of festering into extravagant gossip and rumour.[3] Muhammad was a man who lived in the full light of history. His God did not spare him, recording his human foibles for all to see. Unlike biblical figures such as David, however, Muhammad is blessed with a light reckoning: the Quran never brings in a Nathan to accuse him of anything serious. As the beloved of Allah (*ḥabībullah*), he was always assured of exoneration by his God. Any radical criticism of the Prophet, certainly by Muslims, is therefore forever anathema.

Muslims can, however, well understand the charges brought by the so-called false Christian teachers at Galatia. They must have accused Paul of making Christ, in Paul's version of the gospel, into a minister of sin: freedom from the law must mean, in practice if not in principle, the liberty to act contrary to the law's provisions. Paul's response is fervent, convoluted and woven into the central fabric of the letter (Gal. 2.16–4.31). One distinct strand: by his self-sacrifice on the cross, Christ has rendered forever obsolete the very concept of the holy law. One cannot break a law that has been repealed or made redundant. If the Law is no longer binding, then no one can be a lawbreaker. Paul further fortifies his case by augmenting it: he has died to the law and, moreover, Christ now lives in him. In any case, concludes Paul, looking back at historical precedent, righteousness never came from obedience to the Law since, even before Moses, submission to the law was always insufficient to meet the more rigorous demands of the spirit. Father Abraham's possession of perfect and complete faith, even apart from the works of the law, was meant to teach us that lesson.

The opponents' charge that Paul was seeking to please men (Gal. 1.10) sounds plausible to many readers, especially Muslim readers. After all, Gentiles would be more attracted to a law-free gospel than to a law-observant faith. The latter continuously required constant and unwelcome sacrifices and made unpleasantly exacting practical demands. Muslims often think, with Quranic support, that the reason why Jews and Christians became increasingly unfaithful to their original dogmatic traditions was due to their desire to seek devious escape from the demanding duties imposed on them by God's laws as delivered through his prophets (Q5.57–59). Many professional defenders of Islam preach that Jews and Christians corrupted their scriptures and spread slander about their prophets. Unable to live up to God's high standards, Jews deviously perpetrated a character assassination on their prophets so that Jews could then claim that if even God's spokesmen were not virtuous, then it was absurd of God to demand righteousness of ordinary believers. More narrowly, Muslims are constantly shocked by Christian liberties taken, especially in matters of dietary regulations. It is a two-way traffic. In the past at least, many Christians were amazed and scandalised by Islam's recognition of sexuality as a sacred gift in both worlds. They saw it as concupiscence and blamed it on Muhammad's silken Arabian sensuality.

Paul's *ad hominem* contention is that the false teachers require the Gentile converts to become circumcised submitters to the Mosaic administration in order to avoid persecution for the sake of the cross. Paul's opponents intend to protect Gentile converts from persecution by civil authorities by keeping this new messianic sect within the protective orbit of the parent Jewish faith. Unlike Judaism, the Jesus movement was not even a licit, let alone protected, religion in the Roman Empire. It had to wait until the middle of the fourth century to secure that latter status. Paul accuses his opponents of being cowards for avoiding persecution for the sake of the cross. His bravery, if not his dogmas, must impress even those who vilify him. This is the same Paul who effectively declared 'Jesus is King' when he planted his first church in Europe in Philippi, a Roman city named after King Philip of Macedon. It was an act of subversion. Like his master, Paul was never shy of being subversive, something which can rarely be said of most modern Western European Christians who seem too eager to accommodate their faith to every ephemeral twist and turn of the prevailing secular dance.

VII

I record three literary considerations before returning to thematic issues. Firstly, the genres of evangel and epistle are foreign to Muslims as readers of sacred scripture. The Quran does not contain a biography of Muhammad, let alone four somewhat different biographies. The Islamic scripture's unit of revelation is the surah, containing numbered verses (*ayāt*, pl., lit., signs). A surah is not a chapter in our sense since it contains miscellaneous themes – or, less often, only one – while its title seldom gives a clue to the dominant theme. Like Hebrew scrolls, or papal encyclicals, the title could be a word or words in the first verse or line. Or, unlike Hebrew books, it could be a single occurrence of a strange word – what scholars of Greek call a *hapax legomenon* – which amazed the first audience.

Christian witnesses to the life of Jesus rejected the Greek *bios*, featuring the tragic hero and rejected the Latin *vita*, celebrating typically the life of the triumphant general. Instead they favoured the gospel, a unique literary form developed to express the good news (*euangellion*). Christians claimed that in Jesus they experienced the active holy presence and dramatic disclosure of the moral life of a saving and loving God. This sense of the gospel as gripping reality corresponds not to Muhammad's life (*sīra*) but rather to the recited Quran which is, in the words of the convert Marmaduke Pickthall, 'that inimitable symphony, the very sounds of which move men to tears and ecstasy'.[4]

It is quite likely that the written tradition about Jesus' teaching was, at least initially, in the form of collections of sayings and parables, both moral and apocalyptic. The death of the generation of eyewitnesses became the catalyst for the emergence of a written account of Jesus' life as opposed to merely his teaching. Many Christian writings, including letters, were composed between c.50 and 200 CE. After Marcion of Sinope (84 – c.160), the first important heresiarch, produced his own canon, the desire for official canonisation became steadily irresistible. One should not exaggerate the influence of Marcion in this regard. Our evidence from this period of ecclesiastical history is fragmentary. The anti-Marcionite canon is, as it happens, the most antique statement of canon that has come down to us. A consensus about the final canon is discernible in the quotations of orthodox writers contemporary with Marcion.

The letter is a personal, practical and thus pastoral form of communication.[5] But letters as vehicles for divine revelation, as scripture, are unique to Christianity. Apart from the four gospels, all the books of the New Testament, including Acts, are, at least theoretically, epistles. Indeed, even Luke's gospel is structurally an epistle. The last book of the entire Bible, Revelation, is a letter and, moreover, contains seven short epistles from Jesus to the churches in Asia Minor. Admittedly, given its pace, Galatians reads more like a telegram. In the classical world, we find epistolary parallels only to Paul's shortest epistle (Philemon) and to his medium length letters such as his first letter to the Thessalonians. See for example the *Letter of Isaias to Hephaestion*.[6]

Several Christian writers, including Polycarp of Smyrna (c.69–155 CE), the earliest Apostolic Father, wrote important epistles not canonised in the New Testament. Polycarp was, unlike Paul, a Gentile convert. In his letter of fourteen chapters, sent to the Philippians, Polycarp quotes or paraphrases from the whole of what would become the canon of the New Testament. Polycarp admired Paul for his wisdom and courage and quotes the Apostle in his own letter to the Philippians and also refers to Paul's epistle to the same destination. Polycarp paraphrases Phil. 2.10 in the second chapter of his own epistle. In the fifth chapter of his letter, he quotes directly from Gal. 6.7 ('God is not mocked') and in his third chapter quotes the phrase 'the mother of us all' (Gal. 4.26).

In the Jewish Bible, we find short letters, for example regarding Jewish requests answered by royal decrees (see Ezra 4.7–24; 5.6–17). Jeremiah's letter to the exiles (Jer. 29) is also preserved. Such epistolary efforts are never used to convey doctrine. The art of letter writing is not characteristic of Jewish sacred literature. For modern writers, as a record of their lives, posthumously published letters rest midway between their autobiographies and their literary publications (such as novels and poems).

A practical question: how were messages conveyed? Paul must have known about the imperial postal service for the exclusive use of Roman officials and the military bureaucracy. Both the sender and the recipient had to pay the soldier or sailor who delivered the letter, to motivate completion of the delivery. Arabia had no postal service in Muhammad's day although messages could be sent via trusted messengers travelling from oasis to oasis. Apart from poetry, messages were rarely written down. It seems incredible that Muhammad and his caliphs managed to unite the feuding tribes, scattered in a mini-sub-continental peninsula, into a unified force that subsequently defeated two empires – and all without the facilities of mass communication. No wonder Muslims discern God's invisible hand directing his last and most formidable prophet, a mere man but one who was *sine rivali*.

Christian Arabs use *risāla* to translate 'epistle' although the root word means any message, commission or deputation, independently of its literary genre. It includes the epistolary format. In modern Arabic, a news correspondent is called a *murāsil*. In Arab Christian apologetics, the *risāla* is an apology for a doctrinal position, especially in the context of high-level public debate. We have some 60 extant letters from Timothy I, the Nestorian Patriarch of Baghdad who was in post from 780–832 CE. His *The Apology of Timothy the Patriarch* was delivered in the presence of the Caliph Mahdi, the third Abbasid caliph. It was intended to stimulate dialogue between Muslim religious scholars and the Christian subjects of the Islamic polity.

The Quran uses *risāla* to mean oracle or prophetic message (7.79; *risālāt* pl. at Q33.39). The word shares its root with *rasūl,* meaning messenger, human or angelic. The Quran contains no letter but mentions a diplomatic memorandum (*kitāb*), the classical Arabic word for any written communication. It is sent by Solomon to the unnamed Queen of Sheba and it opens with the Invocation which is used to open all but Surah 9 of the Quran: 'In the name of God, most merciful, most compassionate' (Q27.28). The less literary word for letter (*khaṭ*; lit. transcription) occurs in a verbal form (Q29.48) while *khiṭāb* (address; Q38.23) is used to emphasise that one is *addressing* a generic communication, oral or written, to someone. According to Ibn Isḥāq, Muhammad dictated short letters (*kitāba*) to neighbouring rulers, inviting them to embrace Islam. Most rejected this peaceful offer and opted for armed conflict with the armies of the infant faith.[7]

The letter as a treatise or apology for a religious position is not native to Arab culture. Later tradition offers the quasi-epistolary tracts of the Brethren of Purity (*Ikhwān al-Ṣafā*). Known as *The Epistles* (*Rasā'il*), these 52 treatises were penned by anonymous Ismaili writers active in the 4th Islamic/10th Christian century. The material is part of an encyclopaedia dealing with science, philosophy and numerical symbolism. Equally famous is the *Epistle* of Abu Uthman Al-Jahiz (160–225 AH/ 776–868 CE). This regrettably well-known work defends singing girls and their rich owners, hardly a central Islamic theme.

The letter is more popular in Iranian and Indian sub-continental Islamic cultures than in Arab culture. It denotes the notion of any message, *payghām* in Farsi, addressed and dispatched to someone. The Iranian activist, Ali Shariati, the ideological architect of the Iranian revolution, wrote letters from prison, addressed to his daughter. The collection of the fourth caliph Ali's sermons, *Nahj Al-Balāgha (The Summit of Eloquence)* also contains various letters written by him. This work is revered by Shi'ites, particularly from Iran and the Indian sub-continent, but it is originally part of an *Arab* sectarian tradition. Finally, the collections of legal verdicts (*fātāwa*, pl. of *fatwā*) of Shi'ite jurists are often called *Rasā'il* while the famous *Al-Risāla* of the Sunni jurist Al-Shafi'i is really a legal compendium!

While the 'letter from prison' or captivity epistle is rare, the idea of writing lengthy political tracts, even a commentary on scripture, is a staple of Muslim radicals who often languish in lonely cells, an environment that testifies to their piety. One may argue that if they suffer for Islam, then they must be the true Muslims. Are many of their so-called moderate Muslim detractors merely sycophants who posture a lot, some even pretending to plot a revolution from the safety of their spacious studio apartments in London, Paris or Ottawa? Ordinary Muslims are suspicious of professional Muslims who suffer little for their faith but spend much time behind the anonymous security of social media, in conference halls and television studios. Muslims are bound to admire Paul's courage and willingness to embrace the deprivations of prison and to learn to be contented and joyful under all circumstances.

VIII

Jews and Christians have translated the Quran while, naturally, rejecting its inspiration as divine.[8] No Muslim has ever translated the Hebrew Bible from its original language or translated any gospel or epistle from the original Greek of the New Testament. Some prominent Muslims, such as Sir Sayyid Ahmad Khan, and some Muslim converts to Christianity, may have assisted in Bible translations, but there is no reason to think that they acquired, let alone mastered, the relevant biblical languages. Only Christians (and occasionally a Jew or an agnostic) translate the biblical scriptures while usually it is Arab Christians who translate these into Arabic. No Muslim has published a translation of any Pauline epistle, let alone written a commentary on it.

It is rumoured that parts of the Gospels were rendered into Persian by a sixteenth century Shi'ite scholar, Khatun Abadi. Nothing is known of him. There is no reason to suppose that he translated them from the original Greek. An earlier Persian scholar, however, Al-Biruni, wrote a pioneering treatise on India, *Kitāb Al-Hind*, for which he acquired Sanskrit, in order to translate the ancient Hindu scriptures. While the odd Muslim scholar, such as the Palestinian activist Ismail Al-Faruqi, acquired some competence in Hebrew, a language related to Arabic, none has equipped himself with a knowledge of Aristotle's mother tongue. Early Muslim polymaths were typically either monolingual (Arabic only) or bilingual (Persian and Arabic) but they savoured the treasures of the multilingual scholarship enabled by translations of Greek and Syriac masterpieces into Arabic. This is part of a more general limitation in Muslim intellectual culture in its relationship to the European West. Even seminal Muslim thinkers, such as Abu Hamid Al-Ghazzali and his philosophical opponent Ibn Rushd (Averroës), did not enjoy the privilege of Greek.[9] They relied on

Arabic translations of Greek texts made available by Arab Christian subjects of the Islamic state.[10]

Turning to more controversial matters, the findings of linguistic and philological scholarship, preliminary to translation, can either deepen a devotional reading of scripture or distract from it – or even undermine it. In Christian dogmatics, more than in Islamic thought, theological issues are concealed in apparently merely linguistic issues of translation. One notorious example here is furnished by decisions about how to translate and employ *ibn Allah*, son of God, without implying physical consanguinity. Sometimes a linguistic peculiarity conceals a larger theological motivation, as we shall see in expounding Gal. 6.7 (see Chapter 7, section III). We note that *theos* appears without the definite article, a possibility grammatically vetoed in the case of '*Allah*' which already contains the definite article.

A translation is often a 'trans-creation' or collaboration between author and translator. My translation of Galatians is maximally literal, divesting the original text of accumulated dogmatic accretions and received associations. The translation is idiomatic only where the original is either too elliptical to bear any literal sense that remains doctrinally or liturgically meaningful, or where literal translation is lexically wholly unintelligible. In this comparative exegetical study, I note nuances of Greek and Arabic vocabulary and grammar that should also interest Muslims and Arab Christians.

The common Greek (*he koinē dialektos*) corresponds to colloquial Arabic (*'ammiyya*). In the papyri, the para-literature of the New Testament era, we find private letters but also public records ranging from census and tax returns to marital and trade contracts. This material clarifies the workings of demotic Greek. In terms of range, we find no pre-Islamic Arabic prose equivalent of the *koinē* papyri.

Unlike the New Testament, the Quran claims to base its credentials on the supremacy of its literary classical taste. This claim is hard to assess since *classical* Arabic simply *is* Quranic Arabic. The complimentary epithet 'classical' normally refers to a canon of works but, in the case of Arabic, the canon is only the Quran. By definition, therefore, the Quran cannot be judged defective since it sets the rules of grammatical propriety. In the whole of Arabic literature, the Quran alone uses words with other than their normal meanings, sometimes even with the opposite of their normal meanings – but who can dispute God's eccentric style! Unlike the English of Chaucer and Shakespeare and the King James Bible, the language of the Quran is a living one that is continuous with the Arabic of the seventh century. Even literary *modern* Arabic is essentially reformed and simplified Quranic Arabic, the latter still being the sole basis of modern Arabic grammar, used in the speech and writings of Arab peoples of all faiths living in the Middle East.

Even those Westerners who know Arabic have rarely appreciated the Quran's superb aesthetic taste: it is hard to appreciate the purely literary merits of a book which attacks one's core convictions with such sustained incisiveness, clarity and confidence. No claim of linguistic excellence is made on behalf of the *koinē* Greek of the New Testament – although Luke's gospel is written in diction that approaches classical excellence. The philosopher-classicist Nietzsche joked tellingly: 'How clever of God to learn Greek when he wanted to become an author – and equally how clever of him not to learn it any better.'[11] Ironically, pre-Islamic Arabic and pre-Christian (classical) Greek employed a far greater range of vocabulary than that found respectively in the Quran and the New Testament.

The Quran claims that there was no previous scripture revealed in Arabic, a deficiency rectified by its descent. The previous revelations – the Torah, the Gospel and the Psalms – did not exist, it seems, in Arabic translation.[12] The Torah in Arabic would have amounted to an Arabic scripture albeit in translation. Being in a closely related Semitic language, it would have amounted to a quasi-Arabic scripture pre-dating the *de jure* Arabic Quran. In a rare racial joke, the Quran muses about the possibility of 'a foreign recital' (*qurānan a'jamiyyan*), most likely intending a Persian *qurān* (see commentaries on Q41.44). And how that would have pleased the Persians – some of whom perhaps feel puzzled that God should have chosen the Arabs rather than the more literate Persians for that honour!

One fruitful debate in this field – useful rather than merely amusing to experts – centres around whether or not the presence of a translation of the Bible into Arabic in Muhammad's day would have influenced the Quran's vocabulary, perhaps even inhibited the rise of a new faith bearing a *sui generis* scripture. No such translation was available, a striking failure for a missionary faith. Had the Bible been available in Arabic translation, in Muhammad's time, there could have been perhaps some borrowing of nomenclature. As it is, words such as *Al-Taura* and *Al-Injīl* need not carry their biblical or Christian import and meaning, since these are simply proper nouns transliterated into Arabic. *Al-Injīl* and *Al-Taura* lack native (Arabic) root meanings while Quran, an Arabic word, means recital. It is unclear whether the Quran would endorse the original Greek and Hebrew meanings of the proper nouns *Al-Injīl* and *Al-Taura*.

The Quran has countless neologisms while Paul's vocabulary is largely inherited from the Septuagint. The New Testament Christianized a word such as *hupokritēs* and assigned moral weight to it when it originally merely meant an actor wearing a mask. Paul places an indelible imprint on a phrase such as 'the grace of our Lord Jesus Christ' (Gal. 6.18) and uses some form of it or other so often that Christians have become inured to its novelty. Christ's grace must mean the free gift of his love for sinners as he gave himself up for their sake (see Gal. 1.4; 2.20–21). Muslims associate grace (*faḍl*) mainly with God, rarely with Muhammad or other prophets. The word is, however, both as noun and verb, in wide cultural usage, often associated with human courtesy. It differs in content from the robustly Christian theological import of grace as synonymous with salvation – a radical redemption from sin. The Islamic notion of grace resembles the Jewish conception of a state of divine blessing.

The New Testament contains few genuine neologisms. Paul uses *pistis* (faith), a word found in the Septuagint and in Greek literature in general where it can mean faith in Caesar. By contrast, the Quran's central vocabulary consists of neologisms and old words given entirely novel meanings. *Īmān*, *shirk*, *kufr*, even *Allāh* – respectively meaning faith, idolatry, disbelief and the one God – were recruited and then invested with exhaustively Islamic significances. Thus, *īmān* cannot denote faith in any reality except God. This is the reason why Arabic remains a devotional language in which it is awkward if not impossible to appeal to an underlying secular or pagan meaning.

This makes it hard for Muslims to joke about Islam, to be cynical about it by denigrating religious words or mocking the attitudes thus denoted. It is not in vain that the Quran, as many a modern Arab poet laments, strangled forever the possibility of an outstanding secular poetic canon of the Arabic language. Only Christian Arabs and secularised Arabs of Muslim background dabble in poetry – and their art is invariably imitative of Western existentialist angst and despair.

IX

Let me make a general point about the uses of eloquence before I offer a panoramic view of the Greek and Arabic languages. The basis of oratory, the art of public speaking, is the need to persuade others of views that are at first sight unacceptable. It presupposes the disunity, indeed divisiveness, of the human race. If all human beings shared a single vision of the world, oratory and rhetoric would be neither possible nor desirable. Only the presence of a dissident constituency explains the emergence of persuasive speech. The existence of the politico-literary arts of oratory and rhetoric confirms our intuition that we are political beings, capable of managing intelligent dissent, and in need of communal cohesion and persuasion. Paul seeks to persuade us to reject the views of his enemies who used scripture to argue against his presentation of the Gospel of Christ.[13] The Quran claims that humankind was originally one community but, mysteriously, God did not will for us to remain a single solidarity (Q2.213). The Quran has no equivalent of the Bible's Babel narrative or its reversal in the linguistic miracle of Pentecost. Like Paul (1 Cor.2.1–5), the Quran rejects manipulative eloquence, and both rejected magic and gilded speech that deceives (Q6.112), the sophistry of the ancients.

Rhetoric and sophistry were the innocent arts of pre-ideological ages, the purer and more sincere half of our history, when conquerors did not disguise their intentions but rather proudly proclaimed them. Those were ages of enthusiasm and idealism. Their fanaticism was merely about different matters. What would the ancients make of propaganda and the ubiquitous advertising for rubbish that engulfs us – and leads astray even the religious elect who have, despite their rhetorical condemnation of it, bought into the prevalent commercialisation and consumerism that necessarily requires an ever-evolving technology subject to built-in obsolescence?

This is the crucial question that we moderns forget to ask. Posing it makes us wonder whether the ancient and proud races, in Tennyson's phrase, were as primitive as our vanity leads us to imagine. This is not to seek to reverse the Enlightenment, only to wonder whether we have any ideals worth striving for, any heroes worth emulating. Is the passion of the New Testament and the Arabic Quran incapable of moving our mountains of doubt and hesitation?

X

I comment now on miscellaneous matters of grammar, syntax and lexical-rhetorical features of general relevance. It will give a flavour of the full dish. Specific instances and details are found in the textual commentary. But this survey shall prepare the reader who wishes to discern subtleties of the Greek text. The claims made here about the comparative merits and demerits of Greek and Arabic (and of some other Islamic languages) are my own observations.

As with other Semitic languages, Arabic verbs are based on the trilateral root as opposed to the bilateral roots of Hamitic languages. Arabic is an action-oriented, verb-loving language similar in this regard to Greek which is an 'active participle-loving' language. Arabic has no present tense of the verb 'to be', making for great concision in its key doctrines about God. There is a tense for expressing past existence, also used as an auxiliary verb (*kāna* and her sisters). The verb is strictly for denoting action. Thus, Arabic vetoes the verb 'to have' since possession is not an action. Possession is expressed by prepositions, both formal (with; *'inda*) and informal (to; *la*). In the commentary, I note these prepositions and their Greek analogues.

Greek is more sensitive to time, duration and the status of an action and its consequences. Thus, the Quran's active participial and verbal forms often correspond to English nouns: idolaters are those who idolised (*alladhīna ashrakū*) while Jews are those who Judaicised (*alladhīna hādū*). Like Greek, Arabic has active and passive participles but these are not equivalent to present and past participles since Arabic has no tenses as such. Thus an active participle does not necessarily denote activity in the present but rather emphasises that the agent is known.

Greek has many past tenses all equipped with a sense of time. Semitic languages use verbs with a sense of verbal aspect, not tense: aspect describes a category of verbal inflections that express certain temporal features, including continuity, repetition, completeness and the punctiliar (instantaneous) nature of the action described. In this way, Semitic languages have only three aspects but these can refer to different time periods. Thus the prophetic perfect can be used as a future tense at a discrete future moment (e.g. *qadayto*, I fulfilled, meaning: I shall fulfil; Q28.28). The future in Greek and in Arabic can express actions yet to happen (the so-called punctilinear future), actions that commence now and continue into the future (linear future), for example as in 'they shall abide therein forever' (*wa hum fīhā khalidūn*; Q2.25). Both Arabic and Greek can accommodate the aphoristic future (e.g. what a man sows, he shall reap) and volitional future regarding wishes and commands yet to be issued.

Arabic and Hebrew, unlike Greek, possess a rudimentary future tense which reflects a particular view of prophetic action and a theocentric model of history, making all history sacred, that is, atemporal, since events occur *sub species transcendentia*. Hence, it is permissible to use the prophetic perfect (past) to denote future events (see Q23.1), a feature that complicates the exegesis of apocalyptic books such as Daniel. The Quran contains no formal surah of apocalypse, only past prophecy and the threat of the end-times that herald cosmic death, universal resurrection and human judgement. Though the threatened Day of Judgement seems deceptively imminent (Q54.1), no one knows the time of the final hour which shall come suddenly. Only the wise can read the signs that shall attend it (Q22.1–2; 47.18).

The Greek aorist (unlimited) is a tense of the verb which indicates past action without offering comment on whether it was momentary or continuous. It is used to describe punctilinear action that happened at a discrete (non-extended) moment in the past, a definite, particular and known point of time. It is the tense that does not deal with actions that are imperfect – durative, progressive and continuous – whether in the present, the past or future. Arabic has no aorist tense but it has verbal aspect to accommodate it. Some Islamic languages, notably Turkish, use a grammatical aorist as one of two *present* tenses. Classical Persian (Farsi) employs a gnomic aorist – used for expressing proverbial wisdom transcending time and place.

Arabic has only perfect (completed) and imperfect (incomplete) action. The perfect (or past) tense of the third personal singular (for example, he said) is the standard form of the verb and is used to locate it in a dictionary. The perfect uses the entire verbal root as a stem and augments only the ending to indicate different persons, incorporating gender and number, including dual masculine and dual feminine. The present uses the stem and modifies it with both prefixes and suffixes to indicate the same. Though in some ways much simpler than Greek, the system of verbal conjugation requires alert attention especially when speaking. Even after several years of study, few students of Arabic can speak correctly a single sentence, except perhaps a memorised Islamic quotation!

The future tense and imperative mood are modifications of the imperfect, implying incomplete action. Semitic languages are deficient in tenses and, unlike in Indo-European languages, even the tenses that exist do not denote precise temporal significance. The Quran takes liberties with tenses, being a work of prophetic literature. Greek is marked by a high regard for temporal precision, a feature reflected in the minutiae of New Testament exegesis in all the many epochs of devout as well as religiously uncommitted scholarly industry.

The Greek tense system has idiosyncratic and possibly *sui generis* features. Its main perfect tense, however, shares important features with a perfect tense found in one important language of Islamic scholarship, namely Persian, which similarly restricts it for completed action whose effects are, or continue to be, felt in the present. Apart from inspiring scholarly interest, this feature is relevant to translations of the New Testament (though not the Quran) into this important language of Islamic scholarship.

Continuing with matters temporal, the Arabic conjunction *wa* (and) is indifferent to time. The inseparable conjunction *fa-* (and so) often implies cause and effect and carries a sequential component while *thumma* (and then) is used only as a temporal conjunction and always indicates a later time. In fact, *thumma* is an obsolete classical adverb which functions as a conjunction. The Quran uses it, for instance, to indicate the stages of the embryo's growth (Q22.5; 23.14). We do not find the phrase 'those who have believed and then (*thumma*) did good works.'[14] The Quran never uses the conjunction *fa-* in this context but invariably employs the simple *wa,* a conjunction similar to Hebrew, but without the latter's peculiar power to alter completed (past tense) to uncompleted (present indicative) and vice versa.

If we exclude the vocative case, Arabic nouns have only three case endings, two fewer than the five of *koinē* Greek. Turkish, Russian and other highly inflected languages such as Attic Greek, the most prestigious dialect of ancient Greek, have at least six cases; classical Greek can have up to eight. Arabic nouns are, however, singular and dual before becoming plural. Unlike Greek, English, German and Swedish, Arabic has no neuter (it) for nouns, only masculine and feminine. This causes confusion about the referent of the masculine pronoun *hu* which can be translated as 'he' but also as 'it' in several important Quranic verses, some relevant to interfaith concerns, including Jesus' place in eschatology (Q2.146; 36.69; 43.61).

As in Greek, adjectives can be nouns: the two are not sharply distinguished. There are no adverbs but the accusative case of the noun is best understood as the 'adverbial' case. The action of a verb is modified by an adverbial clause. Thus, for example, 'he hit him with a hard hitting', is a frequent type of construction in the Quran.

The Greek infinitive is a verbal noun. Though not declined, it has at least four forms and takes a quasi-subject (a word in the accusative). It possesses aspect (including the aorist) but no tense. In Paul's letters, see, for example, his theologically significant use of *basileuein* (reigning; pres. act. inf.; 1 Cor.15.25). Arabic has no infinitive but has several verbal nouns, each called a *masdar* (lit. source). These are associated with a different form of the simple verb. An Arabic infinitive functions like a gerund in English.

XI

Unlike both testaments of the Bible, the Quran has, both absolutely and as a proportion of an admittedly much shorter text, virtually no verbatim repetition. But the Islamic scripture would be about two-thirds of its actual size if we excised thematic repetition. However, unlike the dull and prosaic translations of the Quran, the entire original is embellished, displaying an astonishing variety of rhetoric and technique, memorable and memorised by countless millions. In the Quran, word sequence is dictated by the requirements of metre and for musical effect.

Literary elegance and rhetoric also adorn Paul's presentation of themes that are otherwise as arid as the Sinai desert in the Western poets' imagination. Paul uses *expolitio*, a figure of speech where the writer repeats, in greater detail, the same point or argument in alternative but equivalent terms. The Latin *expolitio* (embellishment or refinement), like the *exergasia* (Greek for parallelism) in Greek rhetoric, differs from literal repetition. Rather, thematic repetition is used to express the same idea in different words: typically, the doubling of the thought, through word change, often amounts roughly to a prosaic analogue of parallelism, a popular feature of Hebrew poetry, a feature defined by its own precise rules involving related Semitic, including Ugaritic, versification. We see some evidence of Paul's Hebrew education in his use of techniques involving variant and stylised repetition, reminiscent of the parallelism prevalent in Hebrew poetics. Paul also uses the *epistrophē*, literal repetition, at the end of a sentence or phrase. 'When I was a child. . .' where 'child' occurs four times (1 Cor.13.11).

We can discern in Paul traces of the diatribe, in the original Latin sense of *diatriba*, meaning a learned debate or, as inherited from the Greeks, an intellectual pastime. This technique of oral rhetoric was popular with the Greek Stoics and the Latin

Cynics. We may interpret any rhetorical question as a mild form of diatribe – both in the original neutral sense and in our modern negative sense of oratory aiming at denunciation of an opponent. If so, Paul uses this technique throughout Galatians (see 1.10; 2.14, 17; 3.1–5, 19, 21; 4.9, 15–16, 21, 30; 5.7, 11) – except in the final chapter. In a related technique, the interlocutor, who was not necessarily the hero, pretended that he was having a dialogue with an imaginary opponent, usually a fool (James 2.20; Luke 12.20) or even with one's own unwise self (*psuchē*; Luke 12.19 in the *pericopē* 12.16–21). It is found in Epictetus, a philosopher of the first century, a contemporary of Paul. The Quran has countless passages of dialogue and, in our modern sense of plain denunciation, plenty of diatribe. Shakespeare's soliloquies, addressed to a theatrical audience, afford the closest secular parallel from early modern Western literature.

In the absence of formal punctuation, some Greek words (such as *kai* and *alla* meaning 'and' and 'but' respectively), placed at the beginning and end of any clause, whether coordinate, subordinate or main, effectively functioned as clause markers. Words placed at the extremities, however, normally also carry maximal emphasis. The final placing is for effect similar to the comedic punchline which defers the surprise. Note the juxtaposition of 'something' and 'nothing' (Gal. 6.3) for stress. Arabic achieves emphasis through addition of particles (as in the 'energetic moods') rather than through final or initial location.[15] In ornate styles of reciting the Quran, reciters surprise and delight the audience by placing unexpected emphasis on a syllable, just as they use the more routine method of nasalised stress, often additionally employing the high pitch of an energetic voice–reaching crescendo before falling to a closing low. Owing to fear of offending the *'aẓm* (dignity) of God's speech, no instrument can accompany the human voice which alone must embellish the divine speech. Forms of oral emphasis are thus, in the Quran's case, the most important part of a limited repertoire.

Paul's words were initially formally read out aloud to congregations. The relatively new field of performance criticism examines the recitation of parts of the Bible in order to achieve dramatic impact. Usually the New Testament, and most often the gospels, are being thus scrutinised. There is much less study of specifically Pauline letters. By contrast, armies of experts explore Shakespeare's plays as performed on stage during the dramatist's own age and up to this day. Traditional text-based assessment, a feature of scriptural exegesis, is here eclipsed by the secular concern with theatrical performance and dramatic effect. It shows yet again how modern Western literary emphasis eclipses the concern with the primarily didactic impact of sacred literature. The latter guides conduct morally rather than merely entertaining us aesthetically.

XII

Regarding terminology, I avoid three overly used words and expressions: 'methodological' when it means method, 'hermeneutics' when it means interpretation as opposed to self-consciously intellectual processes of sustained reflection about such interpretation, and 'theology of X' which almost invariably actually means 'an analysis of X' in the context of faith. 'Theology' and its cognates are overused by Christians. Theology is never the whole of religion, even in Christianity, by far the most doctrinally complex – theological – of the Western faiths.

Exegesis is the disciplined attempt to discern the meaning of a text for its first audience. We must neither over-interpret nor under-interpret a sacred text: exegesis can deteriorate into eisegesis. Interpretation is the process of understanding the range of application. Does the scope of the original text extend to our modern context? Hermeneutics is the process of reflecting on the presuppositions of one's exegesis and interpretation of a given text, especially in light of power relations, and race and gender considerations, initial and subsequent, since these latter are our modern obsessions. Islamic theology, insofar as it exists at all, often reduces to hermeneutics, though this is no narrow field, given the vast range of the sciences of the Quran *('ulum al-qur'ān)*, a staple of the madrasah (Muslim seminary) curriculum. Two areas of criticism (redaction and source) might be called *'ulum al injīl* but, given the divergent nature of the two scriptures, the contents of such inquiries could hardly overlap.

The author of Matthew and the Qumran sectarians used the *pēshêr* (Hebrew, interpretation) form of scriptural exegesis, a form appealing to apocalyptic prophets and visionaries. Each scriptural text is thought to have an outer meaning apparent to all readers and a concealed inner meaning that only a few can decipher. It lacks an Islamic counterpart since the Quran contains no apocalypse. But elements of *pesharim* correspond to the *ẓāhir/bāṭin* (manifest/hidden) style of interpretation, popular among Shi'ites, Sufi mystics and other heterodox groups. Among Sunnis, such interpretation is denigrated as interpretation by mere personal opinion since it is thought to lack any tethering authority and may therefore deteriorate into adventurously if not perniciously innovative deviance (*bid'a*) and perversity, condemned by the Quran (Q3.7–8).

'Context', like 'hermeneutics', is a vague word. I define it to mean any or all of the following: immediately adjacent texts in a sacred corpus, the secular historical situation surrounding the emergence of such texts, and cultural and linguistic possibilities latent in them at the time of their initial emergence. In the related field of audience criticism, scholars scrutinise the process of determining the kind of people who were the original recipients of an epistle, speech or text. Who were the Galatians? This is best answered in a sociologically inclined exegesis but it is connected to doctrinal or faith dimensions of identity. In *ḥadīth* criticism, the field of *'ilm al-rijāl* (knowledge of the men) records the names and examines the moral character of the transmitters of prophetic narratives in order to establish the reliability of their witness.

The standard fields of biblical criticism can find no analogues in the case of the Quran. Unlike the Bible, the Islamic scripture is self-described as revelation, making it a text which is canonical by divine decree rather than by human decision. It was merely codified and collated, not edited, let alone assigned canonical status by post-Muhammadan initiative. Once Muhammad had received and recited a particular revelation, it was *eo ipse* canonical. The notion of a process of Quranic canonisation persists because Christian and Jewish scholars assume that the history of the reception of the Quran is similar to the Bible. The latter is an anthology of works which were assigned canonical status, by human communities; often well after their production by their human (if inspired) authors. While there is no process of canonisation of the Quran, there is, naturally, a process of its *transmission*, an act within history. The net result of such Muslim attitudes is that the stability and absolute authority – though not interpretation – of the Quran's text are both placed *ab initio* beyond inquiry or criticism. These vetoes have never been lifted by any orthodox Muslim scholar. Thus, for example, unlike Western non-Muslim students of the Quran, Muslims do not consider 'Uthman's Quran a recension – an edition formed by amendment of an original.

Canon criticism takes the most holistic view of scripture: no *pericopē* should be understood except in the context of the entire Bible. Many exegetes use a modest version of this rule: no passage should be understood except in the context of the biblical book in which it occurs. Thus, for our purposes, we note that much in Acts, especially the three accounts of Paul's miraculous conversion and subsequent fervent missionary activity, complements elements of his confessional autobiography found in Galatians, Corinthians and Philippians.[16] All atomistic interpretation runs the risk of isolating the letter of the text from the spirit of the total message. The Quran too should be understood in its entire context which is easily ascertained since it is a shorter, homogeneous scripture. All its imperatives were, at one time, implemented in an actual society. Parts of the Quran supersede (or in effect abrogate) other parts, though never on matters of doctrine. The authority of the whole Quran annuls the authority of parts of the Quran. Provisional legal verdicts may be abrogated (see Q65.1) but not the notion that revealed legal (and moral) command remains the principal means for the divine tuition of humanity throughout human history.

XIII

We must be charitable in presenting other people's sacred texts. If a coherent argument can be discerned, it should be preferred to a reading that suggests confusion or fundamental contradiction. The outsider must bring a measure of exegetical sympathy which enables tolerance of alien conviction – although tolerance is not embrace.

We may assume that, poetic and mystical verses apart, the primary or first reading of any text is literal. If taken literally it makes little or no sense, we proceed to an allegorical or metaphorical reading. The literal has priority over the allegorical or figurative: no one should begin with the non-literal meaning and then proceed to the literal meaning. It is wise to bear in mind this principle when, for example, exploring Paul's mystical identification with Christ, a theme of Chapter 3, section XVI.

A broader set of implicit concerns centres on claims about the perspicuity of scripture, and related claims about its comprehensiveness and sufficiency for salvation or guidance. Such themes are linked both to the intra-Christian debate about *sola scriptura* and broader interfaith debates involving the relative merits of the Islamic and Christian models of revelation.

The Bible and the Quran both claim perspicuity of scripture. The Quran routinely claims to be lucid and perspicuous, comprehensive and authoritative and indeed wise and infallible (Q2.2; 12.1; 36.2). It concedes the presence of allegorical verses whose meaning is opaque (Q3.7). While claiming clarity and freedom from error and doubt concerning its own teachings, the Quran rejects *de facto* Christian teaching, presumably in the extant Christian scriptures, as being speculative and conjectural (Q4.157), infected by crooked doctrine (Q18.1–5) and therefore compromised, a misinterpretation of originally divinely inspired doctrines. This last claim is implicit throughout the Medinan Quran's highly consistent and systematic critique of Jewish and Christian beliefs. The Islamic scripture is said to contain no crookedness or doubt (Q39.28).

Claims for the clarity of biblical commandments begin as early as the Torah (Deut. 30.11–14). Jesus reproached the Pharisees and the scribes for failing to understand the plain meaning of the Torah texts, especially in regard to justice and purity, and, moreover, in their penchant for preferring man-made rituals to God's laws. Paul claims the clarity of scripture (2 Cor. 1.13–14; Phil. 3.15–16) while the Paulinist Pastor claims the utility of scripture (2 Tim. 3.14–17). 2 Peter claims the total sufficiency and perspicuity of scripture (2 Pet. 1.3–4, 16–21) – although this contradicts the author's claim, later in the same epistle, that some of Paul's teaching is not perspicuous (2 Pet. 3.15–16). In Christian history, the Church Fathers contrasted the clarity of the canon with the esoteric and mystical speculations of the Gnostics whose writings were accordingly rejected.

Paul strikes a different note when he counsels us to set limits to our epistemological ambitions during our earthly life where we can only 'see through a glass darkly' (1 Cor. 13.12) since the natural person is incapable of understanding matters that require spiritual discernment (1 Cor. 2.14). One should discriminate and hold fast only to the good residue (1 Thess. 5.21). Outside of Paul's writings too, this is cited as a sign of spiritual maturity and growth in the Christian life (Heb. 5.14). Paul thinks that a veil prevents Jews from truly understanding the covenant and Law of Moses (2 Cor. 14–17), a veil only Christ can remove. The Quran similarly claims that a veil is divinely placed on the hearts of disbelievers (Q2.7) especially during a recitation of the Quran (Q17.45–46).

In the Galatian, Thessalonian and Corinthian correspondences, Paul writes about matters that were subsequently misunderstood and caricatured by his opponents, most of whom were fellow believers. Martin Luther was fond of the view that our spiritual blindness and perversity accounted for much of the perceived obscurity and opacity of scripture.[17]

The word of God was never intended solely for the elect and scholars – for that would have entailed that only biblical scholars would be saved, a view that is intrinsically absurd. According to the Psalmist, scripture could impart wisdom to the simple man (Ps. 119.105, 130). The Quran claims that whoever is granted wisdom has been granted much good – but adds that only the wise recognise the gift (Q2.269; cf. James 1.5–6).

The author of Hebrews claims, in a passage of visceral vigour, that the word of God is not some defunct document – preserved and reserved, presumably for scholarly scrutiny. No, it is 'living and active (*energēs*) and sharper than every 'two-mouthed' sword, and penetrating as far as the division of soul and spirit (*merismou psuchēs kai pneumatos*), of both joints and marrow – and (thus) able to judge the thoughts and intentions (attitudes) of a (any) heart' (4.12). The Quran employs less violent metaphors as it envisages its own descent on a mountain which is thus pulverised (Q59.21). The Quran claims to have the power to soften recalcitrant and perverse hearts and to grant them tranquillity (*iṭminān*; 13.28; see also 57.16).

The doctrine of the clarity of scripture may be reasonably interpreted to mean that the teachings of the Christian faith are expressed in plain and simple language, requiring no privileged access by qualified professionals, but rather accessible to an ordinary pious believer of average intelligence. This doctrine means that every reader or listener can learn of a clear doctrinal scheme for divine salvation or guidance. It cannot mean that every verse of scripture is linguistically or lexically clear – for that would imply that scholarly scrutiny were redundant.

The Roman Catholic Church denies that all scripture is, or is in all essentials, perspicuous. While it must be believed in its totality, on faith, understanding it requires the official clarification provided only by the interpretive framework of the church and tradition. Although Protestants accept the utility of scholarly commentary, they reject the view that only the Magisterium (teaching office of the Roman Catholic Church) is vested with the power of correct interpretation of scripture. Orthodox Islam has, in theory, no clerical class but in practice only its qualified professionals can produce authoritative commentary.

Those Christians who believe that scripture is clear have historically encouraged devotional study of the Bible and produced much confessional scholarship, some of it rather uncritical. Catholics have often feared that personal interpretation would lead to adventurism and worse, to the production and dissemination of imbalanced and toxic, if not outright, false doctrine.

In Galatians (5.19–20), Paul attributes the lack of communal cohesion to the works of the flesh, produced by the sinful nature. Presumably then the clarity of scripture does not, by itself, ensure a correct reception of its message since it is filtered through a depraved and fallen human being whose faculties have been, especially according to some of the more extreme Protestant denominations, irreparably damaged. This intellectual predicament of the sinner requires the supplementary intervention and illumination of the Holy Spirit, the agency who enables eloquence in believers of ordinary gifts, in situations of persecution and incrimination and, in other situations, endows Christians with at least basic skills to ensure intelligibility of the faith claims they make. While there is no equivalent Jewish or Islamic doctrine of supernatural assistance in such oratorical endeavours, all faiths, despite being equipped with a canon, face the problem of disunity, a phenomenon politely called denominational diversity.

The Quran contains a single if nuanced but consistent view on vital moral and practical themes – for example on the question of personal responsibility and bearing burdens, a central theme of Christian soteriology. The Bible, admittedly a much longer and more heterogeneous scripture, often contains two directly opposed views, leaving the matter to the discretion and interpretation of the reader. Unlike the Muslim scripture, the Christian Bible contains two testaments and therefore has, in the nature of the case, opposing verdicts on some matters since the New Testament supersedes – or fulfils – the old. The Meccan and Medinan divisions of the Quran do not correspond to the two biblical testaments but rather relate as the political empowerment and application of an earlier powerless but sound ethical vision.

This arrangement does lead to some tension, for example, between the Quran's earlier and later notices of the Peoples of the Book – but there emerges a final, practically clear and fully coherent position that is affirmed in Muhammad's own practice and policy, and one embodied in Islamic law, the *Sharī'a*. No doubt, there remain areas of legitimate disagreement among the contending parties of sincere believers who all claim to follow the Quran and the Prophet's example. How else can one explain the endless volumes of commentary on the scripture and on the life of the man who brought it to us! But these disagreements should not arise concerning areas of right belief considered vital to walking on the morally straight path of faith (see Q1.6–2.5). Only fools underestimate the prevalence of human perversity and irrationality.

Christians generally want to harmonise apparent doctrinal discrepancies and oppositions while leaving some matters of practice (such as infant as opposed to adult baptism) open to difference. Muslims are keen to harmonise questions of practice, especially of legal practice, while leaving some peripheral matters of belief unresolved. This is often because they regard any deep inquiry into such matters as presumptuous since the Quran is silent only on matters that are ultimately humanly unknowable but also irrelevant to the attainment of success in the life of faith. Theology, as the study of God's nature as opposed to his will, is anathema.

Finally, both the Islamic and Christian views contrast sharply with the postmodernist view of scripture's alleged lack of clarity. I regard this perspective as pernicious and moreover self-referentially incoherent – since it claims to be the objective truth. It is, in effect, a form of anti-realist relativism which makes a false meta-philosophical claim to be an arbiter providing an alleged Archimedean point of ultimate reference. The claim is that subjective experience is preferable to knowing the original, allegedly objective intended meaning of scripture since no such meaning existed clearly even for the author. Moreover, once a work has been authored, its meanings are simply constituted by its reading community, the original author being merely one member of this group.

A more defensible and convincing variant of this view is that even if there is an objectively correct understanding of the world, of history or of scripture – and it is an open question – there is no reason to assume that we have the intellectual apparatus to acquire such a truth. Which view prevails is a matter of power and the persuasiveness of interpretation, a function of the skill and techniques of the professional interpreter. The texts are infinitely plastic to the needs and desires of readers placed in varied constituencies. Language makes the world: there is only what we can speak of and its meaning is whatever we make of it.

In practice, such reductionist views in effect mock the very notion of successfully seeking guidance from a scripture, not to speak of its allegedly revealed authority. What is being rejected here is the very possibility of the objectivity of the events of external history, a matter of great concern to faiths based on crucial historical events such as the crucifixion. I will not here discuss further the claims that have been articulated in defence of radical doubt that is a feature of post-Enlightenment, Western secular societies.[18] I will only affirm that, unlike the typical post-modernist, I uphold the notion of objective historicity, of critical history, value-free critical inquiry and, more generally, of a realist understanding of some extra-linguistic reality that constrains and confronts us.

The search for an independent, that is, externally constraining, truth is ancient though it is no longer fashionable in the humanities division of Western academia. At best, one can search for a critical rather than objective truth. That is fair enough since, as a man of faith, I believe that the absolute objective truth can be known only by God. In this inquiry, I shall assume that there are putatively historical as well as religious truth-claims in the Christian and Muslim scriptures and that these are offered as truths concerning matters of ultimate moment. I assert that an anarchic (anti-method and anti-realist) post-modernist relativism which questions the coherence of the very idea of pursuing objective truth – in religion, history and so on – is irrelevant, untrue and unworthy of any further sustained reflection. A useful version of the claim is to warn us that though there is indeed a truth to be discovered, there is every reason to be sceptical of the pretensions of those, especially those in power, who claim to know this absolute truth and have appointed themselves as its custodians and guardians. But entertaining such doubt about the pretensions of the powerful is hardly the monopoly of religious people.

XIV

We have arrived at the last turn in the road. There are some turning points in the history of the interpretation of Galatians. The arch-heretic Marcion placed Galatians as the opening epistle in his canon. He cites from Galatians to prove that there was only one true gospel (Gal. 1.8–10) and that false brothers were attempting to divert true believers from it (Gal. 1.6–7). Marcion rightly sensed that Galatians marked a break with the Law-observant faith of the Jews but he probably exaggerated the extent of this rupture. It was certainly a decisive and successful attack on the Jewish inheritance of Christianity. Consistently with the rest of his anti-Judaic stance, Marcion was a ruthless editor of Galatians: he deleted the dense central pericopae that deal with the promises made to Abraham and his descendants (Gal. 3.16–4.6).[19]

No seminal Christian thinker has been indifferent to Galatians, this 'capital epistle', in F.F. Bruce's apt phrase.[20] It was Martin Luther, however, whose passionate advocacy of this letter has, intentionally or otherwise, altered the course of Christian history. Galatians has been used to attack the Roman Catholic doctrine of salvation as being excessively works-based and indeed relying on sacraments. In the history of ecclesiastical commentary on Galatians, the Protestant understanding of Galatians seems to me a proper understanding of Paul's intentions. No church rituals, not even baptism and no human effort at doing the works of the law, can achieve justification. Only faith can succeed here – and that only if received in the spirit of grace.

The Judaisers in Galatia were the archetype of all legalists in religion. Against them one had to shout: 'Justification is by faith alone.' Luther saw in this brief epistle an inspired rebuttal of the dual slavery of the religious bureaucracy of the Papacy and of the rigidly defined rules of monasticism. Luther was Germany's St Paul and shared the Apostle's temperament: sincere, spontaneous, zealous and intolerant of opposition to the point of being, if we may today be so bold, 'fascist'. Luther was more indignant at the Galatians than even Paul was in his letter! The German reformer thought that the Galatians were re-crucifying Christ. Like Paul, Luther saw his opponents as insincere and misguided. He heartily concurred with Paul's temperament, readily seeing opposition to his own views as being rooted in the machinations of the Devil.

Though Luther's exaltation of Galatians was rooted in his own personal religious dilemmas, Galatians was destined to become the manifesto of the German Reformation.[21] With its detailed rules and discipline, monasticism was seen as an acceptable kind of Christian formalism. In this Reformation setting, Catholics had their casuistry and legal rulings. The spirit of Christian liberty was, Protestants feared, perennially at risk, long after circumcision and dietary restrictions affecting the scope of table fellowship had subsided into the oblivion of academic debate. The sovereign freedom of the spirit has been, many Protestants would still contend, curbed by the Roman Catholic Church which domesticated the spirit within the straitjacket of countless regulations.

With the possible exception of some nonconformist churches, most churches publish lengthy manuals of disciplines, rules and regulations. In general, as a Christian sect becomes a denomination, it is normal to have more rules. Some rules, especially constitutional ones, are inherited. Others are moral guidelines specific to a denomination. Thus every Church of England congregation inherits the whole of Anglican canon law while also honouring additional rules of its own for the parish or diocese. Puritan churches typically have more rules, especially moral guidelines. Charismatic and Pentecostal assemblies have few rules.

Perhaps the last attitude noted above is in deference to the maxim 'Let the spirit decide and rule'. That would appeal to Paul, the apostle of liberty – the right kind of liberty which binds without visible bonds and matches freedom with the demands of the duties imposed by the spirit which has the right to rule. Paul was no anarchist and free spirit in the modern sense.

The temptation to be under rules and guidelines still persists even among Christians for it is a human enough temptation. The Apostle himself admonishes many brothers who are unruly (1 Thess. 5.14), and commends Christian discipline (Gal. 6.1) and even threatens those who defile the church with sexual pollution with the penalty of 'deliverance to Satan' (1 Cor. 5.5). Even Paul could never shake off the yoke of slavery to rules and laws, long after he had abandoned the Law in a formal sense. This very fact indicates the possibility of developing fruitfully different understandings and equally valid interpretations of the notion of rules and of the rule of laws. This should reassure his Muslim critics lest they prejudge him and misjudge him. We are now ready for the commentary to commence.

Notes

1 B. Pascal, *Pensées . . . sur la religion, et sur quelques autres sujets* (Amsterdam: n.a., 1712).
2 Among non-Muslim translators, N. J. Dawood rearranged the chapters of the Quran. Kenneth Cragg went further by summarising it; he deleted one-third as repetition. Muslims approve only of abridgement (*mukhtasar*) of law codes, prophetic traditions and commentaries rather than of the Quran. Individual surah, especially Surah 36 ('the heart of the Quran') are, however, often printed alone.
3 This material provides ample ideas for those ex-Muslim writers who want to pander, in fulsome obscenity, to Western curiosity about Muslim sexual prowess. Shi'ite diatribes spare the Prophet himself, naturally, but exploit any potentially scandalous event to portray Sunni heroes of early Islam in the worst possible light.
4 See the Preface to his widely available translation of the Quran. He was the first *believing* translator whose mother tongue was English.
5 For example, the first English novel of the early modern period, *Pamela*, by Samuel Richardson (published in 1740), consisted of a series of letters.
6 For details, see John and K. Court, *The New Testament World* (Englewood Cliffs: Prentice Hall, 1990), pp.123ff. We have no extant lecture-sermons by Paul but we know that he lectured (*dielegeto*) at length to a few of his *protégés*, including Timothy, at Troas (Acts 20.6–12). The contents of this extended conversational lecture are unknown.
7 M.I. Isḥāq, *The Life of Muhammad*, trans. A. Guillaume (Lahore: Oxford University Press, 1955), pp. 652–59.
8 International and pan-confessional committees of competent and anonymous scholars translate the Bible and do it well. Ambitiously but perhaps rather foolishly, the Quran, a shorter but indefinitely complex work, is translated by single named individuals, Muslim and non-Muslim.
9 Al-Ghazzali (1058–1111), especially popular with Sufi writers and with Western non-Muslim scholars, is admired only cautiously by mainstream Muslims since they note his anarchic style of orthodoxy. While they admire him for his stance against Greek philosophy, they note with dismay that his otherwise comprehensive compendium, *The Revival of the Religious Sciences,* is conspicuously silent on military *jihād*, the touchstone of the radicals. In his other works, he expresses the standard views about *jihād* but it is unclear whether that was done only for prudential reasons. Al-Ghazzali lived at the time of the first crusade, proclaimed by Pope Urban II in 1095. It is never mentioned in the premier Muslim thinker's voluminous, eclectic and otherwise comprehensive writings which make it impossible for any single individual to claim expertise regarding the whole of his corpus.
10 Syriac is a dialect of Aramaic, itself a close demotic variant of classical Hebrew.
11 Nietzsche, *Beyond Good and Evil* (Chicago: Henry Regnery, 1955), section 121, translated by Marianne Cowan, p. 81. Nietzsche published this pioneering work in 1886, at an early stage in the development of European critical biblical scholarship.
12 See S.H. Griffith, *The Bible in Arabic: The Scriptures of the 'People of the Book' in the Language of Islam* (Princeton: Princeton University Press, 2013). The Christian failure – as late as Muhammad's day and age – to make the Bible available in Arabic was not only a remarkable deficit and a signal failing in a missionary faith of global pretensions, it also had decisive and enduring consequences relating to the rise and spread of Islam, far and away Christianity's most successful competitor for the hand of grace and for universal influence.
13 The three ancient rhetorical genres are judiciary, epidictic and the deliberative. Galatians is classed as deliberative. See M.D. Nanos (ed.), *The Galatians Debate* (Peabody: Hendrickson, 2002).
14 One verse uses *thumma* (Q90.17) in a puzzling reversal of priorities in the context of 90.11–16.
15 The pair of energetic moods, used for exhortation, is restricted to the Quran, sermons and rhetorical literature. The energetic moods achieve emphasis by making additions to the present indicative. Arabic has no separate optative mood but can accommodate it.

16 The account of Paul's life in Acts should be treated as being less reliable than the one from his own pen, even though I grant that a man can entertain a false view of himself.
17 See his *Bondage of the Will* (Lat. *De Servo Arbitrio*), published at Christmas, 1525.
18 See, for example, my discussion in S. Akhtar, *The Quran and the Secular Mind* (London: Routledge, 2007).
19 Marcion's canon included the *Apostolikon*, a compendium of ten Pauline epistles: Galatians, the Corinthian correspondence, Romans, the Thessalonian pair, Ephesians (called Laodiceans), Colossians, Philemon and Philippians. Marcion also canonised only an edited version of Luke's gospel as the sole authentic gospel. The choice of Luke, with its arguably relatively low Christology, retains substantial implications for an Islamic reading of Christian origins. I argue for this view in the sequel to this work, *An Islamic View of Christian Origins: The Nature of the New Testament,* forthcoming from Routledge.
20 The classicist Christian commentator F.F. Bruce was a religiously conservative but academically scrupulous commentator. His commentary on *The Acts of the Apostles* (Leicester: Inter-Varsity Press, 1990) is unusually catholic in its range of citations: he even mentions Quranic verses condemning idolatry and some verses about *Allāh*'s signs in nature.
21 For a manifesto, Luther's commentaries are rather long! German writers, no less than our own Charles Dickens, needed a ruthless editor. Luther's commentaries are unduly prolix and verbose. He felt passionately about many matters. Nonetheless, his commentary on Galatians contains unnecessary diatribes against Turks (Muslims) and Jews. German commentaries, like other modern Teutonic works on theology and philosophy, suffer from an obsession with arid philological minutiae. In his last work, *Ecce Homo*, Nietzsche rightly boasted of the concision and originality of his German prose: he could say in ten sentences what every other German writer 'said in a whole book - did not say in a whole book!' See *Ecce Homo* (Harmondsworth: Penguin Books, 1979), translated by R.J. Hollingsdale, p. 3.

2

'THERE IS NO GOSPEL EXCEPT THE ONLY GOSPEL' (1.1–12)

Some modern secular readers would perhaps detect in the first dozen verses of Galatians a note of fanatical intolerance of opposed convictions, even the seeds of a fascism, evident in the enthusiastic intra-Christian inquisitions that periodically mark Christian history until relatively recent times. They might sense the same totalitarian impulse in the Jewish confession of faith and be tempted therefore to dismiss it, unfairly, as merely the permanently belligerent pose of some jealous tribal deity. Islam's very *credo* begins with an imperial style assault on all other gods. All Semitic monotheisms are fascist by modern secular standards of toleration for dissident stances. Many would contrast the tolerant polytheistic faiths as lifestyles associated with the green and fertile forest rather than the arid desert of the Semitic tribes.[1] This impression may be questioned: we hear of violent Hindu vegetarians and armed Buddhists in Burma and Sri Lanka killing defenceless Muslims. And many Jewish and Christian martyrs, past and present, have bravely faced, in passive vulnerability, the hostility of brutal and callous witnesses.

Paul shows no love or Christian charity for his enemies in Gal.1.6–10. One could defend him by saying that these are not merely personal enemies but rather enemies of the cause of Christ. And while one should forgive and even love those who persecute and hate one, it cannot be right to love ideological enemies. I find this reasoning to be convincing. But it is striking how few Westerners, if any, have ever been charitable enough to see that this was in fact Muhammad's policy, one seen as noble by Muslims. He forgave his personal enemies but punished and dealt justly with his ideological adversaries – those who mocked the Quran, the Word of God and Muhammad ex officio as the Messenger of God. We return to this in Chapter 5, section XI and in Chapter 6, section XII.

In Galatians, Paul is motivated by three themes that define juridical monotheism. The trio is embryonically present in the masterful opening: the sole true source of final authority for any revelation, whether oral and experiential or as solidified in scripture; the sufficiency of divine grace; and finally, God's promise of delivering human beings from the power of sin. God's revelation of his authoritative truth, his gracious provision of love, and his firm promise of salvation – each offer is of and from God, from first to last. The first concern unites all monotheists who accept the authority of revealed canons. I have expressed the second and third themes in a characteristically Christian idiom since this pair has been most fully explored by Christian thinkers, starting with Paul. The three motifs are not disparate. Paul relates all three to the sovereign and gracious will of the God who manifests himself in Christ Jesus at this late hour.

I 1.1–2 To Galatians

1 *Paul, an apostle (sent) not from men nor through man but through Jesus Christ and God the Father, the one having raised him out of the dead ones,* **2** *and all the brothers (who are) with me, to the congregations in Galatia.*

The letter's title is the superscription. 1.1–5 is the epistolary prescript while the exordium runs from 1.6 to 1.11. In an abrupt opening which invites comparison with the initial verses of several Quranic surahs, we read a plea for the recognition of direct revealed authority. The opening of Galatians offers a salutation but, uniquely in the Pauline corpus, there is neither thanksgiving nor prayer. In *lieu* of a greeting, Paul offers a benediction (1.3). Apart from its ninth chapter, the Quran opens invariably with an invocation which invokes two related attributes of God, both highlighting divine mercy.

Muhammad is never named as apostolic author of any verse of the Quran. Only one chapter opens by mentioning him by name (Q47.2). Some chapters open by addressing him as Prophet (33.1; 66.1) while others open by citing the Quran's wisdom as providing his prophetic credentials (Q36.1–4). 'A wise book, therefore a true prophet' is an inference that some ancients would have drawn instinctively – but, in our secularised age, no philosophically sophisticated believer would even draw it, let alone embrace it uncritically.

The tone of Paul's opening verses and of the exordium that starts at v.6 is aristocratic, autocratic and assertive, not tentative or reflective. This is true of all Semitic revelation. What is unusual about the Quran is that the tone remains autocratic and authoritative throughout the text, not merely in the opening verses. This sustained confidence is never diluted by the milder *pericopae* of pastoral concern, self-doubt or mundane interlude. Its tone is thus that of pure revelation from someone who never regrets even retrospectively the vehemence of prefatory assertions. With the exception of Philippians, Philemon and the Thessalonian pair, Paul's epistles, both genuine and disputed, invariably begin with an audacious tone and magisterial authority that interdicts all contradiction. This is rarely sustained since Paul is human – even though he is inspired by the Holy Spirit, the agent who enables Christians to be eloquent under duress (Mark 13.11; Luke 12.11–12). Paul argues, pleads and asks – but does not know in advance the recipients' responses.

The Galatians are not addressed as saints (*hagioi*), perhaps an early hint of a crisis in Galatia. Sanctification is formally absent from Galatians, deferred to the epistle to the saints at Rome (Rom. 1.7).

1

Writing to the Galatian congregations which Paul established during an earlier visit, he opens with a declaration of his apostolic authority. Even if the Thessalonian correspondence were earlier, neither of its constituent pair of epistles mentions Paul's apostleship. Thus, Galatians could be the first written declaration of apostleship made by Paul. My choice of this Pauline epistle for commentary hardly needs further defence.

Paul claims unmediated divine authority for his apostleship. No one ignores the note of conviction; certainty is seductive. No faith was built on doubt. If the trumpet does not sound a clear clarion call, who shall prepare for battle? Even in print, without the benefit of the recited word and the pulpit that dramatises speech, Paul's passion is audible.

'*Anthrōpos*' means 'man' in contrast to God, not man as masculine and thus in contrast to woman. Compare Gal. 3.28 where male (*arsen*) and female (*thēlu*) denote biological masculinity and femininity. *Anthrōpos* corresponds to the Quran's gender inclusive *al-insān* (humanity), meaning all human beings generically as opposed to non-human beings such as the invisible elemental spirits called jinn. *Zakar* (male) and *unthā* (female) indicate the Quran's world of absolute sexual differentiation (Q3.36; cf.4.1), reflected in the sensitivity to gender in Arabic grammar.

The epistle opens with 'Paul, an apostle'. Note the name change and assimilation to a role. Paul's identity is wholly absorbed into his new commission as the missionary apostle sent to the Gentiles. The bare name *Shā'ul* is used by the risen Christ in addressing Paul, presumably in Aramaic (Acts 9.4). In the Quran and Muhammad's traditions, the Prophet is typically called 'Messenger of God' (*rasūl Allah*) just as Jesus is identified with the role and title of the Messiah (both in the New Testament and the Quran).

No Quranic Arabic preposition captures the precise undertones of continuous and accompanying intimacy found in *dia* (through) although *bi* – the equivalent of the Hebrew preposition *be* (in/with/of) – partly captures this tone. The literary Arabic expression *bi wāsiṭah* (through the middle of/by means of) is closer to *dia*.

The prepositions used with *Allah* include *bi* (in), *fī* (inside), *min* (from), *'alā* (upon, normally indicating obligation), and *'inda* (with). Such Arabic prepositions, however, take the noun or pronoun only in the genitive case rather than also the dative (which we find in *Koinē* Greek) or the locative and ablative (in classical Greek). Arabic uses only the nominative, accusative, genitive and vocative cases. Unlike Greek, Arabic has no dative case but verbs are often doubly transitive – taking two direct objects rather than a direct and an indirect object.

The employment of particular particles, including prepositions, in *Koinē* (demotic) Greek need not always convey deeper theological truths. Unlike modern communication, the medium is not the message. This is, however, less true of the Quran, self-eulogised as a literary masterpiece composed in classical Arabic, a challenge to all readers and writers.

This opening verse contains the only mention of the resurrection in this staurocentric epistle. The resurrection of Jesus Christ by God the Father is the cornerstone of the Christian edifice, the stone the Muslim builders rejected. God the Father justified his servant Jesus by raising him from the dead. This act changed a tragedy into a triumph. Jesus' resurrection corresponds to the descent of the inimitable Quran, a single unrepeatable event that constitutes the central probative credential of Islam.

In keeping with my promise of remarking on features of comparative Greek and Arabic usages (see Chapter 1), note here that only the strong adversative *alla* (but) strictly corresponds to the Arabic *lākin*. Other means of contrasting clauses in Arabic sentences, including the use of the temporally indifferent conjunction *wa*, are not as clear and emphatic in securing the required contrast.

2

The preposition *sun* (with) is more intimate than *meta* (with). These two correspond to three classical Arabic prepositions: *'inda* (at) *ma'a* (with) and *ladā* (on or with) denoting roughly the same level of intimacy as *sun*.

In our day, it is tempting to use gender inclusive terminology. But 'brethren' here naturally means brothers since Greek distinguishes *adelphos* (masculine singular) from the feminine *adelphē*. Theologically speaking, however, in view of the marked inclusivity of Gal. 3.28, the use of sons in 3.26 could include daughters. In Arabic, the indeclinable noun *man* (whosoever) may intend one or more persons of either gender. It is frequent in the Quran (e.g. Q2.8), reinforcing that scripture's radically inclusive scope of address.

II 1.3–5

3 *Grace to you and peace from God our Father and the Lord Jesus Christ* **4** *who having given himself on behalf of our sins so that he might deliver us out of the present evil age according to the will of our God and Father* **5** *to whom be glory for ever and ever. Amen.*

3

Paul's opening and closing references to Christ's grace (1.3 and 6.18) sandwich this epistle. The Apostle greets with grace (*charis*) rather than offering the more secular Hellenic 'Greetings' (*chairein*) used elsewhere and meaning 'Hail!' or 'Health'. See, for example, the letter sent by the Jerusalem Council to the Gentile believers (Acts 15.23).

At the earliest opportunity, Paul mentions the Lordship of Jesus. The word *kurios*, vital in assessing Paul's final position on the alleged deity of Jesus, is a masculine title of respect and nobility used often in the Bible. In the Septuagint, *kurios* refers to Israel's one God and *kurioi* to gods in general. It is a polite form of address, especially to a senior.

It resembles the English use of 'Sir' and the Arabic title 'Sayyid'. In Matthew, we note a representative range: *kurios* is used of human lords, including slave-owners (10.24), heads of households (13.35), property owners (20.8) and Roman authorities (27.63). The Roman emperor is called *kurios* (Acts 25.26). A son can call his father 'Lord' (Matt. 21.30) just as wives can use it of husbands (1 Peter 3.6).

Acts 2.36 reads: 'God has made this Jesus both Lord (*kurion*) and Christ'. Here 'Lord' cannot mean God: if Jesus were (or was) already God or one with him, it is doctrinally incorrect to say that he was *made* (*epoiēsen*; aorist active indicative) Lord.

The Arabic *rabb*, meaning sustainer, carries similar ambiguities. Normally used of God (Q1.2), it can be used of human masters. Joseph uses it to refer to his Egyptian owner (Q12.23, 42). Pharaoh uses the same verbal root when he accuses Moses of ingratitude after he had been nourished (*nurabbika*; Q26.18) in the royal house (cf. Acts 7.22). In modern Arabic, *rabbatu bayt* (mistress of the house) is an affectionate title of the wife.

The peace greeting reoccurs towards the end (6.16), wrapping this angry letter in goodwill.

4

Some mawkish poet – Wallace Stevens comes to mind – might well muse that there are only ages of innocence, never a place of innocence. In Paul's understanding of time and locale, the present evil age refers not only or necessarily to the actual first century, under Roman occupation in Palestine and, therefore, in that sense a secular era. Rather, it refers to any era anywhere – in contrast to that long-awaited age, dear to all Jews, in which divine justice and vindication would finally reign. That would be, for Christians, the hour of the Messiah, set according to the eternally binding will of God the Father. The sentiment is obliquely alluded to in the Lord's Prayer (Matt. 6.10).

Note the hint of eschatological consummation: 'evil' alerts us to the Devil's activities though he is not named in this epistle and, strictly speaking, dealing with divine judgement rather than with the Devil is the core of eschatology. Nonetheless, flesh, referred to later in this letter, serves as a metonymy for his evil domain. That the world is currently governed by the Devil is implied in the Lord's Prayer when the believer prays for deliverance from evil (*tou ponērou*), an ambiguous expression (meaning either 'evil' or 'evil one') which, in late manuscripts, is disambiguated as 'the evil one' (Matt. 6.13). The Book of Revelation makes this stress explicit: Satan is expelled from heaven but permitted to reign intermittently, directly and in disguise, on earth (Rev. 12.7–13.18; 20.1–10).[2]

It is possible to read into this verse and its reference to evil something of the imminence of judgement and the associated apocalyptic stress, admittedly both much more evident in 1 Thessalonians. Only in the final book of the New Testament do we note the millennial situation in which Christ and Satan explicitly engage in battle. This contrasts with the Quran where threats of the imminence of judgement

(Q21.1; 54.1) must be rhetorical and hyperbolic since these did not prevent Muhammad from calmly and systematically building his heavenly city on this side of the grave. Nor does the Quran assert or imply that the present age is evil or under satanic sovereignty.[3]

'According to the will of our God and Father' might be expressing something of the Islamic sentiment implicit in *inshā Allāh*, if God wills, the equivalent of 'by divine permission' (*bi'idhnillāh*). *Inshā Allāh* is a seriously intended conditional expressing divinely imposed limits on the capacity of human volition to translate into action. God corrects Muhammad's confident promise to his Jewish Medinan critics that he would answer them soon through a revelation: he is reminded of the caveat of divine permission (*inshā Allāh*; Q18.23–24). This idiom has now deteriorated in practice into a pious platitude, being often used as an excuse for a failure of punctuality that is humanly avoidable, a trait much prevalent among Muslims, even among Western converts to the faith.[4]

Christian Arab translators render *kata to thelēma tou theou* (according to the will of God) by the Arabic *bi mashatī Allāh* – not a phrase found in the Quran but consonant with its vocabulary and religious purpose.[5]

5

Galatians is the only indisputably authentic epistle in which the initial verses (1.4–5) already contain a doxology. It replaces the more customary commendations. Quranic exordia and endings often constitute a doxological *inclusio* (Q59.1, 24; 17.1, 111; 64.1, 18). Other Pauline letters contain a doxology but it is found fairly late in the opening (1 Cor. 1.8–9; 1 Thess. 1.9–10; Rom. 1.16–18, etc.).

III 1.6–9

6 *I do wonder how quickly you are removing yourself, from the one who called you by the grace of Christ, to another gospel* **7** *which is not (really) another (gospel). Only there are some who are troubling you and wishing to pervert the gospel of Christ.* **8** *But even if we or an angel out of heaven should preach a gospel to you, beside what we preached to you, let him be a curse.* **9** *As we have previously said, also now again I say, if anyone preaches to you a gospel beside what you received, let him be a curse.*

These verses register rather than describe the crisis in Galatia. Being indignant helps one to choose direct, even impolite expressions. Style and content – manner and matter – cannot always be separated. Although dissent is not apostasy, Paul is indignant enough to replace thanksgiving with threat and curse. The typical Pauline thanksgiving (e.g., 1 Cor. 1.4–9) is uniquely omitted here in the Galatian exordium and replaced with astonishment, disapproval and ironic rebuke.

6-7

Although there are four canonical gospels, *euangellion* occurs only in the singular in the New Testament. In secular Greek, *euangellion* means joyful message and can be used in the plural, as in the correspondence relating to the Caesar cult.[6] Paul will not even countenance another gospel. 'No gospel at all' reminds the Muslim reader of the Quranic assertion of an only God, all else being merely 'names (of non-existent idols) which you and your fathers have named regarding which God has sent down no authority from heaven', in the words of Joseph's prison speech (Q12.40).

This is the first mention of the Galatians' intended defection. Such backsliding is a recoverable position as one heads towards outright apostasy. This is the first of several negative notices of the agitators who shall be condemned more and more as the epistle gathers momentum. Elsewhere too, Paul bitterly complains that the Corinthian Christians are far too ready to accept a Jesus other than the Jesus that Paul preached (2 Cor. 11.4).

Paul preaches the singularity of the evangel with the cross and resurrection at its crux. Muslims might think here of *i'jāz al-qur'ān* (inimitability of the Quran) while Christians from the Muslim world might think of *i'jāz al-'Isawī*, the inimitability of Jesus, a popular term in Indian and Persian Christian apologetics. Muslims admire Muhammad as a uniquely formidable representative of God's universal mercy and justice (Q4.113; 17.79; 33.21; 68.4). Appointed (and anointed so to speak) as the final messenger, he is granted the gift of the mighty Quran (Q15.87) and made to be the inheritor of all prophets (Q33.7, 40), a view affirmed additionally in his own sayings.

Heteros in v.6 means different and, moreover, of different type while *allos* in v.7 means different but of the same type. These are declined as *heteron* (acc. sg. neut.) and *allo* (nom. sg. neut.). This distinction, suited to a language that housed rich philosophical distinctions, is not found in Arabic where both types of differences are covered by one word, *ghayr*. However, Arabic is potentially fertile enough to accommodate the complexity of Greek nomenclature, as was proven by the content of the sophisticated Greco-Islamic tradition in philosophy.

8–9

Even an angel from heaven cannot be trusted if he brings another gospel. What matters is the message, not the messenger.

Note the Semitic hyperbole buttressed further by the repeated use of the 'we' of majesty, a literary plural. Conservative Christian exegetes might be tempted to interpret the 'we' as first person plural literally – to refer to Paul's liaison with the orthodox evangelists and apostles who worked together with him for the shared cause of the true gospel. However, given Paul's general reluctance to share authority with other believers and his claim to have kept his conversion secret (Gal. 1.16–17), the 'we' should be taken as a literary embellishment no different from a modern author's use of it. It is now used, of course, only to presume upon the interest of the reader rather than to exhibit one's magisterial authority as a writer.

Those who opt for an alternative view are under penalty of anathema, pronounced once and repeated for effect. Such reverential repetition is found often in Semitic assertion and symbolic conduct – three times or more (1 Sam. 3.8–9), three times in Muhammad's traditions and twice in the Quran (e.g. Q78.4–5). Such reverent or liturgical repetition is, in sacred or secular contexts, for rhetorical effect. Adults, no less than children, need to hear the important lesson repeated. In that sense, we are not an intelligent species.

Anatetheimenon, the full form of the participle which in English yields anathema, means something placed or erected in a temple, thus meaning either consecrated or accursed.[7] In Christian usage, it means only accursed. The Arabic adjective *ḥaram* can mean forbidden or consecrated, depending on the length of the final vowel: *ḥarām* (forbidden) and *ḥaram* (sacred, set apart as holy). The Meccan shrine is the 'Forbidden Mosque' since violence is not permitted in its precincts. Pilgrims are in a state of sanctity (*iḥrām*; Q5.1, 9).[8]

Note the linguistic and conceptual similarity with the Hebrew ban or *chērêm*, a word found twice in *Devar'im* (Deut.) 7.26. It meant the curse of destruction which was originally an ostensibly motiveless, malicious and certainly barbaric, regulation in Israel's holy war, requiring the annihilation of captives and war booty. This was justified as a purgative action which served to prove one's sincerity and zeal for God. How? It showed that one was not motivated by material gain and did so, moreover, as part of one's faith in a God who alone could give such a signal victory over Israel's powerful and ubiquitous enemies.[9] It later came to mean excommunication from the congregation of Israel. That was the penalty for apostasy from Judaism.

In v.9, the preposition *para* (as *par' ho*) strictly means 'beside what' (i.e. alongside or 'other than') rather than 'contrary to' but the local context confirms that the latter meaning is intended. Naturally Paul will not tolerate a gospel with opposed content but his vehemence suggests that he will not even countenance materials supplementary to his teaching, if these affect the salvation of his disciples.

IV 1.10–12

10 *For now do I persuade men or God? Or do I seek to please men? If still I pleased men, I would not have been a slave of Christ.* **11** *For I make known to you, brothers, the gospel preached by me is not according to man.* **12** *For I neither received it from a man nor was I taught (it thus) but (I received it) through a revelation of Jesus Christ.*

10

Paul is the *doulos* (bondservant) of Christ. Thus, Arab Christians call him *'abd al-masīḥ*. Seeking divine favour or human approval appears, to the Apostle, as mutually exclusive. This hyperbolic view is moreover expressed defensively – in a polemical environment. One wonders what Paul would have written instead had his epistle been addressed to a constituency made ready for a joyful availing of his message, perhaps in a *Pros Galatas Beta*, where the Apostle was happier and Galatia was more like Philippi. But this is fantasy.

The Quran condemns ostentation (Q8.47–8), linking it to the Devil's ability to make evil conduct appear glamorous. This attitude, linked to the sin of hypocrisy, may show itself in a tendency to be a crowd-pleaser. Paul was, critics would argue, a politician who was, despite what he says, a 'men-pleaser'. He admits that he became all things to all people – but for the sake of Christ (Phil. 1.18). Hostile exegetical critics of 1 Cor. 9.19–23 might see in Paul's attitude there some traces of the Shia principle of *taqiyya* (dissimulation), a principle of accommodation to hostile circumstances, entitling one to conceal one's faith and true intentions, for the sake of one's faith. The attitude finds support in a narrative unique to the Quran about a monotheistic believer who hides his faith since he belongs to Pharaoh's people – during the time of Moses' ministry in Egypt (Q40.28–45).

Muslims believe that one should cultivate human relationships naturally and accept human assistance, but only as a divinely approved means to a God-ordained end. All help is ultimately from God (Q8.10) – and he suffices anyone who trusts in him (Q65.3). This is the message of absolute and unconditional trust in God, a frequent emphasis in the Quran and in the Prophet's teaching. Prophets and devoted servants of God are expected to rely directly on his help. Thus, Mary receives provision directly from God (Q3.37), thought to be fruits out of season. Admittedly, Joseph asked one of his fellow prisoners to mention him to his master and thus relied on a human network of influence – but only because he was falsely accused and therefore rightly eager to exonerate himself (Q12.42).

As early as this verse, we sense Paul's reservations about formal religious authority and his ambivalence concerning the institutionally approved pillars of the Jerusalem church. This is also the earliest indication of the motif of honour and shame – a concern which dictates regard for certain moral values endemic to hierarchical structures marked by authority and subservience. Christ subverted and inverted the values of the world when he ordered his followers to obey new ethical directives.

11

Before Paul begins his confessional autobiography, he defends his ministry and claims to be called directly by God. See also 1.1 and 1.16 for Paul's relentless stress on the wholly divine provenance of his gospel of grace. It is no human fabrication – no more the product of human effort than the salvation it achieves. 'Preached by me' in the aorist (completed past) passive registers and salutes the absence of any human component or initiative, capturing Paul's mood of total dependence on God. The Greek idiom here translates awkwardly as 'the gospel gospelled by me'. In the Quran's poetic Arabic, however, using a verbal noun with its cognate verb is frequent – as in 'In him let all who trust put their trust' (Q12.67).

Paul uses 'Brothers' (*adelphoi*) in the vocative case. The equivalent address, used often among Muslims, can denote mild coercion, sometimes disguised as frustrated affection, especially in contexts of exhortation. It resembles the use of 'Comrades!' among communists. While one can use an affectionate phrase to capture a statement of fact, it is also possible to use such phrases to mean the opposite of their lexical meaning: 'darling' can be a term of reproach, if used with a negative tone.

12

Paul asserts that he received a revelation (*apokalupsis*) of the risen Christ, not merely a vision, auditory experience or dream. The gospel's origin and authority lie in God's will. Muslims find such claims familiar since they believe that the Quran's genesis is wholly divine: Muhammad's authorship is not conceded even as a literary convention. This emphasis on total literary reliance on God is reflected in, and consistent with, orthodox claims for Muhammad's illiteracy and lack of access to human sources of knowledge. At another level, however, the revelation to Paul could hardly differ more from the one to Muhammad. Paul received a commission, through an encounter with a remarkable person. Paul explained and expounded the idea contained in this experience. Muhammad received a dictation – which contained exhortation and legal commandments that were to be implemented in Medina and seen as the perfect political providence.

Paul cannot mean here that he learned nothing about Jesus from any human being. Persecutors often learn much about the sect they wish to destroy. In the acquisition of ideological information, as we now know in the case of Western secret services – including the CIA, perceived by Muslim radicals to be ruthlessly militant and efficient – hostility is a far more powerful motive than sympathy. Paul claims that he received Christian traditions (1 Cor. 11.23, 15.3), citing only Christ as the transmitter of such knowledge. What did Paul thus receive? It is unlikely to have been some propositions in Aramaic, directly from the lips of the risen Christ. Rather it was the experience of knowing, with certainty, the Lordship of Christ and the priority of grace over the law for receiving the gift of salvation. Paul could have learned some more factual or historical details from Ananias, the devout Jew who baptised him and gave him back the gift of sight (Acts 9.10–19), or from Peter during that fortnight when he met him in Jerusalem and enrolled in a 'crash course' on the life and ministry of the earthly Jesus (Gal. 1.18).

That Paul was sent neither from a man nor through men but through Christ (1.1, 12) implies that Christ Jesus is more than human. In Romans and Galatians, *anthrōpos* can mean man and therefore 'man without Christ', that is, the unredeemed and purely biological human condition. In many Meccan revelations (Q17.11; 36.77–78; 75.3–6; 90.4–11; 96.6–7), *al-insān* means the disbeliever or godless man claiming self-sufficiency and, unlike devout believers and prophets, arguing insolently with God and refusing to submit to his gracious will.

V

We turn to dominant themes in this part of the letter. Paul opens by defining an apostle negatively as being 'neither from human beings nor through a (or any) human being', implying a polemical environment. The prevalence of polemic – God himself indulges in it – suggests that the human race is disunited even though its origins are monogenetic. The human context is always polemical given the perversity of human nature, given our tendency to reject uncomfortable truths in the two crucial matters of moment: truth and power. No responsible theology could ignore the combative context of real existence. To do so would lead us to indulge in fantasy while thinking we are doing theology.

Paul never mentions any human influence unless he feels obliged to do so. Stephen and Ananias are telling omissions. The Apostle mentions the Jerusalem apostles probably only because his opponents mentioned them first and accused Paul of being a second-hand apostle. He sounds at best ambivalent and at worst dismissive of the pillars and, moreover, he opposes Peter in public. The mention of Barnabas appears to be only a courtesy admission. In two vignettes in Galatians (2.5–9, 11–18), Paul is featured as the hero while others come out badly. Barnabas and Peter are even portrayed as fickle enough to be crowd-pleasers who side with the hypocrites. Admittedly, everyone is tempted, when recounting an event, to edit and angle it in such a way as to place oneself in the best possible light!

Paul denies, with Semitic scrupulousness, both a human source (the preposition is *apo*, from) and human agency (*dia*, through) for his apostleship. Paul is an apostle through, not merely from, Jesus. The Quran, by contrast, is revelation from (*min*) God, not through God. Distance is preserved between the revealer and the reality revealed. The mother of the book (*umm al-kitāb;* Q3.7), meaning its essence, is with (*'inda*) God. This preposition, frequent in the Quran (e.g. 9.19), literally means 'at God', that is, in his sight – implying intimate connection albeit at a fixed location rather than, so to speak, during an agent's continuous movement or transfer.

Muslims and Christians agree that the gift of apostleship is directly endowed by God. Paul receives the gift from two divine persons, Jesus Christ and God the Father. Only one preposition (*dia*) is used here, though that need not imply that the two persons are identical. In any case, Muslims reject close identification of the messenger with the sender since messengers remain human and mortal while God remains divine and immortal. Christians never deify Paul or identify him, qua apostle of Christ, with the sender, God as Christ.

Paul was presumably appointed an apostle of Christ Jesus in c.34–35 CE. In the conventional Christian chronology, that would be shortly after the crucifixion. Note that a figure as significant as the author of Revelation does not, unlike Paul, claim apostolic authority although both were itinerant prophet-apostles who travelled widely among the scattered churches. John modestly calls himself only a servant (*doulos*) of Jesus Christ (Rev. 1.1). Apostles were more important than mere mystics or even Christian prophets such as John whose book offers a preview of future events. On one understanding, apostles were those directly commissioned by Jesus; their number was forever fixed. This cannot be Paul's definition of the word which means anyone who was a witness to Christ's resurrection and is sent with the message of the gospel (see also Acts 1.21–22). By John's day, the original twelve apostles had become 'cornerstones' of the heavenly Temple (Rev. 21.14).

In Galatians, Paul calls himself an apostle from the very outset, and a servant as late as verse 10. Elsewhere, he identifies himself immediately as both servant and apostle of Christ Jesus (Rom. 1.1). In the Corinthian correspondence, he introduces himself as apostle (of Jesus Christ) only; in the Thessalonian pair, he is neither apostle nor servant of Christ. To the Philippians, he is merely one of two servants (with Timothy) of Christ Jesus. In the disputed epistles, he is described in Ephesians, Colossians, and in two of the pastorals (1 and 2 Timothy) as apostle of Christ Jesus. In Titus, he appears both as a servant of God and an apostle of Jesus Christ. In the opening verse of the pastoral 'postcard' called Philemon, Paul abjectly but proudly calls himself 'prisoner of Christ' (*desmios Christou*), a prisoner of the one who set him free – a paradox which epitomises the Apostle whose strength was perfected in his weakness.

Paul is variously an apostle and servant of higher beings – and his strength derives from that liaison. To serve a voluntarily powerless Lord is, however, still to serve in weakness. Where is the strength in this arrangement? Christians need to know that such claims, whose charm and truth seem self-evident to Christians, are dismissed particularly by Muslim and also by Marxist critics. They see it as special pleading, self-deluded reasoning and, in any case, ineffective in our kind of world which resists goodness, not evil, and does so with determined force and tenacity. The Christian will no doubt dismiss the critics' dismissal of the Christian stance. And to all alike should be granted the right to their own consciences in such ultimate matters of moral moment.

VI

One theme that makes Islam and Christianity superficially similar is the theme of prophets. Islamic prophetology differs profoundly from Christian views of that office. For one thing, in Islam, a messenger of God is never sent by another man or men; only an ordinary delegate or emissary can be dispatched thus. A divine commission can only be from God. Muslims and Christians concur that God authorises and sends apostles. Jesus sends out the twelve and the seventy but he is, for Christians, a divine sender.

The apostleship of Paul, commissioned by Jesus Christ, however, is unacceptable to Muslims since only God can commission human apostles (and angels) for various tasks – and Jesus Christ is not considered God. In some ways, the Quran's notion of prophet resembles the biblical notion of the angel (or messenger) of the Lord who represents God, speaks his word but does not allow his personal identity to intrude (see Judges 13.3–25). The biblical prophets were, however, humans called by God and sent to the people, commanded to convey God's message with and through their unique character and personal identity. This is not a distinction that can be rigidly applied since prophets in the Quran also retain their personal traits and some local colour and detail while conveying essentially the same message of divine unity. In the eyes of many Jews and Christians, however, the Quranic prophets appear to be all alike – 'clones' of Muhammad preaching a stereotypical monotheism. This is a mistaken perception.

A prophet may assist or be a mouthpiece for another, as Aaron to Moses, but no *rasūl* (Jesus) can commission another *rasūl* (Paul). Muhammad had no co-prophets. A contemporary called Maslama ibn Habib wanted to share prophethood with him. Muhammad dismissed the offer and mocked Maslama – and the Quran does not even condescend to mention the incident. More recently, members of the Ahmadiyya sect have strenuously contended that Mirza Ghulam Ahmad was a satellite prophet, orbiting around Muhammad, jointly commissioned by him and by God. The Ahmadis' ingenuity got them nowhere: they have been declared apostates.

According to their Quranic profile, prophets strive to please God and expect no reward from humans. They faithfully deliver their messages and trusts and are willing to be martyred in battle or in physically passive vulnerability. Prophets are obedient servants of God but can, on occasion, be temporarily disobedient. Jonah is an example (Q21.87–88; 37.139–148).

In biblical Aramaic, a messenger (*sheliāch* from the verb *sh-l-ch*, to send, literally, to stretch or extend) is any secular functionary on an errand. In Arabic, *rasūl* has come to mean only a religious figure although the root meaning is secular, that is, anyone sent with a message. This usage is rare in the Quran but the messengers (*mursalūna* at Q27.35) are thought to be diplomats, an embassy sent from a court in Yemen to Solomon in Jerusalem. Although the Bible and the Quran concur that God chooses mortal human beings as prophets, Quranic prophetology differs since 'prophet' (*rasūl*, *nabī*) is made to carry more weight and depth in the Quran where God sends prophets to communities to warn them of imminent divine judgement and annihilation. This is the case with biblical prophets too but, apart from all the major ones and a few of the 'minor' ones (such as Micah), they also play the less dramatic roles of pure exhortation and censure, as evidenced in the oracles of Malachi or the anonymous book of Jonah.

In Islam, disciples and companions of prophets are, like prophets, human. Unlike prophets, however, they do not receive divine revelation. The Quran contains no sustainable distinction between Old Testament prophets and New Testament apostles, the latter being mentioned in the Quran only in their capacity as Jesus' disciples. Part of the reason for the discrepancy between the Quranic and the biblical notions of the prophetic office is that Christians subtly transcended the Old Testament category of prophet after its perceived fulfilment in Jesus. Thus, New Testament prophets have different, indeed comparatively attenuated, roles. Christians retained the older robust notion of prophet for the prophets of ancient Israel but also adopted, for New Testament times, a broader notion of the prophetic office which could cover older seminal personalities (such as Elijah and Elisha) while also including anyone who prophesied during the time of Jesus and Paul.

As for Paul, he was perhaps too much of an intellectual to be a prophet. Reading the Bible and the Quran has convinced me that God admires men and women of faith, not theologians, let alone philosophers and academics. Isaiah sounds most like the Quran's notion of a prophet. He preached the straight path, condemned crookedness (Isa. 40.3–5) and was no jingoist. Judaism was a potentially universal faith as we see when the great prophet looks forward to a time when God's house will be 'a house of prayer for all nations' (Isa. 56.7 quoted at Mark 11.17). The Quran does not mention by name the suffering servants of the word, men such as Jeremiah, whose matchless integrity reached a level that perhaps appears masochistic to many moderns. The Noah of the Quran, however, resembles a suffering servant whose life is full of agony and meditative sadness (Q11.45–47; 54.9–10; 71). Job is a man of sorrows in both scriptures, the victim of Satan's wiles.

Paul's vocation as apostle to the nations was perhaps unconsciously and partly modelled on the call of Jeremiah, 'the weeping prophet' to the nations (Jer. 1.5). Paul was also the suffering but joyful servant of Christ crucified. Aspects of Jeremiah's ministry resemble Muhammad's, especially the stress on speaking the literal word of God (Jer. 1.7, 9) which suggests a dictation model of revelation. However, Jeremiah's oracle about the new covenant – a future for Israel and Judah when God's law shall be written on human hearts (Jer. 31.31–34) – also reads like a paraphrase of a Pauline epistle! And Paul sometimes sounds like Jeremiah.

Is Paul one of the unnamed prophets of the Quran? Samuel Zwemer (1867–1952), an indefatigable American missionary to Arab Muslims, argued that Paul was to be identified with *Ṣāliḥ*, the pre-Islamic Arab prophet (see Q7.73–79). Zwemer based his argument on a slender basis: *Ṣāliḥ* lamented to his disobedient people after they had perished: 'You do not love sincere advisors' (Q7.79). And love was the mark of Jesus' disciples and of the Christian community, as the Quran concurs (57.27). Zwemer's claim is speculative but not unmotivated. Unsurprisingly, it has never received any attention from either New Testament scholars or Muslim scholars of the Quran.[10]

VII

In Gal. 1.6, Paul accuses the Galatians of deserting (*metatithesthe apo*; verb: *metatithēmi*) the one who called them. In the classical world, individuals changed their minds as they turned from one school of philosophy to another. The deserter, *ho metathēmenos*, not a New Testament word, left one school of thought to join another. This would perhaps resemble a Muslim leaving one of the four Sunni schools of law, into which he or she was born, in order to join a school consonant with his or her adult inclinations.

Hē apostasia (2 Thess. 2:3), not used in Galatians, includes both intended defection and actual apostasy from the true Gospel. It troubles Paul as he worries about the activities of the unnamed agitators. Muhammad had to deal with agitators in Medina, unnamed enemies of the infant Islamic society. Paul fights on two fronts: unwarranted additions to the message and attacks on the messenger. In Muhammad's case, the agitators identified the messenger Muhammad with his message of Islam.

In post-Quranic Islam, apostasy was a matter of great legal import. However, purely theological criteria were often used to decide who should be subject to legal penalty and sanction. In Muhammad's day, we find apostasy being committed privately (theologically motivated) and publically (politically motivated). The latter involved ex-Muslims joining battle against the nascent Islamic state. It amounted to treason against the state, a capital offence. The Quran prescribes no penalty for private apostasy but condemns it as anathema in this world while threatening perpetual hellfire in the next. Muhammad's traditions seem to suggest a death penalty for all types of apostasy – although his words, assuming that they are his words, might reasonably be interpreted otherwise. The debate about the historical accuracy of Muhammad's reported conduct in this matter is no merely academic concern: it remains vitally relevant to the predicament of today's converts from Islam to Christianity.

The Quran also mentions pretended or fake apostasy: a strategically misleading apostasy whereby some People of the Book would pretend to become Muslims at the beginning of the day but, by evening, declare their loss of faith, thus casting doubts in the hearts of Arab polytheist converts to Islam (Q3.72). The Quran is constantly alert to Jewish and Christian mischief. If Muhammad sanctioned the death penalty for this kind of apostasy, it would be somewhat easier to justify it.

The New Testament and the Quran concur that retreat is unacceptable in the life of faith. One must believe and then endure in such belief. Is divine grace revocable or irresistible and terminative? Can one reject grace once it has been received? Faith need not endure, it seems. Was it then always false faith from the start if it later became false? Can true faith end and be replaced by hypocrisy? Or does true faith always endure? If so, is it enabled by grace? Such are the complexities and paradoxes of grace. Though debated in depth only by Christian thinkers, the paradoxes are present in every monotheism.

VIII

Paul mentions angels (Gal. 1.8, 3.19, 4. 14). Unlike the Arabic word for angel (*malak*), however, both the Greek *anggelos* and the Hebrew *mal'ak* are semantically ambiguous. The primary meaning is that of a messenger with a message to convey. The secondary additional meaning is a heavenly being. In Arabic, as in English, a human being can be called an angel but only metaphorically. In the Quran, Joseph's female Egyptian admirers call him 'a gracious angel' (Q12.31).

The Arab pagans regularly challenged Muhammad to bring an angel from heaven to verify his claims (e.g. Q25.7). The Quran interprets this as mockery and retorts that had there been angels resident on earth, the messenger would have been an angel (Q17.95). The request for a warning angel to accompany a human prophet is seen as a kind of mild category error – somewhat analogous to the claim that God became incarnate, dismissed by Muslims as a serious category mistake. Christians and Muslims alike accept that mortals can receive messages from angels. But only some angels are authentic messengers of God (see Gal. 3.19, 4.14). Others may be malevolent and deceptive (Gal. 1.8). The Devil himself, warns Paul, masquerades as an angel of light (2 Cor. 11.14). The Quran has no notion of 'false angels' any more than it has of 'false prophets'. A visitation by an angel is always a good and rare event. However, there is a partial parallel to Paul's claim since the Quran permits the damaging possibility that the Devil may successfully interfere in the reception of revelation brought by an angel to a (human) prophet (Q22.52). The broader issue here is the controversy known as 'the satanic verses', a matter discussed by some commentators in the context of the revelation of Q53.19–23.

For Paul, the gospel is self-authenticating, its credentials constitutive of its message. The Quran's descent and Muhammad's experience of revelation are both seen by Muslims as self-authenticating (Q2.2; 53.2–18). Disbelievers demanded that an interpreting angel from heaven be sent down to confirm its heavenly provenance and truth. The Quran dismissed this pagan demand which, to our sceptical contemporary temperament, seems legitimate. We cannot bridge the cultural gulf between us, in the age of realisation and enlightenment, and previous ages of revelation and mystery. A robust sceptical tradition has accompanied the birth of all faiths. Doubt is not an exclusively modern phenomenon although its contemporary range and intensity are historically unprecedented.

A messenger's moral credentials were deemed fundamental since we must examine these before we can assess the authenticity of the message he brings. A good man must bring a good message. An evil man could receive a divine revelation but, given what we know of God's character, this is unlikely. For this reason, Paul emphasises his virtuous lifestyle, as a Jew and as a Christian convert (see especially 1 Thess. 4–5; 2 Cor. 3.1–2; 11.7–13.10; Phil. 3.3–17). Similarly, Muhammad appealed to his character as the trustworthy one, Al-Amīn, also a title of the archangel Gabriel. In our sceptical age, the truth of a message is not seen as organically connected to the moral excellence of a messenger's character. The ancient liaison between virtue and the reception of revealed knowledge (or wisdom), found in Plato's thought and affirmed by the Quran (Q12.22; 28.14), has been replaced by a sceptical view in which the acquisition and the content of knowledge are both detached from the moral character of the knower. A man may acquire an immense amount of knowledge, even of important moral truths, and yet lack wisdom and even be evil. I would contend that we owe this amoral and therefore potentially dangerous epistemology to Descartes, the father of modern Western philosophy.

IX

Paul preached the gospel (*euaggelizōmai*, v.16) with authority (*kataggellein*; Phil.1.16; Acts 13.5, 15.36, 17.13). *Euangellion* is a frequently used noun in Paul's letters. It means not a factual statement or mere proclamation but rather the power of God in Christ, gripping repentant sinners as they are saved for eternal life through Jesus' death and resurrection. In secular Greek, *euanggelizomai* can be used to describe a slave carrying and proclaiming news of a general's triumph in battle. The noun is found in inscriptions announcing that the birth of Emperor Augustus inaugurated good news for the whole world.

Injīl sounds like an Arabic rendering of the Greek *euangellion*. I have not found any clear instances of a recognisable cognate of *Injīl* in other languages such as Syriac or in Ethiopic, an Afro-Semitic language. The Quran uses *Al-Injīl* as a proper noun; it has no native Arabic etymology. It occurs only with the definite article (*Al-Injīl*; Q3.3; 5.47, etc.). As an indefinite noun, it admits of a plural (*anājīl*). The Quran never mentions any scripture in its (indefinite) plural noun form.

The Quran contains good news (*bushrā*; 27.2), which amounts to wisdom and includes an awareness of God's mercy and justice, practical guidance for attaining paradise –offered to all those who yearn to attain faith and do good works. But *Al-Injīl* is not called *al-bushrā* even though the Torah and the Gospel (given to Jesus) contain perfect guidance and divine mercy for those who fear God and intend to do good and to be good (Q3.4; 5.54; 6.154).[11]

According to the Muslim scripture, *Al-Injīl* is a scripture given *to Jesus* (57.27) rather than an eschatological gospel *about Jesus*. God taught Jesus the Torah and the Gospel (3.48). And the Islamic notion of the Gospel is a world removed from the developed dogmas of its complex rival faith, dogmas such as the order of salvation (*ordo salutis*). This describes the precise process whereby Christ takes on the sins of sinners who then receive his righteousness as they are, through grace, judged innocent for Christ's sake, even though they are (objectively) guilty as charged.

The Gospel is unique and singular, not banal and repeatable. This feature is constitutive of its divine credentials. For if it was of human origin, it could be humanly duplicated. Muslims argue similarly when they seek to establish the inimitability *(i'jāz)* of the Quran as proof its divine origin. The Quran repeatedly challenges disbelievers to produce another Quran like the one given to Muhammad (Q2.23–24). Logically, the challenge cannot be met and the demand is, strictly speaking, incoherent. If the rival work is similar, it is the not the same; if identical, it is a copy, not a rival. Paul could have challenged the perverse Galatians to 'produce another Gospel like it' adding that 'You cannot; therefore believe in the only authentic one.' Paul held that alteration, modification or addition constituted a perversion of the gospel.

If we were to express the kerygma in terms analogous to Islam's creed, we would declare: 'There is no gospel except the only gospel.' This relentless emphasis on the uniqueness of the *euangellion* explains the triumph of Pauline Christianity. Great ideas are always formulated in this way. No faith or ideology was ever founded on doubt, on acknowledgement of diversity or on the literary apparatus of hesitation that accompanies it. Certainty is a form of authority. It is intolerant of alternatives. In temperament, it is totalitarian, the temper of every successful protest and revolutionary movement. Many seek to deny even the dignity of real existence to their enemies – not as people, of course, since they exist biologically and therefore need to be annihilated. Rather, they deny and dismiss their ideas, their self-identification and self-images. The best parallel is the lack of documentation which effectively denies the very existence of an illegal immigrant: a man without papers becomes no one, the invisible man with no human worth. His self is effortlessly reduced to nothing – without any Buddhist-style meditative effort.

'There is no god except the only God' implies that idols do not even exist, except as literary fictions enjoying rhetorical existence, and thus existing only so that their existence can be denied – in style. 'There is no good news except the only good news'. Other gospels do not even exist, let alone matter.[12] For Paul, this sole Gospel was 'the criterion' (*al-furqān*), to borrow here the Quran's self-description (Q25.1). Paul uses it to judge putative claims to heavenly inspiration and revelation. Paul would judge the Quran to be a false Gospel, as many evangelicals proclaim when they refuse to engage Muslims as dialogue partners – since to do so might be a covert concession that Islam has the potential right to assert its truth-claims as being no less valid than the Christian kerygma.

Finally, a postscript here about motives. While Paul upholds that there is only one Gospel, the true one, he also admits that such a gospel can be preached from false motives (Phil. 1.18). One can imagine Paul issuing the following warning to the Galatians: 'You can preach the true gospel from false motives because you can insincerely preach the truth. But if you preach a false gospel, as some of you do, the sincerity of your motives counts for nothing.'

X

I comment further now on Gal. 1.8–9, the locus of the Pauline stress on the singular comprehensiveness of the kerygma. Acts confirms Paul's stance. As he bade farewell to the Ephesian elders (Acts 20.17–35), Paul identified 'the gospel of the grace of God' (Acts 20.24) with 'the whole counsel (will) of God' (Acts 20.27).

Gal. 1.8–9 is one scriptural source for *sola scriptura* – the Protestant view that the Bible contains all knowledge necessary for salvation and sanctification of the sinner. The *sola scriptura* was originally part of a trinity of Reformation '*sola*'s' – only by scripture, only by faith, only by grace – to which others, including only by Christ, were later added. Luther wrote that God alone was to establish articles of faith and that no one, 'not even an angel could do so'.[13] The implication is that Christians need confess only those doctrines that are directly or by implication in the canonical scriptures. Other authorities are normative but remain subordinate to the infallible authority of the biblical canon. It is admitted that the private individual needs a supporting Christian community if his or her interpretation is to be considered authoritative. The revelation to an individual believer must still be communally approved, its interpretation externally authorised. The catholic epistle 2 Pet. 1.20–21 assigns a supplementary role to the Holy Spirit. Anglicans and Methodists hold a modified view (*prima scriptura*) which enables them to add that scripture is illumined by tradition and reason, a modification that moves them closer to Catholicism.

The problem with *sola scriptura* is that it is itself not biblical. Indeed, the canon of the New Testament was established by an extra-biblical authority, the Synod of Rome (382 CE). Moreover, throughout the New Testament, we find references to 'apocryphal' material which is deemed authoritative (Matt. 2.23, 2 Tim. 3.8; 1 Pet. 3.19; Jude 9; James 5.17). Oral and extra-biblical tradition is upheld as authoritative by Jesus himself (see Matt. 23.2–3). James quotes the prayer of Elijah (1 Kings 17.1) but additionally specifies the duration of the drought (James 5.17). Paul refers to a spiritual rock (*pneumatikēs petras*) that followed the Jews as they wandered through the Sinai wilderness (1 Cor. 10.4). Such an idea is nowhere in the Torah and must have originated in some fertile rabbinic mind.

Christians may then differ on the range of 'scripture'. Any truly apostolic, and *a fortiori* ecclesiocentric, hermeneutic must reject the simplistic and ahistorical doctrine of *sola scriptura ad litteram* (scripture alone – and that literally). The latter stance amounts to Biblicism in which Christians could be associating the Bible with the competing revelation of God in Christ. Some Muslim heretics have in modern times argued for 'Quran only', a view that marginalises the role of the Prophet. This view was not even held by Muhammad himself who could have held it justifiably since the Quran, unlike the Bible, does claim self-sufficiency as scripture. But Muhammad, at least in the early years, was asked to seek confirmation from extra-Quranic sources, namely, from those who already possessed scripture. In modern times, anyone – Muslim or non-Muslim – could, of course, revere 'the Quran alone' in the sense of admiring its aesthetic beauty rather than its status as a book of revealed guidance pointing the way to God, the revealer. In my view, this resembles the prevalent modern idolatry of literary art where one merely seeks to be entertained, not morally edified.

Gal. 1.8–9 betrays Paul's tendency towards an exegetical intolerance as he annexes to the new Jesus movement the ideal of the Christ, now shared by Jews with Gentiles but originally exclusively Jewish. He proclaims a partly and subtly opposed appropriation of its content when he rejects crucial parts of its existing but competing traditional – and exclusively – Jewish meaning along with its inherited associated aspirations. Paul's interpretation was destined to prevail. With much reason most Jews see this achievement as, tragically, the most famous successful takeover bid in the history of ideas. They feel dispossessed of their rich heritage. We know that some Christians neither know nor care that Jesus was a Jew, let alone that Christianity is named after a Jewish aspiration consummated. And, to take an extreme example, some of Adolf Hitler's Nazi followers actively tried to prove that Jesus could not have been a Jew at all!

XI

In Gal. 1.4, Paul mentions Christ's self-sacrifice on the cross. 'For Christ, our Passover', declares Paul elsewhere, 'has also been sacrificed' (1 Cor. 5.7). Paul was co-crucified with his master and thus died to the law. Christ now lives in him (Gal. 2. 19–20). Paul adds that through Christ's death, the world has been crucified to Paul as he has been to the world. He cites as proof his wounds (Gal. 6.14, 17). These seem to be phantom – that is, without apparent physical causation – but Paul received beatings and some scars must have endured. Extreme and prolonged suffering of the type Paul endured may have caused injuries in his body, including wounds of a psychosomatic nature.

Jesus and Paul were Jewish martyrs who laid down their lives. In the Quran, with one prominent exception (Q85.4–8), martyrdom is rarely voluntary self-sacrifice. Typically the martyr is not a victim but a combatant and warrior. No doubt, Paul was, like Gandhi, a kind of warrior but he was fighting only a spiritual battle, equipped only with spiritual weapons. Being physically defenceless and thus dependent on God alone, however, marked the Christian style of witness, especially during the early centuries of persecution.

By contrast, the Muslim martyr (*shahīd*, meaning witness, as in the Greek *martus*), is a warrior-merchant making an excellent bargain (Q9.111), as he sells the finite and ephemeral goods of this world in exchange for God's forgiveness and escape from the Fire of Hell. The bonus is entry into the eternal delights of Paradise – without even the strict reckoning everyone else must face. This is the best bargain, the supreme triumph. Muhammad's audience understood it well. This is indeed the message of orthodox

Islam though admittedly it appears problematic to modern Westerners and some contemporary 'moderate' Muslims living in a world of sovereign states rather than faith-based empires. The holy law of Islam lays down rules and guidance for regulating the religious enthusiasm of the warrior.

The expiating death of Christ 'in accordance with the scriptures' (1 Cor. 15.3) was a humanly transmitted tradition Paul received. He also received a direct revelation (Gal. 1.11–12), presumably about the centrality of the cross. Sin, sacrifice and atonement are of vital interest to Christians, but of marginal significance in Islam. Muslims are dismissive of such key Christian concerns. To think that someone else suffered for our sins and that we are redeemed by his blood is unjust. It is our own self-surrender and righteousness, not another person's self-sacrifice and merits, no matter how great, which merits 'salvation'. That God's grace is a prerequisite for Muslims no less than for Christians, is not a disputed thesis. Muslims rarely have the patience and conscientious respect even to appreciate, let alone explore, core Christian soteriological convictions. In what follows, I shall introduce and survey larger themes that shall interest us in the rest of the textual commentary.

Sin not only degrades human beings but it reminds them, Christians would add, that they are already degraded. Sin damages our relationship with God; we crave atoning reconciliation (Ar., *kaffāra*; Hebr., *kapporêth*, Lev. 16:15). In Islam, sin is primarily *ẓulm al-nafs* (self-wronging; Q18.35) but it also injures our relationship to God though not irreparably. According to the Hebrew Bible, this relationship is restored typically through sacrifice – an external form of atonement (Lev. 5–7). An internal or spiritual purification is also required (see Isa. 1.11–17). Muhammad's Islam requires only the internal process. Muslims, like modern Jews, hold that they can repair and maintain their relationship with God through daily canonical prayers, accompanied by supplication and repentance, fasting and voluntary charity.

The redeemer (Hebr., *go'el*) was originally a blood-avenger (see Num. 35.12–29). It later came to mean advocate (as in Job 19.25). Justification (*dikaiosunē*) is God's act in redeeming human beings from a state of otherwise permanent sin by discounting its deserved effect. Protestants insist on God's unconditional acceptance of sinners without necessarily disregarding good works and holiness. Catholics emphasise God's commitment to justice in aligning virtue with reward (and vice with punishment) but also maintain that merit may itself be an undeserved gift of grace.

The Quran affirms the Old Testament perspective on sacrifice as a divinely ordained way to show self-surrender and affiliation to the covenant and the cause of God. All the prophets from Abraham to Moses, from David to Jesus, offered sacrifice as an expression of worship. It was accepted as righteousness but the Quran rejects the dogma that blood cleanses us of sin, a Jewish view inherited by New Testament writers. In the Letter to the Hebrews, written in Italy (Heb. 13.24), not Palestine, Christ abolishes the Levitical sacrificial system by offering himself as a sinless victim. The whole letter reads like a rebuke to those who hankered after the older sanguine but splendid dispensation centred on the Jerusalem Temple sacrifices.

The Quran would see this obsession with eliminating sin through sacrifice, animal or human, as corrupt pagan superstition. The pilgrimage to Mecca, originally instituted by Abraham the iconoclast, provides atonement for sins and absolves believers of accumulated wrongdoings as their piety alone, not the blood or meat of the sacrificed animals, reaches God (Q22.36–7; see also Q6.136 and Amos 5.21–5). The slaughter of animals, the culminating ceremony of the *ḥajj*, provides food for the poor. It is not a propitiatory or penitential sacrifice but rather a prayerfully grateful and gracious commemoration of Abraham's noble conduct (Q.37.102–107; Gen. 22) which pleased God so much that a ransom (*fidyā*; Q37.107) was accepted. This test, known to Jews and Christians as 'the binding of Isaac', embarrasses Reform Jews who see it as merely a daring moral fable. According to Muslims, whatever may have been ordained by God in the past, the revelation of the Quran terminated the need for animal sacrifice as expiation for sin and instead demanded that human beings surrender and sacrifice only their will and purpose to God – the very meaning of Islam.

How does the life, healing ministry, death, resurrection and ascension of Jesus accomplish (for others) forgiveness and reconciliation with God? Christ's death, as opposed to his life and ministry, secures atonement for all humanity as opposed to the few who knew and accepted him in first century Palestine. It universalises what would otherwise have remained a local and parochial transaction. His death was an expiation – redress or compensation – for universal sin.

The atonement for all sin by Christ's death – called satisfaction – is no self-evident doctrine. The penal or juridical theory holds that Christ has borne the penalty (or burden) of sin on behalf of those who deserved it. This enables God to freely forgive human transgressions against him. Anselm argued that since sin is an infinite offence against God, it required a correspondingly infinite satisfaction. And this could only be arranged by God himself. This demand can be interpreted literally to mean that Christ is the substitute for each and every individual who deserves the penalty. In the sacrificial theory, Christ propitiates the deserved wrath of God by becoming the perfectly sinless offering: as victim, he becomes the ransom and thus makes a universal expiation of the stain of sin, Adam's original sin inherited by the human race. Here Christ is the representative of sinful Adam, not a substitute. The atonement is also seen as a dramatic and decisive triumph over the evil of sin personified in the Devil. Christians typically uphold that the amazing extent of God's gracious love revealed in Christ, especially in his voluntary acceptance of an unjust and brutal death, should move sinners to repentance. In the revolutionary initiative of liberation theology, atonement is extended to encompass a corporate redemption of the evil of oppressive political structures.

XII

Paul emphasises the paradox of the humiliation-exaltation of the cross because he rejects the uncomplicated triumphalism of his Christian opponents. The gospel of the cross, like persecuted Meccan Islam, would appeal to powerless victims, often struggling at the lowest levels of Roman society. Such were probably the majority of Paul's hearers (see 1 Cor. 1.26–28). The Gospel, like the Quran, was to be an alternate source of power, sacred power. But the Quran attempted to absorb politics into religion so that utopian politics would appeal not only to the marginalised but rather confront all the solidarities that oppress peoples and societies everywhere at all times. Faith was not merely a school of social criticism but rather the effective weapon of revolutionary change in every structure that resisted universal justice. Muhammad moved from the soothing catharsis of merely moral outrage into the tougher arena of effectively activist agency.

Christians, as slaves of Christ, become slaves to his ideal of righteousness – a full-time and, once accepted, involuntary requirement. In a popular adaptation of such exacting traditional Christian ideals in secular culture, we note some accommodation to liberal ideals of altruism and self-actualisation through an attenuated and thus merely voluntary and part-time service. The original idea was that, as slaves, Christians were merely doing their duty (Luke 17.7–10) – although duty is a semi-legal word with potentially dangerous overtones for a Christian enjoying liberty in the spirit since duty might place some unspecified limits on liberty.

In Arab culture, as in the classical Greco-Roman world in Jesus' and Paul's day, the slave was not simply a hired servant or an indentured labourer. Rather, the slave often felt close ties with and affection for his master. The Quran permitted slavery, an existing practice in Arabia, but ordered believers to give a freewill offering, upon manumission, to their male and female slaves. It encouraged believers to marry their newly freed slaves, male and female (Q24.32–33). While the Quran permits female war captives, euphemistically called possession of the right hand (Q4.3), it also encourages their manumission and expressly forbids Muslim masters from forcing such women into prostitution (Q24.33). Islamic law permits children born to concubines, originally acquired in war, to inherit property.

Muhammad's adopted son Zaid was his former slave and was unduly attached to him. The Arabic for slave (*'abd*) highlights a spontaneous and wholehearted commitment to the master's cause. To modern readers, the word conjures up only images of servitude – of the slave's lack of basic human rights and therefore his abject dependence on the master. If the word had only negative overtones, the Quran would not have used it to describe the believer as the slave of God (*'abd Allah*). *'Ibāda*, the worship of God alone, is from the same root. (The Hebrew cognate *'avodā* refers to service in a primarily secular sense but with some undertones of the spiritual.) The Quran commends those human beings who sell themselves – enslave themselves – to God to seek his good pleasure (Q2.207; 9.111).

To be the slave of an important figure, such as Christ or Allah, implied status. Thus, 'slave of God' as a title of a caliph meant that he was entitled to lead other lesser slaves of God, and, more dangerously, that the caliph was accountable only to God, not to his subjects. Thus, contrary to first impressions, such titles need not encourage political humility. For the title indicates exaltation by association, not humiliation through subservience. 'I serve at the King's pleasure' implies that the servant has status by association with the master. Again, the post of Secretary of State is a position of honour, unlike the usual office of a secretary – although even an ordinary secretary wields power since she, and it is usually a woman, has access to the great man's time and schedule and can effectively bar access to him.

Paul speaks of Christ's humility and of how he offered to be an indentured slave (*doulou*; *gen*.; Phil. 2.7). Such rhetoric is theoretically powerful but it has clear limitations. Christ's status as slave was wholly different from that of real slaves in the Roman Empire and indeed since those times. For example, no slave ever came back to life, resurrected by his master. Again, Paul's being a slave of Christ is hardly comparable to the normal condition of a slave: any man who looks forward to eternal life and glory is hardly similar to a slave beaten to death and shamefully deprived of his or her rights during a nasty, brutish and short life.

The Greco-Roman view of slavery as a natural condition for some people was more or less preserved intact by Christianity. The Hebrew Bible sanctions slavery (Ex. 21.1–8) but also orders Israelites to offer asylum to escaped slaves and assigns them liberty of domicile (Deut. 23.15–16). The New Testament permits the persistence of an existing practice, indeed encourages slaves to be faithful to their masters (1 Tim. 1:1–2) – agonizingly painful verses for African American slaves to read in church during the days of slavery. The Christian scripture also contains many instructions and commands encouraging slave masters to treat their slaves compassionately and in awareness that they both have a single master in heaven (see Eph. 6.9, Col. 4.1, Philemon 10–21). This would be cold comfort to the slaves since such admonitions are at best moral, left to the discretion of the master, who might be a naturally cruel man. To most modern readers, it is self-evident that, given the ideals of Christian liberty and complete equality in Christ, slavery must ultimately be anathema. Admittedly, this institution was never seen in the classical world as being necessarily cruel and despotic, as abject submission. It ought, however, to be clearly condemned. Yet its abolition was neither predicted nor encouraged. Given that the New Testament authors were divinely inspired men, often granted visions of the future, it seems unaccountably odd that none predicted the end of this ancient social evil.

Islam also accepted the existing reality of slavery. However, relatively honourable treatment of slaves was part of its normative tradition, found in the Quran and in countless *ḥadīth*. It was not merely a later ad hoc development. Islam neither initiated nor abolished this institution while certainly ameliorating the plight of many slaves by encouraging manumission as an act of charity and as expiation for certain sins and lapses. Many black converts to Islam claim, justifiably in my view, that their reading of history enables them to claim that it was always better to be a slave in a Muslim household than in a Christian one. Indeed, one dynasty, the Mamluks, destined to defeat the remarkably destructive Mongols, rose from slavery to imperial rule! There are, however, also some black spots in the Muslim record. Arab Muslim traders were involved in the early trans-Saharan slave trade and complicit in the later and wider European commerce in slaves as commodities. Moreover, unlike Europeans, Muslims have never officially acknowledged that such behaviour is evil and in need of apology and retrospective atonement.

This is not to indulge in Muslim triumphalism but rather to state normative Islam's moral strengths – something most committed Christians are, in general, most reluctant to do. The evidence is more than fragmentary and anecdotal; Muslims are therefore entitled to state Islam's strength here simply as a fact rather than as a boast in the context of interfaith comparisons. The Christian record, as judged by its own professed standards, is deplorable in this regard, as many contrite churchmen now acknowledge. No doubt, a more detailed survey would introduce more nuance and balance but I think that my account is not wide of the mark. I am not comparing normative Islam to the worst excesses of historical Christianity. That would be an unfair comparison. Muslims in northern Nigeria and East Africa have been slave traders and some forms of this social evil may well remain even now in some Muslim nations. But we must also note that so compassionate was normative Islam's legal regulation of slavery that many slaves preferred slavery to freedom since masters were obliged, by Islamic law, to scrupulously respect the rights of the enslaved.

When Paul wrote to Philemon, a Christian slave-owner in Colossae, Paul could have condemned slavery in general – but did not do so. Paul's writings were quoted with approval both by American abolitionists and by slave-owners. Tragically, the spiritualisation and moral exaltation of the condition of slavery by Jesus and Paul did not, in practice, effect much practical moral transformation. I see little evidence of this happening on any significant scale in any period of subsequent Christian history. Slavery, America's original sin, required not simply legislation but a civil war to end it. This is not to deny that traditions of radical Western Christian compassion have also accompanied this regrettable record: many brave Christians have campaigned for extending human rights to many excluded groups and have thus contributed decisively to the amelioration of the human plight. Paul's own exhortations to slaves and servants and masters no doubt did affect the practical attitudes of some individual conscientious Christians and inculcated compassion – but the institution of slavery in Christian lands lacked any legal regulation and was one generally marked by cruelty.

The matter of slavery, however, is in a class of its own. Some black sceptics, usually converts to Islam, question the motives for the American civil war and see the matter in terms not of Christian ethical passion for social justice but rather in terms of the emergence of a certain stage of capitalism that necessitated the abolition of slave labour. Given that much of American society, as many Americans admit, has constantly been consumed by the lust for wealth and power, by ambition and competition, it is hard to discredit this apparently cynical but insightful view. Indeed, black historians go further and claim, rightly, that the slave trade provided the material means for the emergence of British and later American capitalism. Free labour was supplied for centuries with the sugar slaves being the oldest industrial proletariat, long predating the workers of the European Industrial revolution.

XIII

Let peace (*eirēnē*), mentioned twice in Galatians, have the last word in this chapter. With the surprising exception of 1 John, peace (or *salām* in Arabic) occurs in every New Testament book: either the opening or closing salutation refers to it. *Eirēnē* translates the Hebrew *shālom*, meaning well-being through divine blessing, a positive word, unlike the more negative Greek analogue which indicates the peace that comes from the absence of strife and conflict. *Salām* and *shālom* are verbal nouns denoting the positive state of soundness and preservation. *Sallama* (he preserved) describes how God saved Muhammad in a battle context (Q8.43). The peace of submission (*salām al-islām*), the peace that is the fruit of submission to God's holy will, is the aim of the life of faith. Politically, this is the state of the world under Islam (*dar al-Islām*) as true peace is only possible with the establishment of universal justice, Islam's central ideal, staunchly opposed by global capitalism and its allies, both religious and secular. Admittedly, the core, especially economic, elements of Islam's conception of such justice is rejected on principle by the capitalist and communist elite classes whose members have their own respective ideals of global justice.

The risen Jesus offers peace when he visits his disciples. Paul's 'Grace and peace' greeting resembles Islam's peace greeting. The Quran orders believers to offer the salutation of peace to fellow believers, the smaller group proffering it to the larger. The recipients are obliged to answer with an equivalent greeting or one better – by adding 'the mercy of God and his blessing be upon you'. Devout Muslims would never offer the *salām* to non-Muslims. In mixed societies, especially India, where Muslims are a persecuted minority keen to assimilate, it is permissible to proffer a religiously neutral greeting to Hindus.

Islam requires the establishment and preservation of peace between believers (Q49.9). Although human beings can be enemies of God (see, e.g., Rom. 5.10; Heb. 10.27; Q41.28), the Muslim scripture rarely notes the state of human (as opposed to merely the disbelievers') alienation from God. An exception is an uncharacteristically mawkish outburst at Q82.6–8. Reconciliation of sinners with a holy and demanding God is a Christian idiom for healing the fractured relationship between creator and creature. In Islam too, however, *Allah* himself invites Muslims to enter 'the abode of peace' (*dar al-salām*; Q10.25) – the peace which is the fruit of submission (*islām*) to the will of the Peaceable One (*Al-Salām*; Q59.23), the source of peace.

Notes

1 In Arab culture, as in Australian Aboriginal and Saharan societies, the desert is not considered arid or lifeless. Its contours are seen as a shoreline: an ocean of sand with camels as ships of the desert (see Q88.17). While one needs effort to survive in the desert, it is a place of fertile mystery rather than arid death.

2 In my view, it is unfortunate that Revelation was admitted into the canon at all – especially in preference to some epistolary candidates, such as the letters of Clement. Jesus is no prince of peace in this violent work about apocalypse and end-times. Its message of conflict is wildly popular in parts of Christian America, a nuclear superpower whose policies – unlike the empty rhetoric of powerless Muslim nations, including messianic Shi'ite Iran – materially affect the whole world.

3 The Quran uses *al-dahr* (Q76.1) to mean Time as agent of change. It occurs in apocryphal traditions such as: 'Do not curse Time – for I am Time.' The speaker is God. The Persian *zamān*, a secular word not appropriated by the Quran, defines time as an era.

4 Hence the witticism, 'according to MST' (Muslim Standard Time). Cf. Mountain Standard Time.

5 *Risālat Būlos Ghalātiyya* is the Arabic title of 'Paul's Letter to the Galatians'.

6 EWNT 2.176–86. For details, see Dunn's commentary on Galatians, p. 41. See Bibliography for publication details.

7 The Arabic *muṣiba* is similarly ambivalent, meaning anything that successfully reaches or touches a person, whether that be misfortune, the usual sense or fortune. God visits (*nuṣību*) his mercy on Joseph so that he rises from captivity to imperial leadership (Q12.56). The verb is *aṣaba*, the IV derived form, meaning 'to reach or to afflict'

8 The adjective *muḥarrar* (Q3.35) is used only by Mary's mother to refer to Mary in her womb – as consecrated – in her state of holy quarantine.

9 Islamic *jihād* does not require such annihilation of acquisitions in war.

10 Zwemer's death marks the end of an intensive era of mission to Muslim lands and the shift towards interfaith dialogue. Towards the end of his ministry among Arab Muslims, Zwemer increasingly saw Islam as a Christian heresy, citing this as the reason for the immeasurable difficulty of winning Muslim converts to Christianity. This is far less true now. Despite strict laws against it, Muslims do convert to Christianity – more in Shi'ite Iran than in the Sunni world, with the notable exception of Bangladesh and Indonesia. Zwemer's argument is, in any case, unconvincing since Christianity could be seen as an Islamic heresy which nonetheless wins over countless Christians – in the largest interfaith traffic of any pair of rival faiths. In such matters, doctrinal proximity between faiths is neither here nor there. It depends more on the temperamental differences between the adherents of the faiths involved.

11 *Yā bushrā* is the shout of the water drawer who finds Joseph in the well: 'Oh good news/ luck! It's a boy' (Q12.19). This verse is printed on the entrances to maternity hospitals in Muslim lands, unashamedly celebrating male births.

12 Dignity resides in the very existence of something, as shown by Orwell's *1984* where the Inner Party removes all traces of memory, the existence that accrues to an idea or word that once existed. The enemies of the state are not martyred – that would ensure them post-humous dignity – but rather erased from the very stream of history. They are vaporised and thus cease to exist even in someone's memory, as though they had never existed, like the 'child' whose very conception was aborted. By contrast, God is the kind of being whose very nature demands that he must exist, the basis of the ontological argument.

13 Martin Luther, *Smalcald Articles* II, 15. This summary of Lutheran doctrine was published in 1537.

3

THE APOSTLE'S APOLOGIA AND GOSPEL (1.13–3.5)

I

How did Saul, a fanatical Pharisee from the House of Shammai, the ones who bound strictly, become Paul, the committed Christian missionary – leaning towards the lenient House of Hillel? Students of the psychobiography of religious genius must wonder whether or not anyone, least of all a man of spiritual profundity, ever really changes. And if so, is an external influence genuinely coercive and imposing? Or do we allow an external force to influence us only where our nature is already aligned with an imminent internal change? At crucial junctures, does not everyone encounter the right person on some road or other? Do we attribute to others the authority to authenticate our experience when it should be self-authenticating – if only we were strong enough to admit our strengths as keenly as we confess our weaknesses?

We shall read at face value Saul's confession, leaving aside such unduly sceptical reflections that are more suited to a secular history of faith origins than a commentary on scripture. Paul, the zealous Christian, reveals to us brief and exciting glimpses of his pre-Christian life. For all their apparent spontaneity, these *pericopae* are carefully carpentered to reveal only facets of Paul, with a view to establishing his credentials as an apostle called directly to be a servant of Christ. A successful career in Judaism is abandoned: a Pharisee moves from being an enthusiastic persecutor of the Jesus movement to become instead its most fervent preacher.

Early Islamic history, stirring and eventful though it is, has only one comparable event. The conversion of Umar ibn Al-Khattab, destined to be the second caliph, provides a partial parallel. He repudiated his pagan past and his passionate hostility to the new faith, only to be transformed into the most fervent Muslim colonialist of all times, intent on conquering the whole world for Islam. While most Christians are invariably and immensely proud of Paul, their greatest missionary, Umar's ambition embarrasses modern moderate Muslims, Sufis and professional Western Muslim apologists whose faith is seen as weak by more committed believers.

Our major themes: Paul's apologia, the confrontation with Peter, and the first formulation of the gospel of grace alone as it arises out of opposition to Peter and the Law-observant Jews. The order of events: Paul is called by the risen Christ, accepted by the Jerusalem apostles, opposed by Peter at Antioch, reconciled to Peter and the Jerusalem church.

After commenting on 1.13 to 2.21, I offer in section IX below a panoramic view of Paul's life and doctrine before exploring seven themes that have emerged thus far in Galatians. We start with three themes that arise directly out of the epistle: the Arabian sojourn, the balance of human and divine influences on Paul, and Peter and Paul in the early church. The fourth concern is supplied by a comparison of dietary laws in Christianity and Islam. In an interlude, we note the Semitic obsession with the right hand. The sixth and seventh themes are related: the 'law versus gospel' polarity, in its first full occurrence, and its concealed connection with Pauline mysticism.

In section XVII below, we resume the commentary by examining 3.1–5. In the following section, I compare how the Galatian pagans and the Arab pagans came to have faith. We conclude with a technical survey of righteousness and justification. Along with the brief exploration of faith/grace and law/works dichotomies, in section XV, this study shall prepare us for a scrutiny, in Chapter 8, of the involved intra-Christian debate about works of the law (*erga nomou*) both in Reformation and later normative Christian exegesis.

II 1.13–19

13 *For you heard of my past conduct in Judaism, that I excessively persecuted the church of God*
and I was destroying it. **14** *And I progressed in Judaism beyond many contemporaries among my*
race (of Jews), being abundantly a zealot, regarding my ancestral traditions. **15** *But when he was*
pleased – the one who having separated me, from (i.e. since I was in) the womb of my mother,
and having called me through his grace **16** *to reveal his son in me, in order that I might preach him*
among the nations (Gentiles), immediately I conferred not with flesh and blood **17** *nor did I go*
up to Jerusalem to (those who were) apostles before me but I went away into Arabia, and returned
again to Damascus. **18** *Then after three years, I went up to Jerusalem to visit Cephas and*
remained with him (for) fifteen days. **19** *But I did not see any other of the apostles except James,*
the Lord's brother.

13–14

As defender of his ancestral Judaism, the pre-apostolic Paul wanted to humiliate Christians and annihilate the defenceless Jesus movement. This active Jewish missionary proselytised non-Jews and persecuted Jesus' followers. This account of Paul's pre-Christian life is confirmed in his other epistles (1 Cor. 15.9; Phil. 3.4–10).

I translate '*eporthoun*' as 'I was destroying' to capture the Greek imperfect active indicative. If Paul felt guilt over his success in his task as Jewish inquisitor, he does not state it explicitly. He certainly felt no guilt or shame when he was engaged in the task, whatever we may say of his feelings as he recollected the details. Paul the Pharisee wanted to guard against dangerous innovation, what Muslim orthodoxy denounces as *bid'a* (Q46.9). Paul abandoned a promising career in Judaism just as Muhammad abandoned a promising career as a Hashemite businessman.

Zeal and persecution stamp this epistle. The pre-Christian Paul progressed in Judaism as a direct result of his persecution of God's church. His persecution of Christians was precisely what demonstrated his zeal as a Jew. Judaism emerges as not only anti-Christian but violently so. Anti-Semitism and anti-Judaism have been, traditionally, acceptable to many Christians since Jews started this fight by persecuting the infant church. This view was standard in the commentaries of conservative Christians such as Augustine and Luther. In an earlier age, the heretic Marcion viewed Galatians as Paul's manifesto against Judaism – as the Apostle's passionate rejection of the Hebrew God of law, judgement and wrath. The dialectic of hate and suspicion continues even today in our secular age: when a Jew converts to Christianity, other Jews are shocked by such religious and cultural treason to the parent faith that has suffered unspeakably and incessantly at the hands of the Christian enemy.

In v.13, as in v.2, *ekklēsia* is not a building but a fellowship of believers. Its physical location is on earth but Christians are citizens of heaven. *Ekklēsia* corresponds to the global Islamic community (*umma*), not to *masjid* which literally means any 'place of prostration' and thus need not mean only a purpose-built place of worship. Indeed, Muslim mystics often say that the whole world is a *masjid*, with nature its entrance. While *masjid* is an indefinite noun which admits of duality and plurality, it can, with the definite article, refer to the Jewish Temple (*al-masjid*; Q17.7). Masjid Al-Aqsa (Q17.1) literally means 'the remote place of prostration' – remote from Mecca's Holy Mosque. It is so named in the late Meccan period, around 621 CE, about a century before it was actualised in a real physical construction erected in Jerusalem in 709 by Caliph Al-Walid. The same is true of Islam's holiest site, the Forbidden Mosque (*masjid al-ḥarām*) which, said to be built by Abraham, was under pagan occupation in Muhammad's day – and thus hardly a mosque. It became a functioning mosque only with the Islamic conquest of Mecca. This early Muslim penchant for architectural annexation of places of worship claimed by others before them continues in later imperial Islam and enrages both Jews (Temple Mount/Al-Aqsa) and Christians (Hagia Sophia). Buddhists and Hindus are also distressed by the destruction of their holy precincts. Many Hindus regard the Babri mosque in Ayodhya in northern India to have been built in the birthplace of Ram. His devotees destroyed the mosque in order to erect a temple there and thus to erase the memory of the imperial Mughal (Islamic) insult to their faith.

15

Paul thinks that he was commissioned from birth – possibly from conception. This seems hyperbolic until we note the supra-historical assertion in Ephesians 1.4 about Christian salvation being supernaturally determined before the foundation of the cosmos. Isaiah, like Jeremiah, claims to be divinely consecrated as a prophet (*navi*) to warn the nations, an event dated to the time when neither prophet had as yet been conceived in his mother's womb (Isa. 49.1, 5; Jer. 1.5). Muhammad was chosen during his orphaned childhood, and then guided and enriched by God (Q93.6–8). Such claims can only be defended on grounds of faith rather than reason unaided by revelation. That is the way of all religion. Before commanding the routine of regular prayer, the Quran stipulates a faith-based condition for its performance: 'They (the righteous) believe in the supernatural' (*ghayb*; Q2.3). Today, many ask: 'On what grounds?' Muslims would retort that only the insolent sceptic can question such a precondition. Given our human nature and innate knowledge of the unseen God, doubting this prerequisite is anathema. However, as sociologists of religious experience teach us, people differ: the experience of faith, of revelation, leads some to believe in the unseen – so that experience can be a precondition of belief that can subsequently mature into dogma.

Paul probably saw himself as being commissioned like an Israelite prophet to warn the nations. Like Jeremiah, Isaiah and Ezekiel before him, the Christian apostle offers an internal critique of Jewish belief and conduct. He predates Muhammad, the supreme Arab critic of Arab polytheism and of Judaism and Christianity.

Paul is the one 'set apart' and 'called' (*aphorisas kalesas;* cf. *kletos apostolos* at Rom. 1.1) to be an apostle. In Modern Standard Arabic translations of Romans (1.1) and of this verse of Galatians, Paul is self-described as *mud'awwan* (one called), a passive participle from the same root as the verbal noun *da'wa*, meaning invitation or call (to Islam). The root verb and verbal nouns occur often in the Quran but this passive participle does not. The idiom 'being called (by God)' is far more popular among Christians than among Muslims. And the one called must call others. Christianity remains a zealously missionary faith, reflecting Paul's enduring influence.

16

Paul does not consult with flesh and blood, a Hebrew idiom for frail humanity, but rather prefers the autonomous authority of revelation in Christ, his tutor and Lord. Paul withdraws to reflect on the Hebrew scriptures in the light of his experience. If this Jesus is indeed the Messiah, he reasons, then the consequences are absolutely incredible, even scandalous!

16a contains the first intimation of Pauline mysticism, the Christian's dwelling in Christ. The archaic verb 'indwell', used transitively, means that Christ inhabits or suffuses the believer; its intransitive use implies that Christ exists or dwells *in* the believer. 16b reflects Isa. 49.6, Paul's apostolic aspiration.

17

Paul goes to Arabia in preference to Jerusalem. This is his personal decision, not a revealed command. Paul links the present earthly city of Jerusalem, the one he visited at least twice after his conversion (Gal. 1.18, 2.1), with Mount Sinai in Arabia. As we shall see later in the letter, he will reject both as outdated symbols of servitude. He will opt for the spirit which is represented by the Jerusalem above (Gal. 4.25–6), a city standing 'proudly' for gracious service and the freedom that enables it.

Paul leaves unspecified the duration and purpose of the Arabian sojourn. He returns to Damascus, the city of his conversion, after his mysterious Arabian travels. Is this Paul's first missionary journey? This Arabian sojourn is mentioned nowhere else in the New Testament.

Such a retreat in religious life is known to prophets and mystics in all traditions, including Islam. In his quest for God, Muhammad would withdraw into the cave at Mount Hira. Modern Christians and Muslims also go into retreat for prayerful reflection. It is unclear whether the practice brings any benefits for the majority of its practitioners. The principle of initial strategic retreat in order to advance afterwards is known in other departments of human ambition and endeavour, especially in sports and war.

For Muslims, Jerusalem was the original direction of prayer before it was superseded by the Meccan shrine built by Abraham and Ishmael. The Quran, like the Pentateuch, never names Jerusalem but alludes to it in the opening verse of its 17th surah. Islamic tradition has it that Muhammad led the previous prophets in prayer in Jerusalem, before his ascension to heaven. Did the prophets literally descend to earth for one communal prayer with Muhammad as *imām*? Is this too literal a thought? Both the beginning and end of history require symbolic (figurative) treatment. Even visionaries are at the end of their purely experiential and linguistic tether as they seek to express and expound these thoughts and experiences at the extremity of human existence in time and space.

In vv.16–17, Paul seems to suggest that he told no one (or perhaps no one important) about his conversion, versions of claims consistent with his account of his 'conversion' in 1 Cor. 15.3–9. This detail in Gal. 1.16–17 makes Paul's own account differ crucially from the third person narrative accounts of his experience given in Acts (see first account at 9.3–9, 10–19). The second version in Acts (22.9) is offered during a speech Paul gives to fellow Jews, after he has been arrested in Jerusalem. These two accounts in Acts seem to contradict each other in important ways but not enough to justify doubts about the historical reliability of the whole of Acts for reconstructing the Apostle's life and mission. The third version, in a speech addressed to King Agrippa (Acts 26.12–23), is consistent with both the two earlier versions in Acts since it makes no comment on whether or not his travelling companions also heard the voice of the risen Christ, a detail that differs between the first two accounts. In the same vein, some further minor details given in Acts 26.12–23 seem to contradict Gal. 1.16–17 and the broader version the latter implies.

18

The first visit to Jerusalem by Paul the Christian is undertaken three years after his return to Damascus. It is his own initiative to go and meet Peter (called here by his Aramaic name of Cephas). Paul is precise about the duration but vague about the purpose. Is it irreverent to say that a fortnight in Jerusalem was a 'crash course' on Jesus?

19

Paul meets only James, the Lord's brother, who is the head of the Jerusalem church and the most Jewish of the apostles. We detect here some early hints of unresolved tensions surrounding hierarchy, honour and shame, themes with contemporary resonances too.

III 1.20–24

20 *Regarding the things I write to you. Look! Before God, I do not lie.* **21** *Then I went into the regions of Syria and Cilicia.* **22** *And I was, being unknown, by face, to the congregations of Judea, which were in Christ.* **23** *But only (this)! 'They kept hearing that the one persecuting us then – now he preaches the faith he was then destroying!'* **24** *And they glorified God because of me.*

20

This verse is parenthetical. Only those bent on vilifying Paul would say that he was deliberately dishonest, an insincere imposter. Paul wants to give a truthful and precise account. Therefore, his vagueness about some details, such as the purpose and duration of the Arabian visit, must be deliberate.

In an oath, we utter words in God's presence. If we lie, we do so before God rather than only other human beings. In Acts 5.4, Peter warns a man called Ananias who has embezzled money from the church that he has lied to God himself – and not merely to human beings. Ananias was struck dead (Acts 5.4–5). What a shame, many devout Muslims would lament, that such immediate punishment does not befall modern liars and evildoers! It might hasten the repentance of some so-called world leaders as they witnessed their fellow politicians decimated by the outstretched divine arm. Sadly, this is only a fantasy.

Paul is determined to speak the whole truth in God's presence – to be truthful for the sake of a truthful God. Clement of Rome, the first of the apostolic fathers, captures this emphasis from the divine angle: 'He who ordered us not to lie, how much more will he himself not lie' (1 Clement 27.2).

We learn from extensive evidence in the Quran that Muhammad was accused, variously, of being a liar, a poet, a magician, a madman (possessed by the jinn), and a man tutored by the People of the Book. The sheer variety of such slander shows that the Quran was a phenomenon that disturbed its hearers. In the traditions, the Prophet often swears by God, 'in whose hand is my soul (life)', in order to reassure his followers concerning his claim to be God's truthful messenger.

21

Between visits to Jerusalem, Paul travels to the regions of Syria and Cilicia. Did he visit his hometown in Tarsus?

22

If he persecuted those churches, it is unclear why he is unknown to them by face. Perhaps, a new generation of Christians had appeared by then. There were, of course, no photos and social media in the ancient world. If 'by face' (*to prosōpo*), however, is meant a personal relationship rather than literally seeing someone's face, then we may surmise that Paul spent time in Arabia, then Syria and Cilicia and therefore the believers of Judaea had little to do with him. When he was a persecutor, they had, understandably, avoided his angry face. When he became a follower of Christ, he had only briefly visited the Judean congregations – and even then established a personal relationship only with Peter (Gal. 1.18).

More broadly, both in the Old Testament worldview and later in the Muslim outlook, one can fervently desire to establish a relationship with God by 'seeking the face of God' (see Q2.115; 55.27, 76.9).

23–24

Paul is delighted that the conversion of the former persecutor of the church, a great sinner (1 Tim.1.13–16), is a cause for glorifying God. We interpret events no less than texts. When we retrospectively survey our lives, we often re-baptise events in our past, assigning some accident the new status of destiny, even honouring an evil event as a good one in disguise – but recognised as such only in retrospect.

Here and in Philippians (1.12–14), Paul preaches that God can bring much good from a sad or evil situation. Since human knowledge is limited, we never know when our immediate choices have long-term good or bad consequences. Muslims often lament with terminative resignation, 'It is written (*maktūban*)' or 'God knows best (*Allah a'lam*), especially in matters that are part of the supernatural (*ghayb*) and therefore unknowable, even in principle. In the final verse of the Quran's chapter named in honour of the sage Luqman, we read that God has arrogated exclusively to himself five areas of knowledge listed, without comment, at Q31.34.

IV 2.1–5

1 *Then after an interval of fourteen years, I went again to Jerusalem, with Barnabas, taking along with me also Titus.* **2** *And I went up according to a revelation and I placed before them the gospel which I proclaim among the nations – but in private – to those seeming (to be important, i.e. with reputation) in case in vain I am running or have run.* **3** *But not even Titus, who was with me, (despite) being a Greek, was forced to be circumcised.* **4** *But on account of the false brothers, secretly brought in, who stole in to spy on our freedom which we have in Christ Jesus, in order that they will (might) enslave us.* **5** *To them, we did not yield in subjection (even) for an hour so that the truth of the gospel might continue (to remain) with you.*

This portion of the epistle records Paul's only clear victory at Jerusalem – over the opponents of his gospel.

1–2

Paul's second visit to the holy city is in response to a revelation but that need not entail that he was given a direct command. He does not, in any case, specify the source of the revelation. Jesus also set his face towards Jerusalem. Was he self-directed by his conscience? Or was he directed by his reading of scripture or by God? It is impossible to decide on the basis of the gospel accounts alone. Muhammad's night journey to Jerusalem was performed miraculously (Q17.1), his only miracle, apart from the Quran.

Fourteen years could be shorter than our fourteen solar years since some Jews, at this time, reckoned with a flexible combination of solar and lunar calendars.[1] Muslims use only the lunar calendar. The intercalary month, inserted into the reckoning to achieve flexibility, was forbidden by the Quran since it enabled pagans to achieve devious escape from the rules regarding the permissibility of fighting in various months (see Q9.37 and any commentary).

Paul takes along his mentor, Barnabas (son of encouragement), described as 'a good man, full of the Holy Spirit and faith' (Acts 11.24). In religious history, many a modest man has enlisted, for God's service, another man of boldness and genius. Barnabas brought Paul to serve Jesus, their master, just as Guillaume Farel brought John Calvin into the service of the church in Geneva. Muhammad's uncle, Abu Talib, secured Muhammad's personal safety without endorsing his cause. Some men from Medina invited Muhammad to their city after accidentally meeting him at a trading fair in Mecca. They vowed to defend him and his cause. A secular analogue is Engels who financially supported Marx and endorsed the cause of communism.

Paul's situation illustrates the dilemma of authority. The revealed authority of Christ accounts for his visit to Jerusalem and yet the fact that the journey is to Jerusalem implies that Paul must seek additional apostolic approval if not authorisation for his Gospel for the Gentiles. Is not Christ's authority sufficient? Authority need not be absolute authority: it still had to be authenticated by witness. Paul sounds apprehensive about the outcome of his visit, perhaps fearing rejection at Jerusalem, a city that had a long history of rejecting prophets and their oracles (Matt. 23.37).

Muhammad similarly faced the dilemma of authority. He thinks he is directly called by *Allah* but is nonetheless instructed to seek Jewish and Christian confirmation of his mission, especially in the early Meccan years, spent in the pagan wilderness. One could argue that apostles and prophets, once they receive their commissions, must nonetheless work in the real existing constituency and, therefore, must acknowledge the strategic need to seek worldly authorisation and allies. The dilemma is always experienced painfully in prophetic struggle, no matter how convincing the subsequent theoretical rationale offered by armchair theologians.

3–5

Liberty in Christ was endangered by Torah-observant Jews. Paul tells us that Titus, a Greek (Gentile), was not compelled to be circumcised. This is the first mention of circumcision, the practical occasion for penning this letter. Paul did not allow Titus to be circumcised, at least not as a requirement of salvation: the law-free kerygma of gracious salvation sufficed to save the repentant sinner. Consider Timothy's case, mentioned in Acts 16.1–3. He came from Lystra, a region of south Galatia. His mother was a Jewish Christian and his father was a Greek. Paul circumcised Timothy. Did he do so merely as a concession to the Jews? Luke suggests that that was indeed the reason (Acts 16.3). Whatever we may conclude on that score, the circumcision of Timothy, if indeed it was carried out, would contribute to creating the crisis at Galatia. If Paul circumcised Timothy before he wrote to the Galatians, then it is possible that the Judaisers cited that case as proof that new converts to Christ had to undergo the rite.

The false brothers could have been from the Judean congregations. Or they might have been the infiltrators at the church in (Syrian) Antioch. The doctrinal issue remains unaffected by this detail of early church history. Paul maintains Christian liberty against the stance of slavery to the Law, a condition symbolised by circumcision. This whole incident anticipates the Galatian crisis. If Paul had left Antioch after a visit in which he witnessed such an infiltration, one can imagine him penning an epistle to the Antiochenes, one which would have contained admonitions similar to those actually sent to the Galatians.

V 2.6–10

6 *But from those seeming (to be important, i.e., to have reputation) – what sort (of people) they were matters nothing to me (for) God does not care for the face of a man – those seeming (to be important) added nothing to me.* **7** *But on the contrary, seeing that I have been entrusted with the gospel of the 'uncircumcision', just as Peter (was entrusted) with that of the circumcision (group, i.e., Jews),* **8** *for he who effectively worked in Peter in his apostleship of the circumcision, he operated also in me for the nations* **9** *and acknowledging the grace given to me, James and Cephas and John, the ones seeming (i.e., reputed to be) pillars, gave to me and to Barnabas the right (hands) of fellowship, in order that we (might go) to the nations and they to the circumcision (group).* **10** *They only (asked) us to remember the poor – the very thing I was indeed eager to do.*

6–9

How can the Apostle maintain *independent* authority? His tone is defensive, his sentences long and convoluted. Nonetheless, he manages to proclaim boldly that God alone knows the truth of the matter and he never judges according to merely human criteria. The Quran similarly elevates divine judgements about human affairs above human assessments of human realities. Indeed, we are asked to trust divine verdicts that run contrary to human ones. Thus, 'You may dislike a thing into which God has placed much good and love a thing in which there is harm: God knows and you do not know'. The verse here refers to the reluctance to do *jihād* and elsewhere refers to the reluctance to live with recalcitrant wives (Q2.216; 4.19; 16.74).

Even if Jerusalem contributed nothing substantially new to Paul's message, the fact that Paul is the one who is visiting Jerusalem shows his felt need for external validation of that message. 'Who visits who says it all', as a saying popular among modern diplomats has it. One may interpret charitably Paul's assertion that the Jerusalem mother church contributed nothing to his message: perhaps that church merely confirmed his message. There might be purpose in Paul's attempt to distance himself from the founding apostles. Perhaps he wants to supervise the emergence of an independent authority in the Gentile church leaders.

I am struck here by Paul's intolerance and dismissal of opposition even from sympathetic rivals. This aspect of Paul's temperament is originally Semitic but, through his influence, European, even occidocentric. Even over a millennium after Paul's day, Muslims can sense a similarly intolerant exclusivity in Aquinas' refusal, often through the silence of contempt rather than the speech of eloquent rebuttal, to concede the intellectual influence of Islamic thinkers on Latin Christendom.

Peter's memory of Jesus not only benefitted the Gentiles (see Acts 10) but also, perhaps via Mark the evangelist, gave us the earliest and shortest of the Gospel accounts. While this notion of Peter's memoirs being preserved in a gospel is an attractive tradition, especially in the eyes of Catholic exegetes, there is no unambiguous textual (scriptural) evidence for it. Understandably, Peter was sent, like his master, to the circumcised – the lost sheep of Israel. Paul and Barnabas were sent to the Gentile nations because God, at this stage, wishes to guide all humanity. This gradual globalisation is envisaged in the Hebrew Bible, via a two-tiered scheme of salvation (Gen. 17.5–18.18), with Abraham's descendants through Isaac having priority. The notion of the nations being blessed through Abraham, through Israel and then through David, can be mined from the Hebrew Bible – but the motives for doing so are supplied by the later vision of the Jesus movement, without which it would have remained largely dormant until the advent of Islam. I admit that one can discern some strenuous efforts at proselytisation of Gentiles even during Jesus' own time (see Matt. 23.15) and, moreover, if Christianity had not appeared, perhaps Judaism might gradually have become more missionary in its outreach.

Leaving aside such speculation about history in the subjunctive mood, and basing their arguments on the advent of the Quran in actual history, Muslims reject the terms of the contrast between Jews and Gentiles as a racist libel against God and accuse Jews of nationalising the ideal of a universal monotheism which was never meant to be the monopoly of an admittedly favoured people. While the prophets sent to the various nations conveyed a message of monotheism relevant to all peoples, their mission was always limited to their own people. Only Muhammad's message was meant to be final, finalising and thus universal from first to last.

In vv. 6–9 'the circumcision' serves as a double metonymy – for the whole Law of Moses and for the Israelite nation. In v. 7, preaching 'the gospel of the foreskin' (*euanggellion tēs akrobustias*) is a literal translation that highlights Paul's physiologically explicit idiom. It means the gospel of the Gentiles, that is, the ministry that falls to Paul's lot in a divinely authorised division of labour. Were there then two gospels – a gospel for the Jews and a gospel of free grace for Gentiles only? Clearly, this cannot be meant literally since there was and is only one gospel.

Although Paul's mission was primarily to Gentiles, usually pagans, he also preached to Jews, especially those living outside Jerusalem. Customarily, along with his mentor Barnabas, Paul first preached in a synagogue, in any city he evangelised; then he invited the Gentiles to accept Christ. Similarly, while Peter operated primarily in the Jewish mission field, he also had a Gentile, including Galatian, audience (see 1 Pet. 1.1; Acts 10.23–11.18).

The Holy Spirit entrusts Peter (and James) with preaching to the circumcision party. Paul did not think of the Gentile extension until it was revealed to him by the risen Christ. Similarly, Peter saw a vision in which he saw the strict dietary laws being abrogated. He is then instructed to visit the house of the Gentile God-fearer Cornelius (Acts 10–11.18). Paul knew that Peter, perhaps consciously following Jesus, ministered only to the circumcised. This supplies evidence, inconclusive but not negligible, that Jesus came only to the lost sheep of Israel, a claim corroborated by the Quran (Q3.49). The Quran nowhere restricts Muhammad's mission to the Arabs – the lost sheep of Ishmael, so to speak – though, admittedly, the Quran was originally addressed to Arabs. The New Testament contains two opposed views about how Jesus can be presented as the saviour of the entire world. According to Matthew and Mark, many Gentiles eagerly sought out Jesus and he deliberately ministered to them. According to Luke and John, however, Jesus restricted his ministry to the Jews and, enigmatically, looked to the nations only after 'his time had come'. The intended salvific scope of Christianity involves matters beyond the scope of this essay but these would assume central place in any Muslim engagement with the totality of the New Testament kerygma.

In this *pericopē*, Paul has subtly claimed equal authority with the senior apostle Peter who is regarded, notably by Catholics, with some scriptural justification, as the chief apostle. As the very need for a visit to Jerusalem indicates, however, equal authority is not autonomous authority. Only God can claim the latter. Those 'reputed to be pillars' in the mother church at Jerusalem are named in order of seniority: James, Cephas and John. According to the Quran, every prophet was sent to be obeyed (Q4.64), presumably implying that all prophets had equal authority. In 'the covenant of the prophets', each prophet was commanded to assist his successor (Q3.81) – to continue the God-given task of establishing monotheism and to remind humanity, during their brief tenure on this good earth, never to forget about God's intention to cause them to return ultimately to their everlasting abode. I say 'each prophet' above though, no doubt, some periods of history were prophetically charged since several prophets' ministries overlapped: the obvious examples would be, according to Islam's view of prophets, Abraham and Isaac and also Jacob and Joseph.

In vv.7 and 9, to underline the humility with which he undertook his commission, Paul uses theological passives (*pepisteumai*; I have been entrusted) and 'the grace given (*dotheisan*) to me'. God through Christ is the active agent. The Quran uses theological passives, both present and past, to mark the same stress on God's sovereign power as the only truly competent agent (Q2.269; 22.24; 47.2). Note the contrast between Paul's humility towards his God-given mission here with his intolerance, noted above, towards his religious rivals.

In v.6, note that the number of the great and good is left unspecified. Some conservative scholars think that when Paul's gospel was approved by all the apostles gathered in Jerusalem, Paul probably met John and Matthew, the first and fourth evangelists. If so, in effect he finally met all the evangelists whose names are attached to the canonical quartet – since Luke and Mark were to become his travelling companions on evangelical tours. The proponents of such claims make up in fervent faith what they lack in historical evidence.

10

Paul is asked to remember the poor, the *only* (*monon*) condition set by the Jerusalem leaders. The use of *monon* suggests the centrality of this moral duty while simultaneously implying that the rest of Paul's message was acceptable to them. In Jewish ethics, inherited by Christians, charitable duty to the poor is prominent (Ps. 35.10, Isa. 3.15, 25.4, 58.7; Luke 1.53). The Hebrew *'êvyon* and *'oni* came to mean, given their context, poor to the point of destitution rather than merely in a genteel way.

Paul's reference to the poor among the saints is not a reference to the Ebionites (Heb., *'evyonim*). This is a patristic label for a Jewish Christian sect dating from the AD 70s. They were dismissed as heretical Judaisers.

Only prejudiced persons could deny the compassionate nobility of the Christian record regarding service of desperately poor people, in all ages and many lands. Many of these wretched of the earth were overlooked by Muslims and Jews although the Old Testament contains more support for liberation theology than the New Testament – and the Quran the most of all. Why did Jews and Muslims fail in this regard? Jews were less motivated to serve the whole of humanity owing to an ethnic taint which was only exacerbated by the search for a king and for national sovereignty. I am thinking of modern Israel now. Unlike Christians and later the Muslims, Jews were not in general motivated to convert the whole human race to a single ethical monotheism. As for Muslims, their failing was caused by a gradual apostasy from the high standards of enthusiasm set by the Prophet and his early disciples (see Q3.102–104) as subsequent generations of Muslims became lazy and addicted to the luxuries of empire and forgot their part of the covenant with God (cf. Q5.14 about Christian lapses).

Paul was eager to serve the poverty-stricken ones. He uses the habitual aorist (*espoudasa*) to indicate that his disposition and character inclined him to care for these unfortunates. Such abjectly poor (*ptōchoi*) folk, mentioned with approval in the beatitudes (Matt. 5.3) and elsewhere (Matt. 11.5; Luke 4.18), are called *penes* in the Vulgate, giving our word penury.

Paul has in mind, even at this early stage of his apostolic career, his sacred duty to the poor (Jewish Christian) saints in Jerusalem. In a speech before Felix at Caesarea, Paul proudly mentions that he presented 'alms and offerings to my nation' (Acts 24.17). In his Corinthian correspondence, Paul recalls his collection among the Galatian churches (1 Cor. 16.1–4). He urges the Corinthians to imitate the generosity of the Macedonian churches (2 Cor. 8.1–7) and indeed encourages his varied congregations to vie with each other in giving charity (2 Cor. 9.1–15; cf. Q5.48). Paul even forewarns the Corinthians to start collecting in advance of his visit in order to avoid an embarrassing eventuality. Let us suppose that some Macedonians arrive early, accompanied by Paul, only to find that their Corinthian hosts are not as generous as Paul had led their Macedonian visitors to believe. Finally, in the final chapter of his longest epistle, Paul informs the Roman saints about his intention to give a gift to the saints in Jerusalem but fears – a touch of realism, not only humility – that it might be rejected (Rom. 16.25–26, 31).

Although Islam has no monastic vow of poverty, Muhammad lived in holy voluntary poverty even after he was the uncrowned emperor of Arabia. His companions were poor, some becoming poor as a result of spending for the cause. The Quran commends poverty (*'aylah*) caused by doing a righteous act – a reference to the final and complete barring of pagan access to the Holy Mosque whose precincts attracted much trade (Q9.28).

Abject poverty is a theme in early Islam. Some men were in real danger of starvation but never begged since they saw that as shameful (Q2.273). 'The people of the verandah', a group of abjectly poor believers, were so named since they lived literally on the verandah of the Prophet's small private apartments! The desperately poor (*miskīn* and *fuqarā'*) were divinely designated recipients of charity (Q8.41; 9.60). The Islamic state accepts responsibility for such poor citizens by levying the zakat tax on the wealthier ones.

The poor Muslim emigrants from Mecca were assisted by the Medinan Helpers (Q59.8–10) in history's most successful example of a practised brotherhood. The Quran praises those who acquired *khaṣāṣah* (lit, anything conspicuous or spectacular, here extreme poverty) by regularly preferring the needs of others over their own. These people have been delivered (theological passive) from their own avarice (*shuḥḥa*) and have therefore succeeded spiritually (Q59.9). Commentators add that many a Helper often only pretended to eat, usually in partial darkness, to enable his Meccan migrant guest to enjoy his larger share of the food, without feeling guilty about his host's poverty. It is hard to imagine a greater proof of unheroic but true charity in such mundane circumstances.

It is worth adding that despite the prevailing material poverty of Muhammad and of most of his companions, there are many strong traditions attesting to the idea of wealth as a sign of God's blessing, so long as the wealthy man or woman spends it, at least in part, to do good deeds that typically secure divine approval. This is in line with the Quran which attaches no inherent spiritual value to either poverty or wealth. Some cynics might add that we know how little value God attaches to wealth by looking at the kinds of people to whom he gives it in abundance!

True faith certainly requires charity, a central obligation also in Jewish piety, carried over into Christianity. Islam shares with Judaism this stress on charity as crucial to piety. The Talmud occasionally extols charity as 'the mitzvah', equal to all other mitzvoth combined. Moreover, the charitable actions of Jews can hasten on the advent of messianic redemption.[2]

VI 2.11–15

11 *But when Cephas came to Antioch, I opposed him to his face because he stood condemned.* **12** *For before some (men) came to him from James, he used to eat with the (Gentile) nations but when they came, he withdrew and separated himself, fearing the ones from the circumcision (party).* **13** *And the remaining Jews became 'co-hypocritical' with him so that even Barnabas was led astray by their hypocrisy (dissembling).* **14** *But when I saw that they did not walk straight with (i.e., in) the truth of the gospel, I said to Cephas in front of all: 'If you, despite being a Jew, live like the (Gentile) nations and not like the Jews, how can you then compel the (Gentile) nations to Judaize (i.e. follow Jewish law and customs)?'*

Conservative scholars typically claim that one part of the church lived as Jews in Judaea, witnessing to all Israel, while the Asian church lived as Gentile believers, witnessing to all the nations. When the Jewish brethren came to Antioch, they lived as Jews – implying that this lifestyle was ideal while the Gentile option was permitted but second best. Paul rejected this view: among the Gentiles, live like the Gentiles. I reject this picture of the early church as unhistorical since it overlooks the bitter divisions and factionalism. Pauline Christianity, the gospel of God's justifying grace, emerged painfully in the polemical crucible of determined Petrine and Jamesian opposition, not merely amiable difference of emphasis. The conflict between Peter and Paul in Antioch regarding table fellowship with Gentiles anticipates the Galatian crisis about the status of the whole law.

Syrian Antioch, on the river Orontes, could well be 'the far country' in the Lukan parable of the errant son. It was the Paris of the ancient world, one of the four major cities of the Roman world. Located on the north-east Mediterranean, it rivalled Corinth in terms of reputation for debauchery. As the premier Gentile church, it was the epicentre of Gentile Christianity. The possibly derogatory designation 'Christian' was coined here. Although Barnabas and Paul were, since their days at Antioch, administrators of the famine relief fund, Antioch is never recorded as having financially supported Paul.

Antioch is modern Antakya (Arabic *Antakiyya*) in Turkey, near the Golan Heights, a part of Syria occupied by Israel since 1967. It was Gentile soil, a few hours' horse ride from Damascus. A bewildered Paul encountered the risen Christ here, roughly halfway between Damascus and the Mount of Transfiguration. Paul had missed out on the experience of the Transfiguration which was witnessed by Peter, John and James (Matt. 17.1–13; Mark 9.2–13; Luke 9.28–36).

11–13

Peter is personally and publicly opposed by Paul at Syrian Antioch. Many commentators believe that this incident – about the proper management of dissent in the early church – should be mined today to yield normative Christian guidance regarding this same problem when it plagues modern congregations. Muslims who build mosque institutions and appoint personnel to serve on mosque committees could also learn a lesson from this example of Peter's humility in the face of Paul's just accusation.

Syrian Antioch was the site of the daughter church of the Jerusalem congregation, founded in the aftermath of St Stephen's martyrdom and the subsequent dispersion of the Jerusalem saints (Acts 11.19–30). Peter withdraws from table fellowship. Even Barnabas is seduced by the circumcision party, notes Paul, with dismay and a touch of triumphalism. The compound *sunupokrinomai* (to dissemble along with), derived from the verb meaning 'to play a role' or, literally, 'to speak from beneath a mask', is found only here in the New Testament. The poetic Arabic idiom for a hypocrite is 'the father of two tongues (*abū lisānan*), not a Quranic expression. The scripture uses the verb *nā/fa/qa* (the third form from the root *na/fa/qa*) whose active participle means a hypocrite. Enigmatically, the causative fourth form of this same verb (*an/fa/qa*) means to spend money (see Q3.167 and Q2.3 respectively). Such linguistic puzzles are common in the Quran, an irreducibly puzzling scripture from a literary perspective.

One could speculate that Paul, after his conversion, perhaps joined some Antiochene circle of Hellenisers, an influence that made him too lenient and tolerant in matters of ritual observance. However, enigmatically, even as late as his epistle to the Philippians, in about 60 CE, he upholds, at least in principle and rather ambivalently, high standards of legal righteousness (Phil. 3.5–11). The context of these verses (3.2–4) is personal, defensive and startlingly polemical. Paul is no diplomat.

Peter is here shown behaving more like a pre-Christian Pharisee despite the pro-Gentile visions and directives (see Acts 10). He openly enjoyed table fellowship with Gentiles in Antioch until the 'men from James' arrived – from Jerusalem, one can safely assume – to oppose table fellowship with (presumably) uncircumcised Gentile converts. Only now Paul feels obliged to publicly oppose Peter. This is justifiable since hypocrites display theatrical virtue which could seduce others from the narrow path: hypocrites are more dangerous than ordinary sinners who usually only go astray themselves without misleading others. For Peter to be proven a hypocrite, rather than merely morally weak and self-deceived, it would require that he was aware of the discrepancy between his professed beliefs about table fellowship and his practical actions in that regard. Although Paul was justified in his strong accusation, his strong disagreement with Peter, after all a fellow Christian, can only be understood against the backdrop of unanimity about the wider gospel. Peter may be rightly judged as acting hypocritically in one instance – having fallen to temptation – without being a hypocrite altogether. No thoughtful moralist would deny that a person can remain good – act kindly and conscientiously – while doing some wrong.

The men from James must have alleged that Peter violated the *kashrūt* laws. The accusation is ambiguous. Was Peter, perhaps encouraged by his Gentile companions, eating foods considered unclean by Torah law (Lev. 11)? Or was he eating foods that were permitted but perhaps, in Gentile hands, not handled or processed properly to maintain their ritual purity? If only the latter, Peter infringed a halakhic ruling about the maintenance of ritual purity of food that can be lawfully consumed. Islamic law similarly distinguishes between food and drink that is intrinsically unlawful (*ḥarām*) from items that are or become merely disapproved (*makruh*) or ritually polluted (*najas*; Q9.28)[3] such as stagnant water whose stagnation renders it unsuitable for drinking and, according to some jurists, even for performing ablutions. Since the purpose of ablutions is usually considered symbolic rather than also hygienic – that is, to remove dirt – even dirty and stagnant water is generally permitted. In general, then, the intention of the law overrides any scruples about the precise means used to achieve it.

14

To walk straight (*orthopodousin*) reminds the Muslim of 'the path straightened' (*ṣirāṭ al-mustaqīm*; Q1.6), the blessed path. Muslims who reject Islam to follow (and worship) Jesus Christ may perhaps see it as abandoning the straight path for the narrow way of eternal life that few can find (Luke 13.24). One can well imagine such a testimony as being typical of a convert of Muslim background, especially one well-informed of the contrasting metaphorical images of the spiritually right path and its scope and width.

The adverb *ethnikos* (after the manner of the Gentiles) is opposed to *iouda-ikos* (as a Jew). In the New Testament, the verb *ioudaizein* (to judaise or be judaicised) means to act like a Jew or to adopt Jewish customs. Originally, it meant the adoption of Jewish ways by Gentile converts to Judaism. *Ioudaios* is a substantive adjective that means Jewish or possibly Judaean. The verbal noun *ioudaizmos* occurs only twice, both times here in Galatians (1.13, 14). In the (apocryphal) books of the Maccabees, *ioudaizmos* is used routinely as the opposite of Hellenisation since Judaism was, at that stage of its history, a religion as well as a prominent political cause. Non-Jews Judaised by trying to become Jewish through adoption of Jewish customs.

Jews often acted as self-consciously Jewish so as to set themselves apart from the heathen nations surrounding them. The motivating issue in the hinterland of the Maccabean struggles, however, was the *religious* legitimacy of assimilation to the Hellenic world. Many zealous Jews supported the *political* cause of anti-assimilation, an empowered commitment to remain different and separate from the Gentile world. When Paul's opponents claim that he is no longer committed to Judaisation – understood as resistance to Hellenisation – Paul replies, as we shall see later, that he is not selling out to the Gentiles. The proof, he argues, is that he stands for the cross, the commitment that invariably invites persecution from an evil world (Gal. 5.11, 6.12). Paul is insisting, quite credibly, that he is no man-pleaser (1.10).

Many contemporary Western Muslims have chosen to reject any wholly submissive and sycophantic assimilation to Western culture. Naturally, they fear persecution as they become the new Jews of Europe and the West, distinguished by their appearance and conduct. Those who insist on their own uniqueness often invite persecution from others, as Jews well know, though the oppressed Muslims of today's world hardly need Jewish corroboration in this matter.

Jews are normally called *al-Yahūd* in the Quran (Q5.64) and in Muhammad's traditions. The verbal formation *alladhīna hādū* (Q2.62), 'those who (have) Judaised', resembles *alladhīna āmanū* (those who have believed, Q2:62) and *alladhīna aslamū* (submitted, Q5:44). The use of the active voice of a verb, in a relative clause, instead of the simpler equivalent of a plural noun (in this case, believers) is not merely stylish and rhetorical: it implies sustained activity, even effort, since 'those who believed' may have earlier failed to believe and may still fail now and in the future. English verbs normally require adverbial support in order to convey this effort of the agent, in the so-called conative sense of the Arabic verb. The Quran often uses dynamic expressions such as 'those who idolise', 'those who dissemble' and so on, instead of their more static noun equivalents (idolaters and hypocrites, respectively). The use of the relative pronoun 'who' and relative clause 'those who . . .' makes the scripture even more in need of interpretation since it specifies classes of people rather than groups with fixed membership.

Hādū is related to *hāda*, (lit., to return to guidance) and might mean 'they guided'. The verbal noun *hudā* means guidance while the Prophet Muhammad is traditionally called *Al-Hād* (the guide), one of his many noble titles. 'Guided ones' (*muhtadīna*; 2.16) is the plural of *muhtad* while *ihtada* means 'he was guided' – all passive forms. One Quranic prophet, probably an Arab, certainly a Semite but foreign to the Bible, is called Hūd, a noun that could mean 'one who guides', an active form from *ha/da/ya*. His name could also mean '(the) Jew' (Q11.50); the same word also means Jews in the plural (Q2.135, 140). *Yahudiyyan* (a Jewish one or Judean) seems to locate identity using a geographical marker while *Nasraniyyan* could perhaps mean a Nazarene (3.67). The usage is unique to this verse. The Quran never describes Christians as those who 'christise/christianise' or 'messianise' since that would, at least linguistically, legitimise the worship of the messiah, something on which the Quran places a firm veto. Even modern Arabic uses the Quranic verbal noun *naṣrāniyya* (Christian) to derive the verb *tanaṣṣara*, meaning, to Christianise, to become a Christian. *Tahawwada* means to become a Jew.

VII 2.15–16

15 '*We (are) by nature Jews and (are) not sinners from among Gentiles (nations).* **16** *And (nevertheless) knowing that a man is not justified by (the) works of (the) law but through faith of (in) Christ Jesus, we too believed in Christ Jesus, in order that we might be justified by faith of (in) Christ and not by (the) works of (the) law, because by (the) works of (the) law, no flesh (at all) will be justified.*'

Before commenting on this section, I need to record a preliminary point. This *pericopē* could be a continuation of Paul's response to Peter, starting at 2.14b above. It is impossible to decide, based either on internal stylistic criteria or content, where Paul's speech to Peter ends and Paul's letter resumes. Many translators and commentators argue that the speech concludes at v.21, the end of Gal. 1. One hint of a larger audience, perhaps a group of conservative Jews, is the use of 'we' in vv.15–17. But Paul also uses the first person singular in v.14a and resumes it throughout vv.18–21. It could be merely a matter of style, to achieve variety. And the 'we' could be one of majesty rather than one intended to include the listener. In some African languages – such as Bantu – and in Malay, the inclusion or exclusion of the person(s) addressed, along with the speaker, is differentiated by the use of two distinct forms of the second person plural pronoun. Malay speakers use *kami* (we) to exclude the speaker's audience but *kita* (us) to include that audience. This subtlety introduces a distinction, foreign to Greek and Aramaic, into the translation of verses such as Matt. 8.25 where 'We are perishing', uttered by the disciples, must not include Jesus himself!

15

Jews by nature are contrasted with Gentile sinners who are, by definition, lawless and thus outside the Law and therefore routinely violating it. In *ex ethnōn hamartōloi* (sinners from among the Gentiles), '*ethnōn*' has no article and thus 'from among [the Gentile] nations' serves as a compound adjective qualifying 'sinners'. A person could coincidentally – without knowing it – live in accordance with God's will and law. Paul states elsewhere that we are all by nature aware of some of God's laws and his eternal qualities of power and divinity (Rom.1.18–21).[4] The Quran would concur. Additionally, it claims that our God-endowed nature (*fiṭrat Allahi*; lit. the creation of God, hence, God's original; Q30.30), the functional equivalent of conscience, enables us to discern God's laws and acknowledge his sovereignty operating not only in external nature but also in human nature. We are congenitally suited to be submitters (*muslim*) to our creator's will.

In his various mission fields, Paul encountered not only pagans but also native Jews (*phusei Ioudaioi*), proselyte (or converted) Jews, and Gentile God-fearers. It is unclear how Paul would have rated these three types of monotheists. In medieval Judaism, perhaps as a reaction against the hegemony of an ascendant if lenient Islam, some Jewish thinkers consciously defended Jewish elitism and, for example, saw election to prophethood as a genetic endowment exclusive to Jews and denied to Gentiles.[5] No doubt Muhammad was the target of the implied exclusion.

16

Starting with this verse, Paul uses 'faith' twenty-two times in this epistle but 'faith in God' never occurs in any Pauline epistle. Starting here, Paul consistently uses *nomos* in the broad sense of Torah. This is likely to be the first written statement of the gospel of grace in Paul and indeed in the entire New Testament.

Pisteōs Christou Iēsou is ambiguous: it can mean the faith/faithfulness *of* Christ Jesus, that is, Christ's being faithful to the covenant and to Israel's God. This is the subjective genitive. Whose faith? The subject's faith: Christ's faith. This genitive occurs as the possessive in English, marked by an apostrophe. The phrase could also mean any saved Christian believer's faith *in* Christ or, collectively, the believers' trust in Christ's power to save sinners, without regard for their merits acquired through works of the law. This is the objective genitive since the believer places his or her faith in the direct object (Christ). Paul must mean here the objective genitive. If he had meant the subjective genitive, there would have been nothing specifically 'Christian' about his claim.

'Faith in Christ Jesus' has no sense for Muslims for the object of faith is God alone, not his prophetic representative. Used absolutely, one can have faith (*īmān*) only in

God, never in his messengers, angels or books – although one can, using the same verb with the preposition *bi*, believe *in* God and his messengers (Q2.285). *Īmān*, a verbal noun, literally means certainty or security of conviction, not merely faith in the sense of mere belief. Prophets alone experienced the total assurance and security of *īmān* despite being put to numerous tests that would easily shake the certainty of lesser believers. In the Quranic version of their woes, both Jacob and his son Joseph receive, from the very beginning, divinely revealed certainty about the final outcome of their trials and tribulations (see Q12.4–101). For ordinary believers, however, having *īmān* does not prevent vacillation in one's level of commitment to one's faith. The Quran distinguishes faith (*īmān*) from mere submission (*islam*; Q49.14) but, intriguingly, never addresses believers as 'O you who have submitted' (*yā ayyuhā alladhīna aslamū*), only as 'O you who have attained faith' – frequently, for example, at Q.2.104, the earliest use of this expression in the Quran's final arrangement.

If 'the faithfulness of Christ Jesus' means the exemplary faith that Jesus, as prophet, had in God, Jesus' experience is no different from that of God's other messengers. Christians would disagree: the faith of Jesus Christ was a faith marked by a uniquely perfect obedience to God's will, and therefore a doubly saving faith. For it was saving, arguably, for Christ himself in his human capacity, though no Christian group holds this view, and derivatively but more importantly for all those who have faith in him. Muslims discern Christian intolerance in such claims since they see the faith of all God's messengers, including Muhammad, as being a faith of perfect obedience. Fortunately, this inter-religious wrangle is irrelevant here since it is unreasonable to suppose that Paul is referring to the human Christ's faith in God as opposed to the believer's faith in Christ as divine Saviour. The latter claim is unique to Christianity. Islam dismisses it as blasphemous mythology.

Arabic has subjective and objective genitives but prohibits a lexically coherent sense for a subjective genitive in expressions such as 'from fear of God' (*min khashiyati Allahi*; Q59.21). It cannot mean the fear displayed by Allah, the subject, but rather only the fear shown by his creatures (or, as in the quoted verse, inanimate creation). Thus, '*Allah*' can function only as the agent – in that sense the subject – causing the fear.

See also Chapter 4, sections III and VIII, for commentary on Gal. 3.11 where Paul quotes Hab. 2.4. There we explore the distinction between faith as propositional belief and faithfulness as trust. Nowhere in Paul can we confidently read a verse that clearly marks this distinction. The same ambiguity infects Rom. 1.16–17 where Hab. 2.4 is again quoted. No such ambiguity is present in Hab. 2.4 itself since there the subjective genitive is clearly in view.

VIII 2.17–21

17 *'But if while seeking to be justified in Christ, we ourselves were found to be sinners too, is Christ then a minister of sin? May it never be!* **18** *For if I rebuild the things I (once) destroyed, I prove myself to be a transgressor.* **19** *For through the law, I died to the law so that I might live to (for) God. With Christ I have been co-crucified.* **20** *And I live no more but Christ lives in me;*

and the life now which I live in the flesh, I live by faith in the son of God who (while) loving me was giving himself up on my behalf. **21** *I do not set aside the grace of God; for if righteousness (comes) through the law, then Christ died without a cause.'*

17

Is Christ a servant (*diakonos*) of moral anarchy? Since Christ does not require good works as a condition of salvation, does he, in effect, encourage sin? Paul was still confronted with a version of this objection to his position when he came to pen the epistle to the Romans in c. AD 57. 'Shall we continue to sin that grace may abound?' (Rom. 6.1).

Judaism required Jews to lead upright lives, defined in terms of Torah observance. The Galatians might have been told by Paul's opponents that Jesus came to fulfil the law, not to abolish it (see Matt. 5.17). Jesus came to call God's people to respect their calling to the full rather than to abandon altogether their commitment to keeping the law. The Judaisers may have reasoned that, for Paul, sin does not really matter! This is not his position, initial or considered; we find nuances and subtleties galore in his total outlook. If we restrict ourselves to the Galatian context, however, the charge is plausible. Moreover, let us be fair to the Judaisers. They probably took issue with Paul regarding only the Law's provisions for ritual purity; there was no suggestion that Paul was keen to promote immorality in general. That latter suggestion would have amounted to slander.

Ironically, Christians often accuse Muslims of entertaining a nonchalant attitude towards sin. But the Christian stance is equally distressing to Muslims. For if sinners can do nothing to achieve salvation except to place their trust in Christ to absolve them of their sins, then sin is, in one sense, irrelevant: while it matters in an ultimate sense, there is nothing the sinner can do about it. The Judaisers' accusation is identical to the one Muslims bring, especially if they are inclined to vilify Paul on other grounds. The work of Jesus, as an eminent *rasūlullāh*, was to enable the Children of Israel to rise to the height of their initial calling as a guided, favoured and blessed community. Muslims lament that Paul wants to make them sink to the low level of the Gentile sinners. This is, however, a misunderstanding of Paul's admittedly rather convoluted teaching.

18

In this enigmatic verse, Paul seems to be condemning the premier Apostle Peter for joining forces with the Judaisers. Paul sees this as a regression to the regime of the Law from which, as he writes in the next verse, Christ's death delivered Christians. By Judaising, Peter is rebuilding the edifice of Judaism which was demolished through Christ's self-sacrifice on the cross. In the Synoptic Gospels, Jesus predicted the annihilation of the old Temple, as he lamented the coming destruction of Jerusalem (Matt. 23.37–24.2; Mark 13.1–23; Luke 21.5–24). His brief ministry assumed the imminent destruction of Judaism itself in its present state. His followers certainly thought that his death would replace the old Temple with the new spiritual temple of the church, the body of the resurrected Christ (John 2.19–22).[6]

Coming some six centuries later, Islam may be seen as a Jamesian-Petrine move in favour of rebuilding a universal version of law-centred ethnic Judaism – albeit with intensified regard for interior sincerity of motive. Naturally, I claim this only in regard to the retention of the legal dimension of their inherited Judaism since these two apostles, like all Christians, differed from Islam (and from Judaism) in continuing to affirm the atoning death and resurrection of Christ, experience of the Holy Spirit and the coming reign and glory of the messianic kingdom.

19

Paul came to see the Law as a hindrance to spontaneous piety and gratitude to God. Paul uses the genuine first person singular pronoun (*egō*) and for emphasis he places it at the beginning of the sentence. He intends his words to be universally valid for Christian readers. Some verses in the short Meccan chapters of the Quran are addressed to Muhammad using the second person masculine singular but are valid for all Muslim readers since they too may interpret the vicissitudes of their own lives as subtly supplying evidence of divine guidance, mercy, and grace (Q93, Q94, Q108).

Paul is co-crucified with Christ, an idea that perhaps originates in the well-attested tradition of the two robbers who were literally co-crucified with Jesus (Matt. 27.38), a tradition found in negligibly different forms in all four gospels. In most editions of the Greek text, this sentence is part of v.19 and most commentaries treat it as such. In translations into English, however, it is customary to read this claim with the opening words of v.20.

20

'Christ lives in me' is, unlike 'I am in Christ', rare in Paul. The former might perhaps reduce Christ's grandeur by limiting him to a smaller human location. Paul is a mystic who, like mystics in other traditions, sees his relationship to a supreme higher power as organic and yet supernatural, as real but occult. Like a Buddhist who wants to eliminate the illusion of the self (atman), Paul in some moods might have wanted to annihilate the nomistic self. This radical ambition is not found clearly in orthodox (original) Islam but it motivates some Sufi sheikhs.

Justification as the preliminary rectification of the believer is organically linked to the resurrection of the new self. Conversion is an ontological rebirth of the self once the ego of desire is annihilated in Christ. Paul's biography is reversed through death to Christ just as Paul reversed Greek wisdom by becoming the first anti-philosopher, the man who offered the world the alternative wisdom of Christ in his triumph over death – the final frontier that all human beings, including atheists, must accept in fear and trembling. Paul rejoices in this victory over death promised long ago by the prophets (1 Cor. 15.54–55, quoting Isa. 25.8 and Hos. 13.14). Secularists must see death, metaphorically and ironically, as a kind of god. It reduces human effort to a handful of churchyard dust – or, for the lucky few, into eight lines of tribute in an encyclopaedia.

21

We reach the climax of this *pericopē*. The law versus grace dichotomy is, in my view, made needlessly (*dorean*) absolute just as the beatitudes, from a Muslim perspective, needlessly make absolute and universal certain spiritual states, including meekness, peace and poverty, which should be relative, localised and conditional. In practice, Muslims would contend, the conduct of the ethical life requires flexibility (though not compromise) since there is a time for meekness and also a time for a certain kind of pride – though never a time for hubris, an absolute wrong. (This Islamic stance must remind Christians and Jews of the sceptical wisdom of Ecclesiastes!)

Paul proclaims with terminative authority and stress that the law nullifies grace. That Christ might have died *needlessly* is the great fear of Christian faith. The confident Islamic proclamation of the irrelevance of Christ's death often reinforces this subliminal Christian anxiety. On a purely rational level, Christians know that everyone must die: the cross of Christ is at one level only a fact of history. But the believer celebrates the truth that only one man died by decision and was then raised to life and to glory.

For Paul, after the coming of Christ, the reinstatement of the Law would contradict the good news of Christ's grace. If the Law remains relevant to and valid for salvation, what is the good news of the Christ? And, if the (whole) law remains intact, for whom is the good news – Jews or Gentiles?

IX

Before exploring seven themes that emerge thus far in the epistle, note how Paul amplifies his case as he moves, starting at Gal. 2.14 onward, from autobiography to the doctrine of salvation by grace via justification. This strategic transition hinges on the unresolved status of the Gentiles in the scheme of salvation. Paul was to become the chief architect of Gentile Diaspora Christianity. In first century Palestinian Judaism, within its sectarian variety, the Jewish-Gentile divide was beginning to be questioned. It was a far cry from the days of Ezra, the second Moses, whose annulment of the marriages of exiled Jews who had married Gentile women, preserved the core of Judaism at a crucial hour (Ezra 9–10). Jesus often challenged and, sometimes in practice, ignored the finer points of the Law and enjoyed dealings with Gentiles, even with the despised Samaritans. This is true of Jesus as portrayed in all four gospels. Paul's mission is an extension and explicit endorsement of what is at best only implicit in Jesus' encounters with those on the margins of Israelite faith and privilege. The Quran, the reader will recall, regards Jesus as an ethnic messenger sent solely to the lost sheep of Israel.

The Law, the barrier between Jews and Gentiles, is a mark of Jewish identity and destiny. A Torah-observant Jew is easy to recognise. Muslims, like Jews, but unlike

Christians, tend to dress distinctively. This is especially true of Muslim women. Muslim men often wear beards and all bear the mark of circumcision in the flesh.[7] Muslim identity is further secured through the five canonical prayers that punctuate the day. The added dietary restrictions, especially the absolute ban on drinking alcohol, accentuate the differences between Muslims and non-Muslims, especially though not only in a secular environment.

Paul renounced the things that mattered to him in his pre-Christian life (Phil. 3.6–11). To revert to Judaism, after the Christ revolution, would be to become a transgressor. Paul was, of course, outwardly quite Jewish in Jerusalem and spent years collecting money for the poor saints of that church. Paul must have looked like a rabbi to the Roman soldiers who escorted him. He offered the hair sacrifice when he shaved his head in Cenchreae (Acts 18.18; cf. Q48.27) to fulfil a vow. So, he sported a beard and long hair, at least up to this point. Such concessions to the Law, however, are compatible with a deep distrust of the continuing validity of the Torah just as a Muslim whose only apparent concession to his faith is a goatee beard – perhaps doubling as a casual statement of fashion – could still be mistaken for a radical, if only by paranoid security experts at airports. Appearances are often deceptive, especially in the case of those whose lives contain unusual ideological trajectories.

Paul has the unique distinction of effectively destroying Judaism while building Diaspora Christianity on its ashes. Muhammad destroyed Arab paganism to found Islamic monotheism but he did not destroy any existing monotheism in order to establish a new one on its debris – although he did challenge, with immense force and sustained clarity, two established monotheisms. Paul's critical stance on Judaism is comparable with Muhammad's quarrel with both Judaism and Christianity, the faiths of the two peoples of scripture and sacred mention and memory (*ahl al-dhikr*, Q16.43). Nothing in Paul's career can be compared with Muhammad's successful attempt to annihilate permanently his native Arab paganism within a mere two decades, a project started by him and zealously executed by his lieutenants. Indeed, the whole of sacred Semitic history can find no parallel for this feat of the Arab Apostle. Joshua did destroy idolatry among the pagan nations surrounding Israel but it re-emerged and indeed co-existed with Jewish monotheism in the holy land for centuries. It was only the fifty-year exile in Babylon which finally cured Israel of its idolatrous inclinations but, sadly, replaced it with the more moral defect of hypocrisy, among the failings of our shared humanity.

The Law, as salvific determinant, was rendered obsolete by Christ's crucifixion. In his mind, Paul was a slave to God's law while in his flesh he answered to the law of sin (Rom. 7.25). This was the doomed struggle of the pre-Christian Paul, the Law-observant Jew, who lacked the decisive help of Christ's grace. In theory at least, few if any Muslims have ever assigned either to the law or to the sin it identifies any such totalitarian powers. Therefore, Muslims do not experience this characteristically Pauline struggle which later so exercised St Augustine – who was, after Paul, the most influential convert who was also a theologian.

I would contend that Paul misunderstood the purpose and scope of the Law. Think here of the power of another agency whose jurisdiction is also hard to define. Think here of the Unitarian novelist Charles Dickens' mature masterpiece *Dombey and Son*, published in 1848, the year in which Marx and Engels published their *Communist Manifesto*. Dickens plotted a story through which he could lament that money could not do certain things: win us love, preserve our health and save us from death. Dickens was partly wrong. Money can give us status – the social love that others give us in virtue of our wealth. Dickens experienced such social affection all his working life. By freeing us from the drudgery of work, money affords us time for leisure and hence a degree of physical comfort which contributes to physical and mental health. As for death, nothing can save us from it. That is why it is always worthy of our wonder. Even personal love, much prized by Dickens, cannot save anyone from the calamity of physical demise. We must all die and no one can buy longevity beyond the few years obtainable through private health care.

Ironically, *Dombey* was the very book whose commercial success finally enabled Dickens to say farewell to a poverty that had plagued him since his adolescent years – and to partly attain the first two goals, namely, love and health. As for mortality, since every person's lease on this physical life is limited, not even someone who had 'twice everything that is in the whole earth' (Q5.36) could avert divine judgement and punishment or extend his or her stay on earth by even a second (Q10.49; 11.3; see also Matt. 6.27; Luke 12.25). The hour destined for the grave can never be spent outside it, not even by those heedless fools, countless millions today, who live as if they will shop and live on earth forever.

Dickens misunderstood the function of wealth – hardly surprising when we note how few of his characters work and how many of them want to lead idle lives as gentlemen of leisure. Analogously, Paul's view of the Law, I would argue, expects too much from it and the Apostle expresses disappointment when it fails to deliver this. What makes this claim hard to identify is that Paul, in his *ad hominem* polemical context, argues that it is his *opponents* who expect too much from the Law – which might also be true but it is irrelevant here to my claim against Paul.

The Law, as Paul knew well, is and was always meant as a restraint on sin, not a way to completely purify one's heart and its intentions. It could be used to plumb the depths of human evil and thus teach us truths about ourselves. Paul's enduringly correct point is that attachment to even the law of God can become idolatrous when we seek to use it to achieve salvation. But this indictment should properly be seen as part of the larger truth that the idolatry of any reality, such as material wealth, art, progeny or pleasure – any reality less than and other than God – is misguided and indeed sinful. I believe that Paul's three modern targets would be Judaism, Islam and, perhaps surprisingly, Catholicism. Why? These faiths encourage their votaries, in varied ways and to different degrees, to pursue merit, even perfection, chiefly through human effort guided by the grace of divine law. Perhaps Catholics would officially dispute my verdict but, I fear, they would be mistaken.

Before I move on to note one intriguing historical detail in this broad survey of concerns, let me admit that I might have misunderstood and therefore, in effect, inadvertently distorted Paul's actual reasoning and motivation here. Be that as it may, the crisis of law observance was not restricted to Galatia. Paul tells the Galatians about two incidents that occurred outside the Galatian congregations. Some Jewish Christians wanted to force their fellow Jewish Christians and Gentile converts alike to submit to the Law. Gentiles had to become Judaised before they were truly Christians. In Gal. 2.4 above, Paul relates that when he was in Jerusalem during what is probably his famine visit (see Acts 11.27–30), certain men sought to force Titus, a Gentile convert, to be circumcised. Paul dismisses them as 'false brothers' seeking to destroy the Christians' new-found freedom in Christ. (Titus is not mentioned in Acts.) The second incident is the restriction of table fellowship at (Syrian) Antioch in the aftermath of the visit of the men from James. The false teachers in the Galatian churches were perhaps implicated in these two incidents which occurred before the more widespread and consequential crisis in Galatia. These zealous missionaries hounded Paul for years, from city to city. Their relentless attacks would justify Paul's two savage outbursts; one at the beginning and one near the end of his epistolary apostolic career (see Gal. 5.12, Phil. 3.2–3).

X

We start a survey of themes by examining Gal. 1.17. I shall start by mentioning some journeys towards Arabia undertaken by biblical figures before examining the location and scope of Paul's Arabia. I then speculate about the purposes and duration of his visit, commenting on Paul's retreat to the wilderness of Nabatea. I conclude by noting the alleged spiritual barrenness of Arabia and a mention of his return to Damascus. For this last purpose, I use both the accounts in Acts as well as Paul's own account in 2 Corinthians.

The Quran's silence about Paul is remarkable since, unlike most other biblical figures, he visited some part of Arabia. The Quran claims that Abraham and Ishmael came to Mecca and laid the foundations of God's House there (Q2.125–129; 14.37). This visit is certainly possible although the trip from Ur to Canaan would not go via Mecca. Indeed, the onward trek from Canaan to Mecca would be as long as the one from Ur to Canaan and possibly more arduous, given the ferocious heat of the *Arabia deserta*. Jews and Christians would see such an extended journey as unmotivated. Why this place called Mecca? And for what divine purpose?

Leaving aside such reservations which are rooted in an a priori rival faith commitment, we may reasonably argue that nomads made caravan journeys of greater or comparable length, as for example in the biblical narrative of the Queen of Sheba (1 Kgs. 10.1–10) travelling to Jerusalem from what is modern Yemen, the *Arabia felix* of the Romans, a land the Quran eulogises as 'a fair land' (*baldatun ṭayyibatun*) under 'an indulgent Lord' (Q34.15). The Queen travelled this distance accompanied by her retinue of servants and camels laden with spices and gold. It is a far more arduous undertaking – stifling heat and brigands galore – than the one Abraham would have had to endure in travelling to Mecca.

In the case of at least one biblical figure, then, biblical archaeologists concur that journeys of comparable length were undertaken. In the Bible, though not in the Quran, Abraham was in Egypt where he feared the Egyptians would seize his beautiful wife. He asked his wife to pretend to be his sister – and would have lost her to the pharaoh had this pharaoh not been a conscientious and godly man (see Gen. 12.10–20). Muslims dismiss such biblical narratives as Jewish mischief and delinquency dressed as humour – furnishing evidence of tampering with scripture. Jews and Christians call this the realism of the Bible and see the Quran as transcendent in the bad sense of being detached from the reality of human sinfulness. The point here – about the credible range of ancient travel – is unaffected by such a larger moral controversy.

In Gal. 1.17, Arabia is not a metonymy for simply any desert or wilderness. It is a real place. Where then is Paul's Arabia? Was the Gospel preached by Paul in Arabia and its precincts? If 'Arabia' means the whole region from the Sinai Peninsula up to modern Syria, including Damascus, it is almost twice the size of the *jazīrat al-'Arab* ('island' of the Arabs), the peninsular region of modern cartography, containing the Hejaz with Islam's two cities of renown. More likely, Paul's Arabia is the restricted area of the north-western kingdom of Nabatea, located in the south-eastern corner of historic Palestine, in modern Jordan.

What is the extent of Arabia in Muslim understanding? Muhammad's deathbed order, to keep Arabia free and pure for Islam, did not specify the geographical extent of Arabia as Islam's holy land. It led to Umar's decision to expel the Christians of Najran who had signed a protection treaty with Muhammad. Umar did, however, resettle them in newly conquered territories in the Levant.

When Paul writes about his Jerusalem visit, he is surprisingly precise about both purpose and duration. The silence about the Arabian sojourn might suggest that the visit was unsuccessful, whatever its purpose, whether religious or secular. For why record an unsuccessful journey? But we need to be cautious. If the visit were not for public mission but rather a spiritual retreat for solitary reflection, then Paul felt no need to formally recount it. The visit was a personal success with public consequences: he re-emerged with a clarified call and purpose. He was reborn and strengthened to live henceforth in the active heat of a seamlessly single emotional commitment to Christ crucified. There are, in all of history, few who can match such a sustained devotion unto death.

Paul claims to have gone to Arabia straight after his conversion, without consulting anyone. It is unclear what it is that he did not consult others about. And a refusal to consult others is not the same as not telling anyone. If, however, we interpret him strictly – that is, to mean that he did not tell anyone at all – this detail would conflict with Luke's account where Paul does share his conversion experience with others (Acts 9.3–22). Leaving this matter aside, we may see it as a desert sojourn similar to the forty days spent by Jesus in the desert, to be tempted by the Devil and made ready for ministry. Did Paul travel there for hermetic contemplation, in the manner of the later desert fathers? Deserts are important in monastic tradition. St Antony lived in the Egyptian desert, a featureless landscape where ascetics could not enjoy even the innocent beauties of nature. Paul was alone in the wilderness of Arabia. Was he near Mount Sinai? Did he afterwards return only to Damascus or also perhaps briefly to his native Tarsus, as he waited for his Gentile commission to begin? We can only speculate and, in the field of Pauline studies, it is hard to come by new factual and historical data as opposed to endless speculative scholarly conjecture bordering on adventurism.

Paul probably retreated to the Nabatean wilderness to meditate rather than to engage in ministry. If he did preach, however, then Paul's uncharted and brief journey there was his first missionary journey. It was unsuccessful since Paul did not plant churches in 'Arabia', perhaps to be rightly seen as a prescient indication of the later failure of the Gospel to take root in the barren soil of Islamic Arabia.[8] Christians flourished in parts of Arabia – certainly in Nabatea, the northern frontier of the Arab peninsula – but by the early seventh century, their presence in the peninsula may have been steadily diminishing, perhaps even starting to become negligible. We do not know for certain. Typically, Muslim historians at any rate see in this situation the engineering hand of providence: the preservation of Arabia from Christian influence is proof that the place was divinely destined for the plant of pure Abrahamic monotheism finally to take root, courtesy of Muhammad. The success of Muhammadan monotheism would enrage the disbelievers of Arabia (cf. Q48.29) as well as many Jews and Christians (Q2.109; 57.29).

Let me add a postscript here about Arabia's spiritual receptivity or lack thereof. Although Arabia has no rivers, only deserts and mountains, it possesses, for Muslims, despite this physical aridity, a marked spiritual fecundity. Christians might lament that it is spiritually fruitless, a vast and barren expanse which remains largely unreceptive to the Gospel. The seed has thus far fallen only on shallow stony soil: Christian ideals of meekness and humility had little purchase in the martial ethos of seventh century Arabia. Muslims would sincerely challenge Christians, however, to indicate any self-respecting, including Christian, society, in any age or land, where such ideals have had much purchase or appeal.

Let me shunt my train of thought onto the last rail. Paul returned to Damascus, a city which had, like Muhammad's Medina, a significant settled Jewish population with some influence. If the ethnarch of the Nabatean king was hostile to Paul, then we may speculate that Paul did evangelise the Nabateans and, predictably, aroused anger in royal Arabian circles. Was Damascus under Arab (Nabatean) rule at this time?

Paul confirms the Acts account when he writes that 'the ethnarch (governor) under King Aretas had the city of the Damascenes guarded in order to arrest me' (2 Cor. 11.32–3). Why was an ethnarch of King Aretas in Damascus? Were his mission and presence connected with Paul's presence in the city? If King Aretas' ethnarch caused trouble for Paul, is it likely that he would choose to hide in this northern corner of Arabia? Or would he, like Elijah, travel further into Arabia proper, *Arabia deserta*? Commentators can only speculate. Dealing with such spiritually irrelevant minutiae amuses an army of experts but Paul's total legacy, like that of any seminal thinker, is so vast that no one can truthfully claim comprehensive expertise even in regard to its more spiritually significant details.

Unlike the account in Acts 9.23–25, however, Paul does not mention Jewish hostility to his presence in Damascus, a city with a sizeable Jewish population. If Damascus resembled pre-Islamic Yathrib (later to be Muslim Medina), there were probably separate Jewish and Nabatean Arab quarters in the city. Jews and Arabs could have joined forces to eliminate Paul. He mentions an undignified escape from the city, confirmed in Acts. The Jews had good reasons for wanting to get rid of this perceived enemy of Moses, the Torah and the Temple.

The Nabateans had no clear motives of their own but they probably wanted to please the Jewish population of Damascus which must have been large – if we judge by how many thousands had left the city or been deported from it.[9] There is no published comparative sociological study of Damascene and Medinan Jewry in the first and sixth centuries of the Common Era. Muhammad's enemies in Medina, especially the Arab hypocrites and many members of settled Jewish tribes, had different motives, personal and ideological, for opposing this new pretender to the throne. Paul too had enemies in various cities – especially Jerusalem, Antioch and Damascus.

XI

The Galatian Paul scrupulously discounts all human influence for fear that some might think he received the Gospel from a man (Gal. 1.12). In his confessional autobiography, Paul never mentions the Hellenist leader Stephen, the first Christian martyr. Yet, Jesus apart, who could have been a greater influence on the former Pharisee than the man who questioned the apparently impregnable institutions of the Torah and Temple? Stephen, thought to be a Gentile convert to Judaism, became a fervent disciple of Christ. Like Paul, he may not have met Jesus. Paul approved of Stephen's martyrdom but did not participate in it (Acts 6.8–8.3). This remarkable incident is not recorded in Paul's letters.[10]

Paul never mentions Ananias, 'sent by the Lord Jesus', to meet him (Acts 9.10–19). Ananias greets him as 'Brother Saul', heals him of his blindness and baptises him. Paul was presumably immersed in water and came out crying, 'Jesus is Lord!' Again, as far as we know, Paul never compliments Barnabas. Perhaps Paul was anxious that, were he to do so, some might suspect that this senior missionary companion, known for his generosity and courage (Acts 4.36, 13.46), had influenced him! Paul separated from him after a disagreement (Acts 15.36–41). By contrast, note how the Apostle is invariably gentle and protective towards his junior missionary associates, especially Timothy.

Paul earnestly denies that he was tutored by the Jerusalem apostles who had preceded him in Christian conviction. 'Neither from a man nor from men' (Gal. 1.1) may intend a denial of human (as opposed to divine) influence but it need not exclude an allusion to Peter (a man) and the three pillars (men). Paul's detractors must surely have argued, not unreasonably, that Paul's gospel was derivative: it was authorised by the Jerusalem pillar apostles. Paul was their subordinate and thus had no right to oppose Peter, the chief apostle, who was then at Antioch. Paul retorts that not only is he the equal of the other apostles but, moreover, the apostles Peter and Barnabas had come to be numbered among the hypocrites at Antioch!

Paul went to Jerusalem to present his gospel to Jerusalem's elite apostles. The three pillars recognised the grace given to Paul. Yet he still calls them merely 'the seeming pillars'. Despite their endorsement of his mission, he remains reluctant to show excessive deference towards them. Although Paul's teaching is in harmony with that of the Jerusalem pillar apostles, he wants to secure *independent apostolic* authority. He must have agonised over the opposing demands of church unity which had to be maintained despite the legitimate division of labour for the missionaries. Analogously, Muhammad received direct divine authority and was thus freed of the need for Jewish and Christian approval – and yet he initially sought nonetheless their approval, partly to secure communal harmony in the multi-faith commonwealth of Medina. This is a sensitive point and touches the honour of Muslim apologists. Some commentators deny that Muhammad sought such endorsement, arguing instead that the Quran asks him, in case of self-doubt, to consult Jews and Christians *only* about verses in their scriptures predicting his advent as Arab Apostle.

In any event, Paul lists all his Jerusalem visits to prove that, after his conversion, he hardly ever went to the holy city. This is again connected with the anxiety of influence that all seminal thinkers constantly feel. Muhammad travelled to Jerusalem only once, it seems, and then only spiritually (based on an allusion at Q17.1 but cf. 17.93).[11] Had he or his companions travelled there often, perhaps during their trading ventures, then the charge of spiritual borrowing from Judaism would have gained greater force. The very fact that Muslims even faced Jerusalem in their prayerful orientation (cf. Dan. 6.10) gave Medina's rabbis enough polemical material against this upstart and his purportedly Arab edition of Judaism. Within a year or so of Muhammad's move to Medina, Islam had shed most of its Jewish doctrinal (though not ritual) affinities. Jerusalem was repudiated in favour of Mecca, a change that was meant to test the continued loyalty of Muhammad's followers and perhaps in order that God might please his Arabian messenger who longed for his native city to be honoured thus (Q2.142–44; 28.85; 90.1–2).

Paul, a Jew by birth, argued constantly with fellow Jews who embraced Jesus as messiah but still wanted to remain subjects of the Mosaic administration. Muhammad was in serious conflict with Jews who rejected his claim to be a prophet in the line of Hebrew messengers even though he brought a revelation that claimed to confirm the truth of the Torah. Although Jesus and Paul quoted extensively from the Torah, and did so perhaps in its original language, they radically reinterpreted core elements of its ancient teaching. In effect, they questioned the Torah's continuing authority rather than, I would argue, merely questioned its correct interpretation. By contrast, the Quran never criticises, let alone rejects, the Torah even though it confirms the Torah's authority only in the abstract – quoting its contents only obliquely and only in translation. Muhammad was therefore sincerely and justifiably surprised when the Jews mocked him. However, as I implied earlier, the Torah in Jewish possession and possessiveness may well have differed from the Torah envisaged rather abstractly in the Quran's many references to it.

XII

I want to raise a larger issue here about the early church, a matter which might seem distracting and perhaps annoyingly speculative but it is relevant to the broadest concerns of this commentary. Modern readers of the New Testament are, I believe, predisposed to give too much credit to Paul for the successful transmission of an allegedly pristine Christian legacy mainly because more of his epistles, even if we exclude the disputed ones, are in the canon than those of James, Peter and John combined.[12] It is tempting to exaggerate Paul's role in the formation of the early church. Thanks partly to the lengthy ambivalence of both Peter himself and possibly of the whole 'Petrine' faction in Christianity about such practical matters as table fellowship with Gentiles, the movement remained recognisably, if reluctantly, a sect of Judaism, as we see in Acts 1–12. Paul's Christian witness, however, emerged almost *ab initio* almost as a new faith which, in its passionate advocacy and singularity of radically novel messianic purpose, challenged the parent faith enough to cause an irreversible rupture.

What is the point of the above claims? I would sympathise with the view that for commentators such as Augustine, Galatians is at root about schism and ecclesiology – the conflict between Paul and Peter, the triumph of Paul, disunity in the body of Christ, and broader matters of mutual rebuke, discipline and apostolic rivalry. Peter at Antioch is seen as making an error of judgement which gave him an opportunity to show the humility one expects of a seasoned apostle, a true disciple of Christ crucified.

Paul indirectly persecuted his Lord by persecuting his followers while Peter, initially, directly but mildly persecuted Jesus by renouncing and betraying him. Both sinners were unconditionally forgiven. Once commissioned, Paul was the complete opposite of, for example, the patriotic prophet Jonah who refused to be a missionary to other nations. As for Peter, even during his time with Jesus, he was impulsive, abrupt and somewhat unstable, often changing his mind – all qualities of a people-pleaser. Was he, like some among the Galatians, rather fickle? Peter changed his stance on the legitimacy of table fellowship with Gentiles. In Galatians, as in all four gospels, he is weak and fickle.

Peter progressed from being a disciple to become an apostle and in the end proved his mettle and merit through martyrdom. Paul shared at best only the last two honours; he was never a disciple of the earthly Jesus. That was one boast denied to him even if we grant, as we must, that Paul worked harder than all the other apostles (1 Cor. 15.10). Paul would say that he was something better: he was a servant of the risen Christ. We can detect a hint about the possible martyrdom of Paul in Jesus' address to Ananias of Damascus (Acts 9.15–16): the risen Christ warns Paul, his chosen instrument, concerning future suffering for his name's sake. For Peter's martyrdom, we have direct dominical authority (John 21.15–19) – though never in the Synoptics.

In Galatians and to some extent in Acts, Peter is portrayed as an ethnocentric Jew lacking Paul's vision. As an uneducated fisherman from Galilee, Peter's first epistle was penned by Silvanus, his amanuensis (1 Pet. 5.12), while his second letter was perhaps written by one of Peter's disciples – just as his own witness of Jesus was perhaps written by John Mark. By Islamic standards, Peter, the uneducated fisherman, is a good candidate for receiving revelation. Only shepherds make better candidates. Muhammad apparently said that all prophets were shepherds at some stage of their lives. The Quran portrays Moses as a wandering shepherd (Q20.18, 40; 27.7) who meets the biblical Jethro, another shepherd (Q28.23–28).

Neither Paul nor Peter is mentioned in the Quran, although the disciples are mentioned as a group. Just as the Quran rejects certain accusations against various biblical prophets, it does not generally envisage that the disciples of a prophet would be fickle and slow to understand and support him while he lived among them. Indeed, the Quran's portrait of Jesus' disciples is quite flattering. The Muslim scripture, however, condemns the cowardice and laziness of some of Moses' disciples, shown clearly during a military expedition. It praises, in the same context, the courage of two unnamed disciples who feared their Lord who had blessed them (Q5.21–24). One of them is perhaps Caleb (Num. 13.30–33). Muhammad's companions enthusiastically reassured their prophet, to his delight, they would never refuse to join battle if he asked them to fight in God's cause (Q9.44–45). They gave such reassurances by explicitly citing and rejecting the unreliable behaviour of both the Israelites – who feared to enter the 'Promised Land' – and their own contemporary lukewarm Arab hypocrites.

In their love for Muhammad, who was only a human prophet, his companions set a record that has not been surpassed by subsequent generations of Muslim believers or by the adherents of any leader or prophet of another faith.[13] However, after Muhammad's death, the power struggles between some of his prominent followers, often equally devout and zealous, were shameful – shattering Islam's unity forever. For Christians, the glory of the story is that the risen Jesus transformed recalcitrant hearts and minds. According to church tradition, of the twelve disciples, only John died a natural death – at a ripe old age. Jesus forgave Peter and he was rehabilitated. We find no parallel to this in Muhammad's dealings with his disciples: those who deserted him never returned to seek his forgiveness. Those who loved him, however, never deserted him at all, not even in the darkest hour. I would argue that sacred history knows no other case of such an elevated and sustained level of courage, dedication and zeal for the cause of monotheism.

XIII

With the exception of Confucianism, Christianity is alone in having neither formal dietary prohibitions nor ceremonial purity laws relating to food and, to a lesser extent, dress.[14] Members of a sect such as the Seventh-Day Adventists do observe dietary restrictions derived from the Hebrew Bible, but many Christians, if not most, do not classify them as true Christians. Like the Unitarians, they are seen as trying to be Christians – as being outside the accepted ecclesial boundaries of all inherited Christian tradition. The Quran itself notes, however, that there were no dietary restrictions before the revelation of the Torah – except for restrictions that Israel (Jacob) imposed on himself (Q3.93).

Unlike Jews and Muslims, Christians, from the very start, have cared only about moral purity, not about any purity rituals or laws that might define and regulate such a quality. Since this is an unusual ambition, the onus is on practising Christians to establish the coherence and possibility of the notion of purity in the absence of relevant regulations to achieve it. In Jesus' and Paul's time, the Pharisees often belonged to purity guilds (*khaberim*): membership of these ensured a Jew that, if he were invited for a meal with someone who belonged to it, the food would be prepared according to kosher (*kashrut*) laws.[15] Jewish law laid a firm prohibition on table fellowship with non-Jews. Such a culinary apartheid was often supplemented by a ban on familiarity, or even casual contact, with Gentiles.

Islamic law dictates that, in dire necessity, all food is lawful or *ḥalāl* (see Q5.3, the last verse to be revealed). Ordinarily, however, the Quran prohibits the consumption of carrion, blood and the flesh of swine, and any meat offered to idols, to any god other than *Allah* (6.145). There is some dispute about the use of other parts of the pig, especially for medicinal purposes such as pig fat being used, until recently, in capsule fillers and, in the nineteenth century, often used as gun grease in the Indian army. All seafood is permitted (*ḥalāl*). Islamic dietary laws are simpler than Jewish ones (Q2.173; 6.145). The Quran reveals that some Jewish dietary laws were arbitrary in content and that even some wholesome things were forbidden, as divine chastisement for conspicuous Jewish iniquities (Q4.160; 6.146). The Quran's shorter list of permitted and prohibited foods (e.g. 6.145), unlike the longer lists (e.g. Q5.3–4), includes the three forbidden items listed in the decree that James promulgated in the apostolic council of Jerusalem (Acts 15.20, 29).

The Quran permits table fellowship with the People of the Book and permits Muslim men to marry virtuous Jewish and Christian women (Q5.5). Muhammad did so. The prophetic traditions clarify the Quranic permission by endorsing table fellowship only with Jews since Jews follow *kashrut* laws. However, Muslims should not accept Jewish hospitality for an overnight stay since Jews are considered mortal enemies. This is based on the Prophet's practice which grew out of battles with three Jewish tribes in Medina. But it need not apply today since most Muslims are not at war with Jews. (I have myself often stayed in Jewish homes, usually with rabbis who were teaching me the *Mishna* or instructing me in the ritual niceties of the weekly *Shabbat*). By contrast, a Muslim can stay overnight at the home of a Christian host – but must decline to eat meat with him or her unless it is *ḥalāl* meat (cf. Q5.5 which surprisingly mentions no such caveat about food restrictions). Most devout modern Muslims do not accept table fellowship where alcohol is served. At Muslim weddings, the host will have a separate table for non-Muslim guests who wish to drink. These dietary restrictions, derived from the Quran and the Prophet's practice, are widely known and fairly widely practised.

The Quran orders believers to obey God's own order in certain matters of food, dress and worship, including the need to perform formal ablutions in preparation for worship. Being direct divine commands, it is no light matter to disregard such rules, let alone to argue for their wholesale abrogation or neglect. Since food is divine provision (*rizq*), it must be consumed in a posture of respect – sitting on the floor, with shoes removed, although only observant Muslims, in the West and in Islamic lands, do this in today's world. In *ramaḍān*, more or less everyone eats in this posture when opening the fast. Observant Muslims condemn as insolently Westernised those fellow Muslims who blithely transgress food laws – often walking casually as they eat *ḥarām* (unlawful) burgers from fast food outlets, when *ḥalāl* meat is readily available.

The main concern is scrupulousness. According to stricter schools of law, eating in a dark room is prohibited, in case one accidentally eats a *ḥarām* (forbidden) food item. Christians, tutored by Jesus and Paul, and thus alert more to the spirit than the letter, would be struck by how observant Muslims follow closely the letter of dietary regulations. In Jafari law (the major Shi'ite school of law) recent *addenda* show sensitivity to modern situations: even candlelit dinners are forbidden for fear that the romantically inclined couples, being engrossed in each other, might break God's law (inspired partly by Q2.230).

The regulations on food are usually in the context of the Devil, an open enemy of human beings. He orders extravagance and wholesale indecency. Part of that satanic ingratitude and wantonness is to indulge in forbidden foods. Drinking alcohol is singled out as an egregious transgression, the handiwork of the Devil. The consumption of strong drink (*khamr*) was progressively discouraged (see Q2.219, 4.43, 5.90 in that order) rather than declared *ḥarām* (illegal) outright at the outset. The imperative *ijtanibū* (Q5.90) is used to order believers to shun totally all intoxicants, so that they can cultivate a God-fearing lifestyle. While originally forbidden in stages, the *Sharī'a* forbids the consumption of alcohol altogether, making no distinction between beverages of higher or lower alcohol content or between social (or pose) drinking and outright abuse or indulgence.[16]

Quranic verses address all humanity regarding the consumption of *ḥalāl* (legally permitted) food, also described as wholesome (*tayyiban*), the latter description interpreted by some today as organic products (Q2.168). Food laws are certainly not seen as irrational relics or mere taboos. Many Muslim apologists write extensively in defence of Islamic rules prohibiting the consumption of all intoxicants, drugs, pork and meat slaughtered in the name of an idol or, in the modern world, meat improperly slaughtered. The conditions of *ḥalāl* slaughter are the pronunciation of the phrase 'In the name of *Allah*' followed by a single deep incision into the neck artery which drains blood efficiently. In abattoirs, mechanised (recorded) repetitions of *Allahu akbar* are permitted since it is cumbersome for a butcher to repeat God's name over each victim, especially during the *ḥajj*, a time of widespread ritual slaughter.

Most Muslims obey the Quranic rules without asking for grounds. The rules are to be obeyed since God is a wise legislator and it suffices that he knows the reasons. An acute problem with this faithful approach arises when we need to apply past case laws to novel circumstances and thus adapt to modern life. Clearly, unless we know the moral grounds for a law, no analogy (*qiyās*) can be persuasively constructed when arguing for an existing prohibition or permission to be extrapolated to a new situation. For example, it is fair to ask, in the context of modern moral objections to wanton cruelty to animals, whether or not it is more humane to stun an animal before slaughtering. One cannot reasonably even pose, let alone answer, such a question if a blind obedience to divine command blinds one to the nature of the grounds for the divine command.

XIV

To enrich the cultural rather than simply the religious dimension of our discussion, I now add an addendum to Gal. 2.9.

As in the highly ritualised Brahmin (Hindu) culture, the Semites also attached much significance to the right hand. 'From the right hand' means from the perspective of truth, right and might – that is, an approach from the most honourable direction or from an angle of deserved power and influence. Two examples from the Hebrew Bible: Joseph's brother is *bēn-yamin*, 'son of the right hand' (Gen. 42.4); 'the cup in the Lord's right hand shall come round to you' (Hab. 2.16). The Quran refers to God's hand and hands (Q5.64) but not to his right hand. In the New Testament, Jesus is seated in glory at the right hand of God (Rom. 8.34; Acts 2.33). Paul refers to 'the weapons of righteousness for the right hand and the left' (2 Cor. 6.7). When Peter heals a man, he takes him by the right hand (Acts 3.7).

In Arab culture and later in most Muslim cultures, the right hand came to be used for all honourable activities, including eating, starting ablutions and offering the pledge of loyalty to a tribal chief. Abraham was the right-handed iconoclast (Q37.28) while God called Moses from the right side of the mountain of revelation, eulogised as the blessed spot (Q28.30).

The Quran mentions two recording angels, named in tradition, who record all good and evil deeds (Q50.17–18).The angel entrusted with making a transcript of good actions sits on the right hand side of the sinner. The book of good deeds shall be received in the right hand (Q69.19) while the damned shall receive it in the left hand (Q69.25). People of the right hand are the people of paradise (Q56.27–38; 90.18) while those of the left hand are the people of Hell (Q56.41–56; 90.19–20).

Among some peasant Muslim cultures, a child who shows early tendencies to use his right hand or right side of his body, even in mundane activities such as tying his shoelaces or mounting a bicycle, is thought to be destined for piety in later life. In some cultures, moreover, the left hand is considered sinister (Latin for the left-hand side). In Muslim culture, following Muhammad's custom, it is used for unclean acts. Left-handed people are, however, except in backward rural settings, rarely stigmatised for writing and eating with their left hands.

XV

For many Christians, including converts, Gal. 2.20 competes with John 3.16 in terms of the profound affection it inspires. As one of the most moving texts in the New Testament, it speaks of personal faith in 'the son of God who loved me and gave himself up for me'. The use of 'me' heightens the pathos and changes an intellectual conviction about a sacrifice into an existentially dynamic force in the believer's life. This passage moves Christian readers in a way that outsiders cannot fully comprehend. A parallel to this is the way that Muslims feel possessed when they hear the Quran recited in an ornate style. Sheikh Abd Al-Basit recalls that when he was reciting Surah *Al-Muzzammil* (named after the Prophet's mantle) in the Prophet's mosque in Medina, he felt as though he was in paradise – and only the shouts of admiration by the crowd, at the end of his chant, reminded him of his earthly location.

Deliverance from the life of the flesh is part of salvation. This stress on deliverance, not merely on forgiveness of sins, distinguishes Christianity from Islam. Paul moved decisively from his inherited Judaism to a new view of faith as essentially salvific, not merely legal and didactic. Islam is not a mystical faith of salvation wholly by external grace through a holy saviour, human or divine, but rather a practical law-centred faith requiring human effort albeit aided by grace. While the divine initiative of grace is the *decisive* basis of human moral effort, it cannot be its *sole* basis since we have free will, which supplies the grounds for human accountability to divine judgement.

Paul sees the way of law as excluding the way of grace. The latter is the way of trust in God's power to effect atonement on Calvary while the former is a hubristic reliance on human effort guided by law and productive of merit. But the former does not represent his opponents' declared position. As Christians, the Judaisers could not have been proclaiming that it was solely by keeping God's law that God's people achieved God-given salvation. They too must have mentioned the indispensability of God's enabling grace in the cross of his Christ. Divine grace and the keeping of the Law were important, perhaps equally so, for achieving salvation. The Judaisers saw the Law as *the means of* staying in God's grace; the righteousness of Christ supplied *the means for* entering into it. Paul rejected this sensible view in favour of a more zealously Christocentric conviction that marginalises both the Law and even God the Lawgiver – as distinct from God in Christ. The believer enters God's grace through Christ and stays in it by Christ – and both are achieved by faith alone. Salvation is, from first to last, from and by faith – to faith.

Those Christian scholars who are eager to locate Paul sympathetically in his Palestinian Jewish context suspect that he confused legalism with nomism. The former is the misguided attempt to gain favour and merit with God by means of Torah observance. It is not clear if any Jews held this view. If they did, presumably none believed that such merit by itself was sufficient to merit salvation. The nomistic stance, canonical in Judaism now as in the past, consists of the response of faith and gratitude to the God who has acted graciously on behalf of his chosen people. All is within a life governed by Torah. It is difficult to attack this position from any credible angle. Christians do so – by rejecting such nomism in favour of the life by the spirit which centres on the individual conscience informed by scripture, the community of faith and by the Holy Spirit who guides all decisions, moral and cultural. The law of God governing the individual becomes, arguably, largely irrelevant. In Chapter 8, sections IX to X, we explore further dimensions of this crucial disagreement by scrutinising the status of works of the law (*erga nomou*) in Paul's writings.

XVI

The indwelling of Christ in the believer signifies the presence of God on earth. Paul affirms this mystical notion of the body – mystical seen as the presence of a supernatural dimension to a physical reality. The believer's body is the temple of the Holy Spirit. Paul implies, by the use of second person plural pronouns, that it abides within the community of believers (1 Cor. 6.19–20) rather than merely in the individual. Thus, the community is the true centre of the social, as opposed to the potentially anarchic individual, process of discernment of moral value. Additionally, Paul is perhaps counteracting the proto-gnostic notion of an evil material body separate from the soul or the spirit.

Before we return to the commentary, I explore Pauline mysticism in the context of Islam. *En Christou* is an intriguing expression, strange even by mystical standards. Christians are inured to it since their theology is metaphysically of a high order of abstraction and complexity. Muslims have '*fī Allah*' (in God or in his case or concerning him) while *fī sabīl Allah* (in God's path; Q9.19) means the cause of God. The signs of God (*ayāt Allah*) in nature make nature sacramental but this does not mean that nature literally contains God, although he is the subject behind the objects found in nature. Expressions such as '*fī Muhammad*' (equivalently, *fī rasūl Allah*; Q33.21) and 'signs in Joseph and his brothers' (Q12.7) are correctly understood only as metaphorical uses. Such expressions cannot mean that Muhammad and Joseph's brothers are personalities in which other humans somehow mysteriously abide.

Paul was a Christ-mystic, in some ways perhaps similar to a Sufi or a New Age shaman. Salvation was a mystical union of the believer with the risen Christ who indwells every Christian believer (Gal. 2.20; Rom. 8.10). Paul identifies Christ's followers with Christ crucified, vindicated, resurrected, and glorified (Rom. 8.1–30). While the believer still remained physically in this world, he or she also entertained the confident hope of an eternally perfect union hereafter. A believer becomes part of the body of Christ so that Christ becomes the believer's identity – a total identification, not merely imitation – but only as a collective, not individual, event. This is possibly the most coherent description of what might, in fact, turn out to be an impossible and incoherent ambition despite appearing possible, plausible and even attractive.

The spirit's presence is the indispensable condition of being a Christian (Rom. 8.9). Understood methodically, Christian believers are given and thus receive the indwelling of the Holy Spirit. They are not possessed *by* the spirit but rather see themselves as possessing the spirit. This is to safeguard the dignity of individual identity despite the indwelling of a superior power. Any person who is baptised and confirmed must possess the spirit, so long as they have faith. The sacrament is empty without faith since the person being baptised must, except in some Anabaptist and Calvinist interpretations, deliberately invite and accept the spirit – and do so in a spirit of contrite heart-obedience. Thus, it might seem at first blush that each Christian is divine while Christ alone remains incomparably divine – in some sense unique to him. But this is a misunderstanding. Only the whole community of believers is the body of Christ and that alone is divine. Although individual Christians are not divine, the community of Christians is seen as being such that 'God is with us and in us.' All that this can coherently mean is that 'in Christ' or 'in the Lord' conveys the notion that Christ is an inclusive person who provides the ethos or habitat in which

Christians live and act, individually and communally. Christ is the spiritual locus of Christian existence and flourishing. His followers are incorporated into him: he is their location and address.

On two occasions, Paul agonises over a choice about whether or not to be alienated from Christ. For the sake of the salvation of his own race, he envisages the possibility of being accursed – anathema is his word. He sees this exceptionally sad state as the equivalent of being separated from Christ although the word 'separated' must be supplied owing to extreme ellipsis at Rom. 9.3, caused by Paul's agitated emotional state as he enters a kind of *ekstasis*. Again, in Phil. 1.21–26, probably looking forward to his own martyrdom, Paul contemplates the pain of being separated from Christ any longer, even for the sake of his beloved Philippians. It is a riveting moment of high pathos that even a non-Christian can sense.

Muslims are permitted to speculate that God does not abide in any temple or mosque but rather in the heart of the believer since only this heart is, metaphorically, spacious enough to contain him. 'The believer's heart is God's throne' (*qalb al-mu'min 'arsh Allah*) is a weakly attested prophetic tradition. Such mystical intimacy is popular in Islamic devotional poetry, especially in poets such as Rumi and Iqbal. Proximity to God, gained through his archangels, has a physical measure in the Quran (Q53.8–9). God is closer to man than his jugular vein and knows the secret whispering of his soul (Q50.16). God intervenes between a man and his own heart (Q8.24) and is close (*qarīb*) especially to those who have faith and supplicate him (Q2.186). The Quran orders Muslims to adore God and to do their best to seek closeness with him through total obedience to his perfectly holy will whose demands are reasonable and wholly practicable (Q2.286; 5.35). Every human soul has, quite intelligibly, a divinely planted conscience (Q75.2) – or, equivalently, a witness (*shahīd*) who is a soul-captain (*sā'iq*; Q.50.21).

What are the motivations and consequences of mystical religion? I shall look only at Paul and leave aside here the motivations for mysticism in other New Testament writings such as John's gospel, 1 John, Revelation and 1 Peter. Paul's mysticism grows as an organic by-product of the doctrine of justification by faith alone. Law is an impediment to mysticism since a law-observant faith needs a distance between the lawgiver and those who must obey the law. Paul's denial of the primacy of the Mosaic law in the life of faith directly leads to mysticism. A faith, equipped with law, is never naturally mystical. It is instead secular and pragmatic, two dimensions and forms of reasoning which usually encourage perspectives opposed to the mystical one.

A law-observant faith is never *spontaneously* mystical. Among the Western monotheisms, only Christian mysticism can claim valid *doctrinal* support. I judge the impulses behind Sufism and Kabbalah (*Qabbālā*) to be foreign to their respective faiths. Much Islamic practice, including orthodox practice, is of course mystical in the sense that its total significance transcends and surpasses human understanding. That is bound to be the case since the Quran celebrates God's presence in nature, mediated by his ubiquitous signs in it. Again, there is a mystical element in the Night of Power, located in the holy final third of *ramaḍān*, when the divinely inspired words of the Quran were given to Muhammad. Such words, recited ornately by reciters can move the entire audience to a state of ecstasy, often expressed with loud pious exclamations that shatter the sanctuary's silence on many a *ramaḍān* evening. And, finally, many unorthodox but popular practices in Muslims lands – exorcism, the veneration of saints, drinking holy water and so on – imply a mystic, that is, supernatural, dimension to physical reality.

I am not here speaking of mysticism understood as a comment on the limitations of human epistemology. Naturally, many of these practices are based on the irresistible human assumption that the natural world is more than natural – that it conceals some unknowable, occult, that is, metaphysical and perhaps sacramental significance. My point is that a religion which provides legal guidance is naturally opposed to mystical subtleties and private sophistications since these are bound to undermine the shared legal stances of the formally constituted community. Despite being formally recognised by insiders and outsiders, the community remains a fragile group always subject to varied sources of dissension which can easily undermine its unity and cohesion – ideals which all faiths desire but never attain. The applicability of this description to contemporary Islam hardly needs effort or rhetorical pleading.

Islamic Sufism is a heterodox development, in effect a Christianisation of early Islam, whatever the details of its historical genesis as a reaction against the luxury and excesses of imperial Islam. Muhammad was not, contrary to what modern Muslim apologists in the West claim, a mystic who accidentally founded an empire. He was a saint-general who feared an independent and judgemental God. Muhammad never saw himself as dwelling in God or the Deity dwelling in him. If that is mysticism – a co-mingling of the supernatural and natural – he was no mystic. The Muslim mystics were, on the other hand, eager to obliterate any spiritual distinction between themselves and God, keen to identify themselves with him, in some coherent sense. But 'Muhammad is (merely) the messenger of God' (Q48.29). No messenger is literally part of the one who sends him, no matter how closely aligned their wills and intentions.[17]

Mysticism inevitably deteriorates into a falsely religious and therefore ultimately mawkish and thus falsely sentimental version of an otherwise authentic religion. The removal of law is a retrograde step in the evolution of religion. I admit however that Paul never denied, in practice or in theory, the goodness of the good law of the good God of Israel and Moses. He merely denied its power to save sinners. But that does not appear to be the view held by his opponents, whether Jews or Jewish Christians. Another question here – no less important – is whether or not Paul relaxed his own conscientious observance of the Law to the point of virtual apostasy from its scruple and minutiae.

XVII 3.1–5

1 *O foolish Galatians, who has bewitched you, before whose eyes Jesus Christ was portrayed as having been crucified?* **2** *This only I wish to learn from you: you received the spirit by the works of the law or by (the) hearing of faith?* **3** *How foolish you are. Having begun in the spirit, you are now being perfected in the flesh?* **4** *You suffered so many things in vain – if* *indeed it was in vain.* **5** *(Regarding) the one therefore then supplying to you the spirit and working powerful deeds among you: did he do it by (the) works of (the) law or by (your act of) hearing with faith?*

Gal 3.1–5 is a semi-pastoral appendix to the first statement of Paul's gospel of grace. It contains the dual testimonies of present faith and past revelation – and serves as a preface to the scripturally based doctrine that shall presently be adduced in support of the gospel whose content is baldly stated towards the end of Gal. 2. For some 1,500 years before Christ, the Israelites had been trying to obey the Law in its totality and they had continuously failed. Christ came to rescue them from their attempt, seen by Christians as misguided only if it aims to secure salvation through human merit. Muslims try to obey the whole of the *Sharī'a* and one can imagine Paul lamenting, 'O you foolish Muslims!' Setting aside God's grace in such a struggle is surely folly. But it is not the Muslim believer's own description of what he or she is attempting to do. The Quran also speaks of the fool but identifies him differently (Q2.130): 'Who abandons the faith of Abraham, except the man who fools himself?'

The dialogue style of teaching and preaching is effective, especially in didactic portions of treatise-epistles (see Rom. 2). The dialogue method is found in the works of dramatist-philosophers such as Socrates, Plato, Hume and Berkeley. It can be used reflectively but also dogmatically – to promote the views of the author, his mouthpiece being the chief or wisest protagonist.

1

This must be the earliest account of the Eucharist as the sacrifice of Christ on the cross, an event that should have disabused the Galatians of worldly illusions of human merit and values. Even believers may be unworthy of the Eucharist if their spiritual state is defective (1 Cor. 11.28–32). A Muslim is not unworthy of the required prayer (*ṣalā*) – it is a requirement for all believers (Q4.103) – but it might be performed unworthily. The worshipper is engaged in a serious conversation with the Lord of the worlds but is perhaps distracted by anxiety about the diminishing size of his bank balance or by a sudden recollection to perform some mundane task, such as shaving the hair at the back of his head.

Paul reckons the Galatians must be bewitched. Certainly, their vision is distorted although for Paul, as for Muhammad, magic was a live reality. Like other Arabs of his day, Muhammad believed that eloquence could amount to magic. The Arab pagans thought that the Quran was magic. The Quran's last two chapters are said to be apotropaic (averting evil), providing protection against magic. Our current fascination with technology conceals a subliminal fascination with magic. And magic is forbidden.[18]

Christ was crucified in public, not in private. The verb *proegraphē* literally means 'previously written about', that is, made the subject of a public notice. Could it be referring to a gospel read in Galatia? If so, it cannot be Mark's gospel since that is usually dated, at the earliest, from the 50s of the Common Era. Could this be a cryptic hint at the Eucharist that is orally witnessed – seen in public as opposed to some written account of it? We do not know. We are on firmer ground when we note that the placard communicated information in the Roman forum, before the age of pamphlets and newspapers. Among Arab pagans, the latest poetic productions were hung on the door of the Kaaba in Mecca. A poet would take down his work if he felt challenged by a superior work appended next to his own. A leading Qurashi poet, according to Ibn Hisham's biography of the Prophet, took down his poem in honour of Surah 55. No Arab poet could even compose a fourth verse to make a quatrain out of the triplet that comprises the whole of Surah 108.[19]

Paul uses the *perfect* participle (*estauromenos*) to indicate the abiding significance of Jesus' crucifixion, a completed past event with present ongoing consequences. Unlike *Koinē* Greek, Arabic is not a participle-loving language and instead uses pluperfect passive, as in 'having been granted' (*qad ūtiya;* Q2.269), which may indicate present significance of a completed past event. The reference here is to the grant of the gift of wisdom which enables a wise believer to do good deeds.

The theology or rather the Christology of justification is centred on the cross. For Paul, the cross was a necessary event. For the Quran, it is an avoidable tragedy, though not anathema. The Quran concedes that there was a will to crucify Jesus, on the part of the sinful Jewish establishment. It only denies that this putatively historical event occurred. It is hard to verify the Quran's claim.

Paul's point is that worldly charm would no longer work on the one whose vision had been sharpened by witnessing the agony of the cross. Muslims dismiss the cross as suffering that is pointless or, in the nomenclature of theodicy, 'dysteleological'. The Quran would not see it as the necessary precursor of the salvific victory of the resurrection.

Does sin possess us? Does sin possess such ontological integrity that only the death of God's only son on the cross could redeem us from its power? Is not God's fiat sufficient? For Muslims, God forgives whomsoever he wills. It is not in vain that he is God! Or does this Muslim attitude betray too casual a view of sin?

2

The verb *manthanō* here means 'to ascertain' rather than to learn, its normal meaning. According to Socrates, the Greek controversialist who, like the Pharisees, loved to trap people in verbal disputes, the teacher merely encourages the student to extract the correct answer which is somehow known to the student. This is Plato's method for recognition (*anamnesis*) of innate knowledge, including buried mathematical skills, stored eternally in the soul. The claim is developed in one of his earliest dialogues called *Meno* – named for a man whose slave boy, through dialectical questioning with Socrates, arrives at correct answers to simple mathematical questions. The Quran is self-described as 'the one full of reminder' (*dhī al-dhikr*; Q38.1) since human beings possess an innate knowledge of their nature and destiny, acquired at a primordial assembly (Q7.172).

Pneuma here means the spirit of God but carries a catholic range of meanings, some secular. Every believer possesses the spirit of Christ, the spirit of God. Assumed in

Galatians, it is explicit in Romans (Rom. 8.9. *pneuma theou; pneuma christou*; both objective genitives).

3

If we may recruit Paul's notion of the flesh and spirit for the needs of our age, we may argue that he upholds the priority of the spirit to flesh, a metaphysical assumption made unpopular by the rise, about a century ago, of a logical positivism as arid as the Sinai desert. Many contemporary philosophers see it as being disguised philosophical polemics. Paul's preference is strongly attested by our experience of the moral and aesthetic life. The primacy of mind over matter is self-evident since the mind directs matter. In more popular terms, we know that the world does not value brute physical strength: we do not reward people who cannot think. Even a man of physical prowess is admired for combining strategy with force. One thinks of the antics of the boxer Muhammad Ali who psyched out his opponents in the ring, talking and singing to them – and thus making them anxious before knocking them out.

4

Is our effort ever wasted in the life of faith? After the change of the prayer direction from Jerusalem to Mecca, many believers wondered whether their previous devotions were rendered void (Q2.143). The Quran reassures them that God never allows our efforts – to sustain faith while trying to do good works – to be wasted. No faith is more confident than Islam regarding the link between faith in God and the performance of legal duty, and the allied liaison between such effort and the assured reward for it in the next world. It would be interesting if the Quran, for all its total confidence about its own (alleged) truth – which cannot be tested decisively in wholly empirical terms – finally turned out to be false. How would the innocent Muslims cope with such a post-mortem trauma? No doubt, some Jews and Christians would then happily shout with satisfaction or perhaps weep: 'O foolish Muslims, we told you so.' Such are the complex ways of a competitive piety not incapable of the occasional tragic sympathy.

5

Paul's question is posed rhetorically or perhaps hypothetically. Did you receive the spirit (*to pneuma*; neuter), the agency that enables faith, by the works of (the) law, or by hearing with faith? Paul repeats the question of v.2 but now mentions unspecified miracles performed among the Galatians, perhaps similar to the ones Paul performed elsewhere when, during Pentecost and afterwards, the spirit was a palpable pneumatic presence (see Acts 14.8–10, 16.25–26; 19.11–12, 20.7–10). The Acts of the Apostles were indeed 'The Acts of the Holy Spirit' (*Praxeis Spiritou Hagiou)*!

The present active participle *energōn*, working with power, refers to God. The associated noun *energeia* (operative power) is divine or occasionally demonic, but always supernatural. A catholic range of uses was maintained in the New Testament employment of this classical word. *Energeia* correspond to three Arabic nouns meaning power: *qadr*, *quwwa* and *ṭāqa*. The last word here means power that might fail to achieve its goal – and is never used of God. It is used once in the context of the difficulty experienced by some believers during the *ramaḍān* fast (*yuṭīqūna*; Q2.184).

XVIII

We explore two motifs embedded in Gal. 3.1–5. Jesus' earliest followers were converts from what was later to be called Judaism. These became his followers during his own lifetime and at Pentecost and afterwards. With few exceptions, converts from paganism came later (as recorded in Acts 10 and onwards). By contrast, virtually all of Muhammad's earliest disciples were converts from Arab paganism. The few exceptions were non-Arabs: Salman Al-Farsi (Persian Zoroastrian, Christian convert, then Muslim) and Bilal ibn Rabah (fate before Islạm unknown).

Greek pagans who became Christians or Gentile God-fearers attached to a synagogue correspond to Arab pagans who embraced Islam. How did the pagan Galatians become Christians? How did the pagan Meccan Arabs become Muslims? In both cases, God's word was preached. Paul preached the gospel to the Galatians; the gift of the spirit marked their initiation into the spiritual discipline of the Christian life. The Law and its fulfilment had nothing to do with it. Faith was instantaneous since to hear properly was to hear with faith. Such hearing begins in faith and leads to increased faith. Muhammad preached by reciting the Quran; pagans entered Islam by confessing, 'There is no god except the only God; Muhammad is his envoy.' 'O Believers', the most frequent divine address (Q2.104, 153, etc.), conceals undertones of struggle and effort to maintain the state of faith. 'We heard and we obeyed' expresses sincere faith (Q5.7) while disobedient Jews mock God: 'We heard and we disobeyed' (Q4.46) and 'We hear and we rebel' (Q2.93). Such Quranic verses capture concisely Israelite intransigence on display in the Latter Prophets of the Hebrew Bible (Jer. 6.17).

At Mecca, the only requirement was the faith confession, which implied avoidance of idols, along with some voluntary prayer and recitation of the Quran, all performed privately. The Arab pagans became Muslims by God's grace, before they started to fulfil the revealed law. The mere preaching of the word of God inspired faith as men and women heard the call and became faithful (Q3.193). This is true of Muhammad himself and of key figures such as Umar who declared his allegiance after he heard by faith. He heard a recital of: 'We did not reveal this Quran to distress you (*li-tashqā*; lit. cause loss of blessing) but only as a reminder to anyone who fears God' (Q20.2–4).[20] God restricts and expands a person's breast (*ṣadr*) to expel or contain respectively the gift of faith (Q6.125; referring only to Muhammad at 94.1). Note that in both passages quoted here, the Quran uses the relative pronoun (*man*, 'anyone who'), a typical feature of the Quranic narration, noted earlier in section VI above, in our commentary on 2.14.

The Christian and Muslim cases are surprisingly similar – except in one key respect. Unlike Christians, Muslims possessed no law to inherit or disown, except theoretically and schematically since their faith required them to affirm earlier laws such as the Torah. In practice, the law was accumulating in Muhammad's day. It fortified the faithful as they expressed their faith through virtuous deeds. The Quran revealed laws and occasionally repealed (Q4.15 repealed by 24.2–10) or promised future amendments (65.1). Neither the Torah nor the Quran are primarily legal texts but both contain legal verdicts. For example, Zelophehad's daughters, widely admired in Jewish tradition, bravely demanded a just ruling on inheritance (Num. 27.1–11; cf. Q4.11–12, 19, 176).

Gal. 3.2 presupposes that salvation by law alone and salvation by grace alone are mutually exclusive options. But 'salvation by law alone' is neither the Pharisaic stance, as Paul must have known, nor the view of the Judaisers. If we are charitable, we must assume that Paul's opponents in Galatia held some middle position. Works of the Law are emblematic of a believer's desire to receive salvation by grace, being neither sufficient nor necessary: not sufficient since divine grace was an undisputed requirement and not necessary since divine grace could, by fiat, bypass rituals and works of the Law. Even if works of the Law are superfluous, from God's point of view, believers may still need to perform them. The choice between 'sheer divine grace' and 'reward for human merit' rests on a false dichotomy. The third alternative combines divine grace with human *jihād* (effort). Note that Paul's defensible and indeed plausible distinction, between entering into a state of grace and staying in it, discussed above, is irrelevant here. For it does not alter the fact that the dichotomy between salvation by law alone and salvation by grace alone is itself untenably overstated.

In Gal. 3.3, Paul is right, however, to argue that what begins in the flesh is perfected (*epiteleisthē*) in the higher level of the spirit or mind. Mind controls matter. When we see, from a great distance, a car moving, we assume, a priori, that some mind or other, perhaps even a robot, is operating it. We do not assume that its motion is self-directing or spontaneous. This is a fair assumption, even in the absence of evidence. *Enarchomai* (to begin) is contrasted with *epiteleō* (to complete). Since the flesh and the spirit are mortal enemies, it is absurd to begin with the spirit in the hope of completing the process through the flesh. In Pauline Christianity, the spirit and the flesh constitute a complete dichotomy. In Islam, it is only a continuum. For Christians, moving from the spirit to the flesh is a regression, the pilgrim's regress. Meanwhile, for Muslims, the flesh-spirit dichotomy is overstated.

XIX

Paul was immersed in the guilt/righteousness paradigm. The Bible may need to be read from the perspectives of shame/honour, purity/defilement and power/fear polarities, depending on the culture in which the Gospel is preached. Paul dealt in legalese: guilt, penalty for sin, judgement, acquittal (or justification). This might not provide the best filter through which to read him today. He has been read in this paradigm by Luther and his successors but Paul was equally, if not more, concerned with shame and honour in community. Although Christianity, even Catholicism, has not produced as many jurists as has been produced by Islam or Judaism, nonetheless, some outstanding Christians were trained as lawyers. Tertullian (c.160–225 CE, famous for his attacks on reason) and Prudentius (c. 348–405 CE) are the best known. Among reformers, Calvin was a trained lawyer who, incidentally, strongly approved of the validity of the works of the law – though, naturally, not for securing salvation.

Legalism, as a pejorative word, describes the human attempt to seek favour with God by means of Torah observance. The attempt is conceited and misguided. Human effort, no matter how strenuous and disciplined, can never accomplish the task that grace accomplishes – and does so effortlessly. With God, all things are possible. Understood neutrally, however, legalism is identical with nomism – a believer's faithful law-observant response to the God who established the covenant and revealed the Torah. Out of gratitude to this God, a Jew lives a life governed by Torah. Paul's claims conflict with the total ethos of such a law-governed lifestyle although, explicitly, he rejects as anathema only the application of the Law to Gentiles *as a necessity*. As a corollary, he also dismisses the legal component of nomism only if the believer comes to think – wrongly in Paul's view – that he or she can stay in the grace of Christ only by fulfilling *the letter of the Law*. Why? If Christ's work is sufficiently efficacious, then to add anything to it, such as the works of the Law, would be to denature it. A Christian is justified by and in Christ, while good works are the fruit, not the root of the tree of righteousness. Righteous deeds are the consequence, not the cause, of righteousness.

Let me say something here before proceeding. While Paul's views are, arguably, internally coherent and consistent, such views remain metaphysical suggestions which need not be true, let alone revealed. The burden of proof, or at least of plausibility, rests on Christian apologetic shoulders. As in the case of the Christian dogmas of the Trinity and Incarnation, Christians often feel that Muslims are putting Christians on trial – while they look paternalistically on and expect to be persuaded that Christians are indeed monotheists. This patronising Muslim attitude angers many Christians engaged in dialogue with Muslims.

The righteousness of God (Gal. 2.15–21) can mean God's own righteousness, a moral quality (of God, a possessive genitive). It would be an attribute displayed in God's distributive justice. In this view, shared by the Quran, God by his nature, is just to his creatures and loves his just servants. For Jews, such righteousness is shown in God's covenantal faithfulness to his people Israel. Protestant Christians understand God's righteousness primarily as God's salvific potency, shown in his love for Israel and now extended in his saving grace towards Christ's global community. Such righteousness is a subjective genitive: it belongs to God, not to human beings.

The righteousness of God, as a genitive of origin, intends the human status of being righteous, a right standing before God, granted by God. In Lutheran doctrine, it is the status human sinners possess, on the basis of faith alone. Such divinely bestowed righteousness comes from God without human contribution or mediation. Such imputed righteousness is not foreign to the Quran where *taqwā* (piety or God-consciousness) and guidance (*rushd*) are granted to select servants (such as Abraham; Q21.51). Again, 'For those who are guided, God increases them in guidance (*hudā*) and grants them their piety' (Q47.17). This amounts to a human quality that counts with

God or, to use archaic language, avails with him. Once approved by God, this otherwise wholly natural quality becomes a divine gift belonging to the believing man or woman despite being from God.

The Quranic equivalent of the justified sinner is *barī* – the one who is innocent (Q4.112) or has been exonerated (Q12.53). Christian Arabs use *tabrīr* to translate justification. Only God's justice and our corresponding human piety are categories native to the conceptual framework of the Quran – a lucid, consistent and highly homogeneous work of single authorship. While such subtle Christian notions can be accommodated, if rather awkwardly, into Islamic nomenclature and 'theology', no perplexity native to the Quran would motivate Muslim thinkers to draw such fine distinctions which have confounded the greatest minds of Christendom for two millennia and continue to challenge even educated Christian believers today.

Notes

1 Muslims use a wholly lunar calendar while Jewish tradition uses a lunisolar combination. The lunar calendar is aligned to the solar by inserting an extra month (called Adar I) in every 'pregnant year', the leap year. This ingenious device stabilises the timing of the religious calendar, ensuring that its festivals fall in the expected seasons.

2 Talmud (*Bavli*), *Bava Batra*, 9a and 10a respectively. The total teaching is complex. *Mishna Pe'a* 1.1 accords honour of parents, charity and peacemaking the top three places, while the study of Torah is, by itself, equal to all three! *Sukka* 49b declares that charity is superior to sacrifice but inferior to a kindly heart.

3 The Quranic word for radical ritual impurity, caused by sexual intercourse, is *junub* (Q5.6), literally meaning distance and thus denoting the state of being foreign or 'alienated'. The impure one is separated or set apart, the opposite of the Jewish and inherited Christian notion that separation (or being at a distance) implies holiness.

4 The only exceptions are those who are congenitally or invincibly ignorant of God.

5 Judah Ha-Levi (c.1075–1141). See his *Sefer ha-Kuzari* 1.88–95, 98–9, discussed in B. Freundel, *Contemporary Orthodox Judaism's Response to Modernity* (Jersey City, NJ: KTAV, 2004).

6 For more on this verse, see D. Wenham, *Paul: Follower of Jesus or Founder of Christianity* (Grand Rapids, MI: Eerdmans, 1995), p. 207.

7 In India's daily but unreported outbursts of communal violence, Muslim men are identified by their circumcision while women are identified by their head-coverings.

8 Some Western evangelical Christians view Arabia then, as now, as being the abode of the Devil, a place of spiritual sterility and barrenness.

9 See J. Dunn, *Epistle to the Galatians* (London: A and C Black, 1993), pp. 70–1, 81, for details on historic Damascus, culled from the works of Josephus.

10 Such a long speech would not have been tolerated from a condemned man, unless part of it was delivered earlier in the Sanhedrin. Compare the case of Sir Thomas More, famous for his oratorical skills, who was asked by King Henry VIII to give only a short speech before his execution.

11 The aberrant rhyme of Q17.1–2 suggests a late redaction, albeit under prophetic editorial supervision. The word *ḥawl*, a preposition meaning 'around' (hence vicinity; see also Q27.8) suggests that God blessed both the place of prostration and the broader holy precincts. The site of the original pre-Davidic township (*qarya*) mentioned in Q2.58 may perhaps have later developed into Jerusalem – just as Fustat eventually became the site of the mighty Cairo.

12 Roman Catholic tradition holds that Peter visited Rome and founded the Roman church in AD 42.

13 Muhammad's disciples are more entitled to being called 'disciples', not merely companions, since he imposed a legal 'discipline' on them. The Latin root meanings of 'companion' and 'disciple' support these insights. The Greek for disciple is *mathētēs*.
14 Can a Christian, in good conscience, eat meat slaughtered in the name of *Allah*? All New Zealand mutton is halal, catering mainly to a massive Middle Eastern market. Incidentally, Sikhs are forbidden to eat halal meat since Sikhism arose in conscious opposition to imperial Indian Islam.
15 The English word kosher derives from the European or Ashkenazi (as opposed to Oriental or Sephardic) pronunciation of *kashrut*, a passive participle of the Hebrew verb *k-sh-r*, meaning to be suitable or appropriate.
16 According to the *Sharī'a* law, drinking alcohol merits 80 lashes, with habitual drunkards, especially schools of dissolute poets, being barred from society. The purpose behind forbidding alcohol is to prohibit the main effect of alcohol, namely, intoxication. One verse implies that wine is an impure substance (Q16.67) although this verse is invariably quoted by deviants to prove scriptural endorsement for drinking wine since this same verse mentions the grape, one of God's blessings.
17 'I become the hand with which the believer acts.' The category of 'holy hadith' (*ḥadīth qudsī*), especially popular with Sufis, invites the query: if such narratives are the literal word of God, why are these not in the Quran, perhaps as an appendix?
18 In his gratuitous attack on Muhammad, Rushdie imagines Mahound as a conjuror. See his *Satanic Verses* (London: Viking, 1988), p. 363 and see my response, *Be Careful with Muhammad* (London: Bellew, 1989), p. 23.
19 This is ironic since the routine exclamation, *Allāhu akbar*, an expression of praise and wonder, used to punctuate the movements of the prayer cycle, could serve here as the requisite rhyming fourth verse. *Allāhu akbar* corresponds to the Hebrew cry *ḥallēlū-jāh*.
20 During a Nasser-era state visit to Moscow, verses from this surah were recited by Sheikh Abd al-Basit to communist leaders, to invite them to Islam. After his revolutionary success, Ayatollah Khomeini had, a decade before the final collapse of the Soviet Union, invited the Russians to embrace Islam. Khomeini was following the tradition of the Prophet Muhammad who had written letters to the superpowers of his day, inviting them to the new faith.

4

THE PROMISE OF ABRAHAM'S GOSPEL (3.6–4.7)

I

Circumcision in the flesh was a sign of the covenant between God and Abraham (Gen. 17.9–14). For Paul, this ritual was the seal of righteousness based on faith – understood as sheer trust in God's promises. The Apostle to the Gentiles appears to take the risk of arguing that the pre-Mosaic justification of the Gentile Abraham is by *faith* as such rather than *faithfulness* to the covenant of circumcision. Such a risk would not be evident to readers unware of the Jewish heritage of Christianity. 'Abraham, the believer' (Gal. 3.9) is a correct translation but, as in the oracle of Hab. 2.4 quoted by Paul (Gal. 3.11), it obscures a crucial ambiguity subject to fierce polemical debate in Paul's day. The difference between Judaism and Christianity hinges on a distinction between *faith* (personal trust in God) and *faithfulness* (commitment to legal duty derived from contractual fidelity to God's covenant). I believe that Paul, as a Jewish Christian, would have readily recognised this distinction. Most Jews and Muslims, however, would regard this as an irrelevant distinction based on misguided priorities.

Paul calls Abraham the father of the (circumcised) faithful Jews and of the (uncircumcised) but equally faithful Gentiles (Rom. 4.11–12). He quotes Gen. 15.6 at Gal. 3.6 to link Abraham the believer to Jesus the Christ, and thus the 'old' testament to the emerging 'new' testament, understood both as scriptures and covenants. Paul asserts with force and clarity that all those who have faith qualify henceforth for salvation, solely by virtue of their faith, regardless of ethnicity and the scrupulously precise performance of the works of the Mosaic law. Slaves of the Law are to be freed by Christ to become sons and inheritors of Abraham and of God.

While the so-called false teachers had one trump card to play in their polemics, Paul was dealing too close to the bottom of his pack for any wild cards to turn up. Let me explain. Now, Abraham was the model for Gentile Christians because he was a man of faith, certainly, but one who also obeyed God's commandment, particularly when he submitted himself to circumcision and later, more dramatically, when he passed the test of the binding of Isaac (Gen. 22) – although this incident is not cited by Paul. The incident is cited in Hebrews (11.17–19) as evidence of faith taking justified priority. It is quoted by James (2.21–24) as evidence that faith and action are organically related while action is paradigmatic since it tests the sincerity of the accompanying faith. The Judaisers are on strong grounds when they proclaim that in order to become sons of Abraham, the Gentile Christians must imitate their spiritual father Abraham, the paradigmatic believer. Notwithstanding Paul, his critics concluded, faith must be supplemented by both an initial (and therefore) prior obedience to the Law, and subsequently by a concomitant (that is, continuing and associative) obedience to the same. This complex attitude to the Law's central status is a condition of salvation. The false teachers combined Christ crucified with submission to the ancient Law of Moses, Israel's greatest prophet. That would be the complete good news to be preached to the mainly Gentile audience in the Galatian congregations.

We should remember that Paul's opponents were themselves missionaries who never rejected extension of salvation to Gentiles. They sought to subjugate Gentiles to the Mosaic legal administration as a necessary but not sufficient condition of Christian salvation. Their stance, unlike Paul's, is consistent with the inherited Jewish view of the purpose of the Torah. They could have quoted the promise of Gen. 12.3 where 'all nations will be blessed in him' – that is, in Abram, a man on the verge of a significant name change (see 'Abraham' at Gen. 17.5). This *promise* would be fulfilled when Gentile believers in Christ Jesus submitted themselves to the Law. Paul's opponents rejected as unscriptural the Pauline polarity of law versus promise since, they must have argued, the Abrahamic covenant (promise) was completed with the addition of the later Mosaic covenant (law). The two were complementary, not opposed.

The false teachers' view is compatible with Islam which effectively endorses gradual and partial supersession through an accumulation of temporally conditioned precedents rather than by outright replacement of entirely obsolete ones. The Quran, through its approval of partial abrogation (Q2.106; 16.101), effectively permits the latter – substituting a new legal verdict for an old one – though only for practical prohibitions and commandments during its own period of incidence. This ranges over concerns such as the gradual banning of alcohol and the revision of earlier judgements about inheritance (see 2.234 cf.2.240; 2.219, cf. 4.43, 5.90).

In this interfaith context, note further that Paul elevates the Abrahamic covenant above the Mosaic one. I wonder what course history would have taken if the Law-observant false teachers had triumphed in Galatia and their successors had settled in Arabia. Muslims would have been spared the scandal of a law-free faith. It is curious, in this context, to note that that the Quran never accuses Christians of being outright 'antinomians'. Did the Arabs of Mecca and Medina, even in their travels to the north of the peninsula, ever encounter Pauline Christians who assigned the inherited Law *a* place but not *the* central place demanded by Judaism and afterwards by Islam?

Paul's claim that anyone who has faith is truly a son of Abraham is confirmed by the Quran (22.78), a scripture which affirms parts of Paul's 'Christian' view of Abraham and aspects of James' more Jewish-sounding view of him. Paul adduces Gen. 15.6 as proof that Abraham was justified by his extraordinary faith alone. This same verse is interpreted by James (2.23–4) to support the claim that faith without works is jejune and barren. The question of prioritising the two does not arise in the Quran's portrait of this seminal Semite.

Does scripture shape the contours of Paul's experience of the Christ-event? Or does the risen Christ define retrospectively for Paul the correct hermeneutical use of scriptural authority? Or is this dichotomy a malformed one, motivated by external probing that betrays perhaps some outsider's mischief rooted in the wrong kind of curiosity and probing? Paul wishes to honour his inherited Jewish disposition to assign autonomously compelling authority to scripture. Yet he wants to celebrate his experience of the unmediated existential authority of the Christ-event. Paul retreats to Arabia, the land we associate with Muhammad, to ponder a question that is never raised in the Quran: 'If Jesus is Israel's messiah, what do the scriptures mean?' Paul's answer is one which sets Christianity apart from its two Semitic rivals: the nations would come to faith through Israel after all – more precisely, through Israel's true son, Jesus, who defeated death, redeemed sin and terminated history. It was the most purposeful of deaths.

Paul grounds his novel understanding of Jewish tradition and its promise of eschatological fulfilment in his unique reading of scripture. Was the Mosaic administration valid now that the age to come had dawned? Who could guide Paul when he tried to answer this question? He could quote no scripture to support a relegation of the Law in post-messianic times.

Paul was in the position of 'moderate' Muslims who can find little scriptural basis for their proposed reforms of classical Islam while their conservative counterparts have countless texts to hand. The reformers, like the Devil, must sometimes distort texts while pretending to merely interpret them for the novel contexts of a new age. Naturally, not all moderate Muslims are misguided; I do not impugn the motives of every reformer: not all are naïve or motivated by ill intent and malice. Nonetheless, some moderates espouse extreme progressive views that seek to make Islam essentially a form of Western liberal humanism. They take liberties of thought that eventually, though only gradually and imperceptibly, terminate in agnosticism if not outright atheism. They effectively undermine Islam – and are best advised to leave the faith altogether and indeed opt for less demanding faiths which are more compatible with secular modernism.

II 3.6–9

6 *Even so, 'Abraham believed God and it was reckoned to him for righteousness'.* **7** *Therefore know (that) those with faith are the sons of Abraham.* **8** *And the scripture, foreseeing that God would justify the (Gentile) nations by faith, preached the gospel in advance to Abraham, (saying that), 'All the peoples (nations) shall be blessed in you'.* **9** *So that those of faith are blessed with the believing Abraham.*

6

This *pericopē* reads like rabbinic *midrash* (commentary) on the verse quoted from Gen. 15.6. Paul mentions Abraham here, as he mentions David in Romans (1.3), to secure the undisputed inherited authority of Judaism. Abraham and David were both justified apart from works of the Law, blessed since they received no reckoning for their sins (Rom. 4.6–8). In Islam, only martyrs for the cause of Islam enjoy this latter privilege (Q36.26–27).

Faith in God's word and promise is true righteousness (*dikaiosunē*) which translates the Hebrew *ṣedāqā*. The Arabic cognates include *ṣadaqa* – sincere or voluntary (as opposed to legal or imposed) charity. Spontaneous charity is righteousness in action.

7

All who are faithful are the (true) sons of Abraham (*banū Ibrāhīm*) since spiritual descent is through faith rather than physical lineage. The Quran mentions *banī (banū) Ādam* and *banū Isrā'īl* but, surprisingly, does not construct similar genealogical constructs such as *banū Ismā'īl* or *banū Ibrāhīm*.

8

The promise quoted from Gen. 12.3 is repeated at Gen. 18.18 and 22.18, implying a consistent scriptural emphasis rather than an isolated strand. Scripture (*graphē*) is not a text but instead personified as a speaker – an oracle predicting the future viewed from the perspective of the quoted scripture. Is it still the future from the perspective of Paul and the Galatians? Or is the Apostle to the Gentiles taking liberties with scripture – for the sake of the Gentiles?

In Paul, as in James (4.5–6), 'scripture' (*hē graphē*, lit. a writing) can refer to the Old Testament but may also include works now considered apocryphal, such as those quoted in Jude 9, 14–15 and 2 Pet. 2.11.

9

Abraham is the prototype of the true and blessed believer. How many of us would put God at the forefront of our loyalties and be willing to sacrifice even our son in order to please God? The secular humanist would hope that this is only a daring moral fable – and even then he or she would discern in it the inveterate anti-humanism of Semitic religion. For that species of religion is primarily focused on the rights of God the creator, not the independent dignity of the human creature.

III 3.10–14

10 *For as many as are of (the) works of (the) law are under a curse. For it has been written that: 'Cursed is everyone who does not continue to perform everything written in the book (roll) of the law'.* **+12** *And the law is not of faith, rather 'he who practises these things shall live by them'.* **13** *Christ redeemed us from the curse of the law by becoming on our behalf a curse – for it has been written: 'Cursed is everyone who is hanging on a tree'.* **14** *(This is so) in order that in Christ*

Jesus the blessing of Abraham might come to (be in) the (Gentile) nations so that we might receive the promise of the spirit through faith.

Paul links the claim that faith and works yield salvation and self-righteousness respectively with the traditional Jewish view that Jews were under the curse of exile. He is referring to the curses (and blessings) summarised in Deuteronomy 29. The Law brought a curse on Israel but this curse, Paul shall contend, has paradoxically become the source of the blessing of the Gentiles.

10

Deut. 27.14–28.68 lists the curses Israel deserves if she fails to keep the whole Law of Moses, which became over time a compendium of hundreds of rules and regulations, the basis of the later accumulated legal minutiae of Pharisaic Judaism. A few blessings are also enumerated here. The Quran seems to affirm some generalised version of the curses and blessings found in the Torah but offers no details (Q14.6–7). The Israelites must obey the whole book where book means law, the context being the laws of expulsion and ransom (Q2.85). The Quran would condemn any smaller preferred canon within the canon of the whole law. The Christian notion of a summative law, examined in Chapter 6, Section XI, might have arisen in part out of a desire to reduce and manage the scope of such an intimidatingly wide-ranging law. But this is only speculation.

Were Jews under the curse of exile – that ended only with the coming of Christ, the true Israelite in whom there was no guile? One can see the attraction of this view for Christians but it lacks Jewish scriptural justification. Israel was in captivity in Egypt – not owing to a divine curse. Fallen Israel is not the same as accursed Israel but a fall from grace is a milder way of expressing God's disappointing experiment with the Israelites. A disobedient Israel is always potentially under the curses of the Torah (Deut. 27–28, Gal. 3.10). Israel in fact failed in its mission and the promised curses must accrue as a result.

The Quran concurs with Paul that Israel had become hardened and blinded to God's message (Rom. 11.7; 2 Cor. 3.14; Q2.74, 88). Their disobedience in the wilderness led God to make them wander blindly on the earth for 40 years before eventual entry into the Promised Land (Q5.26). The Quran quotes the rebellious Israelites saying defiantly 'We heard and we disobeyed' (Q4.46; see Jer. 6.17, 28) and contrasts it with the new 'Arab Israel' whose members exclaim 'We heard and we obeyed' (Q5.7). The disobedient and disbelieving Israelites were cursed by the tongue of David and Jesus (Q5.78). The Quran confirms that Jews lived in exile, often protected under treaties and compacts with Gentile nations, but sees it as just divine punishment for their iniquities (3.112). The Islamic scripture exempts some Jews from these charges (Q3.113; 7.159).

11

Paul quotes a revised form of Habakkuk 2.4b. We may translate and interpret its elliptical Hebrew in the Masoretic text thus: 'Behold, the proud one! His soul is not upright in him. But a just one (*ṣaddiq*) shall live by his faithfulness ('ê*munā*).' A textual variant found in the Septuagint reads: 'the righteous will live by my faith.'[1]

'My faith', with God as the speaker, can only mean God's own faithfulness to the promises he made to his faithful remnant. God has faithfulness rather than faith. In English, 'God is faithful' (to his promises) is perfectly intelligible while 'God has faith' is grammatically possible but theologically senseless.

'The obedience of faith' (Rom. 1.5, 16.26) in effect means faithfulness understood as simple trust in God, its dominant sense in the Hebrew Bible. Paul writes of Abraham (Rom. 4.20): 'No distrust caused him to waver (lit. he did not decide by infidelity (*apistia*)) concerning the promise of God – but he grew strong in his faith as he gave glory to God.' Earlier in Gal. 3.2, 5, Paul uses 'hearing with/by faith' to mean, in effect, listening with trust – that is, being inclined to believe in and obey God's promises.

12

The verse Paul quotes (Lev. 18.5) teaches that those who abide strictly by Yahweh's statutes shall live by them – have life through them. It suggests that disobedience to the Law revealed to Moses could bring literal (physical) death to the Israelites. This is a plausible interpretation in view of the rest of the Torah's stance, especially the way Yahweh kills two enthusiastic but naïve sons of Aaron for breaking protocol when offering unauthorised holy fire to him (Lev. 10.1–3).

The citation does not support Paul's case; at best, it is a non sequitur and at worst it supports the opposite contention. Lev. 18.5 finds a rough parallel in Q8.24 where submission to what Muhammad calls his people to, through the Quran, gives life to the believers among them. But the Quran intends spiritual (or eternal) rather than physical life.

Paul quotes Lev. 18.5 again in the later epistle to the Romans (10.5) and attributes it to Moses: a law-based righteousness enabled the righteous person to live by it but, Paul proceeds, the Torah also preached a faith-based righteousness. He cites Deut. 30.12–14 to argue his case but imposes on it an audaciously Christocentric interpretation (see Rom. 10.6–10).

13

The Torah warned that hanging on a tree is a curse (Deut. 21.23). Christ transformed this curse (Greek, *katara*) into a blessing by becoming a curse for our sake. He thus absorbed and sublimated it in his voluntary death on a cross, the emblem of an accursed death that pollutes the holy land. Paul's interpretation of the messianic vocation is shockingly novel. No existing sect in Judaism, which has left us a record of its views, held this opinion. It explains why the Pauline Christian movement could not be accommodated under the broad, amorphous and tolerant umbrella of sectarian 'Judaisms' prevalent in first century Palestine.

For the Jews, the Messiah was the eschatological but human agent who would achieve Israel's final *political* deliverance and salvation from her hated but ascendant

Gentile enemies. Paul preached that our real enemies are not the Gentiles, who are merely fellow human sinners, but rather the two enemies of the spirit, namely, sin and death. And Paul added that this crucified Christ Jesus had triumphed over both.

Paul knew that Jesus was the Messiah: the experience on the Damascus road, if Luke is to be credited, was wholly compelling. Paul also knew, as a matter of fact, that Jesus had been done to death on a Roman cross. So, he combined a self-authenticating experience with a factual truth. Now, Paul also knew that the Hebrew scriptures taught that death on a cross was punishment for those cursed by God. So, he asked himself: Why was Christ cursed? Paul answered, without citing any scriptural authority, that the Christ was cursed for the sake of humanity, to take on their sins. Paul thought this through on the joint basis of personal experience and his knowledge of scripture. He did not obtain such convictions from the other apostles. He did not even liaise with them (Gal. 1.16–17). If he had met them and learned the gospel from them, then it would have compromised his claim to know the gospel directly and only from the risen Christ. Such reasoning is coherent and self-consistent. It is another matter whether or not it is true – either in the sense of being sound or in the sense of whether or not Paul in fact, historically, reasoned in this way.

What about the Law? Under the Law, Christ was accursed. If so, Paul might also have reasoned, so much the worse for the Law. Paul's encounter with the risen Christ in effect motivated him to demote the Law. The standard Jewish response had been: 'So much the worse for Jesus!' He was no messiah, elected by grace. Was Paul rejecting the Law of Moses in order to rehabilitate the Christ cursed by the Law? Or was he also or perhaps instead rejecting the Law in order to embrace the hitherto excluded peoples, those untouchables of the Jewish world – the despised but, unlike their Hindu counterparts, powerful Gentile nations?

14

Paul concludes that through Christ Jesus, the blessing of Abraham (*hē eulogia tou Abra'am*) finally reaches the Gentiles. They receive the promise of the spirit through faith, here a metonymy for Christ's grace. These radical realities of the newly dawned eschatological age enable us to triumph over the ancient slavery of the Law, the works of the Law, and the dominion of the flesh which was governed by those twin tyrants, sin and death. Paul had reason to boast!

IV 3.15–18

15 *Brothers, I speak in human terms: even a human covenant, having been ratified, no-one sets it aside or adds to it.* **16** *Now the promises were spoken to Abraham and to his seed. It does not say: 'And to seeds', as concerning many, but (rather) as concerning one. 'And to your seed', who is Christ.* **17** *And I say this: the law, which came four hundred and 30 years later, does not annul a covenant which has been previously ratified by God, so as to abolish the promise.* **18** *For if the inheritance is based on law, it is, no more, of (i.e. based on) promise. But God has granted it to Abraham through a promise.*

The blessing of the promise made to Abraham is primary while law (or the Law) given to Moses is secondary. Paul uses legal reasoning to explore theological concerns. Legal thought, unlike theological ratiocination, is typically public, rational, secular and pragmatic – never paradoxical, sentimental or tragic. Hence, the Muslim predilection for jurisprudence and a corresponding aversion to theology, an aversion not found among the less orthodox, arguably heretical, Muslim groups who flounder in the marginalia of Sunni legal orthodoxy.

15

The Greek *diathēkē* translates the Hebrew *berith* and means testament, will or covenant. *Kata diathēkēn* means 'according to the terms of a will'. Paul's proposed analogy is defective since one can add a codicil to a will – as he himself effectively admits when he mentions Abraham's will being supplemented by the advent of the Christ. The covenants with Moses, David and even Jesus were founded on, and complemented, the covenant with Abraham.

Such a discrepancy, possibly an error of fact in law, in part of the analogy need not invalidate the final doctrine, but it weakens the total analogy through which it is supported. Again, it would be pedantic to insist that the mustard seed is not in fact the smallest of seeds. Such a usage could, charitably, be seen as a popular, possibly hyperbolic, use of idiomatic language current at the time, and thus may not be simply a factual error. In any case, it need not diminish the power of Jesus' parable (Matt. 13.31–32) – especially if we also conceded that Jesus, as a human sage, entertained, like Muhammad after him, some false views about areas of empirical knowledge, including agriculture, astronomy and secular history.[2]

To be charitable to Paul, a will can certainly contain a codicil as an addendum and the whole document may even be revoked altogether. Is Paul's point only that both actions can rightly be taken only by the testator, that no one can change another person's will? If that is his meaning here, then that is fair enough. Now, Islamic law requires any adult person, approaching death, to write a will for disposing of any wealth which is not apportioned by divine law. It is sinful to seek to change a will after hearing it. The Quran envisages an unnamed man who 'fears from a testator the insertion of an unjust or sinful clause' (Q2.180–182).

The earliest biblical covenant is between God and the human race after the flood (Gen. 9.12–17) followed by one between God and Abraham (Gen. 17.4–9; Acts 7.8) and then between God and Israel (Deut. 4.13, 23). The New Testament explicitly affirms the *continuing* validity of only the last one (Acts 3.25; Rom. 9.4) and adds a caveat: this covenant is possible only through the self-sacrificial demise of Jesus. The indispensability of Jesus to the new covenant is emphasised throughout the New Testament, from gospels to epistles (see Matt. 26.28; Mk. 14.24; *hē kainē diathēkē* at Luke 22.20; implied at John 6.53–58; 2 Cor. 3.6; of a better testament *kreittonos diathēkēs* at Heb. 7.22; 8.6, 9, 10; 12.24; 13.20).

In a contract (*sunthēkē*), a word not found in the New Testament, a legal bond is created between two parties, usually equal. If we consider marriage as only a contract, as in Islam and in secular legal thought, we expect some parity of conditions and terms. (For Christians, marriage is a covenant and a sacrament). A covenant presupposes that the parties do not meet on equal terms. In this respect, a covenant does not resemble a contract but resembles a will. God offers his human creatures a relationship with its attendant conditions just as a dying person leaves a will which instructs the living about an inheritance whose terms they neither stipulated nor are able to alter after that person's death.

In the Quran, Allah addresses the Children of Israel, ordering them to fulfil their covenant (*'ahd*; Q2.40). The root *'ayn/ha/da* means to stipulate (a condition). Allah orders the Israelites of Muhammad's day to recall the favour and blessing of the covenant (Q2.122–3).One such divine address precedes the narration of the Abrahamic covenant (Q2.124). In previous sacred history, a binding covenant (*mīthāq*) made with Israelites (Q5.70) followed by one with Christians (Q5.14) was not honoured by its human participants and elicited divine disapproval. The covenant of Allah (*'ahd allah*; Q16.91), newly contracted with the Arab Muslims, through Muhammad (Q33.7; 57.8), indicates the shift of divine favour onto a new people. This covenant fulfils rather than annuls all previous covenants since Allah's words and promises can never be annulled.

Despite permitting divorce, the Quran uses *mīthāq* in order to emphasise the enduring strength and value of the marital bond once marriage has been consummated (Q4.21). Jacob extracts from his sons 'a firm covenant from God' (Q12.66). It is a pledge with divine surety (Q2.283; 28.27–8). If even such human pledges are presumed to be final and unalterable, how much more so the divine covenant(s).

16

In 3.16–22, Paul uses *epaggelia* repeatedly of the promise to Abraham. In Rom. 9.4, Paul lists the privileges of Israel, including God's promises (*epaggeliai*). This word for promise refers to decisions made unilaterally, unlike the mutuality of the contractual promise (*huposchesis*), a word not found in the New Testament.

Jews would no doubt reject Paul's tendentious interpretation of Genesis (12.7, 13.15 and 24.7) as Christian annexation and illegitimate colonisation of Jewish scripture. Christian *midrash* continues in earnest in this entire *pericopē*. The coming of the seed (Christ) could even mean the Incarnation.

Jesus often imposed ingenious meanings on the Hebrew scriptures but his interpretations remained, with few exceptions (see John 10.33–36), within Jewish parameters. The Emmaus incident, unique to Luke (24.13–35), is too vague to qualify as a *Christian* annexation of the Hebraic heritage since it lacks precise textual references. And while Philip's reading of Isaiah, instructing the eunuch who desires baptism (see Acts 8.26–38) is revolutionary, it is restricted to understanding the identity of the messiah and therefore remains recognisably linked to inherited Jewish understandings of scripture's prophetic resources. It differs fundamentally from Paul's reading which contains the seed of a wholly novel retrospective annexation, not merely re-reading, of all salvation history through the lens of a later event. The significance, then, of the original promise to Abraham, is not being merely contested within some agreed and inherited framework but rather being in effect rejected as alien and anathema even to its own (original) community.

17

A law established later cannot nullify an earlier covenant or the promise on which that covenant is established. According to Exod. 12.40, the period of total residence in Egypt was 430 years (Exod. 12.40) but, according to Gen. 15.13 and Acts 7.6, the period of tribulations in the house of bondage lasted four centuries. In his *Antiquities*, Josephus mentions these two figures given in Exodus and Genesis.[3]

The number Paul needs is the time between Abraham receiving his promise and Moses arriving at Sinai. It is slightly greater than the figure he quotes. This is a negligible and irrelevant error since it does not invalidate Paul's doctrinal contention. Presumably, the precise period was not Paul's interest. He was using the established traditional Jewish reckoning of the period rather than the literal historical reckoning: he was no academic scholar. Here a biblical author is uninterested in a detail of secular history, though much of the Bible abounds in it. The entire Quran rarely offers secular details, a trait seen as a hallmark of an eternal revelation entering the temporal continuum while speaking of realities transcendent to it.

Paul's point is that the covenant, once ratified, remained valid and operative, independently of the merits of the human partners, some of whom were unfaithful. What God intends or enjoins, no one can alter, unless God himself alters it. Paul's claim that the divine promise is immutable finds ample Quranic support. No one can change God's words (Q18.27). Surah 4 twice asks rhetorically (vv.87, 122): 'Who is truer to his word than God?' God would never break his promise and thus mislead believers and wrong them (Q2.143). With regard to the dating of such events, we have no alternative Islamic dating since the Quran, one incident apart (Q30.2–6), takes no interest in secular history.

18

In his grace, God granted (*kecharistai*; cf. *elogisthē autō* [reckoned to him] at 3.6) the inheritance to Abraham by means of a promise. Promise and legal obligation belong to different categories. In Islam, a human promise is always overridden by a revealed legal duty. Similarly, the informal and apparently contradictory provisions for the maintenance of a widow out of the estate of her dead husband (Q2.34; cf.2.40) were overridden by later precise legal provisions (Q4.12). In general, any informal promise made by a dying person would be overridden by Islamic law, especially if the content of the promise contradicted Islamic teaching or seemed emotional or incoherent.

The Christian position for which Paul argues is that the promise of God is primary and certain, not to be trumped by the law. This view is affirmed by Islam. For example, the martyr is promised forgiveness of sins even though the law is that sins must be reckoned and the sinner held accountable. But the promise and grace of God are greater than the law and justice of God, should a situation arise where one – whether we humans or God himself – must choose between the two.

V 3.19–25

19 *Why then the law? It was added because of transgressions, until the seed should come to whom the promise has been made, being ordained through angels, by (the) hand of a mediator.*
20 *Now the mediator is not of one (party) only but God is one.* **21** *Is the law therefore against the promises of God? May it never be! For if a law was given, being able to give life, then righteousness would indeed have been by law.* **22** *But the scripture has imprisoned all humanity under sin, so that the promise by faith of (in) Jesus Christ might be given to the believing ones.*
23 *But before faith came, we were kept in custody, under law, being excluded from the faith which was about to be revealed.* **24** *Therefore the law has become our trainer (to guide us) to Christ, in order that by faith we might be justified.* **25** *But now that faith has come, we are no more under a trainer (i.e. tutor).*

Paul begins to argue for the superiority of Christ – as the seed of Abraham – to Moses the lawgiver and mediator (*mesitēs*). The cross was destined to replace circumcision; the promise was meant to override the Law. Moses was *a mediator of a good covenant* but Jesus is *the mediator of a better covenant* (1 Tim. 2.5; Heb. 8.6) since he introduces redeemed sinners into God's presence by offering them a privileged access (*prosagogē*; Rom. 5.2) by faith into a new state of grace beyond the Law. Whatever Paul's intentions, Christianity was to fulfil and therefore in effect to supersede, indeed replace and abrogate, Judaism.

19–21

The giving of the Law through angels implies that it has the majestic support of heavenly authority. The hand of a mediator (*mesitēs*) could refer to Moses or to an angel or angels. Apart from the use of *mesitēs* in Galatians in this way (see 3.19, 20), in the rest of the New Testament this word refers only to Jesus Christ (see 1 Tim. 2.5; Heb. 8.6, 9.15; 12.24). The Quran does not mention angels being involved in the giving of the Law to Moses at Sinai but confirms that the Ark of the Covenant was carried by angels (Q2.248). Muhammad received the Quran through the faithful and trustworthy archangel Gabriel (Q2.97). Neither the prophet nor the archangel is, however, called a mediator. The closest Quranic idea is that of an intercessor (*shafī'i*; Q6.51; 10.3, etc.), a role traditional piety assigns to Muhammad, but only on the basis of some of his (authentic) sayings.

'God is one' here means that there is no second god to whom Israelite sinners can appeal when confronted by the unwelcome demands of the Law imposed by Israel's only God. Paul's total view, culled from the whole of his extant authentic writings, is that the Law informs sinners of their obligations under it – without granting them the power to resist the temptation to break it. Nor can it grant the gift of righteousness, a metonymy for life itself. For Paul, human sin created a gulf between human beings and God, hence the need for reconciliation and mediation. The Quran contains no such view of the negative power of sin which is seen as at most a cause of judgement and thus as the ground and occasion of repentance: God created human beings with the dual capacities to sin and repent.

Paul regrets that the Law, interim and provisional as it is, cannot give life. Therefore righteousness is not based on it since true righteousness gives life. I believe that Paul here misunderstands – misinterprets is a milder word – the purpose of the Law. He conflates the power of law with the province of law, its efficacy with its jurisdiction. The Law was not intended to give life but rather to guide conduct. God himself gives life and death. And the guidance of the law, Muslims would add, is not an inert guidance. It requires the agency of a prophet and the actively willed and continuous submission of the repentant sinner.

In v.21, we realise that even some fellow New Testament Christians found it easy to misunderstand Paul. Out of the fifteen occurrences in the New Testament of 'May it never be! (*mē genoito*; aor.mid. optative mood, third sing.), all but one are in Paul. This verse also tells us clearly that Paul does not see the Law as detached from or in opposition to the promises, a view that might otherwise be plausibly imputed to him.

The high level of complexity of Christian doctrine is a standard Muslim complaint and criticism. Of all the faiths, Christianity is most in need of an apologetic accompaniment and has, of all the faiths, the longest continuous intellectual tradition of doctrinal defence against secular and rival religious derision and criticism. In the modern world, it has failed to prevent mass leakage from the vessel of faith, though only in Western Europe. Despite posting its learned tribes in prestigious feudal academia, Christianity continues to face mass desertion at grass-roots level. I believe that all faiths primarily need martyrs, rather than thinkers, in order to survive and flourish – *even in an age of secular reason.*

22–23

The scripture declares that the whole world is a prisoner of sin. Not only do we often do what is sinful, we are prisoners of sin, personified here in its role as jailer. That is why Christians insist that sinners need a saviour, not merely a warner. By proving the impotence of the sinner to avoid sin, the law itself drives the sinner to seek the grace that alone could redeem him.

Before faith in Christ was available, we were imprisoned (lit. hemmed in) by the Law. There still existed a way of faith – but it was faith in the mercy of God rather than the way of obedience to the Law. That is Paul's point but he has no clear scriptural authority for it. 'Faith is Freedom' is Paul's own slogan – and he interprets this freedom as being the kind of liberty that binds without visible bonds. We have been set free in order to be slaves to righteousness. It sounds Orwellian and paradoxical to us – but then Paul is no less a master of paradox than Orwell, the anti-fascist secular humanist 'prophet' with honour in his native land. The law faithfully, so to speak, kept us in its custody, until the arrival of the revelation of the Christ-event.

Although 'faith' occurs 22 times in Galatians, only 3.22 has 'faith in/of Jesus Christ' (*pisteōs Iēsou Christou*) while the related 'faith in Christ Jesus' occurs twice (2.16, 3.26). 'Faith of Jesus Christ' could function as an adjective to indicate a type or kind – a 'Jesus Christ kind of faith', that is, faith originating from or in relation to Jesus. The phrase may simply indicate possessive identity, the faith of Jesus, but it remains ambiguous: the believer's faith in Jesus Christ or the faithfulness of Jesus Christ, that is, his own faith/trust in God.

Apart from the ambiguity of this vital phrase, due in part to the versatility of the Greek genitive case, Paul might even be arguing, on a radical reading of v.23, that in the pre-Christian era of law, there was no genuine faith. The conditions for its emergence were not available. We encounter yet again the serious theological consequences of the sharply defined Pauline polarity of faith and law.

24–25

As moral tutor, the *paidagōgos* taught a boy good manners (*eukosmia*) – *adāb* or *akhlāq* is the Islamic equivalent – to enable the transition from childhood to youth. Paul contrasts the guardian of juvenile days with the father of mature faith when he boasts that he is the Corinthians' only spiritual father even though they have many provisional guides (1 Cor. 4.15).

The Law was our custodian or tutor (*paidagōgos*) which finally led us to Christ, the *telos* (end) of the Law (Rom. 10.4). Christ is the end, in two senses. Faith in Christ is the end (purpose) of law; Christ's advent renders the Law redundant through consummation. Justification will henceforth be by faith alone, as indeed it was in the past, as shown by Abraham's case. Christ's arrival marks the end of the Law's temporary vocation as our tutor. In the New Testament, only Paul uses *paidagōgos*, a word which indicates that the Law is inadequate, since it is merely transitional and provisional.

The Law remains a tutor after Christ's advent since the Law does not stop leading people to Christ. It may be all the more effective in its new role. But it leads people to Christ by highlighting the impossibility of obeying its contents, not by exhibiting its own (earlier) power to enable holy living. That latter task is – always was, according to Paul – the domain of grace. The Law resembles, as the later Wittgenstein said of philosophical reasoning, a ladder one uses to reach the roof of healthy common sense, after recovering from the illness and instability of philosophy. Once we reach our goal, we can kick away the ladder. Or is this a foolish action – both for the man on the roof and for the Christian standing, figuratively, in the elevated state of grace? What then is Paul's final verdict on this matter of great moment?

VI 3.26–29

26 *For you are all sons of God through faith in Christ Jesus.* **27** *For as many of you who were baptized into Christ have put on Christ.* **28** *There cannot be Jew or Greek, there cannot be slave or freeman, there cannot be male and female, for you are all one in Christ Jesus.* **29** *And if you are of Christ, then (you are) Abraham's seed, heirs according to promise.*

Paul is describing the new and now universal eschatological people of God, a community whose identity is derived from its location at the climax of salvation history (see Rom.8.19–21). Paul calls all the Galatians 'sons of God', perhaps subconsciously echoing the message of the book of Jubilees, composed in Hebrew, in the second century BCE. This work is effectively a rewriting of the canonical book of Genesis in the light of the later Law of Moses – with the laws of Moses observed perfectly in the life of Abraham. The author of Jubilees calls all devout Jews sons of God while arguing for a pre-Mosaic liberty from the law. Note the echoes of the canonical Hebrew Bible in the phrases and images used in the following passage where the speaker is God:

> And I shall create for them a Holy Spirit, and I shall purify them so that they will not turn away from following me from that day and forever. And their souls will cleave to me and to all my commandments. And they will do my commandments. And I shall be a father to them, and they will be sons to me. And they will all be called 'sons of the living God'. And every angel and spirit will know and acknowledge that they are my sons and I am their father in uprightness and righteousness. And I shall love them.[4]

28

The unity of Christian fellowship is established by erasing three social distinctions. There remains neither Jew nor Greek: the cross annihilated the Law that distinguished them and then kept them separate, sometimes asserting this division in stark physical, architectural and cultic terms. In Christ, we are all slaves and yet we are all free. The secular demarcation between slave and free must be spiritualised. Only here in the authentic Pauline literature is the gender division explicitly transcended. Elsewhere, Paul shows a certain indifference to gender, atypical of a Jew of his age. In Rom.16.1, he calls Phoebe a *diakonos* (male role of deacon), though admittedly this noun can be both masculine and singular in *Koinē* Greek. In matters of the spirit, one should disregard gender differentiation (see Rom. 16.3, 7). Finally, in 1 Cor. 12.13, all are one in the body of Christ; women are not mentioned here.[5]

In history's most comprehensive erasure of social divisions and barriers, spiritually irrelevant distinctions are abolished in the spirit. The sons of God put on Christ in order to enter a lifestyle where the antinomies of the pre-Christian age are made obsolete. The distinctions of race, class and gender remain in force in a literal sense but are dissolved in and by Christ – transcended metaphysically and thus metaphorically rather than literally. The resulting union is mystical and therefore remains compatible with Paul's social conservatism. It does not supply the basis for a radically novel political solidarity.

Literally, Paul wrote: 'not one Jew nor Greek, not one slave nor free, not one male and female'. This is a substantive verse of sociological identity though Christian exegetes perhaps read too much spirituality into it. It can be understood to be merging Jewish and Greek identities, and claiming that slaves are also free. None of this can be literally or legally true. And indeed Paul senses this in the third quoted clause when he uses the conjunction 'and' rather than 'nor' since he knows that men are not women.

There is much point in Paul's explicit affirmation of human equality and indeed unity – as far as this latter ideal can be coherently affirmed. For Paul lived, as we still do, in contexts where Jews (monotheists) may be considered greater than Greeks (pagans and polytheists); slaves are definitely less free than the free, and men are usually seen as superior to women. The greater and the lesser are all the same in Christ – one and equal. Paul was a powerful man who set an example by disempowering himself and pleaded for everyone to disempower themselves in relationship to others, in order to achieve greater equality for all.

There is no equivalent Quranic unification of believers achieved by abolition of social distinctions. For all its truly revolutionary spirit, the Quran is too practical a scripture to make any such sentimentally attractive but impractical claims. Piety (*taqwā*) renders spiritually irrelevant all tribal and ethnic differences (Q49.13) but, as in Gal. 3.28, the gender division remains ineradicably valid. Men and women embrace Islam as human creatures, certainly, but also self-consciously as men and women, and as members of tribes and ethnic solidarities. Only in their pre-existence, as disembodied souls, their seed (*dhurriyyata-hum*) acknowledged their submission to God's will and lordship, as the progeny of Adam (Q7.172), the repentant sinner. In realised history, they are men and women, free and enslaved, and they are all sinners in the sense that they all break some of God's laws and commands. This is their God-given nature, along with the urge to repent; they are victims of satanic seduction but also blessed with divine guidance. The Quran in effect dismisses the Jew-Gentile polarity as Jewish fabrication – self-congratulation and false racial pride. As for the slave-free distinction, it is, unlike that of believer-disbeliever, merely one of social (as opposed to spiritual or ultimate) relevance and may therefore over time be softened if not erased altogether. This is a point of happy convergence with Paul who also implies this much in his affirmation of the unification of such diversities in the Christ who was crucified for all.

29

We reach the second climax to this *pericopē*. The promise made to Abraham is prior to the Law of Moses – which is now fulfilled and, therefore, at least in some sense, rendered 'superfluous' henceforth in view of Christ's advent, passion, resurrection and ascension.

VII

Jews and Christians treat the Hebrew text of Genesis as a foundational narrative. Muslims do not see the Quranic account as merely a variation on that text but rather a competing and true version of events and promises. The man Abraham was chosen by God. Beyond that, claims about his life and legacy inspire endless dispute and challenge. I offer now a panoramic view of competing scriptural claims about Abraham.

Already 75 years-old, the biblical Abraham must leave his native land for an unknown land that God chose for him. His companions are his barren spouse, Sarah (Sarai), and his nephew Lot. In the Genesis account, Abraham starts his ideological career relatively late in life. Most moderns have no energy for any cause after forty. In the Quran, Abraham is portrayed as a youthful iconoclast who challenges his people's idolatry (Q.21.51–70, esp. v.60). Christians would regard this picture of the patriarch as apocryphal but it does resemble the one found in some Jewish *midrash*.

In the biblical narrative, Abraham is given a divine promise of blessing, a promise that includes land, children and an inheritance (see Gen. 11.27–25.18). The patriarchal covenant is contracted (Gen. 15.6) with Abram (exalted father); the name change to 'father of many' (*av-rāhām*) comes later (Gen. 17.5). Sarai will become a matriarchal princess and be called Sarah (Gen. 17.15). The 'Renewed' (Christian) Testament re-iterates the threefold promise to the Patriarch: the Promised Land (Acts 7.5; Heb. 11.9, 13), the birth of Isaac, and the blessing of the nations (Gal. 3.10–14). During his sermon in Solomon's portico, Peter also singles out the promise of a derivative universal blessing through Abraham (Acts 3.25; see Gen. 12.3).

Gal. 3.10–14 establishes the scriptural basis for the blessing of the Gentiles, a blessing post-Christ and therefore one that the curse of the Law could no longer prevent or nullify. The Mosaic covenant established the works of the Law and thereby excluded the Gentiles. For Paul, the more ancient covenant with Abraham established faith and through it the inclusion of the (uncircumcised) Gentiles. Paul concurred with Jewish tradition that the covenant of law was preceded by divine grace, promise and blessing. He upheld the Jewish tradition that the whole world should experience the divine grace, promise and blessing through the Jewish nation, God's own 'peculiar' people. Paul therefore effectively constructs a Gospel of free grace as a vehicle for extending the mission to lawless Gentiles who represent the defilement of the non-Jewish world.

More generally, the Christian, including Pauline, account of salvation history, starts with Noah, in the covenant between God and the human race. This is its widest extent in geographical or ethnic scope and in the universality of its larger moral and salvific purpose. The Quran concurs (Q42.13). The Christian narrative then proceeds – arbitrarily, in Muslim eyes – to restrict 'salvation' by investing its finality only in Jesus Christ in whom, according to Christian witness, all of God's past promises are finally fulfilled (Gal. 3.19, 29; Rom. 15.8; 2 Cor. 1.20). Furthermore, Jesus has in store, for his followers, whatever their ethnicity, even better promises for the future (Heb. 8.6, 9.15). The Quran would dismiss such claims as Christian fanaticism betraying an overly developed devotion to a mere messenger of God who made no claim to divinity or universality of mission.

The Quran is silent on Abraham's name change, on the covenant of circumcision and regarding two parts of the threefold promise. The Quran does not mention the blessing of the nations through Abraham but instead promises Noah universal blessing of communities (*umam*, pl. of *umma*) as he alights from the ark, after the flood

(Q11.48). Unlike the biblical narrative, the Quran has all believers saved from the deluge, not only Noah and his family, a strong hint of universality. As for Abraham, he repudiates the idea that Jews and Christians will be blessed through him regardless of their faithfulness to God's laws (Q2.124) while the promise of the holy land is associated only with Moses (Q5.21, 26), never with Abraham.

The promise of a son, Isaac, made to Sarah, when this seemed biologically impossible (see Gal. 4.23, 28; Rom. 9.9) is affirmed by the Quran (11.69–74) – without naming the mother. The good news (*al-bushrā*); 11.69) preached to Abraham is God's peace and the promise of Isaac's birth when Abraham is extremely old. Ishmael, the firstborn, and Isaac were sons of Abraham's old age, named always in their canonical birth order (e.g. Q14.39). The Quran, unlike Paul in Galatians (4.28) nowhere states or implies that Isaac alone was born miraculously. A child born to infertile parents or born without natural reproduction altogether is, apart from Abraham, associated only with Christian figures, such as Zechariah and Mary (Q19.8, 20) and, unlike the Bible, not with Hebrew figures such as Samuel and Samson, neither of whom is mentioned in the Quran. As for Abraham, he received the promise of Isaac's birth (Q37.112) and, as proof of grace abounding, also of Jacob as a grandson (lit. as grace, *nāfilatan*; Q21.72; see also 11.71).

Paul adjudicates between competing Jewish and Jewish Christian claims about the extent of the promise, a scope defined by the Torah. The Quran would not see the promise made to Abraham as being fulfilled in Christ but rather, in effect, in Muhammad, the Gentile prophet who universalises Abrahamic monotheism. When Abraham and Ishmael laid the foundations of the house of God in Mecca (Q2.125–7; 14.35–7), they prayed for the emergence, 'from our seed' (*min dhurriyyatinā*) of a nation submitted (*ummatan muslimatan*) to you (Q2.128). They supplicated God to raise an Arab Apostle among them, equipped with scripture and wisdom (Q2.129). (One of Muhammad's many pious titles is *al- 'arabiyy*, the Arab). Through Abraham, then, the advent of the Quran may be seen as enabling a further extension in the scope of the promise – to the final people of God, the Muslims, who may be seen as the Arab seed of Abraham through Ishmael. This is how I would interpret Paul's claims in Galatians in the context of Quranic Islam.

VIII

Hab. 2.2–20 is a prophecy containing five oracles of woe. Paul quotes from this part of the book, perhaps conscious that he too lives in an eschatological era (see Gal. 1.4). Habakkuk is an eschatological work, not dissimilar to the apocalyptic works of Joel and Daniel, in that it looks to the unveiling of future events. Hab. 2.4 is quoted three times in the New Testament – and, assuming the integrity of our transmitted Masoretic text, misquoted each time. In Gal. 3.11, Paul quotes it with stress solely on 'by faith' while in Rom. 1.17 he distributes the stress evenly over both faith and 'the just one'. Hebrews 10.38 quotes Hab. 2.4 to underline both 'shall live' and the centrality of the faith that enables and inspires the endurance and persevering loyalty to truth requisite for deserving and earning eternal life.

In the Hebrew text, though not in the Septuagint, the expression 'his soul is puffed up' describes a typical proud Chaldean (Babylonian). Babylon persists as a symbol of unredeemed evil and urban depravity even in New Testament times. The opposite of the just one is the proud one, the foreign enemies of Israel who are proud of their military might. Some American evangelicals saw a prophecy of the 2003 Iraq war embedded in Hab. 1.6–11. 'Their might is their god' was Habakkuk's description of the invading Assyrian army – ironically as true of modern militaristic America, seen by activist Muslims as today's Babylon, to borrow a New Testament word for any corrupt urban environment which persecutes God's elect people.

'êmunā may refer to a persevering loyalty of any kind, including marital fidelity (Hos. 2.20). 'The way of *'êmunā*' (Ps.119.30) refers to the Torah. It is related to the *aleph-mem-nun* root of the verb translated as 'believed' in Gen. 15.6, also quoted by Paul (in Gal. 3.6). These Hebrew words resemble the Arabic verbal noun, *īmān*, meaning faith (in God). It is derived from the fourth form (*ā/ma/na*) of the simple root *a/mi/na* while an eighth form (*i'/ta/ma/na*) means to trust or entrust something to someone for custody. The simple verb means to be secure from danger, but also, derivatively, from doubt concerning the veracity and truth of dogmas revealed in the Quran. When used of God, with the definite article (*al-mu'min*), the active participle of the fourth form of the verb, means the 'all-faithful' and by implication the unique source, keeper or guardian of security (Q59.23).

'êmunā covers faith in the characteristically New Testament meaning of *pistis* (understood as steadfast faith in God and his promises) but also encompasses faithfulness to the covenant obligations. Arguably, *pistis* covers only the first (generalised) meaning and certainly does not emphasise the distinctively Old Testament sense of faith. In any case, *'êmunā* occurs 49 times in the Hebrew Bible, its primary meaning being faithfulness, sometimes its only possible meaning (as at Lam. 3.23). The idea of fidelity to God, or faith in God as the one who is faithful to the faithful ones, is captured occasionally too, especially in the Psalms (see Ps. 37.3, 119.30). Paul quotes *'êmunā* as if it means only faith. Thus, for Paul, to have faith is to have faith in God, not in oneself or one's actions, no matter how righteous both the action and the agent. That is acceptable to the Jew who feels obliged to obey the Law in order to benefit from it, as promised by God. Only the New Testament sharply distinguishes faith in divine promises from faithfulness to the Law – the right means for being right with God. Paul denies that the law was ever meant to be the right means for being right with God. For Paul, on one possible though implausible reading of Gal. 3.23, faith simpliciter was not even a possibility in the age of faithfulness to the covenant-law! This view would contradict his own (and other New Testament authors') implicit conviction that Abraham, Moses, David and all of their (believing) generations were men (and women) of faith.

In the Quran, *īmān* has a combined epistemological and psychological sense, meaning knowledge entertained with certainty, as opposed to merely the state of belief held on trust in its veracity. The Quran calls the latter kind of belief merely 'speculation' (*al-ẓann*), the word used for the Christian claim that Jesus was crucified (see Q4.157). Such conjectural belief lacks divine attestation and therefore avails nothing against *al-ḥaqq* (revealed or objective truth; see Q10.36). A *mu'min* knows with certainty that there is a God and that his will is supreme. Let me illustrate this point by noting a puzzling but revealing difference between the Quranic Jacob and the biblical Jacob. In the Quran, Jacob is blessed with *īmān*; he *knows* the truth of his son Joseph's circumstances (Q12.18, 83, 86). In the biblical narrative, Jacob is fooled by his sons' claims. Knowing the truth of the matter is, however, of little help in dealing with the raw reality of present suffering. In both the Bible and the Quran, Jacob suffers when he is separated from the son he loves. He does not merely believe, he knows. But so what? For having *īmān*, a form of knowledge, in no way reduces for the faithful the challenge of faith: one still needs to cultivate faithfully and patiently the attitudes of patience and trust (*tawakkul*; Lat. *fiducia*) in the eventual vindication of God's promises, despite appearances to the contrary.

Like *īmān*, neither the Hebrew *'ĕmunā* nor the Greek *pistis* is, except in the unique case of the Devil, ever merely the acceptance of a true proposition. But the point of the Quran's narrative about Joseph's father is that faith (*īmān)* is not mere belief but rather knowledge – true belief held with certainty, about God's control of events, including future events – and yet it still requires supplementary attitudinal components before it can mature into the fullness of faith. The certainty of Jacob's *īmān* does not preclude the experience of intense suffering for him (Q12.84).

IX

How does Paul refute the need for law observance as a precondition of salvation? In Gal. 3.6–14, he contends that Christ's accursed death on the cross separates faith from law observance as a means of obtaining justification, *even for Jews*. The full sons of Abraham are only those Jews who, by dying to the Law and embracing Christ, place the same radical trust in God that Abraham placed. In 3.16–4.7, Paul is in effect arguing that God added the Law and its curse to ensure that even Jews could no longer receive the Abrahamic blessing promised to the nations. Only the spirit could make such Jews the sons of God and thus render them Abraham's *spiritual* seed, via Christ, the one seed. Paul does not attempt to cite scriptural authority for most of these novel proposals.

A minority of Christians have held that Paul envisaged a period before Christ, an age when the Law was interim custodian of Israel. It was an age of relative ignorance (or *jāhiliyya*), even though it was a time of divine guidance for Israel. The Law and the sin that the Law highlighted were alike forces that enslaved people, including the chosen nation. As Israel's guardian angel, the Law actively limited Israel's freedom and therefore participation in the full grace that came only with the advent of Christ Jesus, in Paul's curiously memorable reversal of name and title. This view, sometimes dubbed dispensationalism, is a minority verdict, rather unpopular among modern Christian scholars. The status of the Law, in the totality of this fascinating and nuanced view, is no more implausible than in the plethora of other schemes which offer a perspective on Paul's view of the Law.

Paul does judge the Law to be provisional and limited. For the Quran, the balance (*al-mīzān*; Q55.7–9), a prehistorical and transcendent notion of law, was enshrined in

God's nature as just king. The divine law could not be temporary or interim although its contents were variable, reflecting the circumstances of different prophets. For example, the law on theft in Joseph's Egyptian location – the convicted thief was forfeited as property and became a slave – was acceptable to God (12.75–6) even though it differed from the law revealed later to Muhammad (Q5.38), whose provisions required amputation of the offending hand, for all thieves, male and female.

Paul argued that the Law was never the basis of the covenant but rather its representation and embodiment. The sufficient basis was God's free grace; the response of faith was its expected corollary. Reliance on the works of the Law for acquiring salvation amounted to defection from grace. Sinners pander to human pride when they aim at a nomistic self-righteousness that is, ironically, often quite anaemic compared to the real article which only God's grace can grant – for, in truth, complete legal acquittal (amounting to justification) is impossible for any sinner. The Christian Paul, Christ-saved and Christocentric, came to uphold the moral dimension of the Law rather than its rituals, ceremonies, animal sacrifices and priestly Levite practices associated with the Temple in Jerusalem. In this regard, his focus resembles the Quran which, in its several narrations of the life and career of Moses, only once clearly mentions a sacrifice. The incident is recruited to prove that the Israelites only reluctantly obeyed God's clear command – forever inventing perverse and carping objections to it in order to seek devious escape from it (see Q2.67–71. cf. Num. 19.1–10). Jews are not alone in this tendency: the Quran warns Muslims to eschew perverse readings of the Quran (Q3.7). Only the Sunni majority has, I would argue, heeded this warning. And this is the reason I remain a defender of this mainstream orthodox faith of the universal congregation of the *ahl al-sunna* (the people of the trodden path).

X

Paul is no radical anarchist or post-modernist dissident hell-bent on denying all dichotomies. For example, he could never have written: 'In Christ, there is neither right nor wrong; neither lawful nor unlawful; neither law nor grace; neither faith nor works; neither law nor promise; neither spirit nor flesh.' Instead, we have 3.28, among the most widely quoted of his words. 'You are all one person in Christ.' 'One person' correctly translates 'one' (masculine). Had Paul used the neuter instead, available in Greek but not in Arabic, that would have meant 'a unity' or a unit. No word for 'body' is used here.

Paul's apparently radical rhetoric carries Christians further than the sober substance of his position. No doubt, those inclined to reject slavery, on independent grounds, can read Paul's letter to Philemon as quite revolutionary. Paul returns the slave but along with a letter demanding that the slave be treated like Paul himself – that is, with honour and respect. In practice, slave ownership persisted, even among devout and practising Christians. The Quran too, for all its otherwise comprehensively radical assault on the Arabian status quo, stops short of outlawing slavery. Some progressive Muslims believe that slavery has been abolished by a consensus (*ijmāʿ*) of the jurists but just as many legal authorities dispute this claim. Slavery is theologically puzzling.

For if God had intended one man to be enslaved by another, he would have made slaves to serve Adam in the Garden of Eden. This also applies to polygyny which equally lacks a primordial stamp.

In more general terms, Paul, like Marx, was an educated man, an intellectual aristocrat compared to the people he defends. Paul was creating for ordinary people what Nietzsche would call a slave morality. This does not invalidate the content of Paul's message but we should be aware that he does not intellectually belong to the class whose interests he upholds and whose honour he proclaims, no matter what we might say of his material and economic circumstances.

If we move from mundane politics to the power of the spirit, we find Paul speaking of a mystical unity of the believer with Christ, and in Christ – and thus with all believers. This is not some humanly attained solidarity, say, through armed political struggle. Pauline Christianity gives little warrant for modern liberation theology since even the radical Paul (of the authentic epistles) was politically conservative, indeed quietist. The Hebrew Bible is a better source for a liberation theology. The conservative-sounding 'second Paul' of the pastorals seems to support quite strongly what many now denigrate as a bourgeois middle class stability and genteel respectability which can inhibit progressive and reform movements.

Christ crucified dissolves cultural divisions. To a Gentile, crucifixion was associated with the dregs of society; Jews saw a crucified messiah, a defeated and accursed criminal, as more than folly. It was a blasphemous contradiction. The messiah was to be a victorious military leader of Israel who would lead the Gentiles to worship the God of Israel. A first century Judas Maccabeus would have qualified.

In Gal. 3.28, Paul declares the fullest effacement of relevant divisions: he counters the formal Jewish prayer expressing gratitude for winning life's lottery by being born a Jew, free and male, rather than being born a Gentile, a slave or a woman. 'Lord, I am grateful that I am not a Gentile, a slave or a woman.' Only in Galatians does Paul clearly uphold gender equality in Christ. In Romans (10.12), Paul erases only the Jew-Gentile rupture in the human family. In 1 Corinthians, he omits only the equality of the genders (12.13). In the deutero-Pauline Colossians (3.11), female equality is, unsurprisingly, omitted but the explicit statement of equality of Jew and Gentile/Greek is repeated through a metonymy – the circumcised and the uncircumcised.

The Quran teaches that while piety remains the final determinant of human worth in God's eyes, the societal divisions of Muslim and disbeliever, free and slave and male and female should persist. Distinctions of race and gender are legally if not spiritually relevant and permanent. Thus, differences in created form (male and female) amount to permanent divisions while differences in social organisation, races, tribes and peoples, based on diverse languages, can be transcended for superior religious reasons (see Q4.1; 49.13).

Paul in Corinthians is closer to the Quranic outlook than he is in Galatians with its triple erasure. The Corinthians received a letter that taught that 'The head of a woman is her husband' (1 Cor. 11.3) and 'Woman is the glory of man' (1 Cor. 11.7). This hierarchical and patriarchal view, found in the authentic Paul of the Corinthian correspondence, resembles the voice of the conservative (second) Paul of the pastorals. Social context is decisive, especially with the peripatetic Paul. The authentic Paul writes: 'By one spirit, we were all baptized into one body – Jews or Greeks, slaves or free – and all were made to drink of one spirit' (1 Cor. 12.13). It is no accident that this verse omits the unity and equality of the genders achieved in Christ. Female bishops are also ruled out (1 Cor. 14.34).

Let me leave the canonical gospels to turn to the gnostic Gospel of Thomas. In Saying #114, Simon Peter asks Jesus to order Mary to leave but Jesus says: 'For every female who makes herself male will enter the Kingdom of Heaven.' All the canonical gospels acknowledge women only as disciples, never as apostles. The Gospel of Thomas acknowledges that Jesus had female apostles, including Mary Magdalene and Salome. As for Paul, in Romans, he greets Prisca with love and approval and even mentions her before mentioning her husband, Aquila. Paul does not call them apostles but rather co-workers in Christ, which amounts to calling them apostles. The Apostle also names Andronicus and his wife Junia and calls them both 'outstanding among the apostles' (Rom. 16.3, 7).

The Quran's inveterate sexual dualism (Q3.36; 75.39), allied with its instinct for hierarchy and authority, reinforces its other conservative and paternalistic, indeed clearly masculinist, presuppositions. Islam envisages a society under male leadership but it does not endorse a misogynist theology that preaches *femina nulla bona* (no woman is any good; Eccl. 7.28). Many Muslims, including myself, would see this as the concealed mantra of parts of modern Western culture that claims to empower women while in fact serving the ends of capitalist consumerist exploitation. The Islamic stance is distinctive. Men are appointed custodians over women (*qawwāmūna 'alā al-nisā'i*; Q4.34) and exercise authority over them since they, like children, it would seem, know only their desires and wishes, not their best interests. Men supervise their conduct but it is always assumed, in Muslim tradition, that women need both subordination by men as well as male chivalry and protection. In the quoted verse (Q4.34), the latter stress would be achieved if the Quran had used the preposition *ilā* (to) instead of *'alā* (upon) while retaining the same verb. Many women must regret God's choice of preposition!

Despite such paternalism, the Quran clearly and frequently affirms the human and spiritual equality of men and women, including equality of their reward for righteous deeds (Q3.195; 4.1; 33.35). It is revealing that non-Muslims, including most Christians, rarely ask the most important question: 'Does Islam give women spiritual equality, the right to enter paradise?' Admittedly, some visions of paradise, both in the Quran and the Prophet's traditions, openly express gender inequality by catering mainly to male sexual desire (see Q.55.56, 74) – although the generous number of virgins promised to each (male) martyr, a number that vexes Western critics of Islam, is not mentioned in the Quran. Moreover, one should never ignore the equally pressing question of legal equality on earth, lest one fall victim to the socialist charge that religion parades as the noblest form of egalitarian humanism while promoting sexism and inequality.

Unlike Christianity, Islam institutionalises certain gender inequalities (though not inequities) which are harder to remove since scripture sanctions them. This charge is here being expressed in an external and alien vocabulary and is never made by any authentic Muslim, male or female. The Quran's own professed concern is with gender justice and equity, not simple equality, since the latter can sometimes be inappropriate, even unjust. Woman was elevated, quite literally, from the dust of the earth – the victim of female infanticide – to the one who, as mother, had the highest ideal of Islam, namely, paradise, placed beneath the dust of her feet. She is also eulogised as every child's 'first school (*madrasa*)'. It is impossible to imagine a greater elevation of women in any society, past or present. Admittedly, this exaltation is in the Prophet's traditions rather than in the Quran itself. The scripture singles out the mother as suffering much more than the father (Q46.15) though her suffering in childbirth is not attributed to her primordial sin. The Quran frequently advises respect for both parents (2.83; 17.23–24; 46.17) and even takes an oath – but only in the name of the father and then only at 90.3.

While many free male Muslims feel superior to disbelievers, slaves and women, this potentially unworthy sentiment is nowhere sanctified in prayer. Arab pagan culture already supported the superiority of free to slave, and of man to woman. The '*Arabiyy* (Arab) and *A'jamiyy* (Persian, lit., lacking eloquence) was an inherited pagan racial contrast (Q16.103). Islam added the Islam versus *al-jāhiliyya* (age of ignorance) contrast, the gulf between guided believers and ignorant and perverse disbelievers. Inside the Islamic community, Arab Muslims often feel superior to non-Arab Muslims, a major cause of the fracture in the *umma* of Islam. Muslims could learn from Paul concerning 'ummatic' racial unity – though the blatant racism that has blighted Christian civilisation inspires Muslim contempt for the West. Some Christians, notably adherents of the Dutch Reformed church in South Africa, have even claimed biblical support for white racism, seeing Cain as the black murderer of the victim, Abel the white man. A variant interpretation traces the same racial divide to the three sons of Noah (Gen. 5.32). No such reading can be defended as a correct interpretation of the Bible but such immoral readings have been entertained, often by otherwise thoughtful theologians. As for Muslim cultures, Arab racism towards non-white, non-Arabs, even non-white, non-Arab Muslims, even up to this day, is too obvious for any apologetic denial to be convincing. However, no Muslim, Arab or otherwise, has ever been able to claim any Quranic support for racism.

XI 4.1–7

1 *Now I say, as long as the heir is a child, he does not differ at all from a slave, (despite) being owner*
of everything. **2** *But he is under guardians and stewards until the date previously set by the father.*
3 *So also we, when we were children, were enslaved under the elements of the cosmos.* **4** *But when*
the fullness of the time came, God sent forth his son, born of a woman, born under the law **5** *in order*
that he might redeem those under law, so that we might receive the adoption of sons. **6** *And because*
you are sons, God sent forth the spirit of his son into our hearts, crying, 'Abba! Father!' **7** *Thus,*
you are no longer a slave but a son; and if a son, then an heir through God.

Paul argues for the joint adoption of Christians: Abraham's heirs become God's children since God intends that former slaves mature into the higher status of sonship.

1–2

Here slaves mature into sons while elsewhere Paul describes the infant (*nepios*), the word used for child in v.1 and 3 above, maturing spiritually into an adult (1 Cor. 3.1–3). In v.1, 'slave' and 'lord' are juxtaposed for effect.

In Paul, the child primarily symbolises spiritual immaturity. In Jesus' teaching, the child symbolises the innocence that generates effortless trust in the will of the Father, a trust that qualifies the believer for entry into the Kingdom of Heaven (Matt. 18.3). Philip Larkin, famous for his dislike of children, once said that this one verse in Matthew instantly converted him to atheism! Since Augustine, the child's innocence is seen as a myth although, in medieval Christendom, the monastic child's virtues included the inability to take pleasure in female nudity and beauty. William Golding's novel *Lord of the Flies*, published in 1954, merely a decade after the end of the war, clinches the case against children. (In our age, a work of fiction often affects the cultural climate more than works of fact: I think of Orwell's *1984*.) Since the 1960s, some extremist feminists have argued ferociously against 'breeding trouble by breeding kids'. The Quran portrays children, especially female wards, minors and orphans of both sexes, as dependents who lack both discretion and sexual appetite (Q4.2–3; 24.31, 59). The prophet Yahya (John, son of Zechariah) is said to have been granted wisdom as a child (Q19.12).

In much of the modern West, the minority decade of the child is from six to sixteen. In Islamic law, the age of consent and responsibility, for both genders, starts as early as twelve. This is also the age at which Jesus' parents took him to Jerusalem to visit the Temple and they presented him there – where he stayed to learn and debate (Luke 2.41–47). This is roughly the age at which Jewish boys and girls celebrate their bar/bat mitzvah. For the Muslim adolescent too, appropriate religious duties, such as prayer and fasting, become incumbent. Sins committed before the age of discretion are charged against the parents' account – although this conflicts with the Quran's stringently individualistic model of reckoning and personal accountability.

Paul reasons that before adulthood, a son is under the tutors and servants of the father as decreed by the father. On achieving adulthood, provided that the father is pleased, the son runs the house, along with the father. This is fair enough only in human contexts where both parties, the father and son, are mortal. Paul's case is weakened, arguably invalidated, by his weak analogy: the human testator – here the father who makes the will – is, unlike God, not immortal. A man must die in order to leave a will. No one inherits God since he is immortal. Admittedly, while there is no explicit mention of death in these two verses, talk of heirs does, certainly in the human case, imply mortality through the overlap of generations as one recedes to let the other succeed.

In Greco-Roman law, wills were required only if the deceased had no male issue. In Islamic law, based on three long verses of the Quran (Q4.11, 12, 176), wills are unnecessary since property effectively ceases to belong to the person about to die and is disposed according to divine law. The testator may, however, leave supplementary instructions about a portion of his or wealth concerning which he or she may exercise discretion – such as payment of debts and any bequests to charities and the Islamic state.

3

Paul's reference to the elemental things of the world (*ta stoicheia tou cosmou,* also at 4.9) is perhaps a coded reference to Stoic pantheism. Paul claims that he and his readers were once enslaved under these miserable earthly realities. This slavery ended when God sent his son to liberate his people. God sent the spirit on them and made them heirs (4.4–7). In Second Temple Judaism, the gift of the spirit was understood to be a sign of the restoration of Israel, promised to take place at the end of the ages. Muslims believe that God has impressed on select believers a spirit from him, making them his own party or people, the *hizb Allah.* Their enemies are an equally zealous evil group called the *ḥizb al-Shayṭān* (Q58.19, 22). This is the Devil's Party – in Islam's version of the two-party system! Activist Muslims identify the Devil's Party with Western and pro-Western powers (America, Britain and Israel). This is the Muslim equivalent of the American rhetoric of the axis of evil which, North Korea apart, consists only of Muslim nations.

4–5

Jesus was an observant Jew, circumcised on the eighth day. Paul knew the oral traditions of the nativity, later recorded in Luke (2.21). As for filial adoption (*huiothesia*), it is unique to the Pauline and deutero-Pauline epistles (Rom.8.15, 23; 9.4; Eph.1.5). Paul's *adoptio* is rooted in Roman law. As for the Incarnation, it renders slaves of God into sons of God since God sent his son in order to gain, by adoption, many more sons. Muslims discourage even ordinary adoption, permitted only under stipulated conditions in Islamic law (based on restrictions revealed at Q33.4–5). Paul's notion of filial adoption in the case of God is therefore doubly unsettling for Muslim readers.

6

The spirit here could mean the presence *of* God, *through* Jesus Christ, *in* the believer. In Christ, God the Father actually did what he merely ordered Abraham to do, namely, to sacrifice his only son – the only son of promise (see Gal. 1.4, 2.20, Rom. 8.32; cf. John 3.16).

God the Father sent the spirit of his (only) son into 'our hearts' (*eis tas kardias*) so that we may address God as Father (*Abba* in Aramaic, Jesus' native language). The heart is seen in many cultures as the seat of emotion. In the teachings of Jesus and Paul too, the heart is identified as the inner chamber from which issue forth good and bad motives. The Quran regards it as the inner citadel of faith in the expression 'righteousness of the hearts' (*taqwā al-qulūb*), used during its narration of the pilgrimage to Mecca, a rite instituted by Abraham (Q22.26–7). The inner self is the heart (*qalb*) contrasted with the outer self, symbolised by the mouth, tongue and lips (Q5.41; 90.9). The heart and the liver – the nobler viscera rather than the lower viscera of lungs and intestines – also correspond to the (male) breasts (*ṣadr*; pl. *ṣudūr*; Q11.5). In English, the breast in this sense is an archaic or poetic usage only. In Arab and other Islamic cultures, the liver (*kabad/kabid*) is the locus of deep emotion and travail (see Q90.4). The Arabic *kabad* is cognate with the Hebrew *kavodh* (glory) which means something heavy, thus having gravitas and thus glorious. The liver also corresponds to the notion of entrails or bowels (*splagchna*; Philem.20), used to refer obliquely to one's inner depths, one's heart.

Every Christian possesses the spirit of Christ (Rom. 8.9, stated there, assumed here). The Holy Spirit, declared the third person of the Trinity in later formal theology, seems to begin life, so speak, as an intercessor (Rom. 8.26) promised to believers, by the risen Jesus (John 14.26). It is in effect the gift of faith in Jesus (Acts 1.1–8). In later patristic theology, certainly, the Holy Spirit is a person, not merely a symbolic reference to a power or a spiritual influence of God. Although supplications can be addressed directly to this holy agency – asking him to enter the Christian's heart – this spirit is in general the subject, not the object, of Christian prayer. It enables believers to address God the Father by crying 'Abba!' Thus, the Holy Spirit is experienced by the redeemed believer as being God immanent rather than incarnate. The voice of the spirit is thus the voice of God heard by the believer.

Equivalently, the spirit of God's son enables Christians to become sons of God. They can now imitate Christ and thus supplicate God with the intimate submission – the *islām* – of Jesus' world-famous prayer: 'Abba! Dear Father! Your will be done' (Mark 14.36; Rom. 8.15). This spirit's presence creates the *morphē* (form or character) of Christ within the Christian. But, given human perversity, the spirit can be resisted and even rejected.

7

You are no longer a slave but rather a son and therefore you can inherit your father as an 'heir through God'. Paul approves of the father-son relationship of God to the believer in Christ. Promise is superior to law; sonship is superior to slavery and legal discipline. Islam rejects this filial pattern although it seems odd for a patriarchal culture that valued the father-son bond. Islam offers kingship of a just but merciful God; believers are obedient subjects who know their sinful and unwise wishes but, without God's revelation, cannot adequately know their religious best interests. The Quran cites both Jews and Christians as claiming to be sons of God and rejects this claim: they are mere mortals among God's creation and are subject to divine penalty for their sins (Q5.18).

XII

'None can come to the merciful one (*Al-Raḥmān*, i.e., Allah) – except as a servant' (Q19.93). That is the highest station of which the human creature is capable. Immediately after warning Jews and Christians against exaggeration and extremist hyperbole in their dogmas (Q4.171), the Quran adds: 'The messiah shall never disdain (*lan yastankifa*; Q4.172) to be a servant of (lit. to) God, nor will the angels close to God.' The verb translated as 'disdain' is the strongest verb in (Quranic/classical) Arabic for conveying the undertone of scorn. The particle *lan* is used for emphatic denials of future events.

The Quran uses the word *'abd* (servant) in a variety of ways and teaches that there are, spiritually speaking, entirely different kinds of slaves. The Quran relates the parable of two slave-servants (*'abdan mamlūkan*): the first is a useless burden on his master while the second one does credit to his owner (Q16.75–6). The first slave is a chattel slave who controls nothing while the second is a servant entrusted, by God, with good provision out of which he spends openly and secretly, in charity, acquiring good works. The first slave is a retarded man, with no control of affairs, a man who brings his owner into disrepute, despite being constantly guided. The second slave is intelligent and just and does his master credit as he serves him in a spirit of justice, walking on the straight path (of Islam), conscientiously pursuing virtue. 'Are the two equal? The rhetorical question posed is really a litotes gently inviting the reflective believer to ponder.

No doubt, however, the postures of Islamic prayer suit only a slave, no matter how intelligent and virtuous. A son salutes the majesty of his father, his king, without humiliating himself. He is submissive but not subservient since his place is not in the dust of his father's feet. He is exalted despite being humble. By contrast with Islam then, the Christian style of worship must appear as, to borrow a phrase from a discrepant source, 'a free man's worship'.[6]

Why does the Muslim prayer posture insist on humiliation (associated with fear) rather than mere humility (associated with loving service)? Even when supplemented with gratitude, love is often insufficient to motivate righteous conduct. The ingredient of fear is needed not only to preserve our awe of God but also to secure regular and dependable obedience to God's requirements. Whether our conduct is good or evil, we human beings need more than one kind of motivation. A single pure and seamless motive usually motivates only saints, men and women who can live and die in the heat of one active emotion, namely, the love of God. Similarly, only conspicuously wicked human beings are motivated by a single sinful desire, the love of evil.

Take a completely secular case. In Jean-Paul Sartre's mysteriously motivated play, *Les Mains Sales* (Dirty Hands, 1951), a young communist intellectual, perhaps based on Sartre in his own youth, finds himself incapable of carrying out an official order to assassinate a traitor. The intellectual finds that his ideologically motivated indignation is insufficient to motivate him to kill the enemy of the cause. A supplementary motive is supplied when the intellectual begins to suspect that the traitor is having an affair with his wife. After this, he can see his planned killing as a crime of personal passion. And such passion supplies a more dependably powerful motive.

The Muslim believer's motive for keeping the law may initially be fear but gradually changes into love. While it is right to fear God, such fear is not akin to terror. Nor must it develop into a neurotic kind of despair of ever obtaining God's mercy and forgiveness. Such lack of faith in God's mercy amounts to infidelity. A fine balance saves the believer from an arrogant complacency that assumes an undue familiarity with God and his mysterious purposes, on the one hand, and equally, on the other, from an imbalanced kind of despair that loses sight of divine mercy altogether.

Take Muhammad's own astonishing case. The opening verses of Surah 48 announced a future military triumph concealed in a present defeat and promised Muhammad God's forgiveness for his sins, past and future. His wife Aisha asked him why he had increased his devotions since receiving this revelation, implying that he now had nothing to fear. He replied: 'Should I not be a grateful servant (of God)?' Muhammad obeyed the law even more zealously after knowing that his sins had been forgiven. But his motive is gratitude, a close correlate of love, rather than solely or predominantly the fear of God. This total attitude resembles the Christian confession that saved sinners – once redeemed – are free to do what is good, but now out of gratitude rather than out of a sense of legal duty or fear of divine wrath. Christians proclaim that they are no longer slaves and servants of God but rather his sons and heirs. For Muslims, however, being a servant of God is a terminal honour.

Muslims would regard Muhammad's case as isolated, relevant at best only to the spiritually elect. No ordinary believer can hope to receive such a divine assurance. Although Islam offers no guarantee of salvation, no insurance policy for sinners, so to speak, some believers are, in practice, guaranteed God's forgiveness. Fighters who are killed for the cause of Islam, are in this privileged category – provided their sole motivation is to seek God's good pleasure (*riḍwān*; Q9.21; cf. *eudokia* at Phil. 2.13). They shall have no reckoning, indeed no pre-burial ablution, this being the duty of angels. Funeral prayers are held even though martyrs are considered (spiritually) still alive and those who attend their funeral are required to rejoice, not mourn (Q2.154; 3.169–171). According to some sound prophetic traditions, every Muslim will eventually be pardoned by God and will, after enduring appropriate punishment for sins reckoned against him or her, eventually enter paradise.

Muslims sense the need for their Prophet's intercession on their behalf. Many believe that while they may pass the doctrinal part of the catechism that starts in the grave, they will fail the second part of the examination, the account of good and evil works. The sinners request Muhammad's intercession and ask him to 'save' them for the sake of his *umma*. Thus, Muhammad's merits as the prophet of the last and most successful *umma* will help ordinary sinful Muslims to obtain God's forgiveness. Explicit in popular piety, it receives equivocal support in the Quran (24.62; 9.103). The formal prayers conclude with blessings on Muhammad and his family supplemented by petitionary prayer (*du'ā'*) addressed to God 'through your Prophet's prerogative' (*bi ḥaqqi nabiyyika*).

XIII

Having traversed halfway through Galatians, we take stock by examining, from an Islamic perspective, three central Galatian themes: descent from Abraham, righteousness by faith alone and, thirdly, Paul's stance on the Law.

Paul claims that, as an Israelite, he too is 'of the seed (*spermatos*) of Abraham' (Rom. 11.1). In Galatians, Paul offers varied images of descent from Abraham: sons (3.7) in 3.6–14, seed (3.16, 29) in 3.15–3.29, and children of promise (4.28) in 4.21–5.1. The first and last of these models of Abrahamic descent are relevant to Islam. Christ as the singular seed cannot find a Quranic analogue.[7]

'Sons of Abraham' (Gal. 3.7) designates the received mid-first century CE view that Jews were the physical descendants of Abraham and thus shared his faith by virtue of consanguinity. 'Children of promise' in Gal. 4.28 intends the Gentile believers. These latter have, through faith rather than lineal descent, received the Abrahamic blessing – the spirit of sonship that makes them children of God, not only of Abraham. Addressing the Muslims in Medina, the Quran calls Abraham 'your father' (*abī-kum*), implying that Muslims are, in virtue of faith, the spiritual children of the Hebrew patriarch (see Q22.78). Muslims cannot, of course, literally or figuratively, see themselves additionally as God's children.

John the Baptist's claim that 'God is able from these stones to raise up children to Abraham' (Luke 3.8) undermines the putative ethnic basis for a privileged Jewish identity. It is addressed *ad hominem* to Jewish leaders who boast that Jews alone are Abraham's true descendants. John's lapidary threat cannot be taken to be offering early if inchoate support for an extension of mission to Gentiles since it is uttered during an essentially internal power struggle among Jews. John says it in anger, and rather defiantly, to shame his fellow Jews rather than to make an independent claim in favour of Gentiles.

Jesus' own earthly ministry regarding Gentiles may also be read in the light of this attitude. Given that all the writers of the New Testament, with the possible exception of Luke, were Jews, Semitic hyperbole is to be expected. Thus, Jesus' threat to his fellow Jews about the coming inclusion of the Gentiles bears comparison with the Quran's repeated threat to the Arabs that God will substitute a better people who will serve him and love him (Q6.54; 47.38). Both are strategies to motivate the existing audience to repent and to behave. Such verses should be interpreted contextually rather than literally in order to mitigate their deliberately dramatic tone. In the case of the New Testament, an additional concern is that the gospels are layered like a palimpsest: we uncover Jesus but then also find the evangelists' purposes superimposed on his words. We need to assume that the evangelists did not take liberties with Jesus' words and intentions. To put it minimally, Muslims see that as a precarious assumption.

Now, for Paul, traditional Jewry's affirmation of Abraham's righteousness amounts to justification before God, itself another way of speaking of Abraham's faith in God. In turn, this faith supplied the foundation of the promise to Abraham's children, the Jews, through the line of Isaac and Jacob. In effect, then, for Paul, Abraham's blessing by God exemplifies and exhibits his pure faith in God, an attitude that will justify the Gentile nations.

Paul's appeal to Abrahamic *lineage* is ultimately intended, surprisingly, to refute (rather than affirm) a law-based circumcision. His reasoning for this counter-intuitive conclusion has to be oblique. First he wants to establish that the promised Abrahamic seed must be not only a son of Abraham but also a son of God. Paul insists that Jews and Gentiles alike require incorporation into Christ so that both can become Abrahamic seed. Jews require it so that they can share in the divine sonship recently granted to Gentiles; the Gentiles need it so that they can share in the Jews' ancient Abrahamic sonship. This union of the Jewish sons of Abraham and the Gentile sons of God, in Christ, becomes the single divine Abrahamic seed who inherits the promises.

The Quran bypasses the problem that requires such a subtle and indefinitely complicated solution embodied in the mystical reunification of the human race in the body of the resurrected Christ. By upholding the monogenetic origins of the human race and its continuing unity for spiritual purposes, the Quran can reject as spiritually irrelevant the ethnically delineated distinction between Jews and Gentiles. Salvation did not come to the world via God's election of one people. While accepting the originally favoured status of Israel, Muslims regard the restrictive prioritising of guidance and 'salvation' to a chosen nation, at any stage of history, as unworthy of a just God who is and has always been impartially concerned to actively guide, sustain and 'save' all human beings at all times and in all places. It is hard to imagine a more fair-minded and open-hearted theology of grace – though 'grace' retains importantly different shades of meaning in Christian and Islamic vocabularies.

XIV

Christians do not see faith as a virtue that causally merits justification but rather the divinely approved means or channel through which sinners receive God's gift of grace. God himself, in Christ, justifies sinners; faith as such cannot achieve that state of grace. The object of our devotion is God, not our faith in him, let alone our beliefs about him, expressed propositionally.

A blessing, like grace, is never earned on the basis of merit and effort but rather freely promised and gratefully received. Whether for mid-first century Galatian pagans or early seventh century Arabian pagans, works of the law are never the causal condition of receiving divine blessings and grace. Note that the terms of the contrast here are asymmetrical. Only grace is autonomously administered: it can be rejected by sinners, in virtue of free will, but its (potential) salvific efficacy is not thereby compromised. By contrast, God can reject works of the law – whether arbitrarily (unlikely) or reasonably on grounds of their inadequacy.

Good deeds are performed by God's permission – through the operation of his enabling grace. As God's gift, grace is never integral to the human being (*al-insān*) but rather to the human being as a believer (*mu'min*), that is, a human agent who intends to produce virtue for God's sake. The grace of God cannot originate in a human being. Grace, like any blessing, is external and undeserved. This is the case both in Paul and in the Quran.

Faith in God is a prerequisite of the *acceptance* of a good deed (Q4.124). However, it is unclear if faith is a precondition of the *performance* of a good deed. In the world of the Quran, there are no virtuous disbelievers. If someone hears the word of God and rejects it, he or she is guilty. Sincerity of motivation which makes the rejection conscientious does not ensure God's acceptance of the good deed, if indeed the deed even qualifies as good. Some Muslim philosophers, mainly under Greek influence, conceded that a pagan could be coincidentally good – living in accordance with God's will but in ignorance of this truth. Orthodox theologians angrily insisted that God was under no (moral) obligation even to reward a virtuous monotheist, let alone a virtuous pagan. Both could be justifiably sent to Hell. God does whatever he wills. Paul affirms a similar understanding of God's will when he ponders the mysteries of God's inscrutable sovereign choices (Rom. 9.13–21) which must appear arbitrary to the creature's limited reason.

Two points of nomenclature to close this preliminary survey of large theological topics. The Quran has no word for justification but it has forms of the word *zakiyya*, or cleansing, which includes purification, though not sanctification. Self-purification, in the sense of a self-righteous attribution of purity to oneself, is strongly condemned as hubristic. Jews are accused of claiming such self-purity (Q4.49). God alone can purify any human being (Q24.21; 53.32).

Secondly, redemption is both a biblical and a Quranic notion; sinners can seek *kaffara* (expiation or atonement) for their sins. This is, literally, a concealment or covering for their sins. To buy or ransom is used of believers: God purchases believers as they seek to please him by striving in his way, selling themselves and their goods in exchange for the Garden (Q9.111). This is an ordinary commercial word and retains that simple meaning. Muhammad, like many of his prominent companions, was a merchant. This supplies his most popular image in the Islamic Orient where Islam first arrived, courtesy of Arab traders.[8]

XV

Paul develops a Christian view of the law and of its place – in diametrical opposition to its role in the Judaism that he learned and inherited, an influential and prevalent variety of that faith. For Paul, the Law was a later addition to the original promise, rather than a substitute for it. Jews believed that it helped observant believers to recognise infringements and provided for sinners a way, through offerings, to make atonement for sins committed. Sacrifices were made throughout the year for sins, especially those committed accidentally and unintentionally. All sins were offered to God on *Yom Kippurim*. This comprehensive system enabled sinners to recognise and acknowledge that they were sinners, in God's sight (Rom. 3.20). Only the Law makes a moral offence into a legal offence, a sin into a crime against God, the Lawgiver (Rom. 4.15). Paul's claim is that the Law pointed the way towards Christ, the Son of God. It was never intended to provide a permanent guide for God's people to live in righteousness before a holy and therefore judgemental God.

Paul was arguing that the Law was intended to be only a guide to holy living but not intended to be a way of establishing perfect righteousness. The Law proves only that we are in fact sinners; it does not enable us to become holy. Following the Torah means only that we come in humility to a holy God – as sinners in urgent need of forgiveness. In effect, then, for Paul, the Law only pointed the way towards righteousness – without attaining it for any law-observant sinner.

Muslims would judge as arbitrary the imposition of such limitations on the power of God's law. Either God intended the law to be efficacious or he did not. If he did, then its failure to produce righteousness, partial or perfect, can only be due to the free human creature's perversity and weakness of will. If God ordained a law for his frail creatures but knew that it could not be fulfilled, but ordered them to fulfil it in any case – then we have a deity who set out to deceive his creatures and is therefore unworthy of worship. It is no coincidence that Paul can cite no unequivocal scriptural authority for imposing such limits on the Law's divinely intended or actual efficacy.

'For Christ is the end (*telos*) of the Law so that there may be righteousness for everyone believing' (*pisteuonti*; Rom. 10.4). This verse has inspired considerable commentary, an indication that the matter is indefinitely complex.[9] Owing to the confusing polysemy of *telos* which could mean end, termination or cessation but also goal, purpose, or consummation, intractable ambiguity still surrounds this verse. Its apparent meaning is that Christ abolished the Law (*nomos*) which is therefore no longer binding for Christians. It could instead mean that, in Christ, the Law reached its true and intended fulfilment or goal and is, again, for this completely different reason, redundant. Paul was perhaps deliberately being vague here just as he was in choosing *historesai* (to visit) in describing his attempt to become acquainted with Peter (Gal. 1.18): a substantive decision about ultimate versus derivative apostolic authority hinged there on a suitably chosen verb.

The ambiguity in Rom. 10.4 is even more crucial: it implies a larger ambivalence regarding the options surrounding our view of the continuity or discontinuity of the two biblical testaments. It ought to trouble thoughtful Christians that the most thoughtful German apostate from Christianity, Friedrich Nietzsche, was so perturbed by this conjoining of two disparate scriptures in one volume that he regarded it as 'the greatest literary rape on the conscience of Europe'.[10] We could argue either for a harmonious continuity between Judaism and Christianity (interpreting *telos* as consummation) or for a total rupture between the parent and the wayward child (*telos* as cessation). The latter view makes for a Pauline triumphalist supersessionism which outrages those scholars who see Jesus as a Jewish prophet whose message was hijacked by Paul, the self-styled Hellenised thinker.[11]

While there are strong grounds for opting to understand *telos* in a teleological and completive way, Christian exegetes have entertained other equally plausible but wholly opposed interpretations. Christ alone fulfilled the spirit and letter of the Law of Moses. Thus, the purpose of the Law was transformed after its fulfilment. This is a typical conservative and rather unconvincing description of Paul's position. 'Transformed' is a vague adjective and can, plausibly, only mean 'altered', implying that the original purpose was 'transcended', that is, 'abrogated'. The temporal or terminal reading – *telos* as cessation – makes the Gospel of Christ abrogate or nullify the Law, whether partly or wholly, in terms both of practical content and abstract authority. It means that the Law is no longer applicable. Paul does not say this in so many words but his Jewish accusers saw, surely rightly, that his liberties of thought finally led to him being, in effect, an apostate from the Law.

The use of *telos* with the genitive (*nomou*), however, may indicate purpose and outcome rather than abrogation and termination. Thus, if philological grounds alone were permitted to be decisive, 'Christ has invalidated the Law' would be incorrect. While this textual matter may be allowed to stand in perpetual ambivalence, we may safely conclude that, for Paul, the Torah leads to the Gospel via the fulfilment of the former. This is effectively a euphemism for the redundant status of the Torah. For the Quran, unlike for Paul, the Gospel was a corroborating sequel to the Torah which itself remains valid in principle and in (Jewish) practice. Muslim rulers not only permitted but required their Jewish subjects to abide by the Torah (Q5.68).

For Christians, in practice, whether intentionally or otherwise, Christ's advent effectively relegated the Law from its status as ordinance to being mere taboo and irrational scruple. After Christ, the Levitical food laws and circumcision become, certainly for Gentiles, irrational relics; even for Jews, these laws lost their previous force and binding quality. In all but words, this amounts to an abrogation of the Law's authority to guide conduct, even though this is achieved subtly, subversively and obliquely rather than explicitly – and all the more insidious for it. The era of law was a temporary legal interlude, a period where a provisional law operated as interim guardian while Israel was a child. In the Christian scheme of history, the era of promise (Abraham) and the era of law (Moses) culminate in the era of fulfilment of the age of promise (Christ). The fourth era is the eternal life of faithful fellowship with Christ.

Islam has no corresponding scheme of sacred history. Instead, this world in present history will, for each person, end and lead to death, resurrection and the enduring next life (Q7.24–25; 20.55). For Muslims, the law is not probationary but permanent. The Muslim critic of Christianity can see the motives for eliminating the law – the desire to include Gentiles and the impossibility of obeying the whole law without the aid of grace. But what are the revealed grounds, the dominical sayings, for that stance? The Islamic alternative states that every human being received divine guidance and that we are all individually accountable for our actions. God expects us to do our best, no more. He never burdens any person with more than he or she can bear (Q2.286): 'Our Lord, do not burden us with what we do not have the strength to bear.' Thus, no tragedy or suffering can justifiably lead to loss of faith.

Let me end on a point of vital significance in interfaith interactions. Paul knew from experience that the Law was comprehensive. This can be interpreted as offering complete guidance in all contexts or else as inhibiting all freedom in a virtually fascist – totalitarian is a kinder word – straitjacket of rules. In contemporary Islam, in debates about the *Sharīʿa* law, some Muslims, male and female, view the law as rightly regulating all life situations and thus liberating them from the ubiquitous anarchy and uncertainty of a free-ranging Western secular modernity. The law may sound unduly authoritarian, even totalitarian, especially to some female Muslims born and raised in Western lands. While they want some order in their lives, they do not want to sacrifice the freedom to choose and explore options in a world marked by liberty – rather than by chance and destiny, the inherited traditions and rituals of their forefathers who came from conservative lands. In the eyes of many devout Muslim men, freedom often means only one thing: sexual anarchy. In a regrettably prevalent double standard, many men reject such freedoms for women while celebrating these very liberties as the harbinger of sexual opportunity for themselves.

Notes

1 This textual variant could only have arisen owing to scribal ambiguity in the original Hebrew where 'his faith' (*'êmunātho*) and 'my faith' (*'êmunāthi*) differ only in their final consonant, *wāw* or *yodh* respectively. Such deterioration of the writing on a scroll is quite commonplace: part of the letter *wāw* can flake off to leave a remnant easily mistaken for a *yodh*. Perhaps Paul was aware of that manuscript ambiguity and exploited it for his own purposes.

2 A factual error in Muhammad's sayings in not a problem but any such error, were it to occur in the Quran, would be a grave matter. Similarly, the human Jesus could be mistaken about mundane matters – such as agriculture. More broadly, the presence of factual errors is theologically puzzling but only in a scripture that claims to be the literal revealed word of God. In the Bible, human errors can be attributed to the human component in scripture. The sceptic will, however, argue that if a book can be mistaken in its historical and other putatively factual claims, nothing can prevent it from being mistaken about matters of doctrinal moment and ultimate truth. One cannot, the sceptic insists, separate in a scripture its true doctrines from their false or culturally conditioned accompaniments – without begging the question. Did God himself deliberately insert errors into scripture, to test our minds, rather than merely require us to resist the usual bodily temptations?

3 *Antiquities* 2.318 (430 years) and *Antiquities* 2.204 (400 years)

4 *Jubilees* 1.23-25. Neither Paul nor James quotes from the book of Jubilees which supports James' portrait of Abraham while obliquely undermining some of Paul's claims. Thus, for example, Abraham grows in virtue as he lives in accordance with Mosaic law. More generally, in Genesis, Abraham, Jacob and Isaac did some things that were to be later outlawed in the Law of Moses: the building of altars, especially pillars, ritual planting of trees and the performance of child sacrifice. The Quran also reveals that Jacob (Israel) forbade himself certain foods before *kashrut* restrictions were revealed (Q3.93) to Moses and Aaron in 'the explicit scripture' (*kitāb al-mustabīn*; Q37.117; cf. Quran as clear scripture; *kitāb al-mubīn*; Q12.1, from the same root). Both the Torah and the Quran support the notion of a pre-Mosaic freedom from revealed legislation.

5 In a sculpture by Edwina Sandys, Christa, the female Christ, is God's daughter. Would that pose a problem for traditional Christian theology?

6 The phrase is from Bertrand Russell's essay 'A free man's worship' (1902). See also his later essay 'Why I am not a Christian' (1927).

7 For more, see Bradley Trick's unpublished doctoral thesis 'Sons, Seed, and Children of Promise in Galatians: Discerning the Coherence in Paul's Model of Abrahamic Descent', submitted to Duke Divinity School, 2010. My analysis here assumes Trick's work – though he does not mention the Quranic Abraham.

8 Far Eastern Muslims are uncomfortable with the militant Muhammad wildly popular with many Muslim Pakistani and Arab men and some Arab women.

9 See for example Robert Badenas' published thesis, *Christ, The End of the Law: Romans 10:4 in Pauline Perspective* (Sheffield: JSOT Press, 1985).

10 See his 1886 work, *Beyond Good and Evil* (New York: Random House, 1966), p. 52, translated by Walter Kaufmann. I have translated the quoted passage.

11 H. Maccoby, *The Mythmaker: Paul and the Invention of Christianity* (London: Weidenfeld and Nicolson, 1986) and *Paul and Hellenism* (London: SCM Press, 1991).

5

PASTORAL INTERVENTIONS

Saint Paul as pastor Paul (4.8–20 and 5.2–12)

I

While Galatians should be mined for its eternal theological motifs, we must also let it speak in its initial epistolary contingency, in its original pastoral spontaneity. The occasional nature of this epistle does not detract from its enduring appeal which transcends its initial destination somewhere in rugged Asia Minor. The canonisation of New Testament writings was, of course, not arbitrary. While many conservative-minded Christians are innocent of the findings and conclusions of critical biblical scholarship, others are well aware of such materials, but insist that the writings which came to be canonised were always sacred and revealed. They were, they add triumphantly, merely awaiting official ecclesiastical recognition in order to achieve the status of (written) scripture. All Christians concur that Paul's letters were readily canonised because the early church immediately noted their edifying content.

The unsympathetic reader of Paul's epistles might see only some hyperactive, almost neurotic and obsessive personality. But the gracious and caring aspect of the Apostle's personality shines through as he offers pastoral guidance. As the last of the apostles, Paul discerned God's power in human weakness but he never relinquished his authority as a Christian leader and spiritual father to his churches. The Apostle was a shepherd who strenuously asserted his right to discipline his flock. He was embroiled in conflicts of rank and status but only in matters of mission rather than personal standing. In his practice, Paul showed other missionaries that the Christian mission must remain independent by being financially self-supporting. While the Apostle was, in my view, temperamentally and intellectually an aristocrat, his lower social class, as a tradesman, gave him ready access to all classes of society. This cannot always be said for Western Christians, many of whom come from conservative and often quite affluent and educated backgrounds. In some cases, this background may limit their social vision and restrict the range of their sympathies.

The Galatians were zealous, albeit without having knowledge. They were, however, not lukewarm like the Laodiceans (Rev. 3.14–22) who were indifferent even to Jesus' pastoral advice. Paul wants the Galatians to learn the privilege and responsibility of Christian liberty just as the prophets had once instructed the people of God to learn the joint privilege and duty entailed by being chosen to be a light to the nations. Duty flows from obedience to doctrine: we must discover truth in order to obey it.

Paul rarely if ever treats questions, let alone answers them, at the level at which these are asked by his interlocutors and disciples. Unsympathetic critics would say that this only proves that he was a consummate politician, the man who never gave a straight answer and, instead, answered every question with several more questions. But Pastor Paul, unlike the typical politician, is not evasive when a principle is at stake. He postpones an answer in order to deepen the inquiry; he probes not only into his correspondents' professed motives but also into the consequences of their questions. I see Paul as resembling a Christian journalist of outstanding integrity: a man who reacted to current events with the intention of investigating their causes and speaking truth to power.

Only at one level was the Galatian crisis simple. Should believers coming to Christ, from paganism, be required to be circumcised? Paul does not immediately give his final answer – the outright rejection of circumcision for these men. Rather he makes us and the Galatians wait for several chapters even though he knows from the start the final correct response. He offers a tortuous detour through scripture. He shows that the answer to this simple question is a corollary of the gospel of the liberty of the spirit. Paul's theology and ethics are his indicative and imperative moods respectively. Since X has happened, therefore, you should now do Z. The cross, contends Paul, has subverted the world's values, as he presses his readers to extricate the final consequences of this subversion. Paul ponders, with frustration and affection, the question of why his Galatian disciples are slow, even obtuse, in understanding and applying Christ-inspired values to new moral and practical realities.

The tendency to use an occasional event or remark to identify the deepest root issue and then to use it to extrapolate, enlarge and even universalise a matter, is Socrates' way of proceeding. It is characteristic of Hellenism but not of Semitic ways of thinking – and one does not find it in the Quran. It became the bedrock of later Muslim legal reasoning which took its cue from analogy. By then, Muslims had come under the spell of foreign, particularly Hellenic, modes of reasoning. Rabbinic methods differ from the Socratic technique while sharing a penchant for open-ended dialogue and dialectical exchange. The Quran also contains much dialogue with opponents. Semites are often talkative and argumentative, passionately exercised by ultimate questions.

II

The idea of a pastoral ministry, understood in secular terms as counselling, is largely alien to Muslims since the imam is only a leader of daily canonical prayer with the additional duty to deliver a standard sermon (*khuṭba*) and a supplementary statement (*bayān*) on Friday when the normal early afternoon prayer is replaced by a communal one. Muhammad himself, however, was a caring pastor (Q9.61, 128) and leader-teacher (Q3.159) who helped Muslims to bear their burdens (Q7.157) and even, in a limited way, interceded for them with God (Q9.99, 103). But he was not a priest-mediator, let alone saviour. Through Muhammad, however, the Quran orders Muslims to be united, as believers, against a hostile world, to be supportive of fellow believers (Q3.103, 5.54, 48.29, 49.9) – no longer a feature of life in an increasingly fractured *umma* where every faction puts its own goals and grudges first. After the end of Muhammad's tenure as prophet, on his death, the caliphs led their communities in prayer and managed state affairs but were not primarily pastors or religious functionaries. Indeed, orthodox (Sunni) Islam has, in theory, no official clerical class corresponding to the Christian clergy. In practice, however, mosque personnel and trained jurists enjoy this status in effect since they alone could 'pontificate' on religious matters as they instruct and guide the laity in their quotidian practical concerns.

Only in one respect has the centrality of theology in Christianity been salutary. When Western Christian ordinands train in pastoral ministry, they read theology, an intellectual pursuit that prepares them for an engagement with the secular and secularised – profane, alienated and attenuated – condition of most people around them. Most people now live in societies in which it is impossible to find love, truth and friendship. Instead they find only the worthless ephemera of instant but fake communication and endless material gratification that engenders endless dissatisfaction. Christian missionaries seek to retrieve such people for the right vocation of Christian monotheism – an impossible task though there are random successes.

The blend of religious and secular education, which theology enables, is a strength of Christian training and often gives Christian clergymen a worldly charm – a grace seasoned by a sense of humour – that makes them accessible to people of no faith. By contrast, Muslim mosque personnel often cannot even engage rival monotheists, let alone the broader secular society. Many cannot construct a complete complex declarative sentence in any European language. The result is a narrowly religious outlook on the world, one transmitted faithfully and intact to the next generation, admittedly, but at the expense of being an easy target for secular mockery. Their lack of education and training in secular matters largely accounts for their failure to reach the confused-but-sincere Muslim youth of both genders. If Christianity and Judaism have recently failed to produce morally good human beings, Islam has failed to produce intellectually profound and charming people in its cultures. Western Islam is virtually toothless, unequipped with a sophisticated apologetic to survive attacks from rival monotheists and secular humanists. It lacks the temperament both for apology and polemic. Where are the intellectually aggressive Muslims who can compete with polemical atheists such as Richard Dawkins, Sam Harris, Salman Rushdie and Christopher Hitchens?

Only in secularised post-Ottoman Turkey, since 1928, have imams been trained in the theology faculty of a university and required to learn something of the beliefs and history of other major faith communities. Alone among Muslim nations, Turkey openly maintains friendly relations with Jewish Israel and is the only Muslim nation actively trying to become part of Christian Europe. Despite appearances, the Ottoman Empire did finally succumb to the influence of the European Enlightenment.

In Paul's own case, the formative power of his rabbinic education was tempered with the unavoidable influence of Hellenic culture and education. The Greek heritage directly influenced only Christianity, both linguistically and metaphysically. As for Islam, it encountered the Greek philosophical heritage only late in its formation as a faith. Therefore, philosophy was easily expunged from orthodox Islam and has never been able to make a victorious return. Muhammad, unlike Paul, was spared the formative influence of any philosophical system. The Quran is, uniquely among the world's revelations, wholly uninterested in doubt and theological and metaphysical curiosity. Indeed, it is not even interested in theology, a Greek word and a pagan enterprise – a study of the gods – dating at least as far back as the cold and clinical Aristotle. Original Islam's congenital indifference to theology ended once Umar conquered the Persian Empire. The speculative and mystical temperament inherent in the Persian gene – kindly called genius – gave Islam the dubious enterprise of metaphysics, the equivalent, among Christian nations, of the German penchant for theology.[1]

We are now in a position to proceed with the textual commentary. Paul makes a personal plea as he fears his Galatian flock's possible apostasy and regression into the slavery of (the) law.

III 4.8–11

8 *Formerly, however, when you did not know God, you served as slaves to those who by nature are not divine beings.* **9** *But now, knowing God – or rather being known by God – how is it that you revert again to the weak and poor elements to which you desire to be enslaved afresh?* **10** *You observe days and months and seasons and years.* **11** *I fear for you, in case I have in vain laboured over you.*

8–10

The Galatians had abandoned paganism to become Christians. Paul wants them to know their privileges as Christians. He is alarmed when he learns that his disciples are contemplating adherence to a religious version of the very paganism they had renounced. Paul denounces the temptation to hedge one's spiritual life with rituals punctuated by a religious calendar – if one thinks that this will add anything to a salvation already secured. If you have Christ, you have it all, a message repeated, in a similar context, in the deutero-Pauline epistle to the Colossians (see Col. 2.16–17).

Here in 4.9 (as in 4.3), *stoichea kosmou* are the elemental things or natural principles of the world, analogous to *al-dunyā*, the Quran's derogatory word for the material world (lit. the near or easy one to reach). Paul calls these elements weak and worthless. In the Semitic faiths, neither the physical world nor linear time is illusory but rather materially real and historical – but not absolute since the world's creation and continued existence rely on God's will and power. Although we live in a contingent space-time continuum and a closed system of natural causality, the world is no illusion. This view contrasts with the Hindu and Buddhist conception of the natural cosmos as being illusory. The Quran preaches that we are surrounded by a superb if partly concealed divine providence which offers countless signs and hints of its presence. Only the wise and penitent people note it – and offer praise and gratitude. The regularity and reality of the natural world invites the enterprise of empirical science. It is no accident that India, rich in spirituality, did not inspire the emergence of empirical science, even while excelling in mathematics. That enterprise was stimulated by Muslim scientists working with Christian and Jewish scientists who were subjects of the Islamic empire. Their achievements were then gradually institutionalised – but only in the exclusively Christian universities of feudal medieval Europe.

It seems from these verses (as from 1.6 and 3.1) that the Galatians were rather fickle and easily changed their minds. It would be race-related rather than outright racist to observe that some nations or ethnic groups are more reliable, committed and perhaps stubborn than others! The Quran accuses most of the Bedouin Arabs, the nomadic rather than settled urban ones, of being fickle, insincere and hypocritical in their attachment to Islam (Q9.97–99; 49.14–17). Fake and flaky people who do not honour their word are seen as dishonourable in most cultures. Such people abound in our modern world of instant communication and shallow relationships where many teenagers are 'screenagers'.

11

Paul, the athlete for Christ (Phil. 3.12–14), fears he may have run his race in vain (cf. Gal. 3.4). In the event, Paul's evangelisation of the Galatians eventually succeeded. Pauline Christianity was destined to triumph and to eclipse the Jewish version offered by the Judaisers.

IV 4.12–16

12 *Become as I am because I am also as you are – I beg of you, brothers. You wronged me in nothing.* **13** *And you know that on account of a weakness of the flesh, I formerly preached the gospel to you* **14** *and the trial to you, in my flesh, you did not despise or disdain, but you received me as an angel of God, as Christ Jesus.* **15** *Where then is your blessing (that) you had? For I witness to you that if possible you would have gouged out your eyes and given them to me.* **16** *Have I now become your enemy by speaking the truth to you?*

In this autobiographical *pericopē*, Paul's tone is less defensive than in Gal. 1.11–2.21. The theme is still apostolic authority but Paul refers to a time when his Galatian audience was more receptive, before the sham Christian teachers' insidious infiltration. Paul recalls fondly his initial mission among the Galatian Gentiles. It is time to display a magnanimity and pastoral warmth denied by the total circumstances of this epistle, as shown in the abrupt opening where Paul is virtually incoherent with indignation. The syntax and the omission of courtesy betray both his anger and his love for his flock. The Galatians, Paul reminisces, had received him well despite his poor health and physical appearance. In the event, the Galatians, unlike some modern congregations, actually heeded their pastor! They preserved the epistle and thus gave us an exciting glimpse into the normative patterns of emergent Christian piety.

Paul does not here follow the standard Greek rhetorical procession of pathos, logos and ethos: elicit sympathy, make a case and commend appropriate action in its setting. Instead, he offers the argument before proceeding to appeal to pathos, later in 4.12–16. He ably reverses the Greek rhetorical order because he can build on an already established sympathy and knowledge of his arguments (see 1.11–4.11). The Quran does not use pathos as a technique of rhetoric although it is prevalent in pre-Islamic poetry, especially in the Islamic ode. Traces of pathos can be found only in a handful of Quranic verses (Q22.45; 36.30; 44.25–29; 82.6–8) but these are anomalies in a scripture that lays a firm veto on tragedy, a word that does not exist in classical (Quranic) Arabic. Revealingly, when the Arab rulers authorised the translation of the Greek canon, they omitted the tragedies.

12–13

Paul uses 'brothers' (as earlier in 3.15) when addressing Gentiles, to show affection, even though it was customary for Jews to restrict the peace (*shālom*) greeting to fellow Jews. The Quran orders believers to return greetings offered and to proffer peace to the inhabitants of any, presumably Muslim, household they enter (Q4.86, 24.27). Typically Muslims greet only other Muslims with the *salām*. Muhammad's traditions stipulate that Jewish and Christian subjects of Islamic rule must initiate the peace greeting – which may then be reciprocated.

The Apostle affectionately demands *imitatio Pauli* from his recalcitrant Galatian disciples as he does elsewhere from his other disciples (1 Cor. 7.7). In 1 Cor. 11.1, he even says: 'Imitate me just as I imitate Christ', thus linking the two acts of pious emulation.

Paul relishes the irony that he preached the gospel only owing to an illness, 'a weakness of the flesh' (lit. 'temptation in my flesh') that brought him to Galatia. (See Gal. 1.23–4 for a similar irony.) Paul's physical illness provided the occasion for the Galatians to obtain spiritual health by turning to the living God. Strangely, for a medical doctor, Luke does not record Paul's Galatian illness (cf. Acts 13–14) or any other illness suffered by the Apostle.

Jesus was a well-known healer during his earthly ministry. Why then did he not, as the risen Lord, heal Paul of his physical ailments and of his thorn in the flesh (2 Cor. 12.1–10)? Despite the powerful answer given by Paul in the Corinthian verses just mentioned, it remains easy enough for determined modern detractors to mock and vilify Paul just as it was for his Galatian critics. Fortunately, few Muslims know enough about Paul's life and illness to throw such a polemical hand grenade at him and his Christian admirers.

14

No matter how exalted Paul's moral character may be, his critics can still speculate cruelly that his physical appearance largely accounts for his antipathy to the flesh. (Muhammad was considered handsome but no portraits are permitted.) To what extent were Paul's fervent denunciations of the flesh a reflection of his own lack of physical health and good looks? Paul's denigration of the flesh, admittedly only occasional, is still surprising since Jews celebrated the body albeit within the moral limits imposed by the Torah. While Jews eschewed Hellenic hedonism and anarchic celebration of the senses, they entertained a healthy regard for the body and the pleasures of the flesh. They enjoyed these permitted pleasures with wholesome appetite and without guilt. By contrast with certain Christian reservations about marriage and sexuality, usually among ascetics and monks, almost all Jews saluted and sanctified marriage (along with progeny) as the first *mitzvah* of the Torah (based on Gen. 1.28). Paul criticised the flesh, seen as anarchic and unruly, rather than the body, a good creation of a good God.

15

Was the physical ailment defective vision? Could that be the thorn in the flesh (2 Cor. 12.1–10)? Medieval Christian polemicists claimed that Muhammad suffered from epileptic fits and seizures, a slander used to explain and debunk his experience of receiving revelation. Of course, unlike in the medieval era, we no longer stigmatise epilepsy but see it as an ordinary ailment in need of a cure.

16

Paul probably sensed that he had been too frank in his criticisms of the Galatians. He must have known that the counsellor or pastor who speaks the truth, even to a friend, is rarely if ever forgiven – especially if the insult is true in its substance. Sadly, truth-speaking, even with the best of intentions, is usually interpreted as an insult, even by those who actually elicit so-called constructive criticism from opponents only to reject it later. Paul wants to ask whether he has become the Galatians' ideological and public (rather than personal or private) enemy by preaching the truth to them. It is vital to bear in mind this distinction between public and private foe when we debate the demand to love and forgive one's enemies – and to do so repeatedly – in order to achieve the state of being perfect, in imitation of God's moral perfection. We discuss it in section XI below.

V 4.17–18

17 *They eagerly seek you but it is not good since they wish to exclude you (from us) so that you may seek them.* **18** *But it is good to be eagerly sought in a good way – and not only when I am present with you.*

17–18

Paul the sincere pastor contrasts with the insincere agitators who care about fair appearances in the flesh. Zeal can be wrongly motivated. It is only commendable if the purpose which it serves is good. Zeal can lead us astray; it should be in accordance with knowledge. Were the Galatians fickle, their zeal temporary? Was their enthusiasm for the true Gospel only transient? More generally, we should encourage *rational* religion which does not leave a believer's will undefended against irrational sentiment and misdirected enthusiasm. Rationality must direct, not destroy, zeal. If it succeeds in doing so, its power is irresistible. This is the secret of the Quran's message which remains as powerful and relevant today as when it was first revealed.

In v.17, Paul uses the adverb derived from *kalos* (a good thing). *Kalos*, used in the next verse, denotes what is also aesthetically pleasing. By contrast, *agathos* (Gal. 6.9, 10) refers to what is only morally and practically good. The Arabic *ḥusn* (beauty or goodness), like *kalos*, also contains this ambiguity. The word occurs in the Quran's comment addressed to Muhammad in regard to women's *ḥusn* being pleasing and tempting in the Prophet's eyes (33.52).[2]

VI 4.19–20

19 *My children, with whom I am again in the pains of childbirth, until Christ is formed in you.*
20 *And I wished to be present with you now and to change my voice (tone), for I am perplexed about you.*

19

Pastor Paul agonises over the birth and transformation of each believer into Christ's likeness. Christ-formation, as character formation, provides a criterion for recognising the genuinely Christian believer, leader and institution. A Christ-like pastor will, by the grace of Christ and in the power of the spirit, strive for perfection, 'as your Father in heaven is perfect'. The reader senses the anguished tenderness of Paul the pastor, the shepherd concerned and consumed for the sake of his flock's salvation. This rare tender moment is well captured by the use of 'my children' (*tekna mou*).

Paul's pastoral concern reaches an apex as he sees himself in labour pains. Note the discrepant image of maternity in a letter which carries many undertones of violence, a letter whose concerns seem male-centred, indeed phallocentric, as shown by the explicit word 'foreskin' (2.7). Paul is literally at pains to witness the emergence of Christ in his converts. Elsewhere, he laments and yet celebrates the *cosmic* labour pains that must precede the birth of a redeemed creation (see Rom. 8.22–23). It is a mystical notion that is hard to convey to orthodox Muslims and requires some imagination even in Christian readers.

In Greek philosophical nomenclature, the verb *morphō* and derived noun *morphē* describe essential or internal form, not external shape. The Pauline epistles supply an effective touchstone: if a denomination does not produce the image (*morphē*) of Christ in the inner lives of its adherents, it is not an authentically Christian group, no matter how loudly its allegedly Christian character is externally proclaimed, for public consumption. The lesson for Christians everywhere, especially in advanced capitalist nations, could hardly be louder or clearer. There exists an agreed standard for being a true Christian. One can say, accusingly, 'You are not a true Christian' in a way that one cannot properly or convincingly say of someone who fails to be a 'true' atheist. Perhaps, this is partly due to the relative infancy of the explicitly secular humanist tradition.

20

Paul shows his anxiety and confusion over his converts' future. He is as solicitous as Jesus, the good shepherd (John 10.1–15). Although Paul's heaviest burden was probably the proper and continuing care of his foundations, his anxiety (*merimna*; 2 Cor. 11.28) was not worldly and narrow but rather rooted in a pastoral blend of privilege and duty, grounded in that trust in God which enables true foresight and reliable planning within the mysterious provisions of providence. For the faithful, the anxiety that depresses and disables is always wrong. We should take thought for each other, though not for our own morrow (see 1 Cor. 12.25; Phil. 2.20).

The Quran portrays Muhammad as solicitous and caring to the point of being naïve and gullible (Q9.43, 61, 128). The context is a military campaign when rumour is rife and many seek exemption from duty. Those who follow the 'Gentile' prophet Muhammad, like those who follow the Jewish prophet Jesus, are characterised by conspicuous mercy and gentleness (Q48.29; 57.27) – though, in Muhammad's case, only among fellow believers. Disbelievers must be made to sense Muslim harshness – though only in the context of active hostilities which, sadly, was virtually throughout the Prophet's life in Mecca and Medina (see Q5.54; 9.123; 47.4). Muhammad's pastoral care is much in evidence in his biography and customary practice, less so in the Quran, a mysteriously detached scripture even though its verses deal with zeal and passion, divine mercy and unreserved human submission.

VII

Gal. 4.12 requires extended comment before we move onto the second pastoral interlude. Paul assumes that his Galatian neophytes recognised his high moral character, a basis for the call for imitation, though, strictly speaking, it reads like a call for mutual emulation. In any event, unlike pagan converts to Christianity, Paul did not come from a morally lax background. Indeed, elsewhere he is twice self-described as pure (*katharos*; Acts 18.6, 20.26), a man who is innocent of any crime (lit. blood). In the beatitudes, 'Blessed are the *katharoi* (pl.) in heart (*kardia*), for they shall see God' (Matt. 5.8).[3]

Paul asks Christians to imitate him by paying heed to his lifestyle. Jesus Christ provides the perfect pattern for imitation (*hupogrammos*; 1 Pet. 2.21). This claim is made by Peter on behalf of Christ; Muslims see God himself extolling Muhammad as his perfect servant who supplies the good and beautiful (*kalos*) exemplar (*uswatun ḥasanatun*; Q33.21).

The imitation of Christ has been an imitation of his noble conduct and moral virtues. Sadly, except among saints, Muslim imitation of Muhammad has been a rather mechanical copying of the Prophet's actions rather than of the just and merciful dispositions that motivated those actions. Hence, in my view, it often reduces to a rather arbitrary and pointlessly imitative piety. This is markedly so when, out of love for their noble Prophet, believers' imitation extended into the arena of aesthetic choices, in dress and physical appearance and even tastes in food and drink – a penchant for honey or an avoidance of garlic and of meat of birds foreign to the Hijaz. (Some yearned to die at the age at which he had died!) Unlike this radical imitation, almost identification, with Muhammad, the followers of Jesus and Paul never imitated their culinary and aesthetic tastes, but rather only their moral and spiritual values, their ascetic denial of the major appetites, attitudes which eventually motivated the formal monastic ideal of later ages.

The Quran praises Muhammad's character and extols his receipt of abundant divine grace (see Q4.113; 17.79; 68.4). Thus, there is a scriptural warrant for *imitatio Muhammadi* understood as an imitation of the prophetic consciousness of the world – a penitent awareness of one's place in the world, a place for seeking God's good pleasure in life's varied vicissitudes. This life is lived as an expression of the freedom of the creature's will but also within the limitations imposed by a supreme creator whose holy will is exhibited in a perfect law tempered by his grace.

We now comment on the second pastoral interlude (5.2–12) which secretes much moral substance from its doctrinal underpinnings.

VIII 5.2–6

2 *Behold I, Paul, say to you that if you were to be circumcised, Christ will profit you nothing.* **3**
And I testify again to every man who is being circumcised that he is a debtor obliged to keep the whole law. **4** *You have been discharged from Christ, you who are justified by law; you fell from grace.* **5** *For we, in spirit by faith, eagerly expect (to obtain) the hope of righteousness.* **6** *For in Christ Jesus, neither circumcision nor un-circumcision avails anything – but only faith operating through love.*

2–4

Freedom in the spirit is incompatible with the observance of the Law. Gentile believers must therefore reject the inherited Jewish ritual of circumcision. Two relevant Pauline polarities here are: circumcision versus Christ's offer of gracious freedom from ritual and, secondly, Jewish law versus the gospel of Christ's grace. Keeping a part of the Law obligates one to keep the whole Law. And doing so, whether voluntarily or under compulsion, amounts to submitting to a yoke of slavery (5.1). All who obey the Law, as part of their quest to secure salvation, are alienated from Christ.

Paul repeats in v.4 that seeking justification through works of legal righteousness amounts to loss of Christ's grace. The advocates of circumcision are, he reasons, merely troublemakers. They have no case. *Katērgēthēte* (discharged) is aorist passive while *exepesate* (fallen) is aorist active. In both these voices, and in the middle voice, the aorist tense can treat a future event (normally indicated by the Greek punctilinear future tense) as actually realised in the past or even present. 'You fell from grace' here refers to a future event: you *shall* fall from grace if you are seeking to be justified (*dikaiousthe*) in the *present*. *Dikaiousthe* is the passive indicative of the verb *dikaiō*. The Quran uses the prophetic past tense to refer to future events, especially those that shall occur in the next life. It uses this tense sometimes even for events in this life. Thus, Q23.1 refers to the future triumph of Islam as if it had already happened.

5

Paul declares that through the spirit, by faith, believers are waiting for the 'hope' (*elpis*) of righteousness (*dikaiosunē*). Here pastoral advice is offered as doctrine. The new community of Christ awaits the hope of righteousness where *elpis* does not mean hope in our sense of this word but rather the community's confident and earnest wish for eschatological consummation (see Rom. 8.18–25). Here *elpis* (vb. *elpizein*) amounts to a strong and eager expectation for which there are grounds – hence a justified confidence. It corresponds to one of the few fundamental Quranic virtues, namely, *ṣabr* (patience): temporary acquiescence in present travail and suffering in the assured hope of future vindication by God. The lack of the definite article with *elpida* (hope; acc.sg. fem.) may imply a qualitative usage, meaning the hoped-for kind of righteousness.

The Law, by contrast, inspires despair since no one can obey perfectly the perfectly good Law of God. Many Christians have become more deeply convinced of the truth of their faith as they have watched Muslims and Jews struggling to keep God's laws. The new dispensation of grace (2 Cor. 3.12–17) regards religion not as law and the fear of God but rather as innocent trust in God without the detailed algorithm of merit through works.

The hope (*elpis*) of the resurrection from the dead (1 Thess. 4.13; 1 Cor. 15.19) and the hope of God's glory (Rom. 5.2) are integral to faith. This is hope as total trust, not a mere wish. The hope of salvation means the confidence of safety in this world of peril and perfidy (2 Cor. 1.10). While no one can expect to be safe from life's unpredictable dangers, believers can aim to become independent of life's vicissitudes. Christians can feel safe despite this world's trials. Moreover, unlike Muslims, Christians can feel secure, through the grace of God in Christ, against incurring God's wrath and just judgement. Muslims dismiss this attitude as a presumptuous denial of the awe in which human beings should stand as they contemplate God's mysterious majesty and judgement. Of these two temperamentally (attitudinally) opposed views of God, each experienced by billions, only one can be based on an objectively (factually) true view of his nature and will.

Paul elevates *elpis* to one of the three pillars of the faith, along with faith and love (1 Cor. 13.13). A Paulinist further proclaims that such hope is the monopoly and prerogative of Christ's faithful ones (Eph. 2.12).

6

Both circumcision and un-circumcision are rendered irrelevant in the resurrected Christ who effortlessly enables transcendence of Jewish ritual identity markers. This verse fortifies Paul's declaration at Gal. 3.28 about Christ's radical unification of believers. Here *energeia* is divine power – effective power in action. In the New Testament, it refers only to supernatural force, usually divine but sometimes demonic.

The Christ-event makes the ritual *necessity* of the Law into merely *contingent* practice. One can and should still obey the good law – only now knowing that its intent and spirit rather than its letter and detail are binding. What matters is faith (*pistis*) working (*energoumenē*) through and energised by love (agape). This total arrangement, however, militates against the obligation to fulfil legal duty and, in practice, virtually always leads to a law-free if not 'lawless' or anarchic lifestyle, independent of one's theoretical attachment to the Law. This is to be expected since a fundamental motivation for obeying the Law has been removed. However, in the case of the best Christians, and only in their case, it may lead instead to a greater law-keeping – even without a conscious decision to obey the Law. Such Christian piety, marked by coincidental but scrupulous regard for divine legal restrictions, is rare.

'Faith operating in love' suggests that the only faith which justifies is the faith which expresses itself in good deeds. That alone is true faith – to use a persuasive definition more worthy of the preacher than the philosopher! Whether in intention or only in effect, we cheerfully register that this verse brings Paul's theoretical stance close to contemporaneous Judaism (see James 2.14–26) and therefore to Islam. For details, see the final section of this chapter.

IX 5.7–10

7 *You were running well. Who hindered you from being persuaded by truth?* **8** *The persuasion did not come from the one calling you.* **9** *A little leaven leavens the whole lump (of dough).* **10** *I trust in the Lord regarding you that you will not think otherwise. But the one who is troubling you shall bear the judgement, whoever he may be.*

7

A regression to law-observant Judaism, for the sake of securing salvation, is no better than a return to paganism and a reliance on fake powers. Paul was troubled by the spiritual subversion, indeed sedition, created by those who preached a gospel of law-observant grace. Unfairly, Paul saw the Galatians' intention to return to Jewish law-observance as essentially no different from a return to their pagan past since both positions involved rituals and ceremonies.

8

Paul's confidence (I trust, *pepoitha*, v. 10) in the Lord is contrasted with the Judaisers' mere *peismonē* (a yielding to persuasion, hence assent, in v. 8). The verbal root is the same (*peithō*). For Paul, the other missionaries were propagandists. This is the negative side of religious enthusiasm: it leads enthusiasts to dismiss all doubt, all diversity and dissension as being from the Devil.

9

The proverbial 'A little leaven' refers to the insidious influence of the agitators. In Paul, the yeast symbolises the permeating effect of bad company (1 Cor. 5.1–8) which must be quarantined and cauterised. Part of this sentiment is found in traditional English adages such as 'A man is known by the company he keeps' and 'One bad apple spoils the whole barrel.'

Paul's grace-only perspective leads him to reject the teaching that trust in Jesus must still be combined with observance of the Jewish law. Paul sees this view as contaminating purity of belief and thus as destructive of the whole congregation. The Judaisers' influence was insidious – apparently negligible but potentially devastating. Hence, we are told to remove the offending leaven. In Matthew (13.33), in a parable told by Jesus, the yeast stands for good influence. A small amount of fermented dough exercises a salutary effect on the whole loaf of bread, spreading rapidly but secretly.

There are no references to yeast in any Quranic parable or Quran-derived Arabic proverb. The Quran often condemns the Arab and Jewish hypocrites whose influence, like that of the Devil, was considered insidious and devious (Q2.14; 9.47). The Medinan hypocrites and agitators were few but were keen to spread slander and obscenity (Q.24.11, 19). God's influence, like that of his prophetic representatives, is direct and sincere. The Quran's teachings, like those of the Prophet, were never esoteric – unlike those of some later Islamic heresies.

10

Paul condemns the agitator (singular) responsible for the near defection of the Galatians. He asserts that God does not judge by worldly standing. Could this be another veiled attack on the Jerusalem pillars? Whoever the target may be, Paul indirectly continues his polemic. His earlier sarcastic and polemical tone has now changed into a solemn and pleading one. Paul hints that the Judaisers and the pillars are in the same boat: even if the Judaisers can claim the support of the pillars, so what? Everyone, without exception, is subject to God's judgement. 'He who troubles you' could mean the troublemaker, in several individual cases or the class of agitators as a whole or a single known individual. Paul warns the Galatians that God will judge whoever perverts the gospel: rank, status and reputation cannot protect anyone. How Islamic a sentiment!

In its force and clarity of verdict, Paul sounds like the author of the Quran when he solemnly warns disbelievers that no one and no amount of wealth can shield them against God's judgement (Q5.36). Paul might here be warning the Jerusalem pillars: notwithstanding your reputation for piety and legal righteousness, you too might stand condemned, should you dare to pervert the pure Gospel of Christ's grace. Like his master Jesus, Paul was never afraid of giving offence.

'Shall bear his judgement' is expressed literally as 'shall carry as a burden (*bastasei*) his judgement'. This verb is used three times (6.2, 5, 17), the last referring to the weight of the stigmata. Bearing the burden of divine judgement is not a Quranic image but the Islamic scripture occasionally uses the word for an ordinary physical burden (*thiql*; pl. *athqāl*; 16.7) to convey the burden of sins incurred (*khaṭ'a*; pl. *khaṭāyā*; 29.12–13). The word *wizr* denotes any kind of burden, especially the burden of moral effort, including that of the prophetic office (Q94.2).

Instead God's irreversible judgement is symbolised by the ledgers or transcripts of his creatures' good and evil deeds, presented by angels, as an open book for each sinner, to read and to be self-convicted on the Day of Judgement (Q17.14). The Quran has the image of the sinner, raised to life on that fateful day and ordered to carry the burden of the injustice (*ẓulm*) he had committed to himself and others (Q20.110). How backbreaking will be the burdens of some modern politicians!

Paul seems confident that the church as a whole will not follow the false teaching. Compare Muhammad's confident remark that 'My community will never agree on an error.'[4]

Once again Paul displays his zeal but also intolerance of enemies, especially those who oppose him in matters of principle as opposed to those who merely hurt him personally. Similarly, Muhammad regularly forgives his personal enemies but always brought to justice his ideological enemies. Those who attacked the Quran, the Word of God, were rarely pardoned unless they repented before being overwhelmed by Muslims. As the prophetic representative of divine justice, Muhammad was the human agent who proved that God, despite being merciful, was able to requite evil (*'azīzun dhū intiqām*; Q3.4).

X 5.11–12

11 *But I, brothers, if I still proclaim circumcision, why am I still being persecuted? Then the offence of the cross has been annulled.* **12** *I wish that those who are troubling you would even mutilate themselves.*

11

In this intensely polemical interlude, Paul reminds the agitators of the scandal of the cross, a scandal they too should embrace without fear of the persecution that is bound to follow.

While Paul's courage hardly needs comment or advertisement, his reasoning is unduly compressed here. He preached Christ crucified, not Christ circumcised. He would surely be the last person to preach circumcision! Let me explain.

For Paul, neither circumcision nor 'un-circumcision' mattered. This means that he was ready to circumcise Timothy (Acts 16.3) as a concession to ancestral custom but unwilling to circumcise anyone if that was presented as a requirement of Christian salvation. Titus' case (Gal. 2.3) is obscure. Certainly, Paul's opponents would have noted that he was himself circumcised, as he later boasts to the Philippians (Phil. 3.5). As a zealous Pharisee, he would have preached circumcision as a prerequisite of membership of God's household. He rejects the suggestion, however, that he still preaches this view. Paul argues that the fact that he was still being persecuted was because he did not preach the need for a ritual act such as circumcision. If he chose to endorse circumcision, the Jews would approve of him. He was being persecuted, in effect, for the *anti-Judaic pro-Christ* component in his preaching, regardless of his views on the validity of the Law in general or its application in particular cases.

Paul thought that had he endorsed circumcision, the core ritual requirement of Judaism, the rest of his essential teaching about the cross would have been acceptable but, of course, he preached instead that the Law and the cross were rooted in incompatible aspirations. Only thus could he do justice, he reasoned, to the scandal of the cross. And to endorse the autonomy and exclusivity of the cross in this way would certainly, as Jesus warned his disciples, invite persecution from a corrupt world.

Both baptism and circumcision are rituals. Paul assumes the superiority of baptism, admittedly an easier ritual to perform. Baptism was a Jewish conversion ritual appropriated by the new Jesus movement. Catholics see baptism as essential to salvation even though, like the emphasis on the Gentile mission, it was instituted only by the post-resurrection Jesus. The mode of baptism – immersion, pouring or sprinkling – has been, in ages of enthusiasm, a point of denominational difference. Such niceties puzzle even sympathetic Muslim observers of Christianity.

The Quran mentions neither circumcision nor baptism – the rites of initiation in Islam and Christianity respectively. We find a single and contextually isolated reference to Muslims as being distinguished from the People of the Book through 'the baptism (lit. dyeing or colouring) of God' (*ṣibghat allahi*; Q2.138). Despite inspiring much commentary, this claim remains too enigmatic to be serviceable.

Skandalon means an offence or stumbling block. One could translate it into Arabic as *fitna*, meaning trial, sedition, temptation or seduction. The word has a vast range of meanings including anything that hinders one from walking in the path of Allah. The Quran cites wives and children as a *fitna* if family obligations hinder one from doing one's duty, especially *jihād*, in God's cause (Q64.15; see also 60.3; 63.9; 64.14). Paul expresses similar reservations about marriage and its distracting duties (1 Cor. 7.32–35) just as Jesus questioned the primacy of the family in a Jewish culture that had come to place family first (Matt. 12.46–50). In modern Christian Arabic usage, for example in the Lord's Prayer, temptation is rendered by *tajarba* (lit. experiment or test) rather than *fitna*, a Quranic word endowed, in many Muslim lands, with centuries of accumulating cultural connotations.[5]

Elsewhere, Paul celebrates the scandal of the cross (1 Cor. 1.18–25) – the crucified Christ bears the curse (Gal. 3.13). Paul knows that this must appear offensive to the limited understanding of humans. For Muslims, it is an offence to God, not only to sinful human beings with limited understanding. The folly of God is, Paul preaches, superior to the wisdom of man. But the folly of God is only a way of speaking of the wisdom of God which appears as folly only to foolish humans. Rhetoric apart, there can be no such thing as the folly of God.

12

Paul wishes that the agitators would self-mutilate or emasculate themselves. If it has no spiritual dimension, then circumcision is partial self-mutilation. Why not go all the way? Having the male organ removed or having one's testicles crushed was one ground for excommunication from the congregation of Israel, God's people (Deut. 23.1).

The pagan priests of the cult of the goddess Cybele, the Great Mother, emasculated themselves as a sign of zeal, while in a state of religious frenzy. The cult was centred in Galatia. This Greco-Roman cult is partly analogous to that of the Hindu goddess Kali, also called Mother (*Kali amma*), who demanded brutality though not self-mutilation.

We know on the authority of Aisha that some Muslim ascetics had approached Muhammad to seek permission to castrate themselves. He advised them that while he feared God more than they did, he also lived a normal life: he slept and he woke up, ate and also fasted and had sexual relationships but also abstained. While castration is forbidden in prophetic traditions and only vaguely alluded to in the Quran (see Q24.31 for a possible reference to eunuchs), it was practised by some men who served as attendants in the sultan's harem, especially in Ottoman times. It is an unscriptural innovation. Nor is it certified by the Prophet's normative practice. The Quran does not regard ascetic self-restraint as a reprehensible practice. It criticises celibate monasticism, however, as an ultimately misguided though well-intentioned Christian innovation (Q57.27).[6]

XI

We turn to themes with a marked communal, pastoral or ecclesial dimension. If the Judaisers were watchdogs for the Mosaic law, zealous for the Lord's administration, then Paul was the vigilant watchdog for the faith grounded in the liberty afforded by the new Gospel of Christ. Freedom from the ritual dietary regulations would enable fellowship with Gentiles since strict adherence to such rules effortlessly created an apartheid based on culinary considerations. The Gospel of Christ can be interpreted to imply that Jewish rules and regulations were, for the most part at least, cultural scruples, essentially irrational taboos which belonged to the infancy of the Jewish people. Admittedly, Paul did not see the minutiae of Jewish law as being intrinsically negative. Indeed, he himself respected and probably relished the laws while rejecting their application to Gentile believers. His stance has ensured that, in practice, whatever Paul's own original – and largely undiscoverable – intentions, the Jewish laws would in time come to be seen as superfluous. The course of Christian history proves this beyond a shadow of doubt. If one says loudly and proudly that the Law is irrelevant – if only to the attainment of salvation – it is only to be expected that people shall in time reject the Law altogether.

In the heat of the confrontation, Paul was uncharitable. To most readers, Christian or otherwise, it is evident that the Judaisers genuinely wanted to conform to God's will as revealed in the Torah. They thought, notwithstanding Paul, that submission to God's will required that we subject everyone alike to the Torah's provisions, making both the Jew and the Gentile (convert) stand within the holy law's jurisdiction. If we are charitable, we must admit that while the Judaisers might have chosen the wrong way of pleasing God, their intention to please him was commendable. Both parties accepted, in principle, the authority of the Law. Paul's use of 'It is written' is a standard appeal to the authority of Jewish scripture. The two parties differed in their view of the application of the Law – and did so, as we know from Paul's defensive stance, owing to some significant difference regarding the intention behind the Law.

Paul here shows no love for his enemies, perceived to be not his personal enemies but rather enemies of the cross. The opponents of Paul's message are dismissed as false brothers (Gal. 2.4) although they are still brothers. They stand under a curse (Gal. 1.9). Paul is kinder to those who are merely led astray from his message: they are bewitched (Gal. 3.1). Ironically, and in reverse, as it were, Muhammad's pagan opponents thought that his followers, the monotheists, were bewitched, victims of a magician posing as a prophet.

Paul's attitude towards his ideological enemies resembles Muhammad's attitude towards ideological as opposed to personal foes. Muslims would argue that it is not psychologically possible to love one's enemies qua enemies. But one can and should at least be just towards one's *personal* enemies, a Quranic imperative. Indeed, the Quran goes further in teaching that to forego one's rights, such as some rights in a marital context or in matters of retaliation, is closer to piety and more charitable (Q2.237; 4.92). It is not clear, however, how one can or even should, in any sense, love *ideological* enemies – enemies of God and thus of the human race. Even Jesus did not love enemies of his cause and those who were destined to betray him (see Matt. 18.6; 26.24–25). Christians would add here that, whether or not he loved this category of radical enemy, Jesus did die for such enemies of his cause. This last claim is a matter of faith and not subject to objective verification. To Christians, Muslims grant the right to their Christian conscience. We return to this matter in Chapter 6 (sections VIII and XII) where we debate the proper scope of agape. Here we note only that true believers must always distinguish personal from ideological enemies.

The Quran enjoins justice and proportional retaliation while encouraging unilateral forgiveness and forbearance. Repaying evil with good is a valid translation of Q13.22 although the verse literally reads 'those who prevent evil with good'. Matt 5.41 preaches that we should not resent unjust treatment at the hands of others. In their heyday, Muslims rejected this attitude but today, as a defeated civilisation, many Muslim apologists accept this attitude even though they find no Quranic or prophetic support for it. Some pacifist Palestinian Muslims quote the incident of the two sons of Adam and note that the innocent victim is the true Muslim (Q5.27–31). A weakly attested prophetic tradition counsels: 'Be like the better son of Adam.' This can at best mean that there are occasions when one is unjustly victimised and can do little about it. It cannot be a general principle of conduct since it conflicts with much more prominent emphases in the Quran, such as the imperative: 'Do not do wrong and do not be wronged' (Q2.279). If one is slapped on the cheek, at the very least one should have the courage and the power to challenge the aggressor by asking him or her why he or she took that liberty. Humility is a virtue but it cannot mean that one simply accepts being humiliated by unjust aggressors. This is the Islamic critique of the Christian imperative. Secular common sense also concurs with the Islamic verdict.

Again, some Christian commentators on the Quran commend Joseph's forgiveness of his brothers who had behaved like enemies. They note how the Quranic Joseph moved from being a victim to being a victor – without desiring vengeance. He wanted only vindication and just exoneration from false blame. But this is only possible because Joseph's enemies were personal, not ideological foes of his cause. Joseph was a righteous man who associated himself with an ungodly government, working humbly from within for the common good, without trying to eventually overthrow the polity. Joseph was, unlike Muhammad, not stirring opposition from powerful political enemies of his cause. Few Christian commentators note that Muhammad quoted Joseph's words when he forgave his pagan enemies after the conquest of Mecca, history's least bloody revolution. But these enemies had now capitulated to the triumphant Islamic cause and did not continue their past ideological hostility to the new faith. They were forgiven their past ideological enmity because they ceased to be ideological enemies in the present. As for personal injury, Muhammad was at all times no less forgiving than Joseph, Jesus or Paul – and far less vindictive in such matters than some biblical characters such as David (see 1 Kings 2.5–9).[7]

I want to touch on the broader question of attitudes and dispositions that arise out of Paul's own attitude towards his enemies. Paul has all the negative traits of the saint, qualities often considered typical of seminal Semites such as Abraham, Moses, Saul, Jesus and Muhammad. These qualities have some echoes in the modern secular notion of the genius, admired by many Westerners but dismissed as imbalanced by Muslim societies in which no one, no matter how artistically eminent, is considered exempt from Islamic moral assessment and religious duties.

In hagiography, the man (or less often woman) who is monomaniacal, zealous, self-absorbed and intolerant of diversity of opinion may be made to appear as admirable nonetheless. In the secular psychobiography of religious genius, however, he is seen as a flawed human type. For if a man, wearing only a sheet and sandals, claims to hear directly from God, it is hard to interest him in any human assessment, let alone criticism, of his views and policies. All external criticism is from the Devil; only self-criticism, if one ever produces it, is ever valid. Notwithstanding his pastoral warmth and his diplomacy on behalf of Christ, as his ambassador, Paul is certainly dismissive of his opponents' views.

In itself, this attitude of instinctive intolerance towards what is alien does not distinguish Paul from other seminal Semites, including Muhammad. But Pauline Christianity has also been continuously the nursery of the European character for at least a thousand years. And that has had consequences for the entire human race. I see Paul as the essential European. He has nothing to learn from anyone else. He is even dismissive of the so-called pillar apostles who to him merely *seem* important.

This dismissive attitude has been inherited and is found notably, although not only, in Latin Christianity as it faced a powerful Islamic presence on its borders. John of Damascus and Aquinas were the two earliest examples of this attitude which, courtesy of European colonialism, later became prevalent and persists largely unaltered to this day.[8]

XII

Paul's opponents were not pagans but rather Jewish Christians, prejudicially labelled 'Judaisers', whose prima facie case could easily be strongly attested by scripture. Quite uncharitably, Paul dismisses them as Jew-pleasers who wished to avoid persecution for the sake of the cross (see Gal. 4.17, 6.12–13). They must have argued, deducing from the claims and the tenor of Galatians 3–5, that Paul's version of the Gospel was an attenuated one designed to placate and please the Gentile converts. After all, Paul did not require circumcision, recognised by all Jews to be the sign given to Abraham to denote his special relationship to God and thus qualifying as a mark of God's people.

The requirement of circumcision for Abraham was plainly stated in the Torah; it did not require allegorical interpretation. Abraham was commanded to be circumcised even though he was almost a hundred years old (Gen. 17.1, 11). Luke tells us that Jesus was circumcised on the eighth day (Luke 2.21; see Gen. 17.12). So was Paul, in his own words (Phil. 3.5). Paul would need much skill to argue against the literal meaning of scripture, to say nothing of the normative Jewish practice of which he was aware and indeed participated in. Jesus had never proposed the abolition of the Torah (Matt. 5.17–19). Thus, circumcision remained a basic requirement for any Gentile who wished to become one of God's people.

The Torah was unanimously exalted as ritual guidance for Jews and for God-fearing persons who chose to associate with Judaism. This conviction was shared by all Jews, no matter where they were located on the Jewish sectarian continuum in Jesus' and Paul's day. A Jew might say of the Torah, echoing the Quran's opening comment about its own status, 'This is the scroll, without doubt, guidance for those who fear the Lord' (cf. Q2.2). Judaism minus the Law of Moses is as unthinkable as Islam minus the *Sharī'a* based on Muhammad's career as judge in Medina. If a person self-identifies as a Muslim but openly rejects the applicability of the *Sharī'a*, whether to themselves or to other believers or both, he or she is automatically considered an apostate. However, being observant is not a condition of being a Muslim, even a good Muslim. One can be a Muslim merely by accident of birth and culture – and see oneself as a sinful and lapsed believer but a believer nonetheless.

Paul could not claim that Jesus, a Jew, had denied the necessity of circumcision. Nor could Paul claim that Jesus, during his earthly ministry, had clearly preached the gospel of free grace as understood by Paul. After all, the Christ was no Christian – though he was, Muslims would add, a '*muslim*'. Nietzsche quipped that 'there has only been one Christian and he died on the cross.' This witticism has more style than theological substance.[9]

The Judaisers, then, could truthfully claim that they were merely rejecting Paul's unauthorised interpretation of Jesus' teaching. Paul could not quote his Lord's words to refute the Judaisers' claim. It is not self-evident that the Apostle to the Gentiles is offering the true reading of his Lord's implied teaching on law and grace, on circumcision and the inclusion of the Gentile nations.

XIII

In a critical interfaith commentary, judgements about the *Jewish* element in Christian origins affect the *Islamic* assessment of Pauline Christianity. Any Semitisation or Judaisation of Jesus and Paul, of Peter or of the early Christian movement, may be conducive to an Islamisation of these men and realities too. I shall explain.

Central to our concerns is the identity of the 'agitators'. There is no scholarly consensus about the identity of this group, some commentators suggesting there were two groups of agitators. Were the agitators nationalistic Jews, perhaps a splinter group of teachers of the Law, men who had zealot sympathies? These might have rejected Roman power just as Jews of the Maccabean period had rejected assimilation into Hellenic culture. Were the agitators attempting to preach a gospel without Christ, hence Paul's declaration of anathema? Despite being angry, Paul never curses his Christian opponents in Corinth. Does cursing the Galatian agitators indicate Paul's greater closeness towards these men and thus greater bitterness towards them? Or the opposite – they were less close to him and deserved the curses? Were the Galatian agitators insisting on an eternally valid Torah as the opposite of the Christ and were therefore literally 'anti-Christs'?

The Judaisers were certainly instigators. In the Quran, there were similarly unnamed opponents of Muhammad who were infiltrating the newborn Medinan Muslim group. These were Arab hypocrites with some secret support from Jewish tribes (Q8.60) opposed to a Gentile 'prophet' determined to succeed. The infant Muslim community in Medina feared the political threat of agitators in that city. In one place, they are called alarmists or agitators (*murjifūna*; Q33.60). The Galatian agitators were similarly trying to undermine Paul's leadership of that congregation. Although there are no marked political overtones in Galatians, it is reasonable to speculate that ecclesiastical unity, as a source of solidarity and power, was at stake.

In the end, the agitators in Galatia bear little resemblance to the hypocrites in Medina. For the agitators were, notwithstanding what Paul says against them, sincere in their intentions. It is not even clear that they were mistaken. The Medinan hypocrites were, by contrast, disaffected Arabs, merely pretending to be Muslims. They looked for Jewish and pagan (Arab) support against Muhammad who was seen by both these groups as the Meccan upstart who had quickly risen from being a mere refugee to become the Prince of Medina.

In Philippians (3.2), Paul calls his opponents dogs, animals considered unclean by Jews and Muslims. He might be referring to the agitators first encountered in Antioch and Galatia. Paul is so indignant here that he does not even use the correct word for circumcision (*peritomē*; Phil. 3.3) but instead employs the pejorative *katatomē* (mutilation), a word used nowhere else in the New Testament. One commentator calls this usage a 'studiously contemptuous paronomasia' to indicate that even though circumcision had been abrogated in Christ, it remained in its origins an intentionally spiritual act.[10] Thus, *peritomē* was too good a word to be used of what the agitators were proposing – namely, an act suitable only in the flesh and therefore, in Paul's view, spiritually false and degrading.

Perhaps we should not call Paul's opponents 'Judaisers' or even agitators. Such descriptions predispose us towards a negative reading of their intentions. As a modern proverb has it: 'Give a dog a bad name and you might as well hang him.' We should try to retrieve the situation and reconstruct it without assuming that Paul's attitude towards his opponents is normative or even correct. Did he himself have an inaccurate estimate of his opponents? Paul does not explicitly accuse the Judaisers of being hypocrites or 'wolves in sheep's clothing' but that is his intended accusation. Being unnamed opponents of Paul's Gospel, the Judaisers should, in more neutral language, be called dissenters. But that is of course only for scholarly and academic scrutiny. It is Paul's Gospel which triumphed in Galatia, the Roman Empire and across the world.

Paul in effect claims that the agitators had hijacked the only true Gospel. It is hard to decide here since we know of the agitators, all unnamed, only through Paul's bitter invective. In our day, we hear that some group of extremist Muslims have hijacked Islam. This may sometimes be true – for instance in the case of Islamic groups who engage in anarchic violence and psychopathic cruelty. However, all too often, this claim about the alleged abuse of authentic Islam is made by so-called liberal or moderate Muslims who make no secret of their own indifference to and contempt for Islamic ritual requirements such as daily canonical prayer and the arduous fast and intensified worship of *Ramaḍān*. Many Westerners, especially in academic circles, the media and cultural settings promoting the liberal arts, befriend these kinds of Muslims who are rejected by their own community, their careers seen, rightly in my view, as a triumph of image management, motivated chiefly by the desire to please and flatter white Westerners. It is revealing that few Christians or non-Christians claim that true Christianity has been hijacked by, say, some group of African or American evangelicals – a claim with far more substance.

XIV

Paul does not name his opponents in Galatia, a point of rare but incidental similarity with the Quran. A book destined for universal application should avoid naming names. The Quran answers, via Muhammad, the objections of the unnamed pagans and of the People of the Book. But it does not use the occasion to offer a thematic detour. The Quran answers with a simple *fatwā*, a legal opinion that can amount to a verdict, in this case divinely authorised and therefore binding. This legal permission – to act in a prudent way – corresponds to the Roman *responsa prudentium* rather than the more authoritative papal statement issued ex cathedra.

In the Quran we read of inquiries made of Muhammad: 'They ask you for a *fatwā*' (Q4.176; 12.41) or 'They ask you' (*yasalūnaka*; Q2.189, 215, 217, 219, 222;

10.53; 18.83). The questions are posed in the Medinan and very late Meccan revelations and cover an astonishing range of practical concerns – from the birth of new moons to menstruation cycles, from waging war in the months of peace to the details of inheritance rules. Jews and pagans challenged Muhammad, the former asking for esoteric information, the latter mocking him about his predictions of imminent doom. Believers zealously referred to him every conceivable anxiety no matter how private, confident of his personal sagacity and his access to divine wisdom.

It would be instructive to compile a set of modern questions from Muslim worshippers who had heard and reacted to a typical sermon-address given on a Friday afternoon in a modern Western capital. This would tell us much about how a Quran revealed today would react to the Westernised Muslims' attachment to empty ritual, to Muslim men and women's dilemmas in a secular culture of cynical hedonism and laxity in morals, and to the youth's condition of confusion amid the perplexity of ideological diversity.

The elder Seneca began his *controversiae* with a description of the crisis causing the controversy. In the case of a law-centred faith such as Islam, the occasions of revelation (*asbāb al-nuzūl*) available more abundantly for Medinan than for Meccan verses, matter materially. The Quran decouples narrative from commandment except on rare occasions. Food laws are sometimes given in the context of the Devil's enmity to humanity, his wish to spread corruption and to encourage people to break God's laws. 'Do not follow the foot-steps of Satan' is often part of a more positive injunction to submit unreservedly and wholly to God (Q2.208).

Paul's style is earthier as he engages locally while dealing with themes of universal significance. He reacted to external events and crises, as his discussion of circumcision in first century Galatian churches illustrates. He answered urgent pastoral questions posed – by writing an epistle that was a detour that deepened and universalised an originally parochial and pragmatic concern.

As an original thinker, however, Paul did not always need to wait for an external stimulus. Think of his letter to the Romans, written in relative detachment, almost as if he were in the serenity of a cloistered library. If Paul was a theologian, however, he was no armchair or, as at elite universities, ivory tower or bathtub theologian. His doctrinal arguments are never solely practical, pragmatic and pastoral, let alone merely academic. He is an existentialist: Søren Kierkegaard would have admired Paul because he *became* a Christian, through sheer choice and will, rather than merely *being* a Christian. Moreover, both thinkers admired paradox. Typical Pauline paradox is aimed at inspiring newer human attitudes that would be closer to what is God's will for us. Perceived heresy can be closer to truth than orthodoxy.

The Quran contains no genuine paradoxes – although verses such as 'You may love a thing which is bad for you and hate a thing that is good for you' or 'He brings the living out of the dead and the dead out of the living' can be made to appear superficially paradoxical. Again, 'He brings believers out of the darkness into the light' seems paradoxical – for how can believers ever be in the darkness? The point is only that, as former pagans, believers rejected God and thus lived in darkness. We humans need paradox when we do not have the absolute, clear and literal truth.

We therefore need several ways to express an unclear truth that we cannot grasp. The Quran cannot contain any real paradoxes since God knows the absolute and final truth.

Finally, and at the broadest level, I find Paul to be a wise mentor. I believe that he would advise Muslims to imitate the prophetic Muhammadan consciousness of the world rather than a robotic imitation of his actions. Muslims should seek to cultivate the same dispositions of character rather than merely copy their Prophet's actions motivated by his impeccable performance of the works required by God's law. The potential benefit of Paul's advice to Muslims is a theme for future research.

XV

Before I scrutinise a single verse that summarises the epistle thus far, I explore the ritual of circumcision, seen as sufficiently central to Jewish identity for Jews to be called simply 'the circumcision'. Jewish law permitted circumcision even on the Sabbath so that the Law of Moses was honoured (John 7.22–24). In the pastorals (Titus 1.10), for example, 'the circumcision group talks nonsense' refers to Jewish calumny against the new Jesus movement.

The twin practical problems of eating food offered to idols (1 Cor. 8; Rom. 14) and the circumcision of converts to Christianity have lapsed since the first century and now retain purely academic interest. The rite of circumcision remains integral to Muslim self-identity. In an important Islamic language such as Urdu, spoken by millions of Muslims, the active participle of the verb 'to become a Muslim' (*musalmān hona*) is related to the passive participle of the verb 'to undergo circumcision' (*musalmāni baytana*). The Arabic noun *khitān* (circumcision) bears no relationship to the act of becoming a Muslim which instead requires the dual verbal witness (*shahādatān*) to God's unity and to Muhammad's apostleship. The Urdu word emphasises a rite, a conduct performed on behalf of the newborn child. All newborns, male and female, immediately on birth, hear the call to prayer announced in their right ears, usually by the father. The Prophet's tradition, like the Jewish ritual of *berith milā* (covenant of circumcision), requires circumcision on the eighth day after the male child's birth. Some Muslims circumcise their sons at an older age but still within infancy. Legal opinions about the requirement of circumcision for adult male converts vary.

In Jewish thought, the foreskin was a symbolic offering to God, presumably to recognise the power of sex to perpetuate the human heritage. From the Quran's inaugural revelation onwards (Q96.1–5), we note sustained interest in the miracle of human birth. There are no explicit or clear references to circumcision or the penis. We find reverent allusions to ejaculation and sperm in the context of the natural growth of the farmer's seed, the revival of the dead earth and the analogous possibility of human resurrection (Q35.9; 56.58–63). Restrained comments on the sexual act are found, one verse hinting that believers may encounter God during the sexual act (Q2.223). The Quran contains many euphemistically expressed references to male and female nudity in the Garden, to the female duty to ensure modesty and concealment of female private parts, countless allusions and verdicts on sex-related and gender-related themes such as marriage, divorce, virgin divorcees, menstruation and so on. No one can, however, find any reference to clitoridectomy, the female genital mutilation that is no doubt harmful to the integrity of the female body. This crude practice increasingly incenses many female Muslim activists, along with most Western feminists, but also countless Islamophobes and other racists, including white supremacists, keen to exploit any opportunity to defame all Muslims and their whole religion. It is a coalition of enraged parties.

Unlike the Torah (Gen. 17.10–12), the Quran never orders the circumcision of male infant Muslims even though it is a universal practice among Muhammad's followers. Many, perhaps most, pre-Islamic Arabs, practised circumcision. The Quran is silent on the subject of circumcision, including both Muhammad's and Abraham's circumcision, but its silence could mean that the practice was so prevalent and widely approved that the Quran acquiesced in it and thus there was neither need nor occasion for comment. Islamic tradition holds that Muhammad was born already circumcised (*wūlida makhtūnan*), presumably by angels.

There could however be an allusion to the topic of circumcision in the cryptic saying attributed to the Jews: 'Our hearts are uncircumcised' (*ghulf*; lit. encased; Q2.88). This has overtones of the notion of a spiritual un-circumcision (cf. Phil. 5.6). The Quran curses those who uttered that saying, a situation that might remind Jews and Christians of the way that God forbids the utterance of one offensive proverb in Israel (Jer. 31.29–30; Ezek. 18.2–4).

The rite of circumcision was perhaps associated traditionally with Abraham and thus regarded as a religious rite, just as the pilgrimage to Mecca was seen as being instituted and first announced by the Hebrew patriarch. If so, the practice of circumcision would have been carried over wholesale into Islam. Unlike Islam's original prayerful orientation (*qibla*) towards Jerusalem, circumcision had no political significance – and would therefore have been unaffected by the formal break with Judaism symbolised in the change of the *qibla* towards the Meccan shrine, soon after the migration to Medina.

Islamic law, like the halakhah, requires circumcision for religious rather than hygienic or aesthetic reasons.[11] Circumcision was, especially during the Maccabbean period, a custom symbolically supportive of ethnic Israelite imperialism. It was a Jewish custom that was useful for cultural colonisation or, more politely, conversion, of non-Jews. For Muslims, circumcision has no Arab cultural implications, being a wholly religious custom. A tradition of the Prophet warns that the prayer of an uncircumcised man is automatically invalid. Circumcision is a ritual requirement for a Muslim male to be considered a part of the Islamic community. It is not associated with marriage or puberty and majority – thus not a Muslim equivalent of bar mitzvah.

No Islamic rationale for circumcision is offered in the law codes. Muslim apologists also rarely offer any rationale for circumcision, whether for infants or adults (in the case of converts). It is an order given only by the Prophet and recorded in his traditions but not found in the Quran. Since devout believers assign the same authority to Muhammad's verified orders as to direct divine commandments, they would need no further – independent or secular – reason to obey any prophetic commandment. It remains unclear why Muslims saw circumcision as a religious rather than hygienic mandate, the latter status being cited, for example, for the order to consume only ritually slaughtered meat. Circumcision does not qualify as a morally relevant requirement but rather only as a ritual requirement. That makes it difficult to defend it against modern radical secular challenge.[12]

Until recent times, Muslims have rarely felt the need to defend such cultural practices. The constant current assault on Islam and the ferocious scrutiny of all its beliefs and practices might perhaps lead to the emergence of a more sophisticated apologetic tradition. But it is unlikely: almost all Muslims dismiss Jewish, Christian, agnostic and atheist attacks as being all equally actuated by *motives* of malice rather than *grounds* of reason and conscience.

XVI

We conclude by examining Gal. 5.6. This will prepare us for Chapter 6 where we explore the ethical portion of Galatians. Martin Luther thought that Paul described the entire Christian life, internal and external, in this single verse.

Luther affirms that a man is inwardly a Christian 'through faith in the sight of God, who does not need our works' while this same man is a Christian 'outwardly in the sight of other men, who do not derive any benefit from [his] faith but do derive benefit from works or from our love'.[13] Muslims would concur with Luther's sound reasoning. A believer's worship (prayer, fasting and pilgrimage) benefit him, establish and maintain his relationship to God who needs neither his faith nor his works. This is private piety although even a private Islamic duty has a public dimension. Thus, confession of faith benefits a believer privately but also establishes his or her public membership of the believing community. The private confession has public, including legal, entailments since a believer must now obey Islamic laws. The alms tax purifies a Muslim's wealth, in the sight of God, but also benefits other Muslims. The believer's duty to establish social justice – by ordering good and prohibiting evil – is the one that will most benefits others. God's political providence is expressed through the establishment of the caliphate, a powerful expression of God's Kingdom on earth. This is indeed piety in the public sector.

Paul's phrase 'faith working through love' has inspired much commentary about the precise role of human deeds in salvation. This is especially so in Reformation exegesis, which is presented by Protestants as normative Christian exegesis. In all faiths, faith is authentic only if it is reflexively personal and thus sincerely interior. For Christians, a further requirement is the tool of love through which faith becomes effective and energetic. *Energoumenē* (operating through or working) is in the middle passive voice: the action of the verb does not extend further than the subject.[14] Luther thought that Paul saw love as the tool through which the believer's faith works.[15]

Faith 'arouses and motivates good works through love'. A man does not truly believe if 'works of love do not follow his faith'.[16] 'Works of love' naturally replaces 'the works of (the) law'.

A Muslim can concur with much of this Lutheran doctrine. But there are two Christian caveats. Luther regarded faith, God's free gift, as being infused in the human heart by the Holy Spirit and, secondly, partly as a consequence of this arrangement, incapable of co-existing with mortal sin.[17] A Muslim would, moreover, be surprised at the role of the mediating Holy Spirit – since Allah directly rewards and punishes people.

The notion that Paul is suspicious of good works is due then to a misunderstanding of his view of the ethical consequences and content of the faith that justifies the sinner by grace alone. Works are integral but not instrumental to faith since works carry no merit with regard to salvation. Those who receive from God the free gift of salvation will, out of gratitude, do the righteous deeds that are characteristic of faith. Righteous deeds are done actively but the state of being righteous is passive – since righteousness can only be received by the saved sinner. We must not trust works of legal righteousness (such as those in the Decalogue) but rather wait for God to impute his righteousness to us, apart from the works of the Law. In sum, the righteousness of faith is a gift of unconditional divine grace and mercy. The credit is due to God from first to last. Or, as Muslims would exclaim *alḥamdu lillāh* (All praise is due to God), the opening line of the Muslim equivalent of the Lord's Prayer (Q1.2).

Are Paul's moral instructions only an appendix to his mainly theological aim, namely, to subvert and undermine the hubristic confidence in works of the Law as emblems of unaided human achievement? Paul did not want to be celebrated as the advocate of the lawless man, the antinomian anarchist who lives beyond the law. If, however, as John Barclay rightly points out, we permit that the ethical instructions, the prescriptive ending, is actually integral to Paul's thought rather than a postscript to his epistle, then we are conceding that the Apostle is, after all, promoting the performance of works of the law, what Muslims call 'honourable deeds'.[18]

Paul's whole counsel emerges once we *synoptically* read Galatians *and* Romans: Christian faith is active in agape. The faith that justifies is the faith that expresses itself in works and actions. This considered Christian stance is compatible with the Islamic view of the unity of faith and works, of *īmān* and a*'māl*. The Islamic stance is distinctively Islamic, however, since the *Sharī'a* is permanently binding – terminative rather than interim or provisional. Its fallible details, worked out in the human construction called *fiqh* (jurisprudence; lit. understanding; Q9.122), may vary but the concept, though not the total content, of the divine law is fixed and cannot be repealed by human initiative, individual or communal.

Faith endures as the primary category which integrates Paul's Christology, high as it is, with his ethical advice about practical Christian conduct. This same faith, from the moral end, links his view of justification with his high Christology. Nor does the expression of such faith exclude the doing of honourable works. These have their due role in Paul's soteriology as we shall learn presently when we read his firm ethical exhortations to his recalcitrant Galatian neophytes.

Notes

1 German idealist philosophy, logic apart, resembles Eastern philosophy: a great deal of wild and unverifiable metaphysics. British empiricism is sober and modest, making unambitious claims for reason and for experience. The American school of pragmatism, in its popular – as opposed to classical academic – version is really a practical school of utilitarian positivism masquerading as a philosophical movement. It is, however, an improvement on the scientistic polemics of the logical positivism of the Vienna Circle. As for the (Sunni) Islamic world, as early as the early twelfth century, Abu Hamid Al-Ghazzali had signed the death warrant for philosophy.

2 This verse prohibits the Prophet from contracting any more marriages even if some women's beauty attracts him. Only modern commentators have speculated whether women displayed more of their charms in the Prophet's time than is normally supposed – for how otherwise could their beauty have tempted him?

3 A man who was free of debt was also called *katharos*. Islamic (Hanafi) law requires payment of the deceased person's debts as a condition of burial. The dead person is considered legally alive and liable until his debts are cleared.

4 This tradition has a personal and impersonal version: 'God will not allow my community (or: Muhammad's community) to agree on an error.' It is related by the traditionalist Muhammad ibn Isa Al-Tirmidhi in his collection (*Jami'*) with a fair (*ḥasan*) chain of authenticity. That a community cannot agree on an error does not entail that it must always agree on every truth – although it does entail the conditional truth, namely, that *if* it does agree on some doctrine, *then* that doctrine must be true.

5 Only in violent circumstances do Westerners come to learn otherwise innocent Arabic words such as *fatwā* (legal opinion) and *fitna* (temptation or trial). *FITNA* is the name of a 2008 anti-Islamic film made by the Dutch parliamentarian Geert Wilders. A woman whose outstanding beauty can tempt a man is called *Fatōna*, a rare proper name.

6 Muslims see Christian ascetics and eunuchs as proof of an emasculated faith – though the Crusaders were real men. Some Roman thinkers accused Christianity of being a faith that encouraged men to be weak and passive, thus making them incapable of resisting barbarian assaults on the imperial capital.

7 Kenneth Cragg argued for a pacifist reading of the Quranic story of Joseph in his *Iron in the Soul: Joseph and the Undoing of Violence* (London: Melisende, 2009). However, Joseph was, of course, never in a position to become a ruler.

8 After Paul and perhaps Augustine, Aquinas is the essential European intellectual of Latin Christendom, a precursor of the intolerant European colonisers of non-Christian peoples worldwide. Such colonisers were often men steeped in classical education and Christian faith. Along with the more secular imperialists of their nations, they sought to Christianise and civilise the world in the most determined alliance of the Bible and the bullet the world has ever witnessed. I have argued for this view elsewhere and see it as a fair summary of colonial history, not merely a caricature. See my *Islam as Political Religion* (London: Routledge, 2010).

9 Nietzsche, *The Anti-Christ* (Harmondsworth: Penguin Books, 1979), translated by R.J. Hollingdale, p. 23.

10 See C.J. Ellicott's *Commentaries, Critical and Grammatical* (Charleston, SC: Nabu Press, 2011), commentary on Phil. 3.2.

11 For Jewish justification of circumcision, the seal of the covenant, see the work of the eleventh century exegete-halakhist, Moses ben Maimon (Maimonides), *Guide of the Perplexed*, 3.49. He lists the social, psychological and other benefits of circumcision of the male genital organ. For the first century Jewish philosopher Philo's defence of this custom against Egyptian and pagan derision, see his *The Special Laws* 1.1–11. Both texts are in F.E. Peters (ed.), *Judaism, Christianity, and Islam: The Classical Texts and Their Interpretation* (Princeton, NJ: Princeton University Press, 1990), vol. 2. See pp. 227–29, 225–27 for Maimonides and Philo respectively.

12 In August 2012, a court in Cologne, Germany, ruled that circumcision of young boys, for religious reasons, amounted to gratuitous and grievous bodily harm and was therefore illegal. Other Western nations shall probably follow suit.
13 *LW* 27.30. The translations from the German are mine. See bibliography for details of Luther's collected works.
14 The active voice of the Greek verb is called '*energeia*'.
15 *LW* 27.29.
16 *LW* 27.30.
17 *LW* 27.28.
18 See J.M.G. Barclay, *Obeying the Truth: Paul's Ethics in Galatians* (Minneapolis: Fortress, 1988), p. 7.

6

COVENANT OF THE SPIRIT (4.21–5.1 AND 5.13–26)

I

What are the duties of the spirit in its battle against the flesh? What are the moral implications of the Gospel of Christian liberty? In Gal. 4.21–31, in an allegory ostensibly about Abraham's two sons, Paul argues for the superiority of a pneumatic *diathēkē*, a covenant of the spirit: spiritually liberating and liberatingly spiritual and therefore anti-Sinaitic, anti-Torah, anti-Mosaic. This ostensibly – arguably actually – antinomian covenant is not legally binding. Instead, in a typically Pauline paradox, it is a liberating covenant true to the spirit of the Law. This new covenant is moral and spiritual in its impulse rather than contractual and legal in its contents. Hence, the ethical directives of Gal. 5.13 to 6.10 follow naturally in the aftermath of the allegory, separated only by a pastoral hiatus (in 5.2–12) during which Paul runs to earth the implications of the allegory for the practical concern which had prompted the letter – the problem of deciding whether circumcision retained even any communal-covenantal necessity, let alone salvific value, in the new covenant of grace.

In the apocalyptic allegory of 4.21–31, Paul wants to establish that Hagar symbolises the Sinaitic *diathēkē* which fails to produce children suitable for divine adoption. It produces genuine Abrahamic descendants but these remain Jews who refuse to become Christians. They foolishly opt to share in the general human enslavement to the natural elements (*stoicheia*). Only the adoptive Abrahamic *diathēkē* produces genuine Abrahamic descendants (Christian Jews) whose divine adoption frees them from worldly enslavement to the law, flesh, sin and therefore death, the four tyrants of Paul's theology.

The appeal to Abraham's two children, in the generation that succeeded the patriarch, further undermines the Gentile Galatian believers' current motivation for submitting to the Law. By upholding Isaac as the free son of the promise and thus the progenitor of Gentile and Jewish Christians alike, Paul can assert, if not establish, that promise and freedom have replaced law and slavery. There is thus no need to remain even in principle under the covenant of the law – either in its totality or by obeying any of its ritual obligations.

The two covenants argument, based on Genesis 21.9–10, is an ad hominem contention directed against the Judaisers. This allegorical appendix cites scripture to introduce the spirit-directed conception of the moral life. The allegory accentuates a Pauline polarity: the spirit as the eternal liberator and the law as present persecutor. Gal. 5.1 is transitional since it links the freedom, provided by the spirit, to the establishment of the moral *diathēkē*, namely, the covenant founded on the grace of Christ, a covenant whose liberty will, again paradoxically, bind the repentant sinner but this time without visible legal bonds. This verse provides a preface to the *pericopae* of paraenesis (ethical exhortation) even though it may appear, at first sight, as though it is offered merely as a scriptural appendix to the main arguments about the obsolescence of the law in the aftermath of Christ who exemplifies the singularity of the Abrahamic seed. Gal. 5.1 functions analogously to Gal. 3.6–8, the *pericopē* that introduces the scriptural, that is, Abrahamic, basis for the new covenant rooted in the grace of Christ. Gal. 3.6–8 is the first blast of the trumpet as Paul declares his larger intention – to repeal and replace the older covenant of law.

Gal. 4:21–31 contains more eisegesis than exegesis of parts of Genesis and includes some sentences that are hard to understand or translate. In the hands of adventurous or mischievous contemporary Christian preachers, even commentators inclined to be polemical, one can easily imagine how such verses could be used to extract a negative notice of Islam. Sarah symbolises freedom; Hagar represents servitude. Sarah is the winner and Hagar is the loser. I wish it had not been penned by the Apostle. It is an obscure allegory, plastic to interpretation and therefore one easily recruited for promoting anti-Islamic sentiment. Paul himself did not, of course, intend that it should be used in this way but modern Christians may plausibly claim scriptural sanction for their own anti-Islamic views held on other (non-Pauline) grounds. None of this is to deny the Christian believer's understandable, indeed religious, obligation to defend this allegory since it is scripture and therefore eternally valid. Muslims often defend awkward passages of their scripture. One might regret what scripture has enjoined but it must be revered since human intelligence and conscience cannot, in Islam at least, be placed above God's word.

Throughout Gal. 3–4, we saw Paul using his skills as a logician and dialectician. In Gal. 5, we see him as a thinker whose ethical catechism gives Christianity a sharper moral content and focus than the one provided by the beatitudes, those vaguer '*makarian*' axioms of the messianic kingdom, suitable in their context but open to a wider range of interpretation. For Paul, echoing the Sermon on the Mount from his own comparable heights, virtue is beyond the Law. How so? It transcends the external legal limits through the interiority of the virtuous agent's inner motivation. Paul follows in the footsteps of his Galilean master. However, while he spoke in his own name, Paul grounds the authority of his ethics in a divine Christology, via the spirit. The typical ending of a Pauline epistle is ethical exhortation. The Gospel, if we may rephrase it as a memorable slogan, might read: 'Christ will save, but you had better learn to behave!' Paul's gospel contains ethical implications: the spirit dictates a morally demanding and morally excellent life. A practising Christian need not be a perfect follower of Christ in the sense of obeying all his commands, unless God – with whom all things are possible – wills the possibility of such total surrender.

Galatians 5–6 lists the duties of the saved community, the true people of God. Some scholars speculate, quite plausibly, that the exhortative *pericopē*, from Gal. 5.13 to 6.10, may be a later addition since the theological argument, based on scriptural citations, ends at Gal. 5.1. Nonetheless, no matter how supplementary this material seems, it is not simply an ethical appendix to the theological contentions of the earlier chapters. The link is organic: if this is the theology, then here are the moral consequences which must guide the conduct of the Christian saints. This liaison of doctrine and duty is characteristically Christian. It finds no parallel in the Quranic method of instruction which links faith directly to conduct without offering complex theological grounds relating to God's nature as such, as opposed to his revealed will for his human creatures. Moreover, the Quran invariably associates faith with moral rectitude so intimately that the priority of propositional faith to moral conduct is certainly obscured if not denied. The Prophet's traditions, however, often emphasise the priority, indeed sufficiency, of faith independent of piously appropriate conduct.

Originating motives and drives appear in human nature, itself the arena for supernatural good and evil; the God-given spirit and the Satan-assisted flesh struggle ferociously. These impulses are congenital and thus innate: they date from birth and inhere in human nature. The flesh-spirit dichotomy, as it relates to our moral struggles, is neither pre-Christian nor pre-Pauline. Admittedly, Philo and other Diaspora Jewish thinkers, as well as many Hellenic and Gnostic writers, make this rather obvious distinction. They do not, however, unlike Christian writers, employ it primarily to explain the resources and limitations of the moral struggle. 'The spirit (*to pneuma*) is willing (*prothumon*; lit. mentally eager) but the flesh (*hē sarx*) is weak' is found on the Markan Jesus' lips in the agony of Gethsemane (Mark 14.38). The essential moralisation of the tension between the flesh and the spirit is unique to Christianity. It is not a feature of Hebraic, Hellenic or of Islamic thought.

The spirit, as the spirit of God, is a force active in the conversion, moral education and edification of the Galatian pagans. The pneumatic conception of the moral life as graciously enabled is a crucial Pauline claim. This desire to extricate the ethical dimension of the Law and the related attempt to spiritualise the moral life would both be alien – though not anathema – to Paul's Muslim readers.

II 4.21-26

21 *Tell me, you who are wishing to be under law, do you not hear the law?* **22** *For it has been written that Abraham had two sons, one from the maidservant and one from the free woman.*
23 *But the son of the maidservant has been born according to the flesh and the son by the free woman through the promise.* **24** *These matters may be allegorized: for these (women) are two covenants, one (from) Mount Sinai bringing forth to slavery; she is Hagar.* **25** *Now this Hagar*

is Mount Sinai in Arabia and corresponds to the present Jerusalem for she serves as a slave along with her children. **26** *But the Jerusalem above is free; she is our mother.*

21

Paul now turns directly towards a confrontation with the law-observant group. Here, as elsewhere in the authentic Paul, 'the law' can mean scripture, usually only the Torah portion. Where Paul is referring to God's holy ordinance – as opposed to the revealed legislation of the Torah – he uses *to dikaiōma* (as in Rom. 1.32).

22-23

Unusually, *gegraptai* (it is written; perf. pass. indic.) introduces not a citation but a paraphrase from the Septuagint. We find 32 other instances of scriptural citation using *gegraptai* in the authentic Pauline epistles. The total is 67 in the whole New Testament. 'Abraham had two sons, one from the slave woman and one from the free' paraphrases Gen. 21.9–10, the only place in the entire Septuagint where Ishmael (described as the slave woman's son but not named) and Isaac (named and described by Sarah as 'my son') occur together in the same verse and moreover in their historical birth sequence. In the Quran, as we shall see below, the two regularly occur together and Ishmael is named first.

Only on one occasion does the Quran cite, in Arabic, directly from the Bible – although modified versions of biblical themes and narratives are found often enough in paraphrased translation. The Quran appears, however, to quote directly from Psalms (Q21.105). The quotation resembles Ps. 37.11, 29.

Paul demonises the flesh for it refers to birth according to the laws of nature. It perhaps stands for the despised elemental forces (*stoicheia*), including the power of lust to procreate. The birth according to the promise is birth by miraculous means, by suspending nature's laws in order to display all the more God's power to procreate without mechanical causation and human causal antecedent. We find this mysteriously inspiring theme also in the Quran (3.47; 19.8, 9, 20) but without any attempt to disparage the power of the flesh, which is, after all, God's creation.

Paul does not say here that the son of the promise is destined to be (nearly) sacrificed, or that he resembles Christ, the Son of God, who was, in fact, sacrificed. The Quran does not call Ishmael the firstborn or name him as the intended victim of the binding (Hebr. *'aqēdā*) but most Muslim commentators regard him to be the firstborn son and therefore the intended victim.

24-25

Paul asks us to take these matters figuratively even though the scripture presents itself as literally referring to real historical characters. It seems odd to see the two women as timeless figures signifying eternally valid human qualities. Paul's procedure is indefensible since the literal sense of scripture is, mystical verses apart, always primary.

Only where the literal is problematic does one need to, and therefore should, resort to a figurative reading. The original meanings in Genesis are, however, clear and explicit. Christians might object that if Paul's procedure here seems indefensible, it is only charitable to ask whether he really is doing what one thinks he is doing. In other words, since his apparent procedure would be indefensible as an exegesis of the Genesis passage, therefore, we should not see it as exegesis. Naturally, such a conservative attitude towards Paul reflects a Christian faith-commitment. As a Muslim reader, I am not obliged to defend Paul but I am obliged to read him as charitably and sympathetically as possible while ultimately retaining the right to be critical of his procedure and of his claims.

The primary reading has precedence in the Quran which, although not a legal text, is a scripture containing legal verdicts. The Quran warns against indulging in the adventure of needlessly pursuing figurative meanings (Q3.7). To impose a metaphorical meaning on a literal verse is perverse. Sufi commentators regularly impose figurative interpretations on literal verses. Thus, for example, the *ḥajj* to Mecca is reinterpreted to mean not a pilgrimage to the city of that name but rather to the core of one's heart. While such a secondary meaning cannot be ruled out as inappropriate, on a priori grounds, it is indefensible if it presents itself as the primary – or worse, as the only authentic – meaning. For that would be in clear repudiation of the verse's literal meaning and accepted historical interpretation, including the Prophet's own interpretation.

The two women represent two covenants, one (Hagar) from Mount Sinai bearing children destined for slavery. This Hagar is Mt Sinai in Arabia and corresponds to the present Jerusalem (Pharisaic Judaism). Hagar symbolises Sinai, the mountain of revealed legislation.[1] The law had divine origins but – I am speculating about Paul's thoughts here – its wilderness was perhaps a mystic hint about the sterility of the Law. Its barren future and jejune contents would ultimately be enriched in Christ, as history reached its climax. Sinai also corresponds, in this obscurely expressed allegory, to the contemporaneous Jerusalem of Paul's day, the citadel of Pharisaic Judaism. Jerusalem is in slavery with her children of the Torah Law. The Mosaic legal administration produced only slaves of the Law, not slaves of God. As people of the book, Muslims can also become slaves of the book if, as intelligent heirs of the original faith, they refuse to remove beyond its initial inevitably Arabian scope and compass.[2]

26

The Jerusalem above is free: she is our mother, understood to be the unnamed matriarch Sarah.

Hagar corresponds allegorically to the present Jerusalem which is a metonymy for contemporaneous Judaism centred on the Temple elite in the ancient city. Judaism was doubly enslaved: Jerusalem was under Roman hegemony and moreover the Pharisaic branches of the faith had evolved into a suffocating and complex system of ritual and ceremony undergirded by a casuistic ingenuity that encouraged hypocrisy and devious escape from the Law. This denatured the Torah by depriving it of its original compassionate impulses. The yoke of the Pharisees was sufficiently heavy for Jesus' offer of the light yoke to be appealing to many sincere Jews.

A crucial caveat here is that one must not exaggerate the Roman power presence. It is possible to live in a colonised land without even noticing it, at least on a daily basis. My illiterate grandmother, who was born and lived her whole life in rural Punjab, in what became Pakistan in 1947, once responded in shock when I told her about the British Raj. She did not even know that 'these infidel Englishmen' had been ruling her country, then India! Paul's own attitude towards Rome is ambivalent and, from this distance in time, undiscoverable. There were zealots and patriots who resented the Roman presence but they were not a majority.

Modern scholars, notably E.P. Saunders and W.D. Davies, have convincingly argued that Jesus' and Paul's critique of the Jewish faith and its practices was based on appreciation of that faith. It was the patriot's struggle with his own people – for their own sake. Orthodox Judaism has, moreover, continued to be a law-centred faith. Islam shares that stress.

Jerusalem above, to return to our commentary, is free and corresponds to Sarah's line. The spiritual part of the present Jerusalem represents the infant Christian church and its promise of future fruitfulness in the spirit. If Hagar's descendants correspond to contemporaneous Judaism, the barren Sarah corresponds to the Christian church of Paul's day. She will soon bear the children of promise just as she gave birth to Isaac. The early church's spectacular growth, in a hostile world, followed by its rapid expansion into the Roman universe, and its eventual triumph over the empire of that name, amply confirmed Paul's implied prophecy. His allegorical interpretation of the Sarah and Hagar narrative intends to contrast the enslaved present Jerusalem with the eschatological Jerusalem which is 'above and free'. Although the pillars in the present Jerusalem seemed somewhat reluctant to grant their total authority to Paul, he was free to annex the new authority which derived from the sanction of Abraham's descendants of the promise, that is, the authority of the free New Jerusalem.

Keep in mind here also the heavenly Jerusalem (Heb. 12.22; Rev. 3.12), a different reality. Perhaps, however, it was, from the Apostle's perspective, an imminent reality. In much of Christian tradition, it is held that Jerusalem shall be preserved forever although the Temple would be destroyed. The city had such peculiar holiness that reverence for it inhibited colonising European Christians from naming newly established cities 'Jerusalem' in its honour.[3]

III 4.27-5.1

27 *For it has been written: 'Rejoice barren woman who is not bearing (children). Break forth and shout, you who are not in labour. For many are the children of the desolate (woman) than of the one who has a husband.'* **28** *And you brothers, like Isaac, are children of promise.* **29** *But just as at that time he who was born according to (the) flesh persecuted him (who was born) according to (the) spirit, so it is also now.* **30** *But what does the scripture say? 'Expel the maidservant and her son – for by no means shall the son of the maidservant inherit along with the son of the free woman.'* **31** *So then, brothers, we are not children of a maidservant but of the free woman.*

5.1 *It was for freedom that Christ freed us. Therefore stand firm and do not be subject again to a yoke of slavery.*

27-28

Paul asserts the God-given superiority of Sarah, the barren woman and the line of Isaac. Believers in Christ are children of promise. A verse such as v.28 has, independently of Paul's intentions, subconsciously encouraged Christians to indulge an inveterate triumphalism and self-congratulation. They have entertained a sense of being special and elect. Such an attitude, especially if it is unacknowledged, could and did lead to some official dogmatic intolerance of Jews and then Muslims. The Quran similarly informs the Arab Muslims that they are 'the best community ever raised for the edification of humanity', but, fortunately, it adds the double caveat requiring them to have faith in God while enjoining the good and prohibiting the evil (Q3.110). Insofar as imperial Islam achieved its measure of professed political humility and therefore lenient ascendancy over countless millions, it was owing to this double caveat. The Quranic election, unlike Israel's (initially at least) ethnically grounded one, is not based on unconditional grace. The Quranic election is an unsentimental and pragmatic but nonetheless gracious choice made by God. The offer can be withdrawn at any time (Q5.54; 47.38) since God is no partisan: he expects the two attendant conditions to be fulfilled at all times, for all and any peoples.

On the joint authority of the Quran and of common sense, Muslims reject as arbitrary and unjust the range of God's outreach and promise as portrayed in the Bible. Thus, for example, God's promises did not reach Esau or the wicked sons of Eli or the Israelite rebels who died in their transgressions in the desert. Paul excludes Ishmael. Here Muslims ask why God chose some at the expense of others, perhaps equally deserving people. Were God's promises aborted or withheld? Why were some people forgiven but not others? Muslims demand an explanation. Two of the people mentioned above receive promises despite being outside the chosen line (Esau and Ishmael). But why does God disinherit them in the first place? The other two are from the elect but are judged justifiably if harshly for specified sins. I admit this is fair enough but, even for a sovereign but just God, only in the latter case. I remain dissatisfied but we must move on. The covenant of grace was, in any case, established only with Abraham and his seed through Isaac and Israel (Rom. 9.1–4; Acts 2.39; Gen. 17.7).

29

Ishmael persecutes Isaac just as the flesh persecutes the spirit. The son of the free woman inherited the promise made to Abraham, fulfilled in Christ. Isaac represents Christian liberty. This verse anticipates ethical commands which shall soon be issued, in the hinterland of the antagonism between flesh and spirit (5.13–26).

Compared to Paul's persecution of the infant church, Ishmael's persecution of Isaac is mild enough for *edioken* to be inappropriate although Paul invariably uses the same verb (Gal. 1.13, 23; 5.11, 6.12). His allegory is an *ad hominem* demonstration of scriptural reasoning, directed against the Judaisers and thus against contemporaneous Law-centred Pharisees. It can be readily prostituted to denigrate Hagar, Ishmael, and thus Muhammad and Islam, including contemporary Islam. The faith of Muhammad can be seen as inheriting an ancient hostility to Isaac's line – the Jewish and Christian communities. Islam may also be regarded as remaining active as persecutor of the contemporary church in Muslim-majority lands. Clearly, anti-Muslim hostility was not the intended message of Paul. But it is easy enough to appropriate his analogy – to deracinate it from its original context in order to apply it to a new one. Indeed, it might be plausible to do so since the Muslim movement was, effectively, a vigorous attempt to reassert the superiority of the Judaic component of the Jesus Christ movement. And that would surely infuriate Paul.

30-31

Hagar's son is disinherited while she is expelled and disowned. There is a softening of this judgement in Genesis and in rabbinic commentary that was already available in Paul's day. Paul chooses to quote only the most intolerant parts of the Genesis narrative (21.10) without first noting that Sarah persecuted Hagar (16.6), though admittedly only after Hagar had shown contempt for her mistress who then complained to Abraham. In rabbinic tradition, accumulating steadily in Paul's time, Father Abraham was considered kind and clement, a reputation confirmed in the New Testament and the Quran (Luke 16.19–31; Q11.75).

Paul's claim about Ishmael persecuting Isaac is, fortunately, found only in *haggādā*, the rabbinic amplifications of scriptural narratives. In Gen. 21.9, we read that the son of Hagar was laughing. This could mean that Ishmael, aged twenty, was playing with Isaac, aged six, and teasing or perhaps mocking him. Since this commentary was in place in Paul's time, naturally he took up this reading in constructing his argument. Muslim commentators are very suspicious of such materials, found in the *Isrā'īliyyat* (Israelite materials division). They detect in it Jewish mischief and delinquency dressed as humour. No doubt, the possibility of such persecution cannot be denied a priori since we know that sibling rivalry and other friction exist in all families, even those of prophets (see Q12.5, 8–9). All families are, to an extent, dysfunctional, some being even essentially at war albeit in a time of peace. However, no ordinary family is as enduringly dysfunctional as the Abrahamic one, not even the royal families and dynasties of the past (Solomon, the Mughals) or of the present. After all, which family feud has lasted 3,700 years – and is still raging with fresh vigour?

5.1

This transitional verse moves the reader into the ethical directives issued by the spirit which governs the believer in his or her newfound liberty. Gal. 4.21–31 provides the scriptural background to this shift but has virtually nothing to do with Abraham, the paradigmatic believer. Instead, it exploits, for polemical purposes, the patriarch's troubling family problems, involving two sons by different women. Such material supplies Paul with an ad hominem contention against the law-observant party of the Jewish Christians who must have rejected as unscriptural Paul's stress on freedom from the inherited law, in particular his rejection of the rite of circumcision. Both Abraham and his two sons were, after all, circumcised (Gen. 17.25–6; 21.4).

IV

Before commenting on the ethical part of the letter, I examine the sordid details of Abraham's household and, to use a modern colloquialism, his relationship problems. These are made to yield eternal theological truths. At the end of this section, we explain the direction of this commentary as we move on to examine Gal. 5.13–26.

Sarah proposes that Abraham take Hagar, her Egyptian maidservant, as a second wife so that he can have a child by her. This child would remove the divine curse of Sarah's sterility. Hagar is a slave and, as chattel, has no say in the matter. After Hagar becomes pregnant, she competes in status with her mistress Sarah who resents Hagar and makes life rough and tough for her. Hagar runs away into the wilderness and God reassures her about the coming birth and the future of her child who is to be named Ishmael ('God hears'). God rescues them and promises Hagar that her son will become a great nation – but he shall be both aggressive and a victim. In the meantime, Hagar is ordered to return to her cruel mistress and to submit to her (Gen. 16).

By angelic visitation and direct revelation, God continues to promise the nearly hundred year old Abraham that he shall have a son by the sterile Sarah. Abraham hears the news and laughs sceptically (Gen. 17.17) while, later on, Sarah laughs 'in her heart' (18.12). God hears her laughter and interrogates Abraham about it. Sarah denies that she laughed (18.12–15). Eventually, the repeated divine promise comes to pass; Sarah conceives and Isaac is born (Gen. 21.1–7). The Quran mentions only the unnamed Sarah's laughter (Q.11.71). Muslims would regard as irreverent the suggestion that a prophet could laugh at God's promise.

Anxious for her son Isaac's inheritance, Sarah orders Abraham to expel Hagar and her son Ishmael. Abraham hesitantly obeys. God tells Abraham that Ishmael shall not be the child of promise though he will be a child of blessing. The rejected 'spouse' and her son face certain death in the arid wilderness. But God rescues them by providing water in the desert. The boy grows up and, like a kind of Semitic Tarzan, finds happiness in the wilderness. Hagar finds him a wife from Egypt (Gen. 21.8–21).

Like a good Jewish mother, Sarah is tenacious enough to live on (Gen. 23.1) until she has guaranteed the future of her son Isaac, though not his marriage. After Gen. 21.21, Hagar is silent in the canon but her son remains within it. Apart from Genesis, Hagar is never mentioned in the Bible shared by Jews and Christians; Sarah is mentioned only once in it, in an oracle of Isaiah (51.2). Hagar is mentioned only in Galatians, twice by name and nowhere else in the Christian New Testament.[4] Unlike Sarah, the sole founding mother of the ancestral line, her rival Hagar is inferiorised and eventually silenced – in effect dismissed as foreign, pagan and dangerous.

Hagar is *Hajirah* in Arabic. Some speculate that her very name is linked to *hijrah* (migration), the event which dates the Islamic calendar. Like Ruth, Hagar came to throw her lot with an alien culture. In Muslim tradition, she is seen as coping with two alien cultures – that of the Hebrews and then the Arabs. For Muslims, she is the mother of Ishmael and therefore the matriarch of Islam (*umm al-Islam*), the founding mother of Muslim civilisation. Hagar receives this title long before the Prophet's wives were called mothers of the believers (*umm al-mu'minin*). (Muhammad's first wife, Khadijah, is sometimes also called *umm al-Islam*, being the first female convert.) Though Hagar is never mentioned by name in the Quran, or even alluded to, her memory is cherished in prophetic narratives and in the *ḥajj* rituals enacted annually.[5] The story of Hagar searching frantically for water for her infant son Ishmael, as both suffer in the Arabian wilderness, is found only in the Prophet's traditions. It is a story much cherished in popular Muslim piety. The Quran nowhere names Sarah but alludes to her as the mother of Isaac. Muslim tradition does not portray Hagar as Abraham's concubine or maidservant. Since Abraham, like many other biblical figures, practised polygyny, it is assumed that Hagar was his wife no less than Sarah.

Unlike the Bible, the Quran unequivocally honours both Ishmael and Isaac and always lists them in their historical birth sequence (Q2.136, 2.140, 4.163; 14.39). Ishmael is once named as being, with Abraham, the co-architect of the great Meccan shrine (Q2.127) where both pray for an Arab apostle to emerge. The Quran affirms the placing of the gift of continual prophecy in Abraham's seed, through Isaac and Jacob's lines (Q12.6; 29.27).

In the aftermath of the rapid military triumph of Islam, Arabs came to be seen, especially in seventh century apocalyptic Christian literature and then later in medieval polemic, as Abraham's ugly and illegitimate children through Hagar, the foreign slave and idolatrous maidservant. Ishmael was the wild man of the desert. He was the nomad who, like John the Baptist, probably ate locusts and wild honey and dressed in rough clothes. It is hard to see how one can truthfully impose a constructive reading on the Hagar-Ishmael materials in the Bible!

We shall now return to the commentary to scrutinise the ethical exhortation in Galatians. Recall here that we have decided to examine the ethical material in the context of the new covenant of the spirit, a decision I mentioned in Chapter 1. The point is not to interrupt the flow of Paul's argument, let alone to interfere in the canonical order of the text of this epistle. Rather, I am drawing attention to Paul's novel covenantal theology as being the direct inspiration for his ethical exhortations to the Galatian believers. Some exegetes might object that Paul is hard enough to understand as it is – without a Muslim exegete re-ordering his thoughts. My rearrangement shall help the reader see more clearly the theological rationale for the ethical pericopae that follow, a rationale obscured by the essentially pastoral intervention of Gal. 5.2–12. Paul was no academic theologian: rarely did he have the opportunity to revise and edit his material, a luxury afforded by self-imposed seclusion in the modern ivory tower, though even feudal academia is now becoming increasingly more integrated into quotidian life than in centuries past.

V 5.13-15

13 *For you brothers were called to freedom – only do not (use) the freedom to (seek) advantage for the flesh but through love serve as slaves to one another.* **14** *For the entire law has been summed up in one word, in the (statement): 'You shall love your neighbour as yourself.'* **15** *But if you bite and devour one another, watch out in case you are destroyed by one another.*

Paul now begins to apprise his readers of the moral burden of Christian salvation, the serious ethical consequences of spiritual liberty. It is perhaps a salutary lesson for modern Christians who might feel tempted to relax their consciences in the face of the increasing laxity of the modern world of capitalist excess and ubiquitous vulgarity. Muslims are often amazed to note that Christians, some conservatives and evangelicals apart, seem quite relaxed and happy, especially in the arena of sexual ethics, within the increasingly liberal provisions of secular European and North American states.

13

Do not permit Christian liberty (*eleutheria*)[6] to become an opportunity for the flesh but rather use such freedom, through love, to serve one another. That is true freedom; all else follows, including the pursuit of life and liberty in the spirit that leads us. The exhortation to use freedom responsibly is hardly controversial but it is much easier preached than practised. This is not to say that preaching the moral message is pointless or hypocritical. Some charismatic churches employ 'exhorters' whose sole vocation is to preach Christianity's moral message.

'Called', in the aorist tense, indicates that the single completed act of being called to salvation is located in the past, without any comment on its duration. The moral implications of spiritual freedom are in the future. Flesh is an opportunist, always seeking a base for its operations. The opportunity (*aphormē*) is never hard to find. The equivalent Quranic thought is that the Devil and his tribe are forever looking for a chance to mislead Adam and his children (Q7.27; 35.6). But the Quran does not personify flesh or sin or see these as independent or autonomous agencies. The Devil is a much more active and malicious agent in the Quran's account of sacred history than he is in either of the two biblical testaments. The Devil is a sinister and active agent who is, from the very beginning, hell-bent on destroying Adam and his descendants. The Quran often warns us that the Devil, called variously *Iblīs* and *Al-Shayṭān*, is humanity's declared enemy (Q12.5; 17.53; 43.62). This implies that purely human culpability for sin is higher in the biblical outlook than in the Quran since the latter scripture takes the Devil more seriously as God's rival, a supreme evil being determined to make human beings stumble.

The Devil is not mentioned in Galatians but his influence is implicit in the phrase 'this present evil age' (Gal. 1.4). More generally, judging by New Testament references, the Devil's role expands in Jesus' time. He is by now a clearly evil agent who tempts and seduces human beings, including Jesus himself. While in the Old Testament he was merely an opportunist and a rebel, he is now a rebel with a cause since God has identified with human sinners trapped in the human condition. Once God became '*Immanu-ēl*' (God with us), the Devil decided to take a clear stance against God's salvific work for his human creation. If we may express the Christian predicament in Islamic terms, using the Quran's refrain, 'Certainly, the Devil is to humanity an avowed enemy' (Q12.5).

14

The summative law (Lev. 19.18) resembles James' 'royal law' (*nomon basilikon*; James 2.8). By Paul's time, the Torah was so complex and burdensome that it was quite common to hear of formulations of a putatively summative law. Jewish tradition has it that Rabbi Hillel Ha-Gadol (c.110 BCE–c.10 CE), famous for his lenience, was once asked to summarise the Torah while standing on one foot: the ethic of reciprocity (the golden rule) was the whole Torah, the rest being merely *midrash*. In John's gospel, Jesus gives only *two* explicit commandments to his disciples – to love one another and to show humility, the latter demonstrated in practice when Jesus washed the feet of his disciples (John 13.1–16). (Naturally, the requirement to believe in Jesus as the Messiah sent by God is implicit throughout the fourth gospel.)

Paul affirms the centrality of love in the summative law (Rom. 13.9–10). He emphasises that the commandments, four of which are specified in Rom. 13.9, are summed up in a single order: 'Love your neighbour as yourself.' In this double command, one is ordered to love the neighbour and oneself, although the latter comes naturally to sane healthy individuals. For Martin Luther, a 'Christian lives not in himself, but in Christ and his neighbour'.[7] For the great German reformer, neighbour ranges from a servant to a master, whether king or pope and includes men and women, whether they wear purple or rags, whether they eat meat or fish.[8] For Luther, putting faith into practice involved doing penance (for oneself) as well as charitable works (for the neighbour's benefit).

'You shall love your neighbour as yourself' (Lev. 19.18) is cited by Luke and Paul (Luke 10.27). The person who loves himself is not misguided so long as he loves the true self, rather than worships the false self. That latter attitude constitutes the sin of narcissism. The true or higher self is worth knowing and nourishing. Indeed, it brings us to God as we stare at our own true image. Sadly, for some people in our narcissistic and celebrity-obsessed culture, being in love no longer involves anyone else!

15

'If you bite and devour one another. . .' is expressed hypothetically. Paul's pastoral diplomacy is shown in his mild way of condemning what is likely to be the Galatians' actual conduct.

Paul had perhaps only Galatia in mind when he envisaged such a cutthroat society. We today cannot avoid thinking of all advanced capitalist nations such as Japan, India, South Korea – and especially China and America and those last two nations' allies and satellites worldwide. I include in this indictment some affluent Muslim nations such as Kuwait and Malaysia. While the nations mentioned above are already advanced capitalist cultures, others, especially in eastern Europe, are aspiring to higher standards of economic success and thus, exploitation and, unwittingly, communal alienation. Nor is this limited to advanced capitalist nations: some underdeveloped and communist countries are also succumbing to similar temptations, no doubt a part of the failings of our common humanity.

Whether or not a contemporary analogue to the Galatian churches exists – the question of the modern relevance of the epistle – interests us obliquely in the final chapter of this book. Suffice it to say for now that Paul's phrase provides a vignette of the self-destructive society marked by a culture of competition and litigiousness (see also 1 Cor. 6.1–8). Most advanced capitalist nations, especially America and Japan, have generated welcome benefits such as wealth, efficiency and profit – profit is admittedly not a four-letter word – but their citizens are often alienated and dissatisfied, status-conscious, consumed by the need for wealth, competing with each other and therefore anxious for the morrow. People make deals, not friends. Time is money; one must never waste time merely by enjoying life and other people. I have often heard many patriotic and authentically Christian American pastors lament that their confessedly Christian society now exhibits behaviour that is increasingly a travesty of Christ's ideals. The perverted gospel of prosperity and pleasure is preached; even a Muslim version is popular among Muslim 'motivational' speakers in parts of urban America.[9]

It would be a partisan if not perverse commentary on this verse if I were to pretend that these vices (of the biting and devouring that lead to mutual social destruction) are found only in capitalist or in Western Christian nations. Such vices are to be found in different ways, to varying extents, in all nations and at different levels of any society. Nonetheless, their presence in historically Christian cultures is more shocking since it shows a betrayal of ideals actually professed. To fail to live up to other peoples' ideals is one thing, sometimes lamentable. To fail to live up to one's own is a greater failing – and always lamentable.

VI 5.16–18

16 *Now I say, walk in spirit and you will by no means carry out (the) lust of (the) flesh.* **17** *For the flesh lusts against the spirit and the spirit against the flesh; for these oppose each other so that you do not do the things that you (may) intend.* **18** *But if by spirit you are led, you are not under law.*

Christians are called to walk in the footsteps of Jesus Christ (1 Pet.2.21), to walk in a path worthy of their calling (1 Cor. 7.17). Paul sees the flesh as a 'user' which, once we enlist the spirit to our aid, becomes a 'loser'. In this section, I shall ponder and speculate about flesh and its relationship to spirit and the powers of both agencies. However, I cannot offer any decisive assessment of Paul's view of the flesh since the exegesis of 'flesh' remains tantalizingly provisional in Pauline scholarship up to this day.

16

Walk by the spirit and you will not execute the desires of the flesh. *Peripateite* (to walk around), hence the 'peripatetic philosophers', corresponds to the Hebrew *halāk* and hence the holy law (*halākhā*). One walks by the statutes of the Torah, and thus walks, to use the Quran's frequent refrain, on the straight path. The Quran confirms that the Torah contains a light (*nūr*; Q5.44) which enables Jews to walk safely in the surrounding darkness. Paul's use of 'walking in/by the spirit' is provocatively original since it replaces the Jewish idiom of 'walking according to the Torah'. One can only speculate about what precisely is the meaning of Paul's more spiritual rather than law-bound ambulation. Can the spirit lead one on a path in the way a Jew could walk in the light of the Torah?

The Quran invests the ordinary act of walking with religious significance. Hypocrites are said to walk in darkness that is intermittently illuminated by the thunder that praises God. They stop when the darkness falls on them (Q2.20). Believers have light shining around them and in front of them, on their right-hand side (66.8).[10] Believers walk humbly and modestly in the earth (Q25.63; 31.18–19). The late King Faisal (1906–1975), who was assassinated, was much admired by Muslims worldwide for his walking posture, his fixed radius of vision and his bent frame, especially when cleaning the *A 'ba*. This traditional act of piety is one which all devout Muslims crave to perform but is the privilege only of the ruler as 'servant of the two holy places' (*khadim al-ḥaramayn*).

I understand gratifying the flesh to mean gratifying one's physical and physiological needs and desires, that is, food, warmth, shelter, comfort and sex. It is one plausible way to read Paul for whom some needs and some desires may well be both covered under the notion of 'flesh'. Yet it is unfair to see biological needs as being subject to accusation. Such needs are, after all, only natural.

17

Paul claims that the antagonism between the spirit and the flesh frustrates our intention to do as we wish. The precise meaning of this antipathy depends on an exegesis of this verse which contains the germ of Paul's essentially Hebraic anthropology. 'For the flesh sets its desire against the spirit.' Nowhere else do we find the verb *epithumeō* used with the preposition *kata* and the genitive. One commentator wonders if this usage indicates Aramaic syntax.[11] Was Paul still thinking and writing like a Jew – which is fair enough since he remained a Jew all his life? Paul was as sophisticated as any Hellenic moral philosopher but he was a Jew first and last.

In this verse, Paul uses the conjunction *gar* (for) twice, both times in an explicative rather than causal way. He explains the mechanism of the hostility between the two active agents, spirit and flesh, without claiming that this mechanism directly prevents us from doing as we wish. If it did, the subject would have no free will. Thus, the confused self, the subject or agent, needs the law to inform him- or herself of what is right and what is wrong. But since the flesh is against the spirit, the law cannot empower action *if the law were to rely on the flesh*.

Perhaps the antagonism between the spirit and the flesh *causally over-determines* the actions of the human subject within whom the conflict is raging. This feature of the struggle, contrary to Paul's intentions, in fact renders irrelevant both the law, which Paul demotes, and the spirit he seeks to promote. An analogy will help. Imagine a man keeping a boy pinned to a wall when he is already held in place there by an iron bar. The boy here represents the human agent, in his fallen or evil nature as sinner. He is a victim of the internal struggle between the flesh and the spirit whose active mutual antagonism immobilises him. The iron bar dramatises the paralysing effects of this struggle upon the agent, rendering his actions otiose and, moreover, rendering unnecessary the actions of the powerful man. The powerful man is the law. His actions are unnecessary since these supply a causal surfeit: the removal of the powerful man's hand, like the elimination of the law, makes no difference to the boy's predicament. The powerful man represents the unsuccessful and unnecessary external legal ban on our natural or attendant dispositions, the domain of the flesh.

Our nature and the struggle between its two internal tyrants suffice to explain our predicament without enabling us to escape it: neither the law nor the spirit make any difference. The former cannot control the flesh – it acts as an autonomous agent – and the latter is engaged in a fight that has resulted in a deadlock. Meanwhile, the human subject merely supplies a theatre for the confrontation without being able to weigh in decisively on either side.

Leaving aside such an intricate analogy involving multiple hypotheticals, the mutual antagonism of the flesh and the spirit is at least empirically verifiable by each human being as he or she examines the inner theatre of their warring internal dispositions. The fracturing of ecclesiastical unity finds an analogue inside the human personality. Society is broken and atomised but so is the individual as he or she fragments and loses his or her soundness.

18

If you are led by the spirit, you are under the law of Christ, the law of the spirit, and are thus spared the state of moral anarchy. The spirit's directives liberate us from the law's directives and demands.

I conclude by amplifying earlier comments on this *pericopē* (vv.16–18). As we shall see in commentary on v.25 below, flesh is opposed both to the human spirit and to the divine spirit in us. Here we note the joint antitheses of works of the flesh versus the fruit of the spirit and the notion of walking in the spirit versus being under the law. Even though 'walk' is an active command, 'walking *in the spirit*' is effectively a passive experience since one is being led by an external and powerful agency. The Quran captures this attitude of submissive ambulation in prayers which ask God to guide us in the straight path (Q1.6–7). Being under the law, in English translation, makes it sound as though it were a passive experience when, for Paul, it is an active but misguided pursuit of righteousness through human effort. The Muslim experience of faithful living combines resignation to God's will, in gracious submission, with the active attempt to please him through the performance of divinely imposed legal duty.

The Arabic (and related Hebrew) word for flesh, *bashar*, means a creature, usually human and in need of food. It is used to emphasise a person's creaturely mortality. The Quran stresses Muhammad's mortality in the aftermath of his injury in the fierce battle of Uhud (Q3.144). Every prophet, including Jesus, is merely *bashar*, and therefore neither divine nor angelic (Q5.75; 17.93; 18.110). The word indicates mortality and frailty without implying the immoral desires which the word flesh intends in Greek and to some extent in English. It is used to contrast human beings with angels. For example, Joseph's female admirers call him a perfect angel rather than an imperfect mortal (*bashar*; Q12.31). The word occurs in the devotional poetry of many Islamic languages to indicate the doubly ephemeral status of *frail* human creatures who pass through this *transient* world.

VII 5.19–21

19 *Now manifest are the works of the flesh, which are: fornication, uncleanness, lewdness,*
20 *idolatry, sorcery, enmities, strife, jealousy, angers, rivalries, divisions, sects,* **21** *envyings,*
drunkennesses, revellings and, things like these, which I tell you beforehand as I previously said
that those practising such things shall not inherit the kingdom of God.

19

The deeds of our sinful or lower nature, the flesh, are evident. The fruit of the spirit is more subtle just as a great mind is less evident and palpable than a great body. The catalogue of evils opens predictably with three sins of sensuality: *porneia* (immorality and wantonness), *akatharsia* (moral pollution or impurity) and *aselgeia* (licentiousness). This trio is found also in 2 Cor. 12.21.

Unsympathetic critics might wonder what Paul could have known about sexuality, homosexuality and family life. Unusually for a Jew, Paul probably had a guilty conscience about sexual desire. Luther, a great admirer of Paul, certainly had a guilty conscience about his own concupiscence and sensuality.

'Desires of the flesh' sounds natural enough but 'desires of the Spirit' is not scriptural. The Spirit liberates us from the thrill of evil – itself a desire. For Buddhists, this desire to eliminate evil provides a stimulus to indulge a desire they dismiss as misguided, namely, the attempt to control the self. The Western and Eastern faiths part company on this crucial disagreement about the need to control and discipline the self. Buddhists question the very identity, temporal stability and nomistic integrity of the so-called self. It is hard to imagine a more sceptical thinker than the Buddha, the most famous Indian sage. Though I cannot argue for it here, I believe that Buddhists exaggerate the instability and discontinuity of the self. The self is remarkably stable and, given a sharp memory, easily recalled in its varied stages. Its continuity provides a solid basis for personal identity and integrity, prerequisites of morally accountable personhood.

We move on now to *aselgeia*, sheer shamelessness or wanton and lawless sensuality. It was known to the ancients and is well-known to us in our decadent and increasingly vulgar age. Few people have, in any age, admired or desired the lifestyle of virtuous self-restraint. People envy 'evil' – the thrill and glamour of licence and wantonness.

In Greek moral writings, *aselgeia* described a capricious impudence, an audacious readiness and thirsting after every pleasure. It corresponds to the Latin *lustus*, meaning any strong and overwhelming passion of which sexual desire is a paradigm example. The decent man hides his sin while the *aselgēs*, the shameless one, is proud to sin openly since the love of self-indulgence has mastered him. *Aselgeia* is associated with the animal lust that motivates adultery. In Islamic languages, such as Urdu, the seriously insulting epithet *bay-sharm* (the shameless one) refers to one who publicly and proudly indulges total loss of moral inhibition.

The wanton insolence of *aselgeia* is close to mania, the madness that deprives one of shame. The Quran describes usurers as being driven to mania by Satan's touch. In Ephesians (4.19), *aselgeia* sits close to *pleonexia*, the irresistible desire for illicit goods. During a fierce condemnation of Jewish greed, the Quran dubs such goods as *al-suḥt* (toxic gain; 5.42), one of its countless perplexing neologisms. Jews are accused of being shamelessly covetous (lit. more covetous; *aḥraṣ*; Q2.96) for longevity, seen as a kind of greed for life's resources. The Quran claims that even the grant of a millennium of life would not satisfy a Jew. In an early epistle in which Paul also attacks Jews (1 Thess. 2.14–16), the Apostle implies that outliving others carries no real advantage or benefit. But he says this in the context of comforting the Thessalonians regarding those who have died before the second coming (1 Thess. 4.13–18).

Aselgeia has no single precise Quranic equivalent, the closest being *fāhishah* (lewdness), something the Devil ardently orders his disciples to cultivate (Q7.27–28). Synonyms include caprice (*hawā*; Q53.3; *ahwā'a*, pl., 6.56) and joys (*shahawāt*; Q3.14). The latter includes sexual lust, considered a bodily sin only if indulged without or beyond divine sanction. Both words sustain undertones of uncouthness, anarchy and lawlessness. Sexual desire is seen as a threat to the societal fabric, a social force which must be channelled if not sublimated and, in all cases, placed under strict legal controls. Hence we have, as non-Muslims readily note with dismay, conservative Islam's sexual apartheid. It cannot be denied that traditional Islam has placed harsh and puritanical restrictions on male-female liaisons outside prescribed limits.

20

The catalogue of sins continues with nine more vices. The two sins of paganism, namely, idolatry and sorcery, incensed Jews. Rabbinic Judaism teaches that sexual sins are derivative: idolatry is the root cause of sexual immorality. Paul stresses this liaison in his famous diatribe against paganism (Rom. 1.18–32). Muslims are no less incensed by idolatry and sorcery than Jews and Christians.

Witchcraft was *pharmakeia* since medicine was originally a form of magic using drugs. Indeed, some cynic might say that it has become so again today given the size of the pharmaceutical industry: a few doctors are merely drug dealers, albeit on the right side of the law! If, once upon a time, the doctor was seen as a magician – and some doctors did indeed suffer from the illusion of omnipotence – now we trust hardly any authority figure. Apart from seeking assistance with surgery and short-term traumatic injury, wise men and women manage their own health: medical science contains competing and even contradictory claims while many doctors, often overworked, are interested only in their patients' diseases rather than in attaining their optimal health.

Paul lists sins specific to social life and institutions, sins causing failures in communal harmony and fracturing even ecclesiastical unity. The sins of social strife are: hatred and wrangling, jealousy and outbursts of anger. These can cause three further problems: disputes, dissensions and factions (*hairesis*) as hostile splinter groups emerge. Heresies can be commended as a form of choice (Acts 24.5) but can also deteriorate into partisanship and motivate factionalism (as found in Corinth and Galatia). Read 2 Corinthians 12.20 for a list of forms of these sins as they afflict the Corinthian church: strife, jealousy, angry tempers, disputes, slanders, gossip, arrogance and disorder.

The harmful social attitudes include jealousy, a form of perverted zeal. The quartet of self-conscious emotions consists of jealousy (the desire to compete with others to acquire what they already have) and envy (the drive to attack or destroy what others have). Shame and guilt are respectively the desire to conceal real or perceived (i.e. rational or irrational) personal failings and the practical drive to repair the evil one has done.

The Islamic equivalent of wrangling is *jidāl*, a vice inherent in human nature (Q18.54). Man (*al-insān*) is the most contentious of all God's creatures, often unnecessarily argumentative, seeking devious escape from duties secretly recognised as binding. This vice is especially proscribed during the *ḥajj* (Q2.187), a time of intensified worship. In the modern world of exegetical scholarship, one often encounters this vice: many academics have a gift for needlessly complicating even simple (revealed) truths. This leads to an alienation from the world of ordinary devout believers.

Thumoi are outbursts of anger as opposed to *orgē*, the disposition of settled anger. The Quran uses *ghussa* for passionate anger that chokes a person, the word's literal sense. The food served to sinners in Hell causes them to choke (Q73.13). Muhammad advised his companions to control such anger in order to achieve self-control. Such anger subsides quickly, being of the kind which Latin moralists distilled in the proverb, 'Anger is madness for a short time.' Modern non-Muslim critics of Muhammad often accuse him of being capricious in his own expression of anger: remarkably lenient to some and astonishingly vindictive and cruel to others. Muslims defend the latter as righteous indignation, a requirement of prophetic character which must reflect and represent a just God. Such critics, usually committed Jews and Christians, typically overlook the many instances of much greater and sometimes gratuitous violence committed by Yahweh and by his righteously indignant devotees, including some prophets. Elijah's slaughter of the 450 false prophets of Baal (1 Kings 18.20–40) may be acceptable to Muslim readers. But one cannot imagine the Quran approving of some biblical incidents such as the one where God sends two she-bears to kill 42 young boys who had called Elisha a baldhead (2 Kings 2.19–22).

Eritheia is strife and contention caused by selfish ambition and envy. The word occurs only in James and Paul's writings, five times in the latter, usually in contexts of ecclesial disunity and insincere preaching of the gospel. In Paul, it is an antonym of altruistically driven Christian humility (*tapeinophrosunē*; see 2 Cor.12.20–21; Phil. 1.16–18, 2.3). In James, *eritheia* is earthly and sensual wisdom (3.14, 16). Most modern disputes and professional rivalries are rooted in *eritheia*, that naked ambition which is motivated by power and profit. As an anti-social form of selfishness, it is rampant in advanced capitalist nations, virtually unaffected by the official presence of Christianity in their consumerist cultures. Consumerism is itself a form of concupiscent sensuality and, as such, has seduced virtually everyone – even the elect, including self-righteous Muslims who speak loudly of the self-restraint their faith demands.

21

Paul names three vices (envy, drunkenness and orgies) and hints at additional unspecified ones. If the blatant sins include promiscuity, the subtler ones include envy.

'Don't envy. Be envied.' This is the unspoken motto of capitalist consumerist propaganda as it successfully creates needless competition and dissatisfaction among classes of people. Some self-centred individuals are sometimes spared one vice: being indifferent to others can, I believe, occasionally remove envious comparison with others.

In Islam, envy (*ḥasad*) is condemned as evil (Q113.5). It is cited often as a trait of hypocrites, including desert Arabs (48.15), and of Jews and Christians who begrudge the fact that God has honoured the Arabs with an Arabic scripture (2.90, 109; 4.54).

Paul mentions a pair of sins of intemperance, namely drunkenness and carousing (orgies). These were sanctioned by pagan forms of worship. Paul knew well about the Roman and Greek penchant for nights of Bacchanalian revelry. Plato forbids wine for pilots and judges while on duty; magistrates must not drink during their entire year of office.[12] The great Greek thinker charges that the state of just men in the poets' notion of heaven is 'an eternal inebriation' (*aionios methē*).[13]

Islam saved its adherents from the universal curse of alcohol, unfairly associated with Western culture alone. Apart from the world of Islam, alcohol is widely used and abused across the entire globe. If Christianity introduced the virtue of chastity to the Graeco-Roman world, Islam introduced the virtue of temperance to the whole world, wherever it spread. Islam's largely successful ban on the public and uninhibited use of alcohol, if not on its secret and private consumption by sinful Muslims, has not been rivalled, let alone surpassed by any other religion or ideology.

Christian attempts to ban alcohol have uniformly failed in every age. One thinks of the twentieth century American debacle – the 18th amendment of 1919 – which introduced the prohibition of alcohol. There are teetotallers among Christians but the indulgence in alcohol is no mere tolerated subculture in the West. Judaism and Christianity both lack any clear and consistent scriptural support for principled abstinence – although drunkenness is expressly prohibited in the New Testament.

Thus, a bishop must not be a drunkard (see 1 Tim. 3.3, Titus 1.17). Methodism's strong dislike of alcohol grew not out of any scriptural basis but rather out of *empirical* evidence for its destructive effects on family life, especially during the Industrial Revolution.

The Quran forbids believers from performing the formal prayer (*al-ṣala*) while inebriated (Q4.43) just as Paul condemns drunkenness during the Lord's supper (1 Cor. 11.20–22). The Quran permits wine only in paradise (47.15; 83.25), dismissing it as the Devil's handiwork on earth and recommends that believers shun it. Islamic law totally prohibits it and prescribes a mild punishment for public consumption.[14]

Paul reflects Jesus' concern with the coming Kingdom of God. Paul repeats his warning that evildoers shall not inherit it, implying that it is a gift bequeathed, not something earned or achieved by effort. When the Apostle judges some as being unworthy of the Kingdom of God, we sense an early hint of what is to come from Paul the Jewish preacher to the Romans (Rom. 1.18–32). He is no less judgemental than his master who outraged his audience when he declared that repentant prostitutes would enter the Kingdom before the Pharisees.

For Paul, the Kingdom of God is a future event while, for his master Jesus, the Kingdom of God (or of Heaven) is already here in our midst. In both cases, it is a periphrasis for divine rule rather than a spatial location and, in both cases, there is a present and a future dimension, though the future appears to be more imminent and pronounced in Paul. 'To God belongs the sovereignty or ownership (*mulk*; *malakūt*) of the heavens and the earth' is a frequent Quranic refrain (Q3.189; 36.83). In Islamic law, both land and sovereignty belong only to God, not to the people, since God alone is the true owner and king (*al-malik*) even though he permits his creatures to temporarily own things.[15]

VIII 5.22

22 *But the fruit of the spirit is self-giving-love, joy, peace, longsuffering, kindness, goodness, faith/faithfulness.*

In 1 Cor. 3.6–9, during a discussion of the flesh-centred rivalries in the church, Paul offers a famous arboreal metaphor to depict the progress of the life of faith. The Quran has a rough parallel in the parable of the good and the evil word as resembling the good tree and the evil tree. The good tree bears fruit in every season, its roots are firmly planted in the earth while its branches reach towards heaven (see Q14.24–7). This corresponds to the fruit of the spirit since its growth is by God's leave. The evil word is like an uprooted tree, lacking stability and firmness – hollow and easily destroyed.

22

Note that 'fruit' is in the singular just as the 'seed' of Abraham is in the singular. The harvest yielded by the spirit is described in terms of personal relations and the moral qualities that constitute individual character. The three triplets are: love, joy and peace; patience, kindness and goodness; fidelity, gentleness and self-control. (The last two of these nine virtues appear in v.23).

The spiritual gifts, so prominent in the Corinthian correspondence, are altogether missing here. In his eulogy for *agapē* (1 Cor. 13), Paul places it in the middle of an assessment of spiritual gifts, suggesting that such gifts count for nothing if their owner lacks *agapē*. Here too the list opens with this core Christian virtue which is not merely one virtue among others but rather (and also) the impulse or ground for the others. Paul lists love as the first fruit of the spirit, a view to which he clings persistently for the rest of his life as a follower of Christ. In his ode to *agapē*, Paul places this virtue higher than prophecy (1 Cor. 13.8) which is rated higher than the gift of tongues (14.1–25). Paul places *agapē* even higher than faith in Christ!

For Muslims, divine love is not high on the list. Admittedly, God loves the righteous, the just, the pure, the patient, those who trust in him and the *mujāhidīn* who fight in his way (Q2.195, 222, 3.76, 134, 146, 148, etc.) – but this is the *deserved* love of a wise and just king towards his loyal subjects *on condition* that they must behave in a certain way. There are only two references that suggest that love might be displayed spontaneously as part of divine nature and therefore less dependent on human conduct (Q11.90, 85.14). Divine justice, however, scores high on the scale since God is committed to maintaining the cosmic balance of equity (Q55.7–9).

While pure joy is central to Philippians (4.1, 4), it finds occasion only once in Galatians – and that only in a list! Paul celebrates a joyful availing of the Gospel among the Philippian Gentiles, the first colony of Christians in Europe, and does so again slightly later among the Thessalonians (1 Thess. 2.19–20). Christian joy is uncontrived and spontaneous and, like humour, contains an element of surprise. As a term of salutation, indicating health and bliss, joy is a characteristically Pauline disposition but found also in the Synoptic Gospels.

Nietzsche thought that while Jesus' behaviour was marked by joy and spontaneous gaiety, Paul's demeanour was marked by sadness, sentimentality and joylessness. In his *The Anti-Christ*, Nietzsche castigates Paul as the man who ruined Europe with his brand of Christianity. Hence, the German thinker's two much-quoted aphorisms, 'There has only been one Christian, and he died on the Cross' and 'The two narcotics that ruined Europe: alcohol and Christianity.' Nietzsche offered his own gospel of atheistic liberation from all religion, especially Christianity, in his early and incendiary masterpiece, *The Joyful Wisdom* (1882).

The Quran never cites joy as an aspect of Christian piety. As for Muslim believers, their conduct on earth is typically marked by patience and tranquillity rather than joy *(surūr)* which occurs in verses describing the radiant faces of those in (or about to enter) paradise (Q76.11). It is joy that is being described in 'the radiance of delight' (Q83.24) shining in the faces of believers already in heaven. Martyrs in paradise rejoice (from *ba/sha/ra*, to give good news), knowing that others are about to join their ranks (Q3.170). According to Islamic tradition, martyrs have a residue of joy on their dead faces – their final expression on earth – just as all devout believers' faces show on their foreheads the traces of their frequent prostration (Q48.29). The noun *ṭūbā* (meaning wholesomeness or blessedness) is often translated as joy (see Q13.29). It characterises believers.

Chara (joy), *charis* (grace) and charisma (gift) enjoy linguistic proximity. Quranic Arabic similarly uses a small set of words, each with a common root, to form a surprisingly varied range, including neologisms. For example: *ṣidq* (sincerity) yields the expected *ṣadaqa* (voluntary, hence sincere, charity) but also the neologism *ṣaduqa* (Q4.4), literally, a small but sincere gift, a token of love in a marital proposal.

Paul lists peace, long-suffering, kindness, goodness and faith. Notice the placing of faith (*pistis*) quite late in the list. The Quran would list *īmān* (faith) along with piety (*taqwā*) – the expression of faith – at joint first place.

Christians view peace as the fruit of the spirit. This fruit itself may be seen as an unmerited divine gift and equally as the outward sign of that gift as it produces the fruit. The gift that stimulates the fruitfulness is the indwelling spirit of God. For Muslims, *salām al-islām* is the peace that comes through human submission to God's will, both personally and communally. The effort is human; the reward is divine. God calls us to do good deeds, as an accompaniment of faith – that is Islam – or after we receive the gift of salvation through faith alone – that is Christianity. These stances are similar but Islam stresses peace as a political rather than a private virtue. The faith is, moreover, named after this virtue – eulogised in the attitude that leads to the fulfilment of this ideal in God's political providence expressed perfectly only in imperial Islam.

Peace as the natural result or fruit of exercising love is a distinctively Christian notion although there are echoes of it in Psalms (Ps. 119.165). The New Testament teaches that Christ as the believers' surety assumes their guilt, pays the deserved penalty of sin, fulfils the law, and thus reconciles (sinful) humanity to God, securing peace as the last fruit of the spirit (see Heb. 4.14–10.39).

Peace is a positive and substantive value in Islam, combining the values of divine justice and mercy with human moral excellence. The cosmic harmony thus achieved is a by-product of a sovereignty where Truth (*Al-ḥaqq*), Goodness and Beauty – the last two realities covered by the same word (*Al-iḥsān*) – are grounded equally in a single, utterly real and transcendent will.

Neither the noun *makrothumia* (verb, *makrothumein*) nor the Christian virtue denoted by it can be found in classical Greek. I am speaking of the Christian God's patience and long-suffering with his creatures' faults and sins (Rom. 2.4, 9.22). Abraham had this quality: he patiently endured and therefore eventually received the promise (Heb. 6.15). Every Christian must aspire to this virtue, a major fruit of the spirit. It must be exercised towards all (1 Thess. 5.14), being one of the attributes of *agapē* (1 Cor. 13.4) and a necessary condition of all Christian fellowship. Paul cites it as a probative credential of authentic apostleship (2 Cor. 6.6).

Al-ṣabūr (most patient) is one of God's 99 names in Islamic tradition but, revealingly, it is one of the few absent from the Quran. While God is patient with sinful communities, his justice prevents him from being indefinitely patient (long-suffering). Had Muhammad been in charge, the threatened divine penalty would already have been visited on the Meccans (Q6.57–58). Muslims admire Muhammad as the most patient of apostles but, like his God, he is not willing to wait indefinitely.

Christian critics often accuse him of outright impatience. The Quran's division of labour was that Muhammad should convey the message (*balagh*) while God would do the reckoning (*ḥisab*). Yet Muhammad took matters into his own hands when he conquered the Meccans by force since he conveyed the message but also did the reckoning. Can this be the way to conquer hearts?[16]

In the Petrine pair, 'the patience (*makrothumia*) of God' is the disposition which accounts for the merciful delay in just judgement in Noah's day so that there was enough time to build the saving ark (1 Pet. 3.20). It even accounts for our salvation (2 Pet. 3.9, 15), a view Peter attributes to Paul but adds that some of the Apostle's claims are hard to understand. Those who write clearly often have their readers while those who write obscurely sometimes have more commentators than readers! (One thinks of our Dickens and Shakespeare respectively.)

Paul's catalogue continues with *chrēstotēs* (clemency or kindness) which is listed next to *agathōsunē* (goodness). *Chrēstotēs,* rare in classical Greek authors and moralists, is the kind of New Testament word which enriches Greek philosophical ethics. It is used in the speeches of Isaeus, the fourth century BCE Athenian writer specialising in testamentary law and famed for his skill in forensic oratory. But such secular usage lacks the moral depth found in its Christian recruitment. In Paul, it can mean simply goodness (Rom. 3.12, quoting Psalms 14.1, 53.1 and Eccles. 7.20) but can also denote kindness, goodness and gentleness combined (see Rom. 2.4, 9.23, 11.22; 2 Cor. 6.6), nuances captured well in the Latin translation of this virtue as *benignitas*, hence our word benignity. It has this meaning in the disputed Pauline epistles too (see Col. 3.12 and Titus 3.4) although there it can also carry overtones of beneficence shown as a public or civic virtue (Eph. 2.7). This latter emphasis is rare in Christian ethics but commonplace in Islamic ethics and law since Islam is a compulsively political religion.

The Arabic equivalent of *chrēstotēs* is *ḥilm* (clemency); the adjective *ḥalīm*, (tender-hearted), is used of Abraham (Q9.114; 9.75). The *ḥalīm* shows a magnanimous kindness, a practical generosity close to an anonymous benevolence and comprehensive hospitality. Generosity was the Arab nomad's supreme virtue, its opposite being *bukhl* (stinginess). The pagan tribal sheikh yearned for a reputation for generosity. To call him *al-bakhīl*, the stingy one who gives only grudgingly (Q48.38; 57.24), was the worst insult, especially in pagan Arabia where the chief components of virility (*muru'a*) were chivalry and generosity. The revelation of the Quran retained but spiritualised these pagan virtues. The Islamic scripture praises generosity but condemns hoarding and miserliness.

A point about Christian-Muslim relations here will enrich our survey by modifying our popular inherited understanding of medieval rivalries that still infect our current dealings. Educated secular and agnostic Europeans, aware of Islam's contributions to the 'white Christian continent', will be irresistibly reminded of the Muslim warrior-knight Saladin's dealings with the remarkably unchivalrous Christian Crusaders. However, some conservative Christian preachers, especially in America, are now sympathetic to the *religious* intent of the Crusades, and therefore speculate that Saladin was not necessarily chivalrous but merely concerned to achieve only a reputation for this admirable trait. They see his high reputation as the result of secular Europeans looking for any opportunity to malign the Christian component of European history and achievement. There were often only culturally relevant motives rather than any fully reliable historical grounds for the way that historians, whether Christian or agnostic, described Saladin and his Crusader opponents. This is a subject for another occasion.

Agathosunē is here a synonym for *chrēstotēs* but more narrowly means generosity. While found in the Septuagint (e.g. in Neh.9.25, 35), it occurs in the New Testament only in Paul – here, in Rom. 5.14, and in two deutero-Pauline epistles (Eph. 5.9; 2 Thess. 1.11). The closest Quranic virtue is denoted by *iḥsān*, meaning 'pleasing goodness' of any kind.

The inward characteristics of the spirit's presence are love, joy and peace and so on. Muslims would recognise several fruits of God's grace but it would be artificial and unconvincing to list them as analogues of the Christian repertoire. The relevant theological and ethical presuppositions differ. In any case, the Quran emphasises the practical life of faith, setting little or no store by abstract belief and theology. The Muslim believer cultivates the related states of faith (*īmān*) and piety (*taqwā*) through patience (*ṣabr*), repentance (*tawbā*) and trust in God (*tawakkul*). Precaution and planning, along with patience and prayer, render anxiety redundant and irrational. In religious terms, such anxiety is an act of ingratitude, possibly, infidelity, towards God. The faithful man trusts in God and ties his camel firmly and, having tied it, again firmly trusts in God. Human action is sandwiched between two layers of trust in God. 'Whoever trusts in God, God suffices him': a late Medinan revelation (Q65.3).

The net result is the three-fold fruit: goodness (*iḥsān*), tranquillity (*iṭminān*) and peace (*salām*). All are Quranic words, based on pre-Islamic words but invariably endowed with novel spiritual meanings and immeasurably enriched by the Quran's irreducibly spiritual outlook. The believer has faith in God, fears him and tries to obey his law. He or she actively practises patience in the difficult hour, repents through regular prayer and remembrance of God and places total trust in him. The fruits of such submission to God's will are evident in the doing of good actions, marked by charity, kindness and justice. The final results are a state of peace and tranquillity that come not from a direct attempt to achieve such states, but as a by-product of doing one's divinely revealed and divinely imposed duty. God's grace alone can crown the believer's efforts with success. Joy and love are not prominent in the Quran: I suspect that joy is probably seen as too ostentatious and worldly while love is seen as perhaps being mawkish. I know from personal observation that some strict Muslims rarely smile, let alone laugh: instead they see much to lament and even more to cry about, including their own and the world's sinful state.

IX 5.23

23 . . . *meekness, self-control; against such things there is no law.*

In this section, I shall review Paul's list of the qualities that distinguish the Christian character by adding an additional background – the markedly secular Greek views of the virtues while still recording the Islamic analogues. This will enrich further our exegesis of Paul's Galatian list.

23

The beatitudes obliquely replace the Ten Commandments. 'Blessed are the meek' (Matt. 5.5) whose gracious mildness is listed as a fruit of the spirit (see also Gal. 6.1, 1 Cor. 4.21, 2 Cor. 10.1). Ps. 37.11a is quoted in Matt. 5.5: 'The meek (*praeis*) shall inherit the earth.' In a rare notice of external scripture, the Quran quotes this verse but replaces 'the meek' with 'my righteous slaves' (Q21.105).

The noun *praütēs* is Christian humility or gentleness. 'Meekness' now sounds archaic and pseudo-biblical since modern English, unlike modern Arabic, is no longer easy to employ as a devotional language in any robust sense. The prevalence and the decline of specific vocabularies can reflect and influence religious and moral attitudes.

The Quran often mentions the self-abasement of God's servants (Q22.34), including humility in worship (Q2.45, 23.2). Aquinas also defined meekness as the virtue of 'praiseworthy self-abasement'.[17]

In secular Greek, the adjective *praüs* can describe an animal that has been tamed. Aristotle admires the quality of *praütēs* which he defines as the mean between *orgilotēs* (excessive anger) and *aorgēsia* (excessive lack of anger). The attitude of meekness, however, which Christianity commends and commands, would not have appealed to Aristotle. He would have seen it as a moral defect rather than a virtue since he came from a martial culture that set little store by such an essentially peacemaking virtue. It is not in vain that Aristotle was Alexander the Great's tutor!

Behind the believer's gentleness lies a reserve of strength. In Islamic thought, this quality is characteristic of prophets. The traditions often speak of how the Prophet displayed a mild graciousness and clemency in the face of frequent pagan and Jewish provocation. The Torah, unlike the Quran, confirms this quality in Moses, described as the meekest man on earth (Num.12.3). Such humility is strength under control. Prophets are meek and self-controlled men, exuding dignity and composure in the hour of eclipse and, in their finest hour of triumph, magnanimity and forgiveness. Such self-controlled and God-controlled servants serve their God and his creatures in humility and with humane compassion. It is impossible for a secular humanist or agnostic to exercise such a high level of humility since a necessary condition of humility is to acknowledge a superior if not supremely superior personal power, not merely some vague trust in the authority of an impersonal Reason or Truth. The admission of a superior authority is, however, not a sufficient condition of humility, as watching the behaviour of arrogant religious leaders amply proves.

Paul lists *egkrateia* (self-control), also a pagan virtue, one cornerstone of Stoicism. The appearance of this ninth item surprises us since the Christian ethical system is based on divine grace rather than human effort and merit. The Quran's central virtue of patience is a form of self-control. Self-control occurs nowhere in the Quran unless we translate *taqwā*, self-caution in the life of faith, as a rough equivalent.

The notion of restraint and renunciation in all matters, including sexuality, is popular in all established religions. The verb for practising patience (*ṣa/ba/ra*), indicating an active disposition rather than a passive state of being, literally means to restrain or control oneself. The increased form (IV) of this verb is used thus, in a combined transitive and reflexive sense, in a divine order to Muhammad to restrict himself to the company of devout believers who refuse to hanker after the world's enjoyments and pomp (see *iṣbar nafsak*; Q18.28). Several Islamic languages contain the predictable proverb, 'The key to paradise is patience.'

Weakness of the will (*akrasia;* 1 Cor. 7.5), not mentioned here, is not a vice but rather a failing, most often found in the context of the pressure of sexual desire on the frail human frame and the attendant need for restraint. The analogue of *taqwā* (pious restraint) is sexual self-restraint (*'iffah*), a common female Muslim name. No matter how strong the pious will is, flesh is only flesh. While religious belief systems concur with secular ones about the ethical need to control the self, the Buddhist stance radically challenges this view. If the self has been neutered or annihilated, we need not worry about controlling it. I reject this Buddhist view as radically incoherent, not merely false.

Paul concludes that these virtues have never been outlawed – an understatement (*litotes*). Compression renders Paul's meaning unclear. He seems to capture every legislator's dream: human beings behaving well, without the additional inducement of a prison sentence.

Paul's final position may be described by the slogan: *veritas, libertas, pietas*. The doctrinal truth (*veritas*), the key component of faith, is grounded in the liberty (*libertas*) now afforded by the grace of the spirit. Together, these yield the fruit of righteousness (*pietas*). If we replace this Latin trinity with *Al-ḥaqq, al-hurriya, al-taqwā*, the result is unnatural since Islam replaces liberty with its opposite, namely, submission to both the spirit of the law and to its letter equally – and the former often through the latter.

X 5.24–26

24 *Now those who belong to Christ Jesus (have) crucified the flesh with its passions and its lusts.* **25** *If we live in the spirit, let us also march in step with the spirit.* **26** *Let us not become vainglorious, provoking one another, envying one another.*

24

'Crucifixion of the flesh' is a uniquely Christian way of saying 'No' to temptation. Paul knew that *epithumein* (to lust or covet) was used in the Greek version of the tenth commandment. The Stoics defined *epithumia* as grasping for pleasure beyond the bounds of reason.

Is it easier to avoid temptation altogether or to face it and yet resist it? In modern Western art, especially the novel and the film, the typical Westerner is portrayed as being a slave to his or her inner compulsions. Yet, it rarely occurs to secularists, so hell-bent on seeking absolute artistic freedoms, that an inner compulsion is no less a tyrant than the external demands of, say, the divine law or the law of the spirit. An inner compulsion can humiliate a human being no less effectively than an externally coercive force. One has only to look at 'celebrities in rehab' battling the bottle and indiscriminate offers of sex.

Christians are crucifying the desires of the sinful nature as they kill the lustful Adam who is said to live in each of us. Christ's community has, though usually only in principle, transcended base physical desire. The spiritual basis for this conquest is clear but, in practice, most Christians do not lead lives that are recognisably free of the vices that afflict our common humanity. Indeed, some commentators, especially the late 'sit-down stand-up' comedian Dave Allen, would insist that, whatever we may say of sex, the vices of fanaticism and intolerance are found more often among religious people, especially Christians, than among secular humanists. I do not need to assess this claim here.

The demanding ideal of mortifying the flesh has been endorsed by few Christians. This ideal is admittedly only a secondary component of the monastic lifestyle which seeks primarily to please God in all due humility in all contexts. Most Christians have, like virtually all Jews before them, and Muslims after them, affirmed an affirmative view of the flesh and its pleasures. All these believers – the law-abiding Jew, the Christian under grace, the submissive Muslim – have saluted the goodness of the world. A wholesome enjoyment of pleasure permitted by God is itself a form of worship, as we offer thanks and praise for our creator's goodness towards us. Such divine mercy is demonstrated in the providential system of provision that surrounds us, including the delightful if frustrating male-female division. The monastic tradition does, however, affirm part of the corporeal life, especially the pleasures of food.

Paul's use of passions and desires implies a wide range of human wants. Appetites such as food and drink are, as pleasures of the flesh, different in kind from sexual gratification. Sex often involves a desire to dominate another person or persons, usually of the opposite gender. Even sexual fantasy and masturbation involve reducing other autonomous human beings – subjects – into objects. The appetite of eating, however, does not involve liaison with a subject exercising its will, a being who can resist or embrace us. Dead animals, not living ones, are eaten, partly for this reason.

25

Crucifying the flesh, through living and walking in the spirit, is the new *halākhā*, the Christian way of walking in the way of the Torah. 'Let us march' (*stoichōmen)* instructs us to fall in step with communal walking. In Gal. 6.16, Paul uses the same verb to suggest perhaps that the church, the new Israel, is the Christian army marching – in harmony with the spirit, under its inspiration. Paul uses a Greek military phrase to make the Galatians understand the new discipline of walking – but now in the spirit rather than the flesh.

Paul warns the Roman saints that, being under grace, they must now use parts of the body, not as instruments of lust but rather only of righteousness (Rom. 6.13; see also 1 Cor. 6.15–17). The Quran similarly warns us against using the limbs of the mortal body to extend the range of evil; the body's organs of sense, extremities and skin are personified as witnesses against their owners on the Day of Reckoning (see Q36.65; 24.24; 41.20–22).

Before we end our commentary on these verses on the spirit-flesh dichotomy, we note that *pneuma* can designate the divine spirit or the human spirit. This ambiguity in vv.17–18 is removed in vv.22–23 since *agapē* and other gifts of the spirit are rooted only in divine *pneuma*. One could capitalise the divine spirit as Spirit. Some commentators interpret the human spirit as 'that aspect of the person that is open to domination by the Holy Spirit'.[18] Thus, the human spirit is opposed to the flesh, a word that unambiguously means the human flesh. The spirit is of divine origin; 'God has sent the spirit of his son into our hearts' (Gal. 4.6). Thus the Christian believer has a human spirit and a divine Spirit in him or her. The Holy Spirit is the spirit of God, a gift from the resurrected Christ (Acts 1.5). Note that the Quran calls Gabriel 'the holy spirit' (*rūḥ al-qudus*; 16.102). The Islamic notion of the spirit simpliciter (*al-rūḥ*; Q17.85) cannot, incidentally, be the analogue of the spirit in Paul's thought here.

26

The failings of our common humanity include boasting, challenging (mutual provocation) and envying one another, all causes of disunity. Conceit, provocative behaviour and envy are socially toxic attitudes, especially prevalent in advanced capitalist cultures and those cultures that ape them, including some located in affluent parts of the Islamic world. Such societies, if we may even use such a decidedly lenient and kind word for a group of dysfunctional people, are consumed by the drive for power, profit and personal gain, by hedonism and a thirst for ever-increasing levels of vulgarity, ostentation and brazen display and dissemination of mindless activities. In such image-based and competitive cultures, greed and vanity are virtues, not vices. How can people be expected to be sincere and authentic in cultures that have canonised their own superficiality and vanity?

Paul has much to say on strife as a communal vice. In this letter, his advice is pastorally driven, not merely a by-product of bad temper. Pride destroys unity; humility is a prerequisite for unity. The spirit-led believer walks in humility, maturity, integrity, charity, purity, servility, responsibility and – importantly for church life – in unity with others. One senses a level of party strife inside the Galatian churches – probably no less than in the more obvious case of the Corinthian congregations. Paul is daunted more by the pastoral care (*hē merimna*) of his foundations than by his other cares and burdens as an Apostle (2 Cor. 11.28).

We find similar party strife during Muhammad's life. After his death, the splits and factions were numerous. One famous incident, called 'the mosque of mischief' affair, occurred during Muhammad's absence from Medina, when he was leading the Tabuk campaign. A group of hypocrites built an alternative mosque to oppose him on his return. The Quran records in detail the spiritual dimension of the incident

(Q9.38–110) while commentary supplies secular details. It was the only house of worship, of any monotheistic faith, that General Muhammad felt obliged to destroy.

In revealed faiths, zealous believers often feel confident to the point of conceit, thinking that they alone are always right, that others must be misguided in opposing them, and that therefore it is morally right to overlook community and make camp all by oneself. Nor are prophets and apostles always exempt from such hubristic confidence. After all, a man who receives his counsel directly from God can hardly find reason to consult merely human colleagues. One safeguard here is to distinguish between one's own cause and God's cause – and not to assume that the two must always coincide. The Quran encourages such discrimination (Q4.94; 49.6). Alas how few have zeal for God in accordance with knowledge (see Rom. 10.2)!

XI

I did not want to overburden the earlier sections of this chapter. Accordingly, I shall now comment separately, in more detail, on 5.14 (summative law) and 5.22 (*agapē*).

From the Prophet's traditions: 'None of you has faith until you love for your brother what you love for yourself.' Note the reference to the brother rather than the neighbour. Only those within the Islamic fellowship are your brothers and sisters – in faith. The Islamic version of the summative law is narrower than the Christian one since anyone in need can be your neighbour. That is the teaching of the parable of the Good Samaritan, unique to Luke, the evangelist most concerned with the Gentile mission, an incontrovertible fact if we read both of his lengthy contributions to the New Testament. While Luke commends the universality of compassion, Matthew is markedly less interested in the Gentile dimension. He stresses rather the anonymity of catholic benevolence (Luke 25.31–40). The Christian is indiscriminately kind – kind to all. This stress is conspicuous in Buddhism.

Traces of it are in the Quran too (Q76.8–9), a scripture whose regular emphasis falls more on the ideological notion that believers alone are the truly just and authentic solidarity, composed of brothers (and sisters) united on earth under the only true God in heaven. In total contrast to official Christianity, Quranic Islam is only politically exclusive since it seeks a monopoly on the exercise of temporal power – but it is not dogmatically enthusiastic to the point of doctrinal intolerance. This is shown in the way that Islam tolerated Jews and Christians as errant but privileged minorities while arrogating to itself the absolute right to rule the world, on behalf of God. Until the rise of secularism, it is hard to find any avowedly Christian polity with a similarly lenient attitude towards self-professed Muslim and Jewish minorities residing in its midst.

The Quran orders kindness to the near (related) and the distant (unrelated) neighbour (Q4.36) while the *ḥadīth* commentary on this verse elaborates on the rights of the neighbour, understood as someone living in one's vicinity. The physically close neighbour was assigned such important rights that many companions feared that the Prophet might have been speculating about giving them some inheritance rights! 'The man who eats his fill while his neighbour sleeps hungry is not a believer' is an oft-quoted but oft-ignored *ḥadīth*, often uttered by those who announce glibly, after a lavish meal, that God himself will provide – in a world where many thousands, often in nearby lands, starve daily.

In later popular piety, a recurring motif portrays the man who declines to perform his pilgrimage to Mecca and instead uses the money to feed his poor and hungry neighbours who would otherwise be forced to consume forbidden meat, often domestic donkey meat. In a dream, in which the Prophet appears, the charitable man is pleasantly shocked to be told that his pilgrimage has been accepted, in absentia, on the basis of his pure intention to perform it and owing to his charitable concern for his neighbours. The Prophet's added comment is devastating: the pilgrimages of many who did travel to Mecca, enduring much heat and dust, arrived only to find that their journey and sacrifices were not acceptable to God. This was, the Prophet explained, owing to insincerity of motive (*niyya*). We see yet again both the Quran's and the Prophet's high regard for purity of intention.

We may locate in the Quran two versions of the summative law resembling Gal. 5.14. 'Do not forget grace (*faḍl*) among yourselves' (Q2.237). The other one occurs in the context of an absolute divine ban on usury, the bane of the modern world. The Quran counsels with concision and force: 'Neither commit injustice nor be its victims' (*lā taẓlimūna wa lā tuẓlamūn(a)*; Q2.279).

A version of the summative law occurs as a principle of Islamic law and ethics: whatever promotes the *maṣlaḥa* (welfare) of the Muslim community should be promoted. This principle is maximised in the five pillars where *one* verbal confession undergirds *four* practical duties – prayer, fasting, giving alms and performing the pilgrimage. Each member of this quartet retains a public (or communal) dimension of social benefit despite being discharged individually (and in that sense privately).

The Prophet occasionally ordered people to obey only some key commandments – not because they epitomised Islam's holy law but because he wanted to demand little of new converts to the faith. One neophyte was advised to abjure only two things: to stop lying and to control his anger. On occasion, the Prophet (and after him the rightly guided caliphs) permitted newly converted tribes to obey less than the whole law. One tribe was temporarily exempted from paying the alms tax, a pillar of the faith – and one of the two major sources of state revenue, the other being war booty. Again, the Prophet acted in such a way as to single out a quality, especially mercy, as the key trait of the new faith. He once permitted a (pagan) man to continue openly urinating in the mosque, allowing him to complete the act of desecration. Much to the surprise of his companions, the Prophet simply asked the man to leave. That Muhammad managed to inspire such an uncultured people to rise to world eminence, for the first and only time in their history, remains a feat that challenges secular liberal as well as Jewish and Christian explanations, most of which are facile if not wholly glib.

XII

We move to 5.22. In practice, *agapē* finds a close enough analogue in mercy (*ra'fa*), a quality characteristic of normative Christian deportment. Judaism has love (*ahabh*) but Christians expand it to have a more theologically grounded meaning. The God of the Quran does not love disbelievers but he is clement and lenient towards faithful sinners who repent. Divine love, interpreted as the comprehensive compassion of divine *nature*, is a characteristically Christian dogma. Islam encourages mercy, justice, kindness and humility – but love is not its chosen priority. Sufi Islam, possibly under Christian influence, assigns divine love a central place. The Prophet's traditions speak of God's love as being far more powerful than a mother's love. But such love is directed exclusively only at sinful but repentant believers. The tradition might, in any case, be forged: later mystical movements naturally sought the approval of the Prophet.

Paul rightly fears that an abstract call for love will inevitably deteriorate into a permissive lawlessness, a lax antinomianism that is effectively licence. Paul's Gospel offers liberty – with *agapē* preventing liberty from becoming libertinism. It is hard to accuse Paul of antinomianism since he usually pens a substantial paraenesis to guide, motivate and control the actions of his converts. This moral advice is especially crucial for guiding the church in our secular times when hedonism and laxity rule in the world beyond its borders.

Sensing perhaps that even *agapē* can be or may become mawkish and religiose, Paul prays for the Philippians' love (*agapē*) to be deepened and tempered by sensitive perception (*aisthēsis*; Phil. 1.9), an attitude that resembles the reverent perceptiveness and discernment the Quran dubs *tadabbur* (Q47.24). Paul clarifies that the aim of such discrimination is to enable followers of Christ to approve of what is morally excellent and thus attain sincerity and blamelessness. It is impossible for any monotheist to attack this stance from any credible moral angle.

Paul uses *philia* to refer to the love Christians should show towards Jesus (1 Cor. 16.22). This choice is reinforced elsewhere in the New Testament. In the exchange between Peter and the post-resurrection Jesus (John 21.15–17), Jesus asks him if he loves him. The verb *agapaō* is used by Jesus twice in a question he poses three times to a bewildered Peter, already forgiven for his cowardice and now about to be fully rehabilitated. Peter answers in the affirmative each time but with a different verb for love, namely, *phileō*, a detail lost in translation.

Agapē extends further than *philia*. Like charity, *agapē* begins at home, in the Christian fellowship, but also widens outwards towards the neighbour, reaching even to the enemy. Insofar as *agapē* provides a principle that guides conduct, it can, unlike *philia*, be coherently conceptualised only as an intellectual rather than emotional virtue. It relates to the mind and will, not primarily the heart. Since no human being naturally loves their enemy, *agapē* must be a moral achievement of the will. We certainly cannot be expected to love our enemies the way we love our wives and children. The latter arises spontaneously and, at least initially, requires no effort of the will. Rather it takes effort to resist such natural affection. In committed relationships, matters are murkier. Some couples foolishly opt for divorce as soon as their love is no longer effortless, since they forget that love includes not only feeling – the effortless component – but also continuous moral commitment and fidelity. These people need to take a course in the philosophy of mind rather than see their marriage guidance counsellors. In view of these inconvenient facts of human psychology, the later portions of the Medinan Quran exhort believers to struggle to partly resist even such naturally irresistible familial and marital love if it should conflict, as it often and inevitably does, with the higher struggle (*jihād*) in God's cause (Q9.23, 60.1–9).

Agapē then can only be an unconditional benevolence which we must cultivate in order to be able to imitate the Christian God's own moral attitude towards even his disobedient creatures, including his enemies, as he seeks the highest good of everyone alike (Matt. 5.43–48). Such divine love does not have even a linguistic analogue in classical Greek or in the Arabic Quran. The moral limitation in this Christian dogma is that the comprehensive divine compassion it commends is restricted to earth and cannot extend to the future life – where Christ's enemies and detractors, including Jews and Muslims, are presumably destined for hell.

Quranic Islam rejects *agapē* as false and mawkish love, as irresponsible and vague. The Quran is admittedly a supra-moral, even amoral, scripture – indifferent to purely human conceptions of love and hate, good and evil. However, this is not to say that the God of the Quran lacks compassion or that the Prophet of Islam did not care for human beings. Indeed Muslims regard Muhammad as a truly loving prophet who cared for his companions and some claim that he awaits eagerly to intercede on behalf of his *umma* on the dreadful day of judgement. Popular Sunni piety portrays him as anguished on that day, quietly lamenting '*ummati, ummati*' (my people, my people), asking God's pardon even for the worst sinners among his people (based on *ḥadīth* and on Q4.106–109; 9.84, 103; 24.62). Popular Muslim piety portrays even Jesus as preoccupied with his own salvation on that day, unconcerned with the fate of his community! (This is in shocking contrast to Christian views of Jesus who is worshipped as every Christian's reliable advocate on the day of requital.) Among Shi'ites, Hussain and Ali are intercessors for their own *shī'a* (group of partisans), a view considered reprehensible if not heretical by orthodox Islam which is reluctant to grant such an intercessory power even to Muhammad himself, let alone to lesser Muslim saints.

Finally, in the modern world, there are frequent calls for Muslims to be less sensitive to perceived insults to their faith and to the honour of Muhammad. In the context of Salman Rushdie and also the countless cartoon controversies, Muslims are told to 'hate the idea, love the man'. Many Westerners profess this quasi-Christian motto. Thus, Muslims have every right to be offended but should not harm those who insult them. Muslims typically see the man-idea separation as a psychologically incoherent distinction and moreover patronising since it refuses to take the enemy seriously on his or her own terms. Why should we separate the man and the idea? On a related note, Voltaire is reputed to have said that even if he disagreed strongly with his opponent, he would defend unto death his opponent's right to speak his or her mind. This is surely asking too much of people. Why should I die for my enemy's right to speak falsehood? Surely, it is enough that I should be ready to die for my own convictions rather than for other people's errors.

XIII

Before examining major themes, we note some prominent virtues and vices omitted in the Galatian catalogue. Unlike Christianity, pagan ethical systems, such as Aristotle's, were based on merit – reliance on unaided human effort to attain virtue. For Christians, divine grace alone enables virtue. Christianity disdains (pagan) heroic virtue since every virtue is a fruit of the spirit, an undeserved gift. Christ is the true hero: his humility and voluntary humanity earn him everlasting merit with God. The Quran rejects *muru'a* (virility), the great virtue of the pre-Islamic age of ignorance. The word does not even occur in the Quran.

Three surprising omissions from the Galatian catalogue include the two related virtues of Christian purity or simplicity (*hagnotētos*; 2 Cor. 6.6, 11.3) and godly sincerity (*eilikrineia tou theou*; 2 Cor. 1.12). Such sincerity amounts to integrity – a sifting out of character to achieve a seamless innocence and purification. Paul calls it *eilikrineia* (1 Cor. 5.8; 2 Cor. 1.12, 2.17) and also uses the adjective *eilikrines* (Phil. 1.10). This virtue corresponds to sincerity (*sidq*), a central quality of character, commended by the Quran. Paul's third and crowning virtue here is sanctity or holiness (*hagiotētos*; 2 Cor. 1.12). These three qualities are enumerated in the polemical context of seeking to establish the integrity of his apostolic character and credentials. But the Galatian context is no less polemical than the Corinthian one. Hence, the surprise.

Again, *epieikeia* (mercy), not listed in Galatians, marks the Christian moral life. In a construction rare in Koine, Paul uses the neuter of the adjective as a noun (*to epieikes*; Phil. 4.5) to describe such gentleness or forbearance. The Quran pays tribute to this feature of normative Christian conduct. While mercy (*eleos*) is not listed among the fruits of the spirit, it occurs in the benediction at Gal. 6.16. Christianity, like Buddhism, promotes professions of mercy – such as nurses and therapeutic clowns entertaining terminally ill children in paediatric units. The Quran praises the compassion and mercy found in Christian hearts but rejects key Christian institutions with which we normally associate such charitable concern and outstanding care. Thus, it disowns monasticism as a misguided if well-intentioned Christian innovation (Q57.27).[19]

Paul lists neither courage nor wisdom (as such) as virtues. Is this so because both are too pagan (Hellenic) to be authentically Christian? Strictly speaking, no fruit of the spirit is a virtue. Each is a gift. If we may shelve this distinction, for the sake of argument, then the absence of *andreia* (courage) merits attention. Insofar as courage is engendered by human effort exerted in order to make our empirical nature conform to our higher spirit-led nature and thus achieve self-mastery, it is not a Christian virtue. After making an active confession of human helplessness, the Christian must passively receive the gifts of courage and peace and so on, gifts that come from sheer dependence on God. The noun *andreia* is found nowhere in the New Testament but we do find 'play the man' (*andrizesthe*; 1 Cor. 16.13), an imperative in the middle voice. In Acts 4.13, Peter and John display the related quality of *parrēsia*, (boldness) and exhibit a degree of articulate confidence surprising in men who are *agrammatoi* (unlettered) and *idiōtai* (lacking special individual gifts).

The Arabic noun *shujāʿa*, meaning courage, is used as an increasingly popular male Muslim name and occurs in the proverb '*Al-shujāʿa fadila*' (Courage is an excellence), understandably popular at a time when Muslims see themselves as weak and persecuted, no longer masters of their destiny. This word does not occur in the Quran just as the noun *andreia* is absent from the New Testament. The classical Greek *tharsos*, meaning good cheer, does occur (Acts 28.15) and is conjugated at 2 Cor. 7.16 (see also Matt. 9.2). But it does not mean courage as a disposition or determined attitude but rather a casual indifference to vicissitude, a deliberate disregard of circumstance. This might often require courage but it is not the same thing.

I do not want to read too much into the absence of a single word. For the fact that a word is missing need not entail that the attitude denoted by it is absent or cannot be expressed in alternative ways. Indeed, the ethos and the associated attitude might both be too prevalent to require an explicitly linguistic register. Paul had courage in abundance. Although Christians typically use meek symbols, such as the Lamb of God – a description of the sinless Christ – Paul has been rightly lionised as *Great Lion of God* (1970) by the conservative Catholic novelist Taylor Caldwell (1900–1985) in her fictionalised account of his life.[20] Muslims, especially Shi'ites, are irresistibly reminded of Ali, the Prophet's cousin and son-in-law, whose courage in battle earned him the sobriquet 'the Lion of God'.

Although prudence is not listed as a virtue here, it guides us, among its other roles, in deciding when to be courageous. In the life of faith, courage is not merely one virtue among others but rather the core virtue: those who uphold justice and truth in this corrupt world can safely expect determined opposition. And no one can hope to survive relentless hostility to their virtuous ambitions without the will to constantly exercise courage.

Paul claims that tribulation produces *hupomonē* (Rom. 5.3; see also 2 Cor.6.4; 2 Thess. 1.4), the quality of patient endurance under affliction. It corresponds to the Quranic virtue of endurance (*ṣabr*). This virtue inherited some components of the pagan Arab virtue of *muru'a* (virility) – a cluster of traits duly spiritualised and re-baptised by the Quran in order to qualify as the Islamic virtue of patient courage, now to be exercised for God's sake. Like *hupomonē*, *ṣabr* would be active rather than resigned acquiescence in present tribulation. The Christian cultivates *hupomonē* as part of a strategic acquiescence in present suffering in the active hope (*elpis*) of future glory and success (Rom. 5.3).

Among Christian virtues, *hupomonē* is one for which one can easily find an Islamic equivalent. Indeed in Islam. I would assign it a central place. In its own context, in 4 Maccabees, for example, it stood for the spiritual stamina that enabled Jews to opt for martyrdom and to repeat solemnly the noble word *êḥād* (One (God)) until the brutal end. It enabled devout Jews to resist Gentile encroachment and aggression. James, as Jewish as ever despite being Christian, claims that *hupomonē* perfects faith (1.3)! The word occurs, along with the verb *hupomenein*, some 30 times in the New Testament, being quite frequent in Revelation (1.9; 3.10; 13.10), the book that exalts martyrs.

In Senecan Stoicism, indifference (*apatheia*), not listed by Paul as a Christian virtue, was the classical form of courage in the face of adversity. It combined moral grandeur and intellectual dignity in the hour of eclipse coupled with a magnanimity bordering on indifference to fortune's vicissitudes, especially in the hour of triumph. (This is an apt description of Muhammad's career as a prophet-general.) More broadly, however, pagan thinkers, including Seneca, were sympathetic to the view, held also by monotheists, that 'virtue gains much by being put to the test' (*multum sibi adjicit virtus lacessita*).[21] And being tried and tested requires one to manage one's emotions, for God's sake, rather than merely suppress them, out of fear of others or in self-deception.

Paul omits a few vices, some pertaining to sins of speech. Prominent in James, these vices centre on bias and partiality (James 2.1–13). The Quran regards baseless suspicion, paranoia and spying as sinful (Q49.12). It often praises pure and gentle speech on earth and in the next life (Q22.24; 78.35) but permits vulgar speech in public by 'one who has been wronged' (Q4.148). In one of its many vignettes of paradise, God himself removes traces of any residual rancour (*ghill*; Q15.47), malice and ill will in the hearts of believers, so that they may sit facing each other, as brothers with purified hearts (Q83.22–23).

Would Paul compile a markedly different list today if writing to, say, one of the American churches in a country characterised by free market anarchy and the 'pastorpreneurs' of the megachurches? Would the Apostle compile a different set of vices if writing to a group of Saudi Muslims, offering them pastoral advice in the spirit of interfaith ecumene? Certainly, vices such as anger and selfish ambition are among the enduring failings of our common humanity. The Apostle need not dramatically revise his list. Has the world morally progressed much since the days of the glory that was Rome?

XIV

In Galatians, flesh, a metonymy for our sinful nature, is the main opponent of freedom. As the antagonist of the freedom to do (and be) good and to obey God (Rom. 7.7– 8.17), it stands for the impelling motives and dispositions of the natural human being – the being not energised by the spirit. Thus, man minus Christ is dominated by flesh, by what the Quran calls 'the evil-commanding soul' (only at Q12.53). The *jihād* (struggle) of the believer, as spirit and flesh fight it out in his or her body, is present in all Christians despite having Christ in their lives. This was the practical and ethical aspect of the fight, the crisis, in Galatia, requiring Paul's pastoral intervention. In the anguished *pericopē* of Romans 7.7–24, the 'I' (*egō*; 7.9) could refer to the pre-conversion Paul's struggle, to the hopeless striving of the man devoid of Christ – and, by extension, to the continuing strife of all Jews and Muslims since they wilfully reject Christ by denying his power to redeem them from the clutches of their sinful nature.

Paul's point is that in the theatre of dispositions, in the battleground between flesh and spirit, the antagonism between these forces does not result in paralysis: the two forces are not equally powerful. The spirit is more potent than the flesh, an agency whose relative weakness suggests that we should resist the Teutonic temptation to capitalise it.

Life in the flesh is driven by desire. The New Testament declines to recruit *eros* for religious employment, but other words for desires do occur. Paul preaches that a Christian replaces a sinful life by a virtuous life in the spirit (Gal. 5.15–21, 24). This can be compared to similar concerns in James (see 1:14–15, 3:14–16, 4:1–3) who assigns to wisdom (*hē sophia*) the task which Paul assigns to the spirit. For James, it is the wisdom from above (*hē de anōthen sophia*) which produces the fruit of the spirit. James' stance is closely echoed by countless Quranic verses about the gift of wisdom. Indeed the Quran itself offers revealed wisdom (*ḥikma*; Q31.12; 36.2; Hebr. *chokhmā*), along with the God-given sense of judgement and discretionary caution (*ḥukma*; Q12.22;28.14) taught to prophets, sages and even ordinary human beings who seek to submit fully to God's will (Q2.269). Paul and James concur about the kinds of people who are likely to inherit the Kingdom of God (cf. Gal. 5.21 with James 1.12 and 2.5).

Paul argued in Gal. 3–4 that the era of the law ended in the age of Christ, with the advent of the spirit. Paul now posits a dual opposition: the spirit is opposed both to the flesh and to the law. The spirit opposes the law and the works of the flesh, namely, overt deeds and attitudes nurtured by any human being, whether a believer or otherwise, under the domination of the flesh and its demands. But the spirit triumphs over both, by Christ's grace. It is not clear what role, if any, is played by human effort or initiative at this stage in the process of salvation. Perhaps none. A Christian apologist would object that faith – the decision to believe by mind and body, in thought and deed – is itself an assertion of human will and freedom. If so, this claim downplays the role of grace in the election of the sinner who is to be justified. Recall that for Paul, even prior election, not only justification, is by grace, not by works (Rom. 9.11–12). Paul's mature thought clearly contains an element of predestination, a core element of Calvinist theology.

A conservative Christian could question my claim that the spirit is opposed to the Law. Life by the spirit is opposed to living life by the Law but the spirit itself is in harmony with the Law in terms of the moral wisdom of the content of the Law. Thus, the argument could proceed, the believer asks for wisdom – to be given by the spirit, presumably – in order to know what to do in practice. This argument, based on James 1.5, but not found explicitly in Paul, is based on a confusion about the nature and status of the spirit. The spirit, unlike the Law, is here only a vague and context-free agency which answers to the human need for practical guidance. In effect, then, the spirit, insofar as it is not opposed to the Law, reduces to being merely a surrogate for it.

Does the spirit oppose the Law? Or does it somehow fulfil it, or fulfil it by transcending it – or perhaps simply transcend it? Certainly, for Paul, living by/in the spirit is opposed to living in/by the flesh. Moreover, being led by the spirit is opposed to being under the Law. But Paul seems to shy away from directly polarising the law and the spirit. For the Apostle, it seems to be rather a question of which agency (law or spirit) can help in decisively triumphing over the undeniable power of their common opponent, the flesh. While both the law and the spirit are opposed to the flesh, Paul seems to imply that the spirit is more efficacious than the law.

The flesh clearly remains irreconcilable with the spirit. Paul believed further that the latter can ultimately be (or at least become, thanks to grace) more powerful than its rival. Is there any wholly empirical evidence for the Apostle's bold claim on behalf of the spirit? Is it true only for saints? Is it true even for them? Listen to that imbalanced German genius, Friedrich Nietzsche, who answers such questions in his critique of hagiography. In one of his many unforgettably pithy aphorisms, he tells us that both our reason and conscience, a secular way of referring to the spirit, bow to 'the tyrant in us', namely, our most powerful drive.[22]

Is the spirit more powerful than the *sinful* will? The flesh lusts against the spirit because the flesh lacks an outlet for its energies along the path of the spirit. Islam rejects this battle by proposing that the *lawful* gratification of sensual desires is a spiritual act. The spirit of lust is a sign of life so long as it is subordinated to the spirit. The Quran speaks of sex even in the context of godliness (Q2.187). Celibacy is not sanctity. Muhammad did not see his spiritual quest as being compromised by his enjoyment of divinely permitted pleasures which he indulged with a wholesome appetite rather than with guilt. He told his companions that if they made love to their wives, they earned merit. They were pleasantly surprised to learn that pleasure could be thus rewarded. Muhammad replied: 'If you transgress the law, you are punished. So, if you obey the law, why should you not be rewarded?' Only a pervert would dispute such wisdom – from any credible angle.

Secular cynics and some Christian critics, especially Aquinas, charged that Muhammad deferred part of his wanton and silken earthy sensuality to his Heaven. The American poet Thomas Lowell corroborates this claim, in modern idiom, when he claims that Muhammad got religion during a mid-life crisis.[23] By contrast, Nietzsche, to list a discrepant ally, admired the Prophet of Islam. In his late rhetorical masterpiece *The Anti-Christ* (1888), he extols the Arab apostle for being a real man who said 'Yes' to life's few pleasures even in the barren desert.[24] By contrast, the German thinker singles out Paul for special censure – castigating him for his masochism, distrust of the senses and his elite utopian sexuality. Nietzsche was probably inspired by Muhammad's case when he said that the degree and kind of a man's sexuality reaches up into the very summit of his spirituality.[25] To be fair to Paul here, he would not have equated sex with flesh since the works of the flesh do not, of course, include lawful sexual activity, that is, sexual desire satisfied only within the holy state of matrimony.

XV

In this final section, I analyse human intention and action in the context of deciding the capacity and scope of spirit-based guidance. The background is the presence or the absence of explicit legal directives, as preached by Islam and Christianity respectively.

Thoughts may cross one's mind without solidifying into beliefs or dogmas. We can believe without consciously believing something. Mysteriously, an intention is a thought, not a belief, but it is able to guide action. A decision involves intention but several vectors – including reasoning, inclination, desire and intention – jointly lead to a fully rational decision. We avow our intentions to God who knows whether we lie or speak the truth and we avow our intentions to other human beings who may or may not trust us. According to many well-authenticated *ḥadīth*, Muhammad preached that the intention (*niyya*, not a word occurring in the Quran) which precedes an action, wholly determines its status with God. Actions are judged solely by their intentions, not their consequences, since the former, unlike the latter, are within the power of the agent performing the action. The intention is material to the action and wholly determines its reward. The Prophet's teaching reinforces the Quran's singular stress on sincerity and quality of motive, in Medinan no less than in Meccan locations (Q2.139; 4.146; 7.29; 39.2, etc.). 'Human beings can only attain to what they sincerely strive for' (Q53.39–41).

In an unpremeditated action, such as action wholly motivated by strong desire, the conscious intention follows rather than precedes the action. The formation of an intention typically precedes the execution of an intention. In a premeditated act, one can intend repentance before committing the sin that requires it. Thus, Joseph's brothers anticipate that they can, after harming Joseph, still become a righteous people, by repenting of their evil deed (Q12.9).

Unlike our intentions, we cannot change our desires at will. In the absence of desire, a belief about the good can lead to virtuous intention. Naturally, none of these beliefs or desires exists autonomously but is rather a part of a web that may not be known to the agent unless he or she is exceptionally self-aware. Sin arises whenever overwhelming desire competes with moral convictions which forbid that sinful action.

How does the spirit guide independent human intention? The ethical directions given by the spirit replace the algorithm of the law which died on Pentecost when the Holy Spirit – God's spirit poured out on his people – rendered contingent, if not obsolete, the law's explicit rules. This is one Christian position. Paul's own view is rather confused or, if one is kind, nuanced. In Rom. 8.1–4, Paul preaches that condemnation by the law (rather than the law itself) has ceased with the advent of Christ. The implication is that the law has been transformed from being a way of staying close to God to becoming the optional and contingent foundation of the life in the spirit. In any event, for all Christians, the new inner compass is now the Holy Spirit, a notion also found, if rather nebulously, in the Hebrew Bible (see Joel 2.28–29). Christians see the fulfilment of Joel's prophecy on the first Christian Pentecost (Acts 2.17), a view that requires Christian faith. The divine presence (*shekinā*) is the closest analogue from Judaism since the divine presence could purify the human agent's intentions without completely overriding them.

The Muslim objection is twofold: the spirit fails to guide conduct and, moreover, even if it does guide it, the guided agent cannot know when this has happened. How do we know when our own intentions and motives have been surpassed or been modified? Muslims regard the guidance of the Holy Spirit as too nebulous to be a redress for the moral anarchy we enter in the aftermath of a lawless faith. The justified fear is that we will be left with a plethora of pious and evasive platitudes that fail to guide daily practical conduct and moreover divide the community as each charismatic makes camp all by him or herself. The current objection is that Christianity is 'the Buddhism of the West':

vague and sentimental self-help passing for spiritual wisdom. This indictment, partly unfair, remains the prevalent Muslim assessment of the ethical and legal deficiencies of its great rival.

Alert Christians would retort that Christianity is a spiritually mature faith which offers us a liberating theism. Islam offers us only a juridical theism that is repressive of human potential, a faith whose God is an omnipotent despot, notwithstanding his repeated claims to being merciful. Christians would add that Paul's writings emerge out of his experience and make perfect sense: there exists in truth a Holy Spirit of God who indwells believers, transforms them and writes the law in their hearts. This is, however, the voice of faith, the experience of the life of faith. It is hard to publicly verify it.

Leaving aside as we must such wider points of contention, the crucial issue here is about the benefits and drawbacks of having a religious law in the context of the moral and spiritual evolution of Semitic faiths. Is a moralisation of legal ordinance a retrograde or progressive step? We may all concur, however, that we need moral principles and values, not merely rules and rituals. We need relationships, not only rules and formal guidelines. Principles demand creative variation. We should not turn major principles into trivial rules. Reflective believers do not submit blindly to divine commands. As free agents who interpret and assess God's word before submitting to it, they are obedient but they are not robots without choice or voice. Submission (*islām*) without reflection (*tadabbur*) would be like a man lost in a supermarket, walking obediently and blindly behind an employee who guides him to the desired item. It hardly suits the majesty of the just servant of God, Islam's ideal.

Notes

1 The Quran mentions Mount Sinai (23.20, 95.2) but not the cave in which Muhammad received his inaugural revelation.

2 For a critique of Muslim bibliolatry, see my 'Slaves of the Book' in *The Times Higher Education Supplement*, October 1997.

3 On Christian ambivalence about Jerusalem and Islam's claim on it, see my feature article in *The Times Higher Education Supplement*, February 2000.

4 The Book of Jubilees retells the Sarah and Hagar narratives in a way that is somewhat closer to the Islamic tradition. The first Hagar/Sarah narrative (Gen. 16) is edited. It omits the tension between Sarah and Hagar and thus removes any reason for the latter's flight to the wilderness. The second narrative (corresponding to Gen. 21.1–20) is amplified since it offers, plausibly, jealousy as Sarah's motive for protecting Isaac's inheritance. For a close analysis of family rivalries, see P. Trible, *Texts of Terror* (Philadelphia, PA: Fortress press, 1984), especially the chapter on Hagar.

5 Unlike the Bible, the Quran rarely names women and does not mention any prophetesses. Women speak in the New Testament but often do so abruptly: no conversational (stalling) particles ease their opening or transitional comments (see e.g. Mark 16.3). In the Quran, only important religious women – such as Sarah and Mary – speak (Q11.72; 19.18). The unnamed Queen of Sheba speaks to her male counsellors (Q27.29–34); her subversive observation at Q27.34 has made Saudi rulers feel uncomfortable. Two wives of the Prophet have their domestic gossip reported in indirect speech and later we read a prayer of the believing wife of the Pharaoh (Q66.3, 11). Some ordinary woman complains about a pagan prelude to divorce and is overheard, so to speak, by God himself. (Q68.1).

6 Eleuthera is an island in the Bahamas, a British colony founded in 1656.

7 *LW* 27.31. See bibliography for publication details of Luther's collected works.
8 *LW* 31.371.
9 In my experience of living in North America, *Mammon* is an only god who has shot down democracy, the Gospel and Islam too. Most young North American Muslims are 'un-mosqued' as they become assimilated into the worst aspects of Western culture. Some among the youth are hedonists who care only for barbecues and sunshine, 'people of the kebab' (*ahl al-kebāb*).
10 In modern cultures, perhaps starting with George Orwell's *1984* (published in 1949), we associate bright light with torture and sleep deprivation.
11 J.L. Martyn, *Galatians* (AB 33; New York, 1998), p. 493.
12 *The Laws* 674b.
13 *The Republic*, Book 2, 363d.
14 Alcohol is particularly dangerous for women; their smaller bodies cannot handle it. In pregnancy, alcohol and smoking might lower a child's intelligence. The Quran showed prescient wisdom in banning alcohol, a carcinogen and an addictive drug. Red wine may be beneficial but one can derive its benefits from other sources and avoid its greater harmful effects (cf. Q2.219). Islamic dietary laws maximise health by avoiding excess and the diseases that result from the consumption of forbidden items. Health concerns are certainly foundational to the prescription of Islam's dietary laws, whatever may be said of the analogous guidelines in the Torah. Incidentally, while wine is permitted in heaven, there is no mention of pork being permitted in the next world.
15 Abraham is shown disputing with someone, perhaps Nimrod, who denies that it is God alone who owns the Kingdom (Q2.258). The Quran never calls Jesus a king even though it recognises kingship as valid (Q5.20).
16 This view is implicit in Montgomery Watt's crucial decision to divide the career of the Prophet into 'Muhammad at Mecca' and 'Muhammad at Medina'. The idea is developed by Kenneth Cragg. For purposes of heightening the contrast between Muhammad the warrior and Jesus the pacifist, both writers overlook the historical details and complexities. Muhammad performed a peaceful pilgrimage and signed an apparently capitulating peace treaty a few years before he eventually marched on Mecca. He had already peacefully conquered most Meccan hearts before he conquered the city by using minimal force – and forgiving its inhabitants.
17 *Summa Theologiae*, 2a2ae, q.161, a.1, ad 2.
18 D. Harrington and J. Keenan, *Paul and Virtue Ethics* (Lanham: Rowman and Littlefield, 2010), p. 110.
19 A moral quality such as compassion is rooted in a disposition. And no disposition can be reduced to a ritual formality: even feigned compassion can touch the hearts of others. Successful acting is based on this possibility.
20 She also eulogised Luke in a novel entitled *Dear and Glorious Physician* (London: Sheed and Ward, 1959).
21 Seneca, *Epist. Moral.*, XIII, 3.
22 *Beyond Good and Evil* (1886), Part IV, section 158, 'Epigrams and Interludes'. For publication details of all of Nietzsche's works, see the bibliography.
23 R. Lowell, *Selected Poems* (New York: Farrar, Straus and Giroux, 1976), p. 163.
24 *The Anti-Christ*, see sections 59 and 60.
25 *Beyond Good and Evil*, aphorism number 75. My rendering is not literal. I prefer 'spirit*uality*' to 'spirit'.

7

LAW OF CHRIST, GOSPEL OF THE CROSS (6.1–18)

Galatians 6 contains an appendix (6.1–10) in which Paul recommends practical implementation of the exhortations of 5.13–26. Then we read an epistolary postscript (6.11–18). Paul is nearing a spiritual climax, perhaps a state of emotional exhaustion, which contrasts with his initial abrupt burst of anger and enthusiasm. The Apostle fervently restates his case against the agitators and insists on the obsolescence of a key Jewish ritual and of the salvific value of the whole law it epitomised. The cross emerges as the instrument of the new creation in Christ, including a new people, the eschatological Israel of God. Final greetings conclude this concise but seminal work, incomparably the most influential letter in history. No other epistle or pamphlet has been the revolutionary constitution of a global solidarity of such enduring significance.

I 6.1–6

1 *Brothers, if indeed a man is caught in some trespass, you – the spiritual ones – restore such a*
one in a spirit of meekness – (while) considering yourself in case you are also tempted. **2** *Bear*
one another's burdens and so you shall fulfil the law of Christ. **3** *For if any-one thinks he is*
something, (while) being nothing, he deceives himself. **4** *But let each one test his own work*
and then he will have (reason to) boast in regard to himself alone, and not in regard to another.
5 *For each one shall carry his own load.* **6** *And let the one being instructed in the word share all*
good things with the one who is instructing (him).

1

Temptation is universal in range; even the spiritually elect are not exempt. The particle *ean* can be read as 'if', 'even if' and 'whenever', the last translation suggesting correctly that such a scenario was likely to be commonplace rather than rare and unexpected. This particle indicates the subjunctive mood: *prolēmphthē* (should he be taken by surprise; aor., pass. third sing.).

No sinless perfection exists even in the redeemed life. A Christian seeks to be perfect (*teleios*; Matt. 5.48) but his perfection, unlike that of his father in heaven whom he seeks to emulate if not imitate, cannot be total flawlessness. Aristotle, the pagan moralist, to cite a discrepant but wise ally, advises us that for each thing, one should expect only the kind of perfection appropriate to it.[1]

Committing sins remains a continuing liability even after baptism. The transgressor here, as in the incest case (1 Cor. 5.1–5) is a fellow believer. The fallen one must be approached in a spirit of Christian meekness. The verb *katartizein* (to adjust into unity; see also 1 Cor. 1.10) indicates that fellowship requires harmonious if not perfect adjustment, a compassionate restoration of discordant elements into a unified gathering. As any pastor, rabbi or imam well knows, such things are easier preached than done.

Manuals of church discipline and bureaucracy can be heavy tomes written with a Teutonic level of attention to detail. Ideally, if even the best of us were not so inveterately sinful, there would be no need for rules: only the spirit would rule. Leaving aside here the matter of grace's precise bearing on the redemption of sin, a complexity which complicates Christian anthropology, the practical life of faith requires simply that discipline be publicly witnessed – perhaps so that fellow believers may also be duly warned (1 Cor. 5.1–5; 1 Tim. 5.20). This last practical concern is shared by Muslim disciplinarians (based on Q24.2).

What is the point of Christian discipline? It should never be sadistic vengeance on the sinner but rather an attempt to repair him or her and thus the world. Sinners are often damaged and injured people, not always evildoers hell-bent on sinning. They should therefore be sought out and forgiven rather than condemned. The Quran concurs with this sanguine and compassionate view only in the case of sinful believers who repent, preferably immediately, and certainly before death (Q4.17–18). As for those who disbelieve and persist in their disbelief until death overtakes them, such are condemned repeatedly as deliberate and determined enemies of God and of the welfare of the human race (e.g. Q2.39; 9.17). This view of sinners is truer today than in Muhammad's day. Contemporary Muslims rightly lament the far greater prevalence of sinfulness today as a declared and insouciant defiance of God's revealed laws. They survey with dismay the astonishing variety of modern evils and evildoers, especially venal and mercenary politicians from almost all nations, working hard day and night to preserve their undeserved privileges and to resolutely deny justice to their fellow human beings. Many even claim that their privileges are earned and deserved, a clearly false view accepted by their countless gullible followers.

Christians and Muslims can concur that humanly delivered justice is often only *distributive* (rewarding virtue) and sometimes only *retributive* (punishing evil and destroying evildoers). True justice should additionally aim to be *restorative*, seeking to cure through compassion and grace. Here we cannot stop our tale to probe the nature of divine justice as understood by Christians and Muslims. But, contrary to initial expectations, the differences are rooted in emphasis rather in total disagreement about principles. All monotheists concur that divine justice is tempered by God's grace and mercy. Unlike most (if not all) Jews and Christians, however, orthodox Muslims are religiously obliged to see God as wholly removed from the sinful consequences of human evil. No authentic Muslim would hold God ultimately accountable, let alone responsible, for the evil and injustice rampant in the human condition. Unlike Christianity (and Judaism), Islamic doctrine is entirely innocent of the temptations of theodicy since Muslims recognise no puzzle here. In the free human creature, God created the evil component, along with the counterbalancing good component. He had foreknowledge of the human liability and practical ability to flout his law. This fact did not, however, make him in any way responsible for the evil that results from our abuse of the freedom of our human will.

2

As at 5.13, Paul speaks of mutual love and service on the model of Jesus' lifestyle on earth (Mark 10:43–45, John 13.34–35). The law of Christ bears an apocalyptic sense since Christ is the eschatological *torā/sharī'a* of God. He orders his followers to love one another just as he had first loved them. Insofar as Christ's acolytes have taken this commandment seriously to heart, they have reliably attained a level of intra-religious compassionate fellowship that parallels the quality of compassion found routinely among devout Muslims in their mutual dealings. This marked feature of Muslim conduct starts with the Prophet and his companions (see Q5.54; 48.29) and continues throughout Islamic history, up to this day. Nor is this to compare the *ideals* of Islam with the *practical achievements* of Christianity. Islam has, in my assessment, successfully secured a degree of courtesy, generosity and compassion among committed believers, on a scale that finds no parallel in any other faith-based solidarity.

Paul wants Christ's followers to help each other; Christian service to others includes mutual bearing of burdens. Muslims would concur with this charitable stance and, along with key Christian leaders such as Pope Francis, extend it to the sharing of financial burdens. The Quran commands believers to postpone payment of debt and recommends to creditors that they remit the debt altogether as an act of charity (Q2.280). Prophetic traditions reinforce this recommendation. The debtor should be allowed to postpone payment due, that is, the creditor should defer the requirement to pay if the debtor is in difficulties. Such kind attitudes would be welcome today in our unjust world of advanced capitalist usury, greed and rapacity. As recently as Victorian times, the debtors' prisons, made famous by Dickens' life and novels, were places of degradation for the victims of the Industrial Revolution, the original sin of the Victorian age.

3

Paul cautions us against thinking too highly of ourselves. 'Something to be' (*tis einai*) and 'nothing being' (*ti mēden ōn*) are juxtaposed for effect.

If a man thinks he is something when he is nothing, he is self-deceived. This maxim is more complex when a person lays claim to being a prophet or messiah. Muhammad tells his pagan detractors that he is no false pretender, only a sincere warner who asks for no payment (Q34.46–47; 38.36). Yet even the greatest men and women, of all faiths and none, may suffer from self-deception. Is there a safeguard against self-deception, psychologically a deeper malaise than hypocrisy? In academia, as in other professions and careers, including law, medicine and the church, one often meets highly educated but self-deceived people. Indeed, some enter academic careers, including the humanities, perhaps because they want to avoid answering life's urgent questions.

One significant difference between a Christian and a disbeliever is that the latter deceives and is deceived by others (see 2 Tim. 3.13). The Quran condemns those who seek to deceive (*yukhādi'ūna*) even God (Q2.9). The third form of the simple verb – meaning, in this augmented form, 'they seek or vie to deceive' – is used since no human being can successfully deceive God. The simple verb is used at the end of the same verse to mean simply 'they deceive' since such miscreants do successfully and straightforwardly deceive themselves – and only themselves.

4

Paul distinguishes self-importance from self-respect. Boasting with respect to oneself is self-affirmation, a legitimate ambition. Boasting in regard to another is self-advertisement, a personally sinful attitude with negative social consequences. One should treat both excessive praise and excessive blame from others as, in Rudyard Kipling's famous advice, alike as imposters. How few of us would then fall victim to flattery or abuse! Paul would have agreed with Kipling's wise advice.

This verse wisely discourages competition and comparison with neighbours, the bane of post-industrial capitalist society. Boasting in regard to oneself is acceptable so long as one is not belittling others. This is sound advice for pedagogy too where teachers and tutors encourage people to excel in regard to their own talents and potential over time rather than in sterile competition with others blessed with different gifts. The curse of comparison starts in the playground of childhood and lasts a lifetime. Envy of others, similar to us, blights human interaction more today, especially in meritocratic societies, than it did in the rigidly hierarchical cultures of the world's feudal past. While the scourge of envy was destructive in all ages and cultures, in the past it was never part of some ubiquitous and relentless marketing strategy as it has now become in our market-driven cultures for which the term 'cultures' is decidedly generous.[2]

5

Bearing your own burden (*to idion phortion*) is to individually carry a weight – a description of the pack each Roman soldier carried on his back. This burden, unlike the one carried by a slave, is honourable. In v.2 above, *ta barē*, yielding 'barometer' in English, denotes the weight which, like the atmospheric force of gravity, bears (or weighs) on all alike. It is thus a widely shared burden. To express the notion of a constraint that becomes an individual or shared burden, the Quran uses the 4th (causative) form of the root verb *ra/ha/qa* (see Q18.73, 80; 74.17).

The *ethical* attitude, rooted in the appropriate dispositions, recommended jointly in verses 5 and 2, implicates and reflects the deepest *dogmatic* pressures of Christian soteriology. The Quran's views of individual accountability and corporate responsibility are opposed to Christian expectations, especially if these are understood discretely, on the basis of single isolated verses. The dispositions and attitudes recommended by the author of the Quran are incompatible with the overall Christian proclivity here. Consider, for example: 'You are in charge of your own souls' (Q5.105). The attitude of personal dependence underpinning this verse cannot be characteristic of Galatians even if the core moral message runs parallel with v.5 here and is not opposed to v.2 earlier. Take another Quranic maxim which is central enough to be a frequent refrain: 'No burdened one can bear the burden of another' (see, e.g. Q35.18, 53.38). The burdens of sin or injustice and disbelief are not transferable although sinners may foolishly offer to bear another sinner's load (Q16.25). Adam's innocent (unnamed) son, about to be murdered by his brother, desires to see his unjust brother 'bear my sin and his own' (Q5.29) – but this is only the wish of a fallible human being.

6

Koinōneito (let him share) reminds the Christian reader of *koinōnia* (fellowship). A *koinōnos* is a business partner, the equivalent of the *secular* meaning of the word *mushrik*: one who shares, participates in or associates with any enterprise. The Quranic (religious) meaning is restricted to one who associates a partner with God.

Elsewhere Paul claims that Gentiles owe Jews their (Gentile) material blessing since they have now come to share the Jews' spiritual blessing (Rom. 16.27; 1 Cor. 9.11). This view is plausible only if one endorses the assumptions that nourish it. It is unacceptable to Muslims since the Quran teaches that guidance was always, at all times, freely and equally available to all human beings, simply by virtue of being human.

The Christian student should materially support the teacher or preacher. We have a similar arrangement in our universities since professors are remunerated from the tuition fees paid by their pupils. The opposite tradition is maintained by senior Shi'ite clerics who pay for the education and maintenance of their pupils. Thus, the richer a Shi'ite cleric, the greater the number of student-disciples supported by him. Some wealthy land-owning ayatollahs have thousands of student-disciples who endorse *taqlid* – unquestioningly submissive obedience – to their chosen ayatollah's edicts.[3]

II 7–10

7 *Do not be led astray; God is not mocked. For whatever a man may sow, this he will also reap.*
8 *For the one who sows to his own flesh shall from the flesh reap corruption, but the one who sows*
to the spirit shall from the spirit reap eternal life. **9** *And in doing good, let us not lose heart. For in*

its own time, we shall reap, if (we are) not failing (i.e., growing weary). **10** *Therefore then, as we have time, let us do good to all people, and most of all to the members of the family of the faith.*

7

The moral law of consequences is based on the principle that God cannot be mocked. In the traditional Palestinian Judaism of Jesus' parables (see Matt. 13.1–23), the imagery of sowing and reaping is used to teach spiritual lessons not only to simple peasants but also to their more sophisticated religious leaders. It also applies to Paul's teaching, in his more cultivated cosmopolitan and urban settings. His teaching evokes imagery which yields vivid agricultural metaphors for eschatological reckoning (1 Cor. 3.6–9). The Apostle commends the one who provides seed to the sower and assists in the growth of the harvest of righteousness (2 Cor. 9.10), the context being the commendation of generosity in charity.

The ethical application of the metaphor of reaping what one sows, the law of retribution or karma, was appealing to the Arabs, especially in Medina, a settled agrarian community. The believers are the farmers (*al-mufliḥūn*), those who reap successfully (Q2.5; 23.1). Modern Arab culture affirms the conventional wisdom of the saying 'You reap what you sow (*mā tazra'*, *taḥḥid (hu)*)'.

'Whatever a man may sow' perhaps implies habitual and persistent action, good or bad. Islamic law classes a minor but persistent sin as a major sin on account of the sinner's persistence in committing it.

Since God cannot be mocked, we must reap what we sow. The Quran concurs obliquely as it offers more commercial-sounding versions of this ethical maxim. 'A bad bargain for the bad' or 'evil is the transaction for the evildoers' (Q18.50). The motto 'Evildoers shall never prosper' (*yufliḥu*; lit. reap the harvest) punctuates the Quran (6.21, 135; 12.23; 28.37), especially 'the morally excellent story' (Q12.3) of Yusuf (Joseph), the prophet who proceeded from captivity to imperial rule, from victim to viceroy – and never with a trace of anxiety about his future. While the maxims about God vindicating the righteous apply to Yusuf, in the first instance, these rules are universal and thus apply to all believers who prefer good to evil and refrain from the latter (Q12.22, 56, 76, 90). Such universally valid moral hiatuses punctuate the Quranic tale of Yusuf but are conspicuously absent from the story of Joseph, portrayed as the divinely guided Hebrew hero in Genesis (37, 39–50), a conceited youth who matures into humility via slavery and exile.[4]

The conventional wisdom of many nations contains ambivalent maxims about sowing and reaping. 'You sow, another reaps' is a popular proverb in many Arab lands, expressing bitterness about how rewards are misaligned, at least in this life. In agricultural endeavour, as any disappointed farmer can testify, we have the blighted harvest. Only the lucky reap what they sow – equally true in the moral life. We have the testimony of disappointed misanthropes and of those whose children turned out badly, despite their best parenting efforts. 'You reap only what you sow' is naturally true in agriculture. In human affairs, the maxim can be disputed. Luke 19.21 has 'You reap what you do not sow, Master' as a description of the despot.

The maxim can, however, be made to be true in the moral life. This insight inspired Kant's moral argument for God's existence. Only if there is a God, a supreme being who can and will rectify the errors in the moral administration of this life, can we humans be confident of the truth of the moral law. It is clearly a poor argument since it begs the question against the secular opponent – by assuming what it is trying to prove, namely, the existence of a supremely good and powerful agent equipped with suitable moral convictions.

In a system with deferred eschatological sanctions, justice delayed is not justice denied (see Q88.25–26). In the godless universe, however, only the lucky reap what they sow – just as, to wax poetical, only the lucky really die at the end of their lives: many die earlier since they spend their twilight years in pointless suffering.

The believer, then, anxious about the harvest, is bound to add: 'if God wills it'. The secular humanist dismisses the divine caveat as wishful thinking. There are only us in the universe: no benevolent supervision safeguards or guides us. Thus Paul's moral maxim is a truism only in the spiritual life – and then only if the God of ethical monotheism exists.

8

The liaison of flesh with things corrupt (and perishable) and the association of spirit (or soul) with eternal life is more Hellenic than Semitic. Paul's thought is an amalgam of both. As for the Quran, it sees flesh as God's creation; therefore, it is not corrupt though it may be corrupted. Sensual delights are part of paradise though the vision of God is the crowning pleasure. Aspects of popular Islamic culture, however, resemble aspects of Paul's thought: the passions (*nafs*) are considered anarchic, corrupting and thus in need of tight control.[5] A Persian proverb captures the attitude: 'To repent during one's youth – that is the hallmark of a prophet.'

Paul's idiom 'sowing to the spirit' is obscure: it perhaps means the cultivation of the spiritual life, its patterns and habits, dispositions and inclinations, so that one can reap the harvest of goodness, probably even righteousness.

9–10

I paraphrase Paul's advice: 'Perform good works, out of gratitude, now that you have been saved by grace. Never tire of doing good actions. Do good as much as possible.' Paul wants Christians to do good works (*to kalon*; v. 9) and to do good (*to agathon*; v.10) to all human beings. The Septuagint uses *kalos*, meaning good and beautiful, to translate the Hebrew adjective *tov* used to describe the pleasing beauty of creation (Gen. 1.8). The Arabic adjective *ṭayyib* ranges over a similar semantic domain.

The law is *kalos* (Rom. 7.16; see also 1 Tim. 1.8) but, regrets Paul, its goodness is no bulwark against our tendency to flout it. James implies that the name of Christ is beautiful and good (*to kalon onoma*; 2.7), the equivalent of the Quran's description of God as owner of beauty and glory (*dhū al-jalāl wa al-ikrām*; Q55.78). The trinity of beauty, goodness and truth was a unity whose members were not, originally, sharply distinguished in Hellenic, Christian or Islamic thought.

Note that when commanding the good we ask people to do their best. The prohibition on evil, however, is absolute. It would be odd to command: 'Do not commit adultery – as much as possible'. It is more natural to say: 'Avoid adultery, as much as possible.'

Paul urges his readers to be good to all while they have time – during our brief lease in this physical life, as tenants on God's good earth. While 'Time is money' is a vulgar capitalist slogan, the spiritual person recognises that time is the only resource that is absolutely limited for every human being. Theoretically, one can continue to indefinitely accumulate goods such as knowledge and wealth.

Paul's moral horizon has thus far extended only to the Christian fellowship. Finally he wants care and mercy to reach all human beings. More charitably, we could read v.10 as extending an already society-wide focus even further to all human groupings – all of which deserve the same special though not exclusive focus. This would be a summary statement of Paul's intent.

Modern readers would admire the comprehensive range of Paul's compassion. But they might lament that, in his day and age, compassion for all sentient life, especially for the higher animals, was not expected, even of the kindest people. This would be a Buddhist reservation about Christianity, its Western cousin, 'the Buddhism of the West'.

In v.10, Paul uses *oikeios* (household or members of a family). The law, in its contents and as a principle, could tear apart the Christian house of faith. Pagan converts and Jewish Christians would not be able to cooperate. Thus, moral choices decided the unity of the universal *ekklēsia.* Galatians is about ecclesiology as well as soteriology.

While the Quran distinguishes and seeks to separate believers from disbelievers, it affirms the unity of the human race. It does not encourage compassion for those who are stubborn in their infidelity and perversely reject God. Most Islamic charities, however, in practice, distribute to all the needy, with priority assigned to Muslims. This is justified since many of those who are perpetually oppressed – and certainly the overwhelming majority of the world's displaced refugees and migrants fleeing war zones – are Muslims. Indeed, many are victims of direct Western or indirect Western-supported aggression. Muslims often lament among themselves that war, not democracy, is the West's largest export to Muslim nations.

III

Before commenting on what remains of the epistle, I note a remarkable feature of Gal. 6.7 which requires knowledge of Greek syntax. The absence of the definite article for God (cf. *ho theos*) here suggests that 'God' can be understood qualitatively. This grammatical fact hints at two different conceptual understandings of God's unity and nature, differences that the reader will be able to discern in due course.

The context: God is not the kind of being or person who can be mocked – or, for that matter, overpowered or killed, against his will, least of all by his imperfect human subjects. Christians can concur with Muslims that God has absolute power and knowledge (Q2.20, 29) although only Muslims reject as blasphemous, rather than as merely mistaken or shallow, the view that God's purposes could, temporarily or permanently, be outwitted or frustrated by humans (Q12.21; 29.39; 34.5; 65.3; 77.39 etc.). Christians argue that God *in Christ* could voluntarily allow himself to be killed – just as a Christian philosopher might add that God, in his divine fullness, could permit his boundless foreknowledge to be limited in order to allow his human creatures a measure of genuine free will. Only God in Christ – God incarnate – could be killed; the fullness of God remains forever imperishable. Muslims dismiss out of hand such reasoning as devious subtlety that reduces Christianity from an already errant monotheism to a form of refined, disguised and ultimately idolatrous bi-theism, possibly polytheism.

The proto-Semitic *'ilah*, like the Hebrew *elo'ha*, denotes the generic sense of divinity (god). The former varies in its referents but does not refer only to the only god, God. In Arabic, *'ilah* means any deity or even idol. If we interpret Allah as a contraction of *al-'ilah*, the (only) God, '*Allah*' has the definite article built into it just as *al-lat*, the proper name of a rival deity presiding in Ta'if, near Mecca, could mean 'the only goddess'. Philology has many speculative aspects and we cannot pontificate about the linguistic evolution of obscure words even if we know their current significance. Nonetheless, if the definite article is part of the word Allah, it would be a linguistically-based accentuation of his uniqueness as deity, a bid for exclusive divinity embedded in a semantically enforced veto on associating partners with him.

Unlike Greek and English, Arabic restricts a qualitative usage to *'ilah* (God) and vetoes it for 'the only God', Allah. Consider Q25.43: 'Have you considered the one who took his own lust to be his god (*'ilah*)?' It is senseless to substitute Allah for *'ilah*. Even grammatically, then, the only God is placed in a class of his own.

In the Quran, as in pre-Islamic Arabia, *Allah* was considered a proper name, not a title or adjectival noun. In English, god and God function as nouns and titles – as variables, not constants. As a proper name, like the Greek god Zeus, *Allah* has a unique and constant referent. Consistently, therefore, Arabic grammar vetoes the possibility of '*Allah*' as the subject being possessed in an *objective genitive* construct. In Arabic grammar, the definite genitive that would normally indicate possession is forbidden in expressions of the type 'The God/Allah of Abraham'. However, 'a god of Moses' (*ilahi Musa*; Q28.38) is allowed. Since Allah cannot function as the first part of any genitive construct, an equivalent such as *'ilah* or *rabb* (lord) is used. Thus we have 'the Lord (i.e. Allah) of Muhammad' while 'the face of Allah' (2.115) and *rasūl Allah* (Muhammad's central title) are of course acceptable. There is no analogous restriction in the uses of God/god in English grammar.

The noun Allah resembles the definite adjectival noun *Al-Raḥmān* (the merciful one; Q55.1), one of Allah's attributive names. Allah is his sole substantive name. Neither *Raḥmān* nor Allah admit duality or plurality. *Al-Raḥmān* is the opening verse of Q55, the only surah named after one of God's beautiful names. In the Quran, *Raḥmān* occurs only with the definite article and is identical with Allah.

The word for devil (*shayṭān*), however, functions like the English 'god' (or devil) since *shayṭān* admits of plurality (Q26.210). It can be used with the definite article – to mean the Devil (Q12.5) – but the article is not built into it. The word can be used literally and metaphorically. It resembles Christ in that it functions like a titular adjectival noun, not as a proper name. Allah is a substantive name, not a title.

That God can only properly be part of a *subjective genitive* construct might conceal some theological implications: linguistic restrictions may double as theological vetoes that radically limit the comparison between God and humanity. God's nature is that of a unique, incorporeal, eternal spirit – self-placed beyond time, space, direction and beyond duplication, humanity, contingency, death, birth and, therefore, beyond any complete human comprehension. 'Nothing resembles him' (Q42.11). In this way, Islam prohibits any conceptual space for *Christian* theological possibilities that are theoretically contained in '*Allahu akbar*' and expressible in languages other than Arabic. God is greater – but, queries the Christian, how great can he be if he merely sends prophets and reveals books but never comes in person, ready to suffer in love and humility?

This apparently innocent and coherent question can only be formed meaningfully if one commits a category error. Allah is not to be compared to any lesser (or, God forbid, greater) deity. His very name proclaims his uniqueness and incomparability which correspond well to the matchlessness (*i'jāz*) of his last revelation, the miraculous Quran. It is an Islamic version of the ontological argument – directed against incarnational monotheism. The Christian is reduced to retorting: 'How great is that "God" whose nature is limited by human categorisation and thought about him.' This objection appears ultimate but is in fact spurious and indeed incoherent since there is no alternative to a human – and thus humanly limited and defined – conceptualisation of the deity, whatever his true nature may in fact be or be revealed to be.

The reasons for such linguistic peculiarities are unclear. Why should polytheists have such a word along with attendant grammatical restrictions in their vocabulary? Every language contains unrealised possibilities. The linguistic luxuriance of Arabic – typically containing single root clusters which spread out into many dimensions, physical and metaphysical – hardly needs proof. Nonetheless, we wonder why the vocabulary of a polytheistic people contains such an emphatic word for divine unity. It could be argued, though only on theological grounds, that it reflects the innate and universal human disposition to believe in one God. Muslims would argue furthermore that a pure Abrahamic monotheism was older than the polytheism of Muhammad's Meccan forebears. Some commentators suggest that Luqmān (mentioned only at Q31.12–19), a sage unknown to the biblical wisdom tradition but known to the pre-Islamic Arabs, was a relatively local African preacher of monotheism. Arabic vocabulary perhaps reflects the pro-monotheistic stages of pre-Islamic Arab and African history.

IV 11–15

11 *You see: In what large letters I wrote to you with my (own) hand.* **12** *As many as wish to look well in (the) flesh, these compel you to be circumcised, only in order that they (may) not be* *persecuted for the cross of Christ [Jesus].* **13** *Not even those who are (being) circumcised themselves keep the law, but they wish to have you circumcised so that they may boast in your flesh.*

11

To show the authenticity of this letter – in effect to guard against forgery – Paul takes the pen in his own hand (see also 2 Thess. 3.17). The Thessalonians are also warned about letters falsely bearing Paul's name (2 Thess. 2.2). The warning is there issued against contrary advice appearing in different forms, including 'a spirit or a spoken word or a letter apparently from us' which implies a pseudonymous epistle. The difficulty here is that these warnings occur in an epistle that is itself perhaps 'forged' by a Paulinist admirer. In an oral culture, where teachers were held in great respect, the use of a teacher's name in a text still amounts to forgery, though this word is a harsh one. Ancient notions of authorship and intellectual copyright were, however, more relaxed and fluid than ours. What we would now call forgery was therefore commonplace.

Muhammad did not write; he had an amanuensis. In an oral culture, however, being illiterate (or even lacking skills of basic numeracy) was not equated with being uneducated or unwise.

12

Paul dismisses the possibility that his Christian opponents are sincere. Their only (*monon*) motive is to avoid persecution for the sake of the cross. Paul is uncharitable and intolerant. His otherworldly cross-centred faith (what one might call 'Cross-tianity') contrasts with that of his detractors who are portrayed as being interested only in a superficially fair showing in the flesh. This was a well-known pagan obsession, especially as shown in Greek writings about the aesthetic appeal of the male body and, among the Romans, in gladiatorial contests exhibiting masculine prowess and stamina.

For Greeks, physical beauty was almost a moral concern. The good, the beautiful and the true coincided. Greek thinkers typically admired the male physique, especially when stripped for athletic contests. Many dismissed the female body as being merely functionally appropriate (for reproduction) rather than intrinsically aesthetically pleasing – a preference that would baffle those in the world of modern advertising! The New Testament introduced notions of physical modesty and restraint of sexual desires against the opposed Hellenic and later Roman culture of virtual worship of the body and its appetites. Though considered perishable and corrupting, especially by the Greeks, the body concealed a powerful force urging us to a relentless pursuit of pleasure. A major motif of Plato's *Republic* is that sexual desire is a tyrant who will not release us until we are old or dead. The ideal of chastity was virtually foreign to the classical world even though there was official if theoretical recognition of its worth – as shown by the ceremonial veneration of the Vestal

Virgins, the cult of Diana, and of the *Bona Dea* (the good goddess). Such reverence is sometimes a sign that the ideal is honoured only in theory just as one effective way to forget the past is, paradoxically, to officially or regularly commemorate it, and thus cauterise it. Some cynics might say that is the best way to assign it to the oblivion of the safe slot on some Sunday afternoon television show. It has been properly remembered – so that now it may justly be forgotten.

The Quran affirms the beauty of the human body and its shape. The female body is beautiful by design but not for public display or for capitalist exploitation. The Quran speaks of sexual intimacy between men and women as resembling the mutual placing of a raiment (*libās*; 2.187): the sexes privately protect and adorn each other's naked and vulnerable frames. Clothing is a divinely approved form of elegance (*rīsh*, lit. feathers, a metonymy for elegance; Q7.26). The Quran's moral and spiritual rather than wholly aesthetic or erotic image of nudity contrasts with the aspirations of much modern art, entertainment and of commercial pornography. The last-mentioned is totally divorced from the trust in human dignity, required by sexual encounters, since bodily vulnerability is a necessary precondition of authentic relationship. The sexual act is otherwise reduced to recreation or pleasant distraction or, worse, shorn of trust and tenderness, a mechanical intrusion, from the male angle, into the integrity of an alien body with different private organs.

13

At Gal. 2.14, Paul accused the born Jews – believing Jews who follow Jesus – of being lax in regard to the law despite claiming to follow it zealously. Here he extends the charge, in effect, to anyone who chooses to be circumcised.

Reading Paul here, I am irresistibly reminded of a comment in the Quran about why the Jews and Christians of Muhammad's day mocked and rejected Islam. The book of Islam asserts with its customary force and clarity that the People of the Book are not in earnest about their own faith, no matter what they verbally proclaim in this regard (Q5.57–8).

In this residual trace of the former Pharisee, we glimpse the pre-Christian Paul's consuming zeal for the observance of the Torah by all Jews. Like the great Israelite prophets such as Jeremiah, Paul condemns Jewish hypocrisy. He sees circumcision as a sign of ethnic Jewish pride, not a universal symbol of true faith. He views it as a sign of the obedience of faith but one that applies only to Abraham's descendants. The obedience of faith is thus the true circumcision – expressed in symbolic rather than physical form for Christ's Gentile followers. This view is fully developed in Romans (2.25–3.1). The Apostle argues that circumcision is valuable only if one obeys the law and that those Jews who break the law reverse or undo their circumcision. Indeed, the uncircumcised Gentile who keeps the law is, in effect, circumcised. Thus, the physically uncircumcised but law-observant Gentile can condemn the Jew who is circumcised and has the law but breaks it. Both being a Jew and being circumcised are not merely external features of a person but rather inward and spiritual attributes. That is the true – spiritual – significance of this physical ritual.

V 14–15

14 *May I never boast except in the cross of our Lord Jesus Christ through whom (i.e. which) (the) world has been crucified to me and I to (the) world.* **15** *For neither is circumcision anything, nor un-circumcision, but a new creation.*

14

The cross performs a mutual crucifixion of the world to Paul and he to the world. Paul is relatively restrained here compared to his outbursts and boasting in the Lord throughout 2 Corinthians (ch.10–12) where he strenuously defends his apostolic authority against the super-apostles (2 Cor. 11.5, 12.11).

The follower of Christ is an alien (*xenos*) in this world, a temporary resident whose citizenship is in heaven (Phil. 3.20). The believer is advised to abstain from soul-destroying lusts of the flesh precisely because he is a stranger and pilgrim (1 Pet. 2.11), an alien even in the land of promise (Heb. 11.9), passing through the world which is only a bridge to a better and enduring world. The earliest Muslims also held this view about the fragility of life on earth, often reflected in the unassuming early mosques made of mud and straw, reflecting the transience of this world. Later mosque architecture became grandiose, to exhibit imperial glory. The vast innards of the mosque sanctuary offered a subliminally duplicitous hint: the all-encompassing spiritual power of God, certainly, but also the totalitarian power wielded by the feudal caliph demanding submission on this earth.

Here cosmos is analogous to the flesh. Both stand for the order of material or mechanical causation which is recalcitrant to the will of the Holy Spirit. Insofar as the cosmos, a wholly empirical reality at one level, resists the comprehensive control of the spirit, at an elevated level, it acquires negative ethical undertones. The created order rebels against the superior wisdom of its creator. This notion of a newly transformed humanity, made ready for holiness, albeit a derivative one, is implicit in the Quran's stress on clean and godly living. Human beings were created with spiritual capacity and need to be aware of this spiritual heritage (Q95.4); being 'the absolutely holy One' (*al-quddūs*; Q59.23), however, is reserved for God.

As in his other staurocentric epistles, especially Philippians (see Phil. 3.7–8), Paul's motto must be: *Nisi Dominus vanum* (without the Lord, all is in vain). And the Lord is Christ crucified. The scandal of the cross is embraced with irreversible and irresistible zeal. Paul preaches its ever-widening significance: Jesus is crucified, Paul is co-crucified, Paul and other followers of Christ are crucified to the world – and a reverse cosmic crucifixion. It is a vision with no Islamic or Jewish analogue.

15

The new creation in Christ renders obsolete Jewish rituals and physical markers which once served as symbolic precursors of genuinely spiritual identity. Emblematic of Judaism since the time of Abraham, circumcision is rendered otiose by

God's 'new creation'. Paul recognises both the past value and the present irrelevance of circumcision (1 Cor. 7.18–19; Rom. 2.25–29) and rejects it as an obsolete racial sacrament, merely a rite of passage for ethnic Israel. By the time of the composition of Colossians, almost certainly a deutero-Pauline letter, we are startled to read of 'the circumcision of Christ' (Col. 2.11), an operation performed without hands, going beyond branding the body with physical stigmata.

Paul's immediate concern is that Gentile circumcision denies the sufficiency of Christ. The concealed anxiety is perhaps that the pressure to accede to circumcision would make the Gentile follower of Christ yield to other legal pressures, leading eventually to full-scale Pharisaic legalism. Although Paul was mistaken in this fear, he was right and prescient in claiming that too many rules and regulations kill; a wholesome liberty, rooted in constraints of conscience and sincerity rather than formality and dead custom, inspire life and zest. One need not be a student of religions to notice this fact. The bureaucracies and legal systems of most advanced industrial nations, especially in matters of criminality, immigration and taxation, would yield sufficient proof. The legal quagmire of many a contemporary migrant case and its attendant appeals supplies ample evidence of this thesis though we cannot stop our tale to probe it here.

The law is not abrogated as false but relegated as irrelevant, a matter of indifference. It is rendered otiose by Christ's salvific accomplishments on the cross at Calvary. The key inherited ritual of Jewish identity is discarded as irrelevant. All that matters is the new creation out of the old (*creatio ex vetere*). Paul is speaking of a reformed, transformed and holy community that is only now fully human, having finally become what God had always intended it to be. Paul associates Christ's cross with Christ's gracious love – the two together redeeming and recreating creation.

The resurrected world is a sacramental rebirth; the cross recreates the cosmos. This doctrine is, in the final analysis, incompatible with Islam's insistence on the unalterable and continuing integrity of the inaugural divine creation. Although the God of the Quran will resurrect and restore creation (Q27.64; 75.4), he made no errors, physical or moral, in his initial creation (Q67.3–4). He has no regrets as he always was and remains in perfect control of his creation (cf. Gen. 6.6–7). In rejecting the cross, Islam dismisses as anathema the Christian notion of cosmic rebirth but also opts, in doing so, to ignore the riddle of evil – in a world created by the God of mercy.

Finally, note the pathos in this *pericopē*: while Paul looks forward to a new creation, he remains in his own body, subject to ageing. Looking into the future, Paul was to remain committed and zealous until the very end of his life. From the time he penned Galatians, arguably his earliest epistle, to the time he is, in all probability, on the very verge of martyrdom (see Phil. 3.12–14), we can discern the same sustained dedication to the chosen cause. Similarly, in the case of the ageing Muhammad, one is struck by the indefatigable activist enthusiasm of Surah 9, a late Medinan revelation. Most people relax their iconoclastic consciences as they age. Today, most idealists abandon their youthful idealism, under the relentless and increasing pressures of marriage and mortgage, usually by age forty, the very age at which Muhammad was called to be a prophet. Forty marks the watershed of spiritual life, placed a decade after the age which marks the physical prime of life. In secular culture, forty is the time for a mid-life crisis and a nervous breakdown. Cynics would add that a fool at forty is a fool forever while communists often quip that everyone becomes bourgeois by the time they reach this four-decade milestone.

VI 6.16

16 *And to as many as shall walk by this rule, peace and mercy (be) on them, and on the Israel of God.*

16

Those who choose to live in the world transformed by Christ are the true 'Israel of God', an expression unique to Galatians. The final greeting of peace and mercy is addressed to this new spiritual Israel. In a single verse, the old ethnic Israel is superseded; ancient Judaism was to be, in effect, annihilated. Uniquely, Christians claim that the Christian climax sees Judaism historically fulfilled at long last, spiritually transformed in the process and thus decisively consummated. Muslims make an even more daring claim: Islam is the perfection and rectification of both ancient Judaism and of its Christian successor. The Quran asserts this view with such formidable force and clarity that all committed Muslims find this controversial assertion to be virtually uncontroversial, seeing the continued Jewish and Christian rejection of Islam as merely perverse rather than principled and conscientious.

Paul's benediction on the Israel of God is not a benediction on ethnic Israel but rather on a multi-ethnic, multilingual, community created by Christ. Paul blesses the 'Pentecostal' community, in the widest sense, as it now inherits the charisma of the Christ and thus absorbs all races and ethnicities, including Arabs (Acts 2.11). Theoretically, it is a highly consistent vision of a unified humanity but Christian history has regularly fallen much short of this noble ideal.

Through the ethnic *communitas* of Israel, God's firstborn son, God scripted the story of universal salvation. Jesus fulfilled the role of Israel as firstborn son and many are now called, from all nations, to be children of God (Luke 24.47; John 1.12). Paul's 'Israel of God' is the spirit-filled *umma*, the renewed people of God, now destined for universal scope and inclusion. The Apostle to the Gentiles is the chosen agent, the spiritual catalyst who helps to give birth to a spiritual solidarity suited to the new apocalyptic age.

The first *umma* of historical Islam was an Arab community, formed by an Arabic Quran. But the criteria for entering this community were such that it was universal from its birth. The God of the Quran elected a special group of people as a witness to the rest of humanity. This resembles the notion of Israel as a light to the Gentile nations. The Arabs would, however, unlike the Israelites, actively seek to extend their witness to the rest of the world and share their religious good fortune with the nations. The imperial mandate for expansion was no afterthought but already inside the Quranic revelation. The remarkable idea that *islām* was the true and original religion of all humanity would aid in the project of history's first and indeed only self-consciously imperial yet authentically religious globalisation movement. Revelation led to revolution. The Quran recognises the fact of religious pluralism before the advent of historical Islam, attributing some of it – the sectarianism – to human perversity. But it vetoes as illegitimate, in the aftermath of Islam, all *politically empowered* religious diversity. Only the God of Islam must rule the public space, even of monotheistic worship.[6]

While the Psalmist sends peace upon Israel (Ps. 125.5), the Quran sends peace upon all of God's messengers as it establishes a noble reputation for them (Q37.181), especially for Abraham (see Q37.79, 109, 120, 130). Similarly, the Quran orders believers to join God and his angels as they send blessings on Muhammad (Q33.56), a highly spiritual recommendation in a surah that deals also with mundane gossip and sexual scandal involving the Prophet (33.37, 57). The Quran would never bless only the Israelites or only the Arabs. Some Muslim nations, such as Pakistan and Algeria, have a religious self-image since these countries were created specifically to be Muslim. Nonetheless, it would be religiously unthinkable for Muslims, patriotic though they now are, to have an equivalent of the jingoistic blessing 'God bless America.' At most, the strikingly prosperous Gulf nations now think of themselves as recipients of God's bounty as they read the Quran's words 'a fair land, a forgiving Lord' (Q34.15), originally applied to the Yemen but part of a larger message containing a warning about God's judgement on all luxurious lifestyles (see 90.5–7; 104.2–3). Few of the affluent Gulf Arabs note that they might be within the scope of the warning!

Christian greetings often combined Semitic and Hellenic components which jointly comprise the cultural essentials of primitive Christianity. The Islamic greeting is not a blend of religious and secular (pagan) components. The full greeting of 'Peace and mercy of God and his blessings be upon you', used only by self-consciously pious individuals and in correspondence by institutions run by such people, is found in a truncated form in the Quran (only at Q11.73). The context is the visit of angels to inform Abraham and an incredulous (and unnamed) Sarah about the birth of a son. The Quran mandates the offering of the peace greeting (Q24.27) along with its reciprocation, equal or better (Q4.86), and quotes Abraham as returning the peace greeting even to unknown visitors who proffer him peace (Q51.24–25).

Muslims are delighted to note how the post-resurrection Jesus says to his disciples 'Peace be upon you' (John 20.21, 26; Luke 24.36). In Matthew (28.9), Jesus offers a surprisingly secular greeting. In Mark, in a late addition to that gospel (16.14), the risen Christ abruptly offers a reproach instead of a greeting, a gesture reminiscent of Paul when he offers a short peace greeting followed by a lengthy reproach (see Gal. 1.3, 6–9).

Paul's salutation of peace here (Gal. 6.16) contains a hint of hidden menace. It resembles the way that the Quranic Moses offers the Pharaoh a qualified greeting: 'Peace be upon those who follow the guidance' (Q20.47). This verse is quoted in letters sent by Muhammad to surrounding hostile imperial powers. It sounds antagonistic and judgemental. It is used often in the late Osama bin Laden's hostile addresses to 'Jews and Crusaders'.

God's direct address uses the sacred name of Israel (as in 'O Children of Israel'), in honour of Jacob's pre-eminence in Islam. As in early Christian literature, the Quran treats Israel as a *nomen sacrum* (or *nomina sacra*). 'Those who have Judaized' (*alladhīna hādū*) and *Al-Yahūda* designate Jews in confrontational contexts (Q5.51, 82; 62.6). These appellations correspond to *Iudaios* (*Iudaioi*; pl.), found in the Gospels and in Paul's letters, in openly polemical or subliminally hostile contexts.

Respect for Israel is combined with condemnation of the behaviour of some Israelites who are Jacob's seed (Q3.93–4).[7] The Quran often contrasts the behaviour of seminal Jewish figures with their followers (Q5.78). While it rarely if ever criticises the seminal figures, it routinely condemns the bulk of their followers (Q3.110–114; 5.25–6; 57.27).

VII 6.17–18

17 *From now on, let no-one cause troubles for me, for I bear on my body the brand-marks of Jesus.* **18** *The grace of our Lord Jesus Christ (be) with your spirit, brothers. Amen.*

17

Paul suddenly sounds tired of trials and tribulations. This abrupt ending resembles the abrupt start to this epistle. The stigmata are physical evidence of Paul's mystical identification with Jesus, called here only by his name. Paul's body bears the testimony of Christ's presence. The more neutral word *soma* (body) is used here instead of flesh. *Soma* refers to the physical body; it is used in describing the sacrament of the Eucharist (see Matt. 26.26; Mark 14.22; Luke 22.19).

As we saw earlier in Gal. 2.20, 3.26–28, the mystical and sacramental presence of the Christ, dwelling in Paul, comforts him in his sufferings as it comforts the entire church of the faithful saints. This emphasis on suffering and stigmata can easily lead to the kind of masochism found in monastic Christianity.

'In Christ' (*en Christō*) remains, if taken literally, a strange if barely comprehensible expression while comparable expressions, such as 'in Muhammad' or 'in Hitler', are certainly senseless. The expression 'in the Prophet of Allah' (Q33.21) means 'in his case', not in his body: believers are told that in him they shall find an excellent exemplar of godly living. Even Sufis do not abide in Muhammad though many among them often remember him more than they remember God alone.

Christ dwells in Paul; this messianic presence became evident to those who knew the Apostle well. He became the sign (*ayah*) of the messiah: the stigmata make him *ayatu al-masih*. The Quran calls Jesus and his mother signs of God (19.21; 23.50). Again, in Joseph and his brothers, there are signs for those who inquire (Q12.7). Shi'ite clergy assume the title of ayatollah (sign of Allah), conferred by popular acclamation for piety and religious scholarship.

18

Paul reverts to using the full name of his liege, lord and master for whom he was ready to suffer, even unto death on a cross. Paul wants the grace of his Lord Jesus Christ to be with his misguided Galatian brothers, to guide them to the truth of, in, with, through but not beyond, the Christ. The spirit is (and has) virtually the last word in this revolutionary epistle; it succeeds even the words *Iesou Christou*! The grace and peace of 1.3 is now shortened to 'the grace of our Lord Jesus Christ'.

Paul closes the letter with two salutations which amount to benedictions (vv.16, 18). The Quran's longer and medium-sized surahs often end with doxologies (e.g. Q17.110–111; 37.180–182; 59.22–24). Thus, in both scriptures, the opening and the final *pericopae* effectively bracket the relatively more mundane concerns of the body of the text.

VIII

I end by commenting on an organisational feature of this epistle. Note that Gal. 6.1–10 is an appendix to the ethical portion (Gal. 5.13–26). The spirit (Gal. 5.16–18, 22, 25; 6.8), as the spirit of God, is more powerful than the flesh. In Isa. 31. 1–3, the flesh of Egyptian horses, a symbol of military stamina – reflected in our 'horsepower'– is contrasted with Yahweh's greater strength, displayed in the absolutely formidable power of the spirit (Hebr. *ruāch*; Ar. *rūḥ*). Paul's proposal to live beyond the law, to live *kata pneuma*, means accepting supererogatory obligations as one goes beyond ordinary duties and the doing of good works and seeks the supernatural stamina to live habitually in spiritual caution, to live with what the Quran calls 'God-consciousness of the hearts' (*taqwā al-qulūb*; Q22.32). The contrasting life is *kata sarka*, lived conventionally, often materialistically – the unexamined life that Socrates condemned.

Paul had displayed confidence in the flesh when he boasted of his ethical achievements as an observant Pharisee, during his pre-Christian life (see Phil. 3.4–6). But he condemns his opponents for boasting in the flesh, in the law. He reminds them that no one should boast except in the spirit, in the Lord (2 Cor. 10.8–17). The false teachers want to take credit for motivating the Galatians to accept the Abrahamic rite of partial genital mutilation. Paul argues that even the false teachers, who are circumcised, having been born as Jews, do not keep the whole law with perfect obedience. It is Paul, as Christ's apostle, who offers the Galatians the certainty of salvation, and that through faith alone – and they already have it. If you have Christ, you have it all. Paul's point, pointedly relevant to Muslim readers, is that since the sham teachers themselves are not assured of being declared righteous, they could never assure the Galatians of their salvation.

The note of certainty about salvation appeals to Christians and indeed to Muslim-background converts to Christianity. Muslims reject it as a presumptuous complacency and an over-confidence that seeks a unilaterally human annexation of divine grace. In Christian eyes, however, it would be presumptuous only if the believer had reckoned matters without the mediation of Christ and his merits. In matters of moment, Muslims and Christians alike have a right to their own consciences. While philosophers of religion are eminently qualified to adjudicate between conflicting religious claims, they should not rush in where even the theologians of both faiths fear to tread.

Notes

1 Aristotle, *Nicomachean Ethics*, Book 1, Ch. 3, 1094^{b}24.
2 For a development of this thesis, see Alain de Botton's *Status Anxiety* (London: Hamish Hamilton, 2004). For a critical negative assessment, see Steven Poole's review in *The Guardian*, March 27, 2004.
3 *Taqlid* is derived from the word for a collar worn around a camel's neck marked for slaughter (*qalā'id*. pl. at Q5.2). It denotes meekness. The highest Shi'ite clerical status is that of the *marja-e-taqlid* (centre of blind imitation), someone who inspires unconditional loyalty.
4 In the light of Quranic criteria, the biblical tale of Joseph appears to be quite secular and ethnically triumphalist. The Quran consciously rejects what its author sees as the restrictively ethnic stress found in parts of the Hebrew Bible. Some verses uphold the universality of Israel's mission (Gen. 12.3; Ex. 19.6) but this claim is, unlike in the Quran, an isolated and incidental one, and therefore unlike the Quran's stance where this claim is a regular and repeated stress. Universalist claims are found more in the New Testament – and even there, apart from Paul, I see it as an equivocal notice since it alternates with more ethnically exclusive emphases placed more prominently in the same context. The Quranic Joseph, like all prophets, preaches the truth of universal monotheism.
5 This traditional pious theme of the need for self-restraint is prominent in the poetry, folklore, music and films produced in many conservative Islamic nations, such as Pakistan, Iran and Egypt.
6 For a rare, if not unique, defence of this classic imperial Islamic view among Western Muslim academics, see my *Islam as Political Religion* (London: Routledge, 2010).
7 In the Quran, the word Israel never refers to the land or nation of Israel but is used as an alternative name for Jacob (3.93). A place called 'the holy land' (*al-arḍ al muqaddisa*; Q5.21) is assigned to Moses and his people. Its location, and a fortiori borders, are both left unspecified.

8

CRISIS OF LAW, PROMISE OF GRACE

Interfaith interfaces in Galatians

I

In closing the textual commentary, we take stock of major themes in Gal. 6 and indeed of the entire epistle, themes that run throughout the New Testament. For Jews and Muslims, the law of God is the light of day (*lex Dei lux diei*), an instrument for experiencing grace. Moses was the proto-prophet of law, hence the Quran's repeated narration of his story. In 6.14–15, Paul exalts the cross of Christ above the Law of Moses. As a consequence of the Christ-revolution, Paul had a revelation: the law, once the enabler of righteous living, was at best the tutor for salvation, not a means to it – and at worst an enemy of salvation. The law and the flesh persecute the spirit. Judaism, allegorically represented by Hagar and her son, along with the Torah and the pre-Christian Paul, constitute a trinity of persecutors. The victims are Sarah and Isaac, and the church – the new Israel of God.

Martin Luther, like his compatriot Meister Eckhart (c.1260–1327), the greatest of the fourteenth century Rhineland mystics, might say, appropriating Paul's message: 'servants of Christ do not do good in order to please God but rather do good because God is pleased with them.' Muslims would dismiss this as a false and misleading dichotomy which raises an unnecessary question about correct priorities. A believer can do both and do so organically since the two states are both states of grace which can and do coexist simultaneously and one reinforces the other.

Leaving aside that larger question, the law itself, for Paul, is a temptation to do wrong. Though Paul might not approve of my example, I would liken the law to outstanding beauty in a woman, if such a feature is prominent and provocative enough to define the woman's whole personality. If so, such beauty could perversely arouse hostility rather than normal attraction in a man and tempt him to transgress the rules of self-restraint, modesty and chastity. This quality is organically related to the woman's larger personality; but taken in isolation it could be reduced to being merely the cause of male desire – and hence immoral conduct. Perhaps this analogy would appeal only to a conservative Muslim male since it implies that a beautiful woman is morally obliged not to use her beauty as a cause of male temptation, a view not shared by most non-Muslims.

Even if the law is not a source of temptation to do wrong, Paul is certainly suggesting that the law is no longer the enabler of virtue. Therefore, Christ is the end of the law. Whether we call that fulfilment or abrogation cannot be decided in isolation: it depends on one's wider agenda, to use an unpleasantly political-sounding word. Muslims would judge Paul's overall stance as a retrograde step that widens the rift with the third Abrahamic faith unknown to him.

Note that Gentiles are located prior to or, equivalently, outside the law. They are therefore sinful while being ignorant of God's law. They are not, however, coincidentally sinful, as it were, since their nature, through the innate endowment of conscience, informs them of their evil actions and convicts them (Rom. 2.14–15; Q75.2). Concurrently with this, the Jews, including Paul and the human Jesus, are under the Law. With the exception of the human Jesus, they are sinful and thus in need of redemption and righteousness. Furthermore, they are not only conscious of their sinful actions and sinful nature but also, rather frustratingly, long for deliverance from this state – in the hope of receiving righteousness and justification, and, eventually sanctification and glorification. This would enable them to enjoy a closer relationship with an absolutely holy God. But alas, it is not to be, without a costly ransom.

The Christian stance, though radical, is not an abruptly placed appendix to Jewish ideals and concerns. It grows gracefully and organically out of an existing Judaic predicament about obedience to an exacting law. Freed from the Mosaic law, the Christian Galatians were placed under the law of grace, 'the law of Christ', an enigmatic expression Paul probably borrowed from his missionary rivals who were also active in Galatia. The net result is that the Galatian Christians were justified by Christ and became law-free in Christ – while simultaneously becoming slaves to a righteousness that goes beyond the law.

'The law of Christ' has no place in Islamic thought about Jesus, who is only a messenger of God, confirming the Torah of Moses which remains valid since it contains God's judgement. As such, the Torah can never be abrogated in its essentials, a view central to Islamic orthodoxy. Thus, the Mosaic dispensation can only be confirmed or supplemented by later revelation. Islam is no less supersessionist than Christianity and has an auxiliary competing colonial history to match. Unlike Christianity, however, it supersedes its two predecessors by subsuming and augmenting and, especially in the case of Christianity, explicitly rejecting, their doctrines. The Quran also discards some Jewish dietary laws, dismissing them as obsolete for the Muslim community (see Q6.145–6).

Christians typically regard the primary scripture, the First Testament, as being augmented and fulfilled, not refuted or contradicted, by the addition of the Second Testament. They would be disappointed that Muslims typically reject both testaments of the Bible as being, in their extant forms, corrupt or at least humanly revised. If Christians read the Quran itself, they would be surprised and pleased to note that this irreducibly enigmatic scripture contains subtly ambivalent notices of the Bible's overall authority, of its constituent texts and messages. I admit that this is, taken as a whole, a confusing situation for Christians who wish to engage conscientiously, with confidence, integrity and clarity with those who claim access to an alternative ultimate revealed truth.

For Muslims, the divine law can tolerate, even invite, the complement of divine grace. For Paul, in much of his thought, the divine initiative of grace cannot tolerate, let alone invite, the complement of human (legal) effort. Paul's assumption is not self-evident. The Quran would reject the contrast in the Pauline polarity. For Paul, this assumption of the complete incompatibility of law and grace, vis-à-vis the achievement of salvation, is axiomatic although he does occasionally argue for it. For Muslim readers, the sustained Semitic vehemence of Paul's idiom in Hellenic dress, undiluted by any retrospective regret over its employment, in any of his extant letters, does not amount to a convincing argument. Dramatic dogmatism is a fair description of it although as much is found in all authoritative, especially revealed, teaching. But the Semitic temperament is not ours today. Many today would reject both the style and the content of Paul's preaching.

Paul, the pastor for the Galatians, has nonetheless much to teach Muslims. His reservation about the law as a kind of symbolic imperialist – dictating Jewish norms for a Gentile world – is relevant to non-Arab Muslims who often adopt Arab tribal customs as though these were Islamic requirements. Does a convert to Islam need to be Arabicised in order to become an authentic Muslim? Or does that requirement confuse Islam with ancient and religiously contingent Arab cultural norms? Does it conflate form (Arabic, local, legal) with meaning (human, universal, spiritual)? Or has the Quran forever rendered sacred some parts of what was originally merely contingent, indeed profane and secular, Arab culture? I myself think that Quranic Islam has neither a theology nor, less controversially, a culture. But this commentary is not the place to defend such apparently extravagant claims about the true and enduring essence of Islam.

II

While 'born-again Muslim' lacks cultural and theological traction, 'I have been saved' is an oft-heard and joyful hymn sung by many a convert to Christian faith, at countless rallies of the type the late Billy Graham made famous in America but which would find no cultural footing in a more irreversibly secularised north-western Europe. This may be changing with the influx of charismatic and evangelical Christians from Eastern Europe, Africa and South America working in parts of the United Kingdom and Scandinavia. One wonders whether this enthusiasm will endure into the next generation, among the children of these migrants born and raised in a secular ethos. Let me use this observation in social commentary to introduce a less contingent matter, namely, the theology of Christian salvation. In principle, at least, theology aims to be free of the vicissitudes of cultural secularisation, transcending such a mundane reality and even seeking to challenge if not triumph over it.

We find three stages of salvation, especially in its urgent evangelical version. The transformation of the believer begins on earth but reaches post-mortem completion. Salvation is received, through the symbolic rite of baptism, on accepting Christ as one's personal Lord and saviour. (One can be saved without baptism, of course, as in the case of the repentant thief who was crucified with Christ in Luke 23.32–43). This is spiritual rebirth: by being born again, by receiving the spirit like the Galatian Christians, each believer becomes a child of God. This is Paul's doctrine of justification, mentioned in Galatians but elaborated in Corinthians and Romans.

'I am being saved' affirms this conviction in the present. God's ongoing work continues despite our weaknesses and sinful lapses. This divine work will make us into the complete human beings God created us to be, beings capable of enjoying eternal fellowship with a holy God who is himself, as spirit incarnate, no stranger to human suffering and the temptations of the flesh. The end of this stage is sanctification.

'I will be saved' places present and past salvific realities in the perspective of the believer's future as he or she looks forward to the consummation of the process that started on earth but will be completed when God receives the saved believer into his holy presence after death. This is the third and final stage of salvation – one that is, like sanctification, absent from Galatians but expounded fully in Romans. It is glorification: the believer receives a new and glorious body in which he or she experiences final salvation.

In sum, we have been saved (justification; completed past); we are being saved (sanctification; continuous present). And we shall be saved (glorification; future perfect). God's gracious actions are not restricted to saving individual souls. He can save entire communities. Despite containing high doctrine and high Christology, this sketch omits metaphysical and theological presuppositions about how God planned the salvation of believers before the foundation of the world (see Eph. 1.4–5). This predestined plan has now come to bear fruit, in the fullness of time, as the present evil age ends. Thus, reckons the Christian, God plans our salvation, provides for it and calls us to it. It is hard for a Muslim to avoid admiring the comprehensive faith and trust implicit in this attitude while wondering what role, if any, is left for the believer wanting to exercise his or her free will.

III

Although Galatians contains a juridical soteriology, the epistle is simultaneously about ecclesiology – about identifying the unified new community of believers and establishing a single fellowship, a wish also expressed by Jesus in his prayer as High Priest (John 17.20–23). Doctrinal and dogmatic complexity can exacerbate ecclesiastical disunity but other equally powerful sources of disunity also persist. In the Christian case, a dominant source is exegetical ingenuity with one's scripture. In the case of Islam, enduring disunity originates, at least in modern times, in an entirely different source. A battle rages between those who seek true faith – true to its originating principles – and those who seek merely to accommodate themselves to the powerful non-Muslim Western world, at all costs. This conflict is also accompanied by an exegetical ingenuity but this plays only an auxiliary role – in the service of an ulterior and indeed perverse agenda motivated by concerns unrelated to the search for the eternally valid truths embedded in the Quran.

Paul struggles for Christian unity through a power struggle with the Judaisers. There is no gospel except *the* gospel of Christ while the other gospel, the accursed gospel, may just as well be the gospel of Caesar, some kerygma of profane interests – in the interests of Mammon. For Paul, the gospel that preached Christ crucified could move mountains. He knew it first-hand from the Christophany he experienced on the road to Damascus. Muslims make comparable claims about the Quran's descent which, like the epiphany of God himself to Moses (Q7.135), is capable of shattering a mountain (Q59.21). For orthodox Muslims, the Quran is the only reliable link between human beings and their creator. It offers guidance to every sincere seeker for God while unifying all such true believers.

In Galatians, the noun *koinōnia* (fellowship) does not occur but we have the polite imperative (or jussive) 'Let us share' (*koinōneito*; 6.6). *Koinōnia* is the equivalent in meaning to the Quranic word *umma* which can mean the universal fellowship of Muslim believers. But, unlike *koinōnia*, *umma* is a concrete noun. *Koinōnia* is, however, like *islām*, an abstract noun. *Islām* means submission while *koinōnia* means 'joint participation' or 'sharing'. The Christian fellowship thus created, in and through the Holy Spirit, is the concrete result of such abstract sharing. It yields fellowship in the devotional sense of the concrete English noun 'fellowship'. *Umma* never means sharing or participation but rather a group of related people.[1]

Ironically, the Quranic word *shirk* which means sharing or participation denotes a sharing that is anathema – the misguided human attempt to share and thus compromise God's sole sovereignty, unity and incomparable majesty with any human or other creature. The very creed of Islam condemns it as the one unforgivable sin. Christians are sometimes accused of committing it when proclaiming 'Christ is Lord'.

In the gospels, only Matthew uses *ekklēsia* exclusively in the sense of an assembly of believers, a 'church'. Luke uses it also in its secular sense, meaning any assembly, including a rioting mob (*demos*) of pagans in Ephesus (Acts 19.32). In Galatians, this word occurs only once – and it is in the plural (1.2). The Quranic word *umma* can mean nation but has come to refer only to the universal Muslim fellowship. The original *umma* at Medina, with no police or standing army, was not a state but rather, like the early church, a voluntary organisation or an association of people enjoying an intensely shared vision. This is evident in the early church (Acts 4.32–6.7): its scale was that of a family rather than a society or state. This modest scale also explains Paul's realistically attainable pastoral ambitions and his attempts to secure unity in his congregations. Today, the (functioning) state is an organisation, established formally by law, having collective resources of violence superior to any individual within it. Both state and church have typically been vast organisations which manage internal dissent while claiming the sole right to adjudicate conflicts, internal and external.

In Galatians and in Corinthians, Paul condemns factionalism and party strife as he seeks to secure Christian unity. In 1 Cor. 12.14–26, especially vv. 25–6,

Paul confirms the unity of the body of Christ. The Quran orders believers to be united as an *umma* (Q49.9–10) while Muhammad famously remarked that 'disbelief (*kufr*) is a single system.' The Quran twice cites Arab tribal unification as a divine miracle (Q3.103; 8.63) – something quite credible when we note how the modern 22 Arab nations, despite virtually all being officially Sunni Muslim, are constantly at each other's throats, putting their own goals and petty grudges before the unity of the Arab peoples and *a fortiori* of the global Muslim community. Muhammad's traditions report that if a part of the *umma* is sick, the rest of it suffers its pain and shares in it. Rhetorically, all Muslims accept this but, in practice, Arab Muslim suffering, like Jewish suffering in the post-Holocaust West, seeks and finds a privileged place.[2]

Finally, and more broadly, in our world, the church, like the increasingly secular academy, is marked by the sins of social malaise: strife, contention, naked ambition and competition. And all this is so, despite the working of the spirit. Take America, for example, the most important nation today. It is an officially secular state founded on freedom of religion but in practice a nation whose citizens often proudly salute their Christian identity – with many even seeing themselves as the last hope for Western Christianity. Yet, for all that, a climate of distrust, competition and envy can mar social interaction, even in many church circles, whether urban or rural, where I have myself heard many a sincere pastor preach loudly the need for social grace, mutual charity and communal unity. A weekly reading of Galatians should be made compulsory in all such congregations!

IV

Like the Torah, the Quran offers *hudā* (guidance), a more comprehensive word than our word 'law'. *Al-Hudā* as an honorific for the entire Quran resembles the Jewish view of their Torah, a Hebrew word best translated as instruction, as detailed practical guidance rather than merely some vague notion of moral wisdom.

The Islamic scripture is self-described as '*hudā* for humanity', first sent down in *ramaḍān* (Q2.185). The guidance of God – that is the guidance (*al-hudā*; Q2.120). The promise of such revealed guidance was the first divine promise made to a disgraced but forgiven Adam and his future progeny (2.37). The relationship of the opening surah to the rest of the Quran is that of a prayer (Q1.6) and a divine answer to it (Q2.2) which is, basically, the descent of *hudā*.[3] It includes law, etiquette, general wisdom and teaching, the promise of God's grace for believers, warnings against Satan as the open enemy of humanity, awareness of our own nature as being innately good but tempted by our evil tendencies, and the knowledge of the channel of apostleship as God's chosen means for educating Adam and his descendants.

Neither the Lord's Prayer nor the opening chapter of the Quran mentions law. But in both cases, the reference to God's will implies it. The imperative 'Guide us on the straight path' is addressed to God (Q1.6). Classical consensus sees this Islamic path as lying between the paths taken by Jews and Christians respectively: 'those who are victims of divine wrath' and 'those gone astray' (Q1.7). Both flouted God's laws.

The Quran sees its laws as liberation from ignorance, providing defence against human avarice and the aggression of the strong against the weak. If the law is ever unnecessary, it can only be so for the elect. God wishes to make the duties of the faith easy, not harsh (Q2.185; 22.78) since the Quran was revealed not to distress humanity (Q20.2) but rather as a gracious reminder of the creator's rights and the creature's duties. The book was sent down as a mercy and a healing, the event of the Quran being seen as an undeserved gift of grace: Muhammad had never expected it (Q17.17.86–87; 28.86) since, unlike key biblical figures, he was not, in any obvious sense, located in the line of prophecy.

While Muslims see their Quran as revealed guidance, a universal blessing, countless modern non-Muslims increasingly wish there had never been a Quran, Muhammad or Islam: the world would have been a better place. Sir William Muir unwittingly spoke on behalf of many modern Westerners when he famously declared, in 1861, that 'the sword of Muhammad, and the Quran, are the most determined enemies of civilisation, liberty and truth which the world has yet known.'[4] Muslims would answer this charge by pointing to the Quran: God is determined to perfect his light, no matter how averse Islam's enemies might be to it (Q9.32). We have violent deadlocks between Islam and Christianity mainly because the official leaders of both faiths are often men who see any compromise as a weakness, not a strength.

V

To understand how Muslims react to Paul's core offer, in Galatians, of a law-free faith, we need to understand the divinely revealed commands of the law found in the Quran, a book one might see as an Arabic Torah (implied at Q28.49). Out of its 6,236 verses, the Quran contains only some 500 verses with positively legal or combined ethical and prescriptive import. Through direct divine command, address and moral exhortation, the Quran inculcates a culture of submission, of duty and responsibility. In the original and orthodox Islam of the Quran, God is a lawgiver and educator. Law is the epitome of positive and certain knowledge (*'ilm*), enshrining divine guidance (*hudā*) which decisively dispels the total misguidedness and false zeal (*hamiyya*) which marked the pre-Islamic age of ignorance (*jāhiliyya*; Q2.16, 175; 48.26).

The ethos of Islam is at odds with the New Testament world where, for reasons connected with Christian origins in the Pharisaic crucible, liberty from oppressively ritualistic codes is frequently stressed. Christian critics naturally see Islam, with its divinely revealed law as a repressive *Sharī'a*-based theism. The Quran reminds Muslims that the provisions of the revealed law are a divine mercy (Q2.178–9; 5.38; 24.1–10) even though they may not appear as such since, as the Quran adds, God knows and human beings are ignorant and unaware of their religious best interests (Q2.216).

In considering the catholic range of the commands in the Quran, covered in this section and the next one, the reader is advised to consult a copy of the Quran since it would burden the text unduly if we cited a comprehensive set of references from the Quran and the Sunnah for each order. Occasionally, I cite a reference if it is found only in one or a few places in the scripture. The order of presentation is here governed by who is being addressed by the Quran, ranging from Muhammad's own community of believers, freshly retrieved from Arab polytheism, to other monotheistic communities, indeed the human family itself and, as postscript, some mystical imperatives whose addressees vary.

The first commands were addressed to Muhammad and through him to the small, persecuted community of converts, male and female, in Mecca. These commands remain valid for all Muslim readers. In this category is the order to worship God alone while abjuring pagan idols. The believers are frequently exhorted, in both the Meccan years of persecution and the Medinan years of eventual success, to be patient in adversity and to seek divine aid in the struggle against their own lower natures as well as against external enemies of the faith. Muslims argue among themselves whether or not the command to wage martial *jihād* has lapsed after the first Medinan community. Less controversial are the commands to offer the peace greeting to fellow Muslims and thus fortify and unify the *umma*, continually praise and glorify God through timed prayer, spend charitably in his cause, fast in *ramaḍān*, to abjure meat offered to idols, totally reject carrion, the flesh of swine and the consumption of alcohol, restrain lust as much as possible, and to go on the pilgrimage to Mecca at least once (if financially able to do so).

Some direct commands were addressed only to the first community of believers and are therefore inapplicable today in Muslim cultures – or applicable, in non-Muslim societies that wish to convert to Islam, but only with modifications and appropriate qualifications. Thus, for example, the first believers had to be retrieved from ignorant pagan customs and were commanded not to kill their females at birth or their children in times of famine and to enter houses by their front rather than back entrances. The first two imperatives would apply to societies that practised those two outrages while the third imperative can be interpreted to mean that God does not approve of perverted conduct. Thus, the last order becomes an eternally valid imperative – for immoral conduct is always wrong. Again, similarly, the divine order that believers should not raise their voices above the Prophet's voice (see Q24.63; 49.1–5) has been elevated to the everlasting requirement to show respect for him, long after his physical demise.

Let me highlight this last point for it is topical and contains an obligation that is taken seriously up to this day. It remains a point of unnegotiable difference between Muslims upholding Muhammad's honour and their Western and Westernised opponents. Many satirise Muhammad, with impunity in their legal systems, and appeal, hypocritically, to the right of absolute freedom of speech in this matter – though not in matters of racist, especially anti-Semitic, and obscene speech or publication in general. The double standards are evident even to obtuse observers.

Let me end this important digression. Some direct orders, usually about the Prophet's domestic life, apply only to the Prophet while some apply only to his wives and, according to more liberal commentators, need not be applicable in all respects to all female believers at all times. Many injunctions about the Prophet's mystical and devotional life are applicable to all believers as they seek to imitate his spiritual life but a few are restricted to him in his unique role as God's last prophet (eg.Q17.79).

The Quran addresses the Children of Jacob (Israel) four times inviting them to fulfil their covenant with God (Q2.40, 47, 122; 20.80). There are direct orders to various prophets, including Adam, Moses, Jesus and others. The People of the Book are addressed as a group. God often addresses all humanity, ordering them to fear God by submitting to his laws. Believers are frequently ordered to fear God and to seek nearness to him. The order is accompanied by the promise of peace and justice on earth and everlasting bliss and success in the next life.

We humans are constantly invited to reflect and ponder God's signs. Some verses address only the penitent believing reader. Some such verses are merely rhetorical questions – inviting gratitude towards our creator – without any accompanying order. Finally, some divine orders, usually given only once, involve mystical realities – such as inviting 'the tranquil soul' to enter Paradise (Q89.27–30). The earth is ordered to quell and swallow its water (after the flood; Q11.44), the heavens commanded to submit to God's just decrees (Q41.11).

VI

The Quran contrasts the submitter (*muslim*) with the disbeliever or ungrateful one (*kafir*). It contrasts the submissive believer (*mumin*) with the criminal or lawbreaker (*mujrim*; pl. *mujrimūn*; Q36.59; 55.41; 68.35). 'Criminals never prosper' (Q10.17) is the Quran's confident verdict. The more frequent refrain is 'wrong-doers never succeed', famously at Q12.23, a crucial moment in the life of Joseph. The implication is that those who flout God's laws are evildoers and that such criminals are doomed. Conservative Muslims would see the Christian liberty granted to the Galatians as being criminal and as encouraging criminal conduct.

More broadly, Muslims would caution Christians that we need the law in order to experience the awe of God and to safeguard ourselves from each other's evil proclivities. Muslims would concur with Martin Luther King who once shouted, at a civil rights' rally, that the law, referring to human law, 'does not change the heart but it does restrain the heartless'. Paul would concur since his quarrel is with the law as a means to salvation, not the law as restraint on evil impulses.

Muhammad as prophet was a lawgiver whose authority ex officio was stressed by the Quran (Q4.59, 65; 53.3–4; 59.7) not only for judging his own followers but also for settling disputes involving the People of the Book (Q5.42–43). His practice was normative for his followers and became legally binding when incorporated or codified in the *Sharī'a*. In practice, however, it remained only morally recommended even when it was highly recommended in the law codes. Thus, for example, few Muslims regard the keeping of a beard as mandatory for all adult male believers though it is virtuous to grow one in imitation of the Prophet and therefore many Muslims grow enough to nominally cover the face. (Having a clearly visible beard is a job requirement only for key mosque personnel such as a prayer leader!)

More broadly, Muhammad clarified and expounded on matters left unclear or unmentioned in the Quran. Some rules are based on the Quran while much of the rest derive from Muhammad's example. All revealed imperatives, sometimes vague and elastic, even plastic to human interpretation, were initially interpreted and, if appropriate, implemented by the Prophet. This includes, for example, the gradual but eventually total ban on alcohol, mentioned in different parts of the Quran. The relevant verses are cited and explained in section XIII of Chapter 3 of this essay.

Muslims have inherited a massive body of laws, based on the Quran, the Prophet's rulings and varied jurists' legal compendia reflecting the learned community's consensus, including derived novel verdicts on a vast range of matters. Issues mentioned skeletally in the Quran are amplified by examining the Prophet's observed practice. The *ḥadīth* narratives often clarify the Quran's poetically expressed or ambivalent ordinances. For example, the protocol for ablutions, found concisely in Q5.6, is amplified by the Prophet's practice as observed and then imitated zealously by his companions.

The *Sharī'a*, a word which increasingly alarms virtually all Westerners, carries for all sincere Muslims welcome overtones of a comprehensive divine grace and mercy for humankind through guidance that ranges indifferently over law, ethics and etiquette. The range of the legal compendia is catholic and includes: the protocol for private and public Quran recitation, ablutions and personal hygiene, canonical prayer, and other duties of the faith including payment of zakat tax and performing the *ḥajj* and fasting during *ramaḍān* and at other times, observing festivals and new moons, conducting funerals and even prayer manuals and catechisms for the examination in the grave in preparation for the afterlife.

The rules of the four major Sunni (and one major Shi'ite) law schools regulate marriage, polygyny, menstruation, divorce and inheritance, while stipulating conditions for adoption of children and ordering circumcision of all newborn males. Clear and explicit laws provide for treatment of female orphans, rights of spouses, relatives, domestic slaves, children, parents, neighbours and friends and enemies. There is an ethics of waging *jihād* and treating war captives while protocols for diplomacy with other tribes and neighbouring empires and nations are laid down in the legal codes. We read about the rights and duties of the People of the Book and rulings on apostasy from Islam.

The compendia list rules about commerce and the ban on usury and gambling, detailed dietary restrictions, halal slaughter, the punishment for publicly consuming alcohol, and guidelines specifying time, locales and methods for hunting game. We read in the law compendia about flogging fornicators, stoning adulterers and adulteresses, exemplary punishments for theft and highway robbery, public disorder and for sexual deviance. The Prophet's traditions include qualified bans on secular love poetry (continuous with pagan Arab practice pre-dating Islam) and prohibition of magic (sorcery). This random selection gives a flavour of the full dish.

VII

The Quran promises that 'those who do honourable actions shall abide in the merits of their righteousness forever' (Q18.2–3). The original but unrestricted context is a direct assault on the core Christian dogma of Jesus as the Son of God (Q18.1–5). The opening verse of this pericopē (Q18.1) hints that this is the crooked doctrine that the Quran's descent rectifies. Think here of the opposite and equally confident verdict at 1 Tim. 6.3 where we read that it is precisely the teachings of Christian faith which alone qualify as sound and hygienic.

Historically, as we shall see briefly in the Epilogue, only Mu'tazilite (rationalist) theology requires faith, along with good works and avoidance of major sins, as requisite for entrance into paradise. Sunni orthodoxy, represented by the Ash'arite thinkers, upholds that all sins, major and minor, are forgivable. The only exception is Islam's one and only irremissible sin, the error of associating partners with the only God (Q4.48, repeated at 4.116). Stricter Muslims sects, however, restrict divine forgiveness to minor sins and some even add, depressingly, that any minor sin committed persistently is a major sin! As for God forgiving all sins to anyone he wishes, the rationalist school of the Mu'tazilites urged that that would mean that God acted arbitrarily and indeed unjustly, something that would contradict his nature as revealed to us in the Quran and corroborated in the Prophet's traditions.

Before we discuss works in Islam, we note that the preliminary stage in Islam, as in Christianity, is belief; the central sin of unbelief is neither forgiven nor forgivable. The disbeliever rejects God and his ways and thus has no hope and will be punished for his or her unbelief. For us human beings, the goal of divine creation is God and to him is the return, the end of the journey of mortal life (Q40.3; 53.42). To reject this is to reject the reality of the meeting in the afterlife, the climax of this life (Q6.31). Only the believer experiences the mercy of God and knows the forgiveness of sins, both major transgressions and the minor infringements – such as dietary transgressions committed before one became a believer (see Q5.93). In the Christian case, those who reject the grace and mercy of God, as made manifest in Christ Jesus, shall carry the burden not only of their own sins of misconduct but also the greater sin of rejecting Christ.

As for works, the God of the Quran 'renders pointless the works of disbelievers' (Q47.1). Allah withdraws his grace and favour by nullifying the deeds (*ḥabitat a 'māluhum*; Q9.17) of infidels. This present theological passive indicates that their deeds are made fruitless. While this expression is not found as frequently as the past active 'those who have believed and have done good deeds', it remains a frequent Quranic threat. God renders vain and void the deeds of disbelievers and hypocrites, naturally, but even of heedless believers (Q49.2). The works of infidels are described as being similar to the ashes which the wind blows in every direction on some tempestuous day (Q14.18; cf. Ps. 1.4). Such actions resemble a mirage in a desert, misleading the disbelievers (Q24.39). God scatters their deeds like dust (Q25.23). He assigns them no weight or worth (Q17.104–5). Heavy scales of deeds indicate success (Q101.6–11). Some of the Quran's poetic power is concentrated in verses about the futility of infidelity and the transience of this life, passages which approach a pathos uncharacteristic of the Quran's total tone.

God places faith in believers' hearts, adorns it and renders disobedience and infidelity hateful (Q49.7). He aligns divine and human wills in order to empower believers to correctly perform good actions. The resulting welfare amounts to success by divine enablement (*tawfīq*; Q11.88) and reflects partial but decisive divine control of human destiny. Sometimes, God reconciles the hearts of estranged spouses; the same verb is used (Q4.43). Being under God's law does not imply, however, that one is a robot (Q16.75–6). Within divinely prescribed limits, human submission and service presuppose liberty of will and conduct – and these are granted to us, within the revealed parameters of God's revealed will.

Faith precedes, supports and accompanies good works. Justification, to use a characteristically Christian word, is by good works – but not by such works alone. 'God rewards out of his grace (*faḍl*) those who believe and do good works' (Q30.45). As we note in a speech by Solomon, works are required but their reward is through divine blessing (*n'ima*) and grace (Q27.19). While the supremacy, priority and primacy of Allah's grace is not a disputed thesis (Q24.10, 14, 20, 21), the notion of a *saving* grace, a *characteristically* Christian idiom, is not a characteristically Islamic one though it does occur in the Quran in verses that emphasise the fact that human affairs come to ruin without God's grace as the reality that intervenes to save sinners in their spiritually short-sighted and morally retarded conduct. In this sense, it is used as a refrain throughout the early verses of Surah 24 (vv.10, 14, 20), which refer to a sexual scandal in the Prophet's immediate family. Nonetheless, the notion of grace as saving us *tout court* from the very condition of sin, as opposed to individual sins, is – at least in its fulsome development and detail – answering to an *exclusively* Christian anxiety about salvation.

In Islam, faith (*īmān*) does require divine grace (*faḍl Allah*) to enable it, being a higher state than merely submission to revealed law (see Q49.14) and to the state authorities who enforce it. Faith is, accordingly, more meritorious, than mere political submission. Only the man or woman of faith can reasonably expect to secure God's good pleasure (*riḍwān*, Q9.21) and the bliss of everlasting life in his presence, the central, highly consistent and homogeneously repetitive message of the entire Quran.

Sinners in Hell vow that, if they could only be returned to earth, they would do righteous actions. The emphasis is on works, not faith alone (see Q32.12; 74.42–45; see also Luke 16.19–31). Faith is merely the supplement to good works, implies Surah 90, since performing honourable actions is the *al-'aqaba*, the hard climb, 'the ascent of man'. Muslims maintain that belief matures into faith only when it produces right action. Faith is sincere belief in God and his books, angels and so on, coupled with and validated by honourable works (Q2.177, 285). Faith is inward and private while actions are its outward expression. Mere faith in God is irrelevant: one must at least intend to complement (and also demonstrate) such faith by practical observance enshrined in the law. Paul's Galatian opponents of Jewish extraction would agree heartily with this Islamic perspective. Again, James remarks that the demons believe (*pisteuousin*) in one God and even fear him (James 2.19) but presumably lack the kind of faith that enables righteous action.

For all the similarities with Islam's alternative perspective here, Jews and Christians interpret these polarities and the search for some appropriate balance within their foundational understanding of God's gracious covenant which ultimately frames the totality of his relationship with believers. This comprehensive dimension of God's covenantal relationship to those he calls, enduring as it is, remains at the heart of the New Testament perspective too. Muslims need to note this distinctively biblical worldview while appreciating the abstract theological level at which essential similarities concerning faith/works and law/grace divisions obtain between the members of the trio.

Despite noting this larger context, some Christian readers might still feel uncomfortable reading the last few paragraphs: surely we human beings cannot, through our own efforts alone, climb Jacob's ladder to heaven. Exoneration or legal acquittal is the basis, not the completion, of righteousness. The Quran has, admittedly, an essentially forensic (judicial) theory of justification: 'God will acquit (*yukaffir 'an*; lit. cover, redeem) you of your evil deeds' (Q8.29). For Christians, faith in Christ the Saviour is all-sufficient provided that it is real and genuine enough to motivate a new life lived in the spirit of love and marked by a zeal for good works. For such believers, all sins are not only forgivable through God's grace but have in fact already been forgiven.

In Islam, as in Judaism, a believer does what is right, prays regularly and fasts and so on while believing in God. In Christianity, faith precedes action and then informs it. A believer believes in God and his mercy made manifest in Jesus and that enables him or her to lead a godly life (John 8.32–33). This difference can lead to mutually exclusive practical options but often it simply highlights alternative emphases and priorities. The differences on a theoretical level are fundamental. For the Christian, an ethics of law – as human duty whose performance produces merit – must be replaced by an ethics of virtue enabled decisively by grace. We need grace to transform us, not only revelation to guide us: what we are by nature can only be rectified by what we may and should become by grace. Such grace in Christian thought refers to a robustly divine agency ensuring salvific efficacy and must therefore mean more than the Quran's *faḍl*, the commonest Quranic word for this state. 'God suffices you', the Quran also frequently reassures the Prophet. If God and God's grace (*faḍlallah*) effectively mean the same thing, in such contexts, only then can we begin to see an analogue between, though not equivalence of, the category of grace in Christianity and Islam.

The Christian offer appears morally more robust and indeed impossibly demanding. For example, in Islam, forgiving others is a commandment addressed only to elite believers while other believers may ignore it as only an optional recommended ideal. Christians, by contrast, see the unconditional forgiveness of others as a commandment of the new covenant of grace since God forgave them in the same manner. For true disciples of Christ – and alas how few are these in any age! – forgiving even one's enemies is a direct dominical demand. The Christian has no choice and can claim no merit for choosing the noblest option (Matt. 6.14–15, 18.23–35).

VIII

Paul's ethical teaching grows naturally from his theology of the spirit-led community in which history has proceeded from creation to new creation. As a man of the cross,

Paul's sole *merimna* (anxiety) is for his own (and others') salvation, never for material provision and comfort beyond his daily bread. He dismissed his inherited Jewish privileges as cow dung (*skubala*; Phil. 3.8).

Does Paul, from an Islamic perspective, qualify as an apostle of God? Much in the Quran would appeal to Paul the ascetic. The holy warrior (*mujāhid*) despises material comforts and affluence – and especially longevity, a kind of greed for indulging life's pleasures for as long as possible. The warrior is ever ready to lay down his life in God's cause and sees worldly life and its pleasures as garbage compared to the everlasting bliss of Paradise. But this is not a vision of life lived in the spirit in Paul's sense since Islam promises its followers a paradise of sensual pleasure along with God's good pleasure and forgiveness.

The Quran rejects as misguided only certain aspects of idealistic Christianity, especially its stringent sexual ethics. Some Christian ideals are seen as merely human inventions – but not unworthy or insincerely motivated. Thus, we read the Quran's scrupulously fair if rather ambivalent comment on Christian monasticism: noting with approval the component of compassion but judging the total ideal as an impossibly difficult one, lacking revealed sanction, but sincerely motivated by Jesus' followers' wish to please God (Q57.27). As early as Paul, a life centred in and on Christ defeats the power of the flesh so that the Christian leads a life which, literally, leaves nothing to be desired. Even the Buddha would have been envious of Paul – though the very idea of an envious Buddha would shock Buddhists!

The God of the Quran makes provision for the lusts of the flesh. The body is not evil and its desires and physical drives are God-given, subject both to a right enjoyment and an unhealthy and sinful excess. This view is found in Judaism and prominently in Paul's first Corinthian epistle (1 Cor. 7.1–9) though generally rejected, in the practice of later monastic Christianity. The Quran often celebrates the fact that God's providence (*rizq*) includes all provision, including provision for the sexual side of our nature – legitimate sexual gratification in both worlds. Knowing that 'Provision is from God' (*al-rizqu min Allah*) and 'God is the best of providers' (Q34.39; 62.11) gives Muslims security against fear of hunger and poverty (Q106.4–5). It motivates poor Muslim migrants, even in the most hostile of lands, to set up camp and work hard to provide for their families.

Muslims see our desire to sin as part of our human constitution as designed by God. Sin did not enter the world with the fall of the human species. It is part of being a human being (or being a *jinn*) as opposed to being divine (or angelic). Gen. 3.19 teaches that our return to dust is a punishment for sin. In summarising every human career from birth to rebirth via death, the Quran records the universality of death as a simple biological truth (Q7.24–25; 20.55). The God of Islam created us so that he could, within 'a limited span' (Q6.2), test the righteousness of our conduct. The span of life ends with death. Both are natural and divine. In the Bible, death is an expression of divine wrath (Gen. 3.3–19), a judgement (Rom. 1.32), a condemnation (Rom. 5.16) and a curse (Gal. 3.13).

The *Sharī'a* is not intended to eliminate desire but only to control and regulate it. In the New Testament Christianity too, redemption is not in general from desire but rather from sin. Christianity is not the Buddhism of the West! Like the other authors of the New Testament, Paul wants believers to transform, by Christ's grace, wrong desire into right desire. The Apostle is remarkably passionate in his desire to have the redeemed and baptised believer, on earth, already starting to live in Christ – while looking forward to the permanent sanctification and bodily glorification of eternal life. In this vision, our humanity has been transcended, thanks to a saviour from heaven.

Christians and Muslims are fighting a decisive battle for the true image of humanity. Now, human responsibility and initiative are greater for Christian ethical decision-making since Christians reject the formal compass of a revealed *Sharī'a* that provides precise rules for every imaginable situation – through fatwa and analogy. Thus, for example, the *Sharī'a* does not even recognise tragedy, a situation where the categories of wrong or right are both inapplicable since every option is wrong (and therefore equally right). Tragedy requires ethical neutrality, a stance wisely rejected by the *Sharī'a* since that certainly conflicts with its aim of achieving, in practice, not merely in theory, a radical inclusivity of scope. Although Christianity does not endorse tragedy in the same way as Greek thought does, the faith of Paul does originate in a tragedy that was painfully transcended – albeit as a post-mortem postscript in the spiritual triumph of the resurrection.

IX

Since 1977, the 'new perspective' on Paul, championed by a contingent of formidable New Testament scholars, has relegated the predominantly Reformation debate on faith versus works to a polemical postscript to Paul, sometimes coming close to dismissing as a distraction the entire paradigm of justification by faith versus that of works of the law.[5] Martin Luther had forcefully argued, using some nice distinctions, that the era of legalism was terminated by Christ when he condemned the self-righteousness that comes from pride in our own unaided ability to achieve salvation. All works, good or bad, are irrelevant. Only Christ's own justification counts for he alone is worthy of such justification. As for the law, its own demands drive us to take refuge in the Gospel. Luther argued that we cannot achieve merit-producing blamelessness or sinless perfection. We need Christ's merits. Sinless perfection can only be imputed to us as a result of the works of the law *performed by Christ*. This new state of perfection is gradually realised in sinners who have been saved by Christ's grace. This state of gracious *agapē* is present in the saved but is established by Christ himself. As for the law, it is either abolished or fulfilled as a way of salvation.[6]

According to the so-called new perspective, a legalistic Old Testament and a legalistic Jewish believer are myths inspired by egregious misunderstandings. The Hebrew scripture and the dominant Jewish sects are seen as upholding covenantal nomism rather than legalism in the pejorative sense of Jewish ethnic pride in ritual and rite. After all, the Torah discourages the Israelites from thinking that they are entering the land owing to their own righteousness or special strength or qualities (Deut. 9.4–6). The credit is due solely to the God who chose them.

We should, it is argued correctly, interpret the rejection of the covenant of works as Paul's way of condemning the *Jewish* legalism of his day, an abuse of the Torah by fellow Jews. It is not the law that is at fault but rather the Pharisaic interpretation and estimate of its salvific power. The law teaches the correct way to have faith in God. Legalistic Jews are to blame because legalism, as opposed to merely observance of the law's demands, nurtures personal attachment to law and encourages a false view of its power to save the law-observant sinner. One's theological view of the status of the law, not its practical observance, causes problems.

The second issue, related to the first, is the new perspective's rejection of the Protestant interpretation of works of the law (*erga nomou*) interpreted as acts of the virtuous will.[7] The new perspective argues that works of the Law specify practices that identify a person with the Jewish nation, the solidarity of Israel. Such works refer not to virtuous deeds but rather only to Jewish ethnic identity markers that serve to distinguish Jews from Gentiles. I believe that it is implausible to interpret *erga nomou* as intending merely that subset of the Torah laws which specified ethnic markers – understood to be symbolic precursors of Christ. These were, we are told, to be seen in retrospect as only provisional, superseded by Christ as he fulfilled the law and replaced it with his sufficient grace. The law can, then, be partitioned into morality and the ethnic markers; ancient Judaism, out of which Christianity emerged, was often more attached to ethnic ritual and cult than to their broader moral foundations.

'For we reckon (*logizometha*) that a man without works of (the) law (is to be) justified by faith' (Rom. 3.28). This verse was interpreted by Luther and Calvin to mean that Paul had rejected the Jewish insistence upon good deeds for attaining salvation and had instead proclaimed salvation through faith alone. This interpretation best explains Rom. 10.4 which suggests that Christ is the fulfilment of the moral content of the ancient law, not solely one whose advent renders obsolete the merely ceremonial rulings of that law.

Apart from Romans and Galatians, we find other clear evidence, both in the authentic and disputed Paul, for interpreting works of the law as righteous deeds – understood in antithesis to the saving faith that was granted as a gift of grace (see Phil. 3.8–9; Eph. 2.8–9; Titus 3.4–7). It is unconvincing that such a long and intractable debate was merely about observing boundary markers. With due respect, though not deference for E.P. Sanders, N.T. Wright and James Dunn, this view fails to explain the perceived tension between Paul's stance and James' stance, internal to the canon. It downplays the significance of the important accusation that Paul became in effect an apostate from the law, a central charge from the Judaisers in Galatia and elsewhere. Furthermore, it fails to explain why Christians, in all ages, have not felt obliged to obey the Torah obligations. Admittedly, circumcision is a ritual whose content is not a moral matter. But unlike circumcision, not all dietary rules are without some intended moral considerations relating to human welfare. Eating meat and drinking alcohol remain matters of moral concern in many faiths. Moreover, obeying God's laws, independently of our human assessment of their content, is itself a way to cultivate the supremely moral attitude of humility which such obedience presupposes, encourages and reinforces.

X

Christians believe that ritual purity laws, the sacred calendar and especially circumcision are ethnically Jewish identity markers which have been transcended in Christ. My point here is that the range of *erga nomou* was not, in Paul's day and in his view, restricted to such essentially ritual and ceremonial considerations but rather extended to include legally sanctioned acts of the virtuous will. Paul's 'works of the law' intends the whole law, not some legal subset or boundary register denoting ethnic identity markers. The *erga nomou* emphasis may be dismissed as legalism, in a pejorative sense. But that is a polemical reading of the Jewish scriptures. Paul was perhaps misinterpreting the Pharisaic tradition but his considered position is not necessarily opposed to his Pharisaic origins: good works are indeed necessary for salvation – but only as the fruits of faith. In the last analysis, Paul's idea of the works of the law corresponds to the deeds of the Law/Torah (Hebrew; *ma'asē ha-torā*).[8] Both resemble Islam's honourable deeds (a'*milāt ṣālihāt*).

The law/gospel polarity can certainly be overstated and is perhaps ultimately irrelevant to a true understanding of Christian soteriology. Thus, for example, E.P. Sanders correctly held that law and gospel were equally valid principles in Galatians. He identified an irresolvable problem which Paul faced: Judaism is not Christianity, the latter being in Paul's time a nascent faith that was emerging, indeed mainly as a direct result of his thought and effort. Some six centuries later, Muhammad faced a version of the same problem: Judaism is not historical Islam. The 'parent' faith stubbornly resisted two attempts to annex it, reform it or reduce it to either of the new faiths – two apples that fell too far from the Jewish tree. Furthermore, Muslims had to face the problem that Christianity was not (historical) Islam, that is, not the same primordial faith which, according to the Quran, was proclaimed indifferently by all the prophets, including Abraham, Moses and Jesus. In the context of Christian origins, located within the astonishingly rich sectarian diversity and variety labelled Second Temple Judaism, this whole anxiety is well expressed by Sanders: '[H]ow does God's recent revelation in Christ relate to his former revelations to Israel?'[9]

In Gal. 3.10, Paul boldly curses those who rely on works of the law insofar as their attitude creates pride and division in the human family. Paul made genuine progress towards creating a universal faith when he noted that the ethnic pride, implicit in the Jew-Gentile division in the church, created a rupture in the body of Christ.

Paul exploits the broader *purposes* of the Torah, namely, its call for faithfulness in a spirit of love, as an argument against the narrower *applications* of the Torah, exhibited in its encyclopaedic range of legal provision. Islamic jurisprudence relies on an analogous distinction: the *maqāṣid al-sharī'a* (purposes of the holy law) overrule any individual legal application that might be harmful to the larger interests (*maṣlaḥā*) of the Muslim community. One troubling deeper question motivates the believer's attempt to understand the status and place of the holy law in the context of discerning God's will. Is obeying God's law equivalent to obeying God? Some Christians would say: What matters is what is in the heart. But do we know what is in other people's hearts – or indeed even our own hearts? We need an externalisation of the inner through the outer, through the law. The letter of the law can, no less than its spirit, give life, for a ritual need not be ritualistically performed. It can certainly be abused – but that is not a reason to abolish it any more than the fact that people disobey laws means that laws are redundant.

While one cannot deny the inherited Jewishness of Paul's Christian practice, equally one cannot avoid conceding that he wanted to remove the genealogical (if not outright racial) slant (if not taint) of historic Israel – as merely one ethnically defined *umma* – in order to do justice to the potentially universal ethical spirit of Judaism, a spirit obscured by the emphasis on Jewish cult and ritual. Paul probably abandoned the letter of the law, certainly ceased to be a Pharisee and perhaps even a practising Jew (see 1 Cor. 9.20; Acts 21.21, 27–29; 24.5). He was a new Jew with a new view: he believed that the messiah had come and that it was therefore high time that the Jews should lead all the nations to worship the God of Israel. These newborn Jews were to read the Old Testament law in a new light – the light of Jesus the Messiah now reigning in heaven – and then to teach it to all the nations. Many Jews accused him of being an apostate from the law and of preaching against it but they must have been puzzled by the behaviour of the Christian Paul who sacrifices at the Temple, purifies himself and shaves his hair, and offers alms (Acts 21.23–26; 24.16–18; 25.8). Was he only pretending to be a law-observant Jew? Such matters of academic curiosity apart, Paul liberated Judaism for a more international role, by building the church, an achievement with enduring consequences. Had it not been for Paul's labours centuries earlier, Islam's imperial spread would have been, I believe, even more dramatic.

XI

In concluding our textual commentary, we must address briefly a key doctrinal current that runs throughout the New Testament. While God is numerically one, the Christian deity desires relationship with his human creatures in a relational and Trinitarian monotheism rather than in a unitary and juridical one. Paul claims that the character, essence and nature of God become evident only in a relationship of faith as trust – and that this was always so. In ancient times, God was in relationship with Abraham and Israel. Otherwise, Pauline Christian thinkers would argue, monotheism is sterile and inert: it is noble but, like the noble gases, it does not react with other entities or persons. For Paul, God is in relationship again: the one and only holy God of Israel has now become identified with the messiah Jesus – though, in view of post-Pauline doctrinal developments, not exhaustively so.

For Paul, Jesus was, however, God's only Son – sent to provide the righteous standing with God for which the Torah proved useless. Among human beings, father and son belong to the same order of beings. The son is inferior only in rank, not in nature, since one proceeds from the other. Although the reciprocal love of father and son is uniquely profound, it acquires such profundity only after the son matures beyond selfishness. I am constructing this analogy on the human level and therefore mentioning the temporal context of the evolution of such love. Christians do not consider such a caveat: they exclude this temporal dimension, present in the human analogy, since it is damaging to their case concerning Jesus' relationship to God the Father.

At his resurrection and later exaltation, Jesus was appointed 'Son of God' (Rom. 1.4) which suggests, according to liberal Christian scholars, that this title denoted merely an office or function in salvation history, an appointment fully compatible with its Jewish origins and heritage. In the later creeds and dogmatic formulae, this phrase was, it is believed, used to denote a metaphysical quality of essence and possession, a far cry from its rather innocent original meaning. Conservative and evangelical scholars normally dismiss such reserve and scepticism and argue that such views fail to do justice to the implied high Christology of John's Gospel, especially John 1.1–18, and indeed arguably to Jesus' self-identification in some of his sayings and parables in the Synoptic gospels. Some see further support for a high Christology in Paul.

This initial Christology may be dubbed adoptionist but it remains wholly orthodox. Adoptionist in its later heretical sense is the view that Jesus, having been initially purely human, was later adopted as son and promoted to divinity. This Christian heresy, held perhaps as an orthodox view by some Arab Christians in Muhammad's Arabia, is a frequent target of the Quran's condemnation (Q17.111; 18.4; 25.2 etc.). In sound Christian doctrine, Jesus is 'appointed' or designated (*horisthentos*; Rom.1.4) but not 'adopted' since the latter is rightly reserved for the derivative status of Christians as sons and daughters of God (*huiothesian*; acc. Gal.4.5).

The title 'Son of God', fully invested with metaphysical meaning, was destined to become the church's preferred Christological accolade. In Acts (9.20), 'Son of God' is part of Paul's post-baptismal message and is a synonym for the messiah. The risen Christ confers filial adoption on believers (Gal. 3.26, 4.4–7). As the Son of God, Jesus Christ was empowered to usher in God's Kingdom which admitted other sons and daughters. The conservative New Testament scholar Richard Bauckham represents the consensus of normative Christianity, outside the academy, when he claims that Christ is the eschatological Son of God through whom others participate in a newly transformed and redeemed humanity. The fatherhood of God is the newly eschatological relationship of God to men and women while Jesus is uniquely the Son of God through whom others can become sons. As the agent of salvation at the end of sacred history, Bauckham concludes, Jesus admits the rest of redeemed humanity to a new relationship with God his father. While conceding that the later Christology of pre-existent Johannine (or protological) Sonship differs from this earlier eschatological Sonship, Bauckham discerns a developing Christology in the crucially formative half century of the New Testament period (40–90 CE). He suggests that the later understanding is latent in the earlier: the later Christology is a working out of the implications of Jesus as the eschatological Son of God.[10]

Let me comment here briefly, addressing both Christian and Muslim readers. I find the conclusions of Bauckham's research to coincide rather too neatly with his Christian dogmas. These latter are held on independent, pre-existent, grounds which might not always be separable from motives of faith. This precarious situation is a normal liability of such historic-theological research, especially if it is conducted in ways innocent of the cautious refinements that philosophical reasoning enables.

XII

The second issue is the prevalence of characteristically Pauline teaching in Christianity and the related question of the former's compatibility with Islam. Unlike belief in Jesus as Saviour, justification by grace alone is not an explicit teaching that pervades the entire New Testament. It is most abundantly located in Paul and in the deutero-Pauline letters. This makes it a quintessentially, though not exclusively, Pauline view, aspects of which are also prominent in Hebrews and the Johannine components of the New Testament.

I admit that this is too simplistic an overview of the New Testament teaching. If one sees the framework for organising the Pauline position as the tension between faith and works, arguably a real one, then one might miss the vital point that the debate throughout the New Testament, both in its Pauline and non-Pauline components, is about the place of faith rather than merely the object of faith. In Paul, moreover, what is at stake is not some detached or theoretical account of faith but rather the salvifically urgent question of the sufficiency of Jesus and the cross, via Jesus on the cross. Paul's outlook is therefore virtually a 'Crosstianity', as I dubbed it in my commentary on Gal. 6.12.

Such an understanding of the Apostle's theological emphasis bears crucially on any Islamic reading of his thought, especially of his earliest thinking as evidenced in his letter to his Galatian disciples and detractors. The main point to note here is that Paul's teaching on justification by grace alone is, in the final analysis, only rhetorically and superficially opposed to Islam. The reformer, John Calvin, who was blessed with the clarity of mind of a philosopher even though he was a lawyer, wrote that while 'faith avails by itself for justification', such faith is 'always joined with good works.'[11] For Muslims too, in a way that Calvin might have approved of, faith is effectively a key way to obey God, to submit to his will by doing good works – works of the holy law.

I note a point of nomenclature. The Quran speaks only of justification of God's word as it proved true against the disbelievers (Q36.7) – and justly convicted them of infidelity and therefore divine punishment. Muslims expect a time of judgement (*yaum al-dīn*; Q1.4), an eschatological day when the reckoning is established (*yauma yaqūmu al-ḥisāb;* Q14.41). In this regard, Muslims do not differ from Paul who also warns those who trouble the Galatians that they will incur God's final judgement (Gal. 5.7–10).

The Quran reveals, to return to matters of doctrinal substance, that no soul can have faith without God's permission. Faith is decisively but not solely enabled by grace. The Prophet's traditions confirm that entry into paradise is by God's grace, not by works of the law. Only the rationalist Muslims, the Mu'tazilites, saw the works of the law as decisive: God's justice obliged him to reward good doers with paradise and evildoers with hell. Sunni (Ash'arite) orthodoxy stipulated God's grace as the sole requirement of entry into paradise but tended to see such grace as a synonym for the arbitrary if sovereign nature of the divine will which human creatures had no right to question. Paul defends this view of grace at length (Rom. 9.11–24). Modern secularised readers would be alienated by Paul's dogmatic tone which discourages open reflectiveness on an issue that invites human curiosity and concern.

There is some equivocal support for the priority of righteous deeds. A weakly attested tradition of the Prophet has it that God would never send to Hell any man who called people to prayer for seven consecutive years. In such a case, works of the law can save – by God's grace, that is, his permission. A Bedouin asked the Prophet: 'When is the hour?' He replied: 'What have you prepared for it?' The need for righteous action is implied in this counter-question. The Bedouin answered that he had little by way of works (prayer and fasting and so on) but he loved God and his messenger, presumably a way to express his trust in God's grace. The Prophet approved of his answer.

Grace permits the performance of good works – requiring human agency – but grace is never elicited or deserved by such works of human agency. A single, symbolic good action can accomplish a sinner's 'salvation'. For example, according to a well-attested prophetic tradition, a prostitute placed water in her shoe in order to quench a stray dog's thirst – and was forgiven her sins solely for that one act of virtue. Grace can override works of the law. But works can never supersede grace and force salvation through merit alone. Jewish covenantal nomism, Christian libertarianism and Islamic 'legalism' all presuppose that the *raḥmat Allah* (God's mercy) is the only basis of forgiveness of sins and hence of 'salvation' or its equivalents. The crucial differences relate to how one lives out one's faith, its practical demands and the role of the revealed law. Such differences are not superficial. Nonetheless, all monotheists must agree that God alone knows our true motives and intentions, that he alone forgives sins, and that he alone decides our final destiny. God's mercy and grace – the two are related in Islam more intimately than in Christian thought – are his prerogative. He forgives whom he will, though we know that his reliably good nature prevents him from being capricious or arbitrary in his decisions. Only a fool – and there are plenty among the heedless – would be complacent about the final outcome of the human struggle that leads to failure or success in the life of faith.

XIII

In the Old Testament, God is the redeeming one (Heb.; *ha-go'el*; Grk. *ho lutroumenos*) of Israel. Gal. 3.13 reads: 'Christ has redeemed (*exēgorasen*) us from the curse of the law.' A slave could buy his freedom by becoming the property of a chosen god, by depositing money in his temple, thus becoming free from human owners. Paul's use of *doulos Christou* echoes this pagan Greek practice. 'For freedom' (*ep'eleutheria;* Gal.5.1, 13) is frequent in Greek temple inscriptions. In the papyri, the verb *lutro* means to redeem a pledge: to repossess something for its rightful owner, and thus rescue it from the possession of an alien power.

Once the purchase price is paid, the sinner is redeemed and belongs wholly to God in Christ. Jesus came to give his life as a ransom (*lutron*) for many (see Mark 10.45,

Matt. 20.28). The redemption (*apolutrōsis*), effected through his blood (see Eph. 1.17, Col. 1.14, Heb. 9.15), enables Christians to enter into a new relationship with God (Rom. 3.24). Past sins are forgiven; Christians are adopted into the family of God (Rom. 8.23).

In my view, there is a *lacuna* in Christian soteriology: to whom is the price of redemption paid? If paid by God to God himself in a different personal form or incarnation of himself, it makes him a narcissistic and avenging deity rather than the allegedly loving and generous God of Christian faith. It could not have been paid to the Devil since that would make him God's morally equal opponent. Are such questions inappropriate – rooted in the mischief of outsiders and polemicists? Some Christians would concede that the inquiry here is a legitimate one though many would no doubt appeal, eventually, to an escape clause, an *exit in mysterium*, once all rational explanation and accessible human moral reasoning have been exhausted.

The Quran does not address such characteristically Christian views but contains related doctrines which establish a direct opposition between Islamic and Christian perspectives. 'No bearer of burdens can bear the burden of another' (Q6.164; 17.15; 39.7; 53.38) expresses a strict view of personal responsibility which is, at every significant level, incompatible with Christian soteriology. The Quranic claim is not merely that forgiveness can only be between the sinner and God, involving no third party, a view also held, in a related form, by Christians. The Quranic stance implies that since Jesus is not God, Jesus' atoning sacrifice on behalf of sinners would make him into the third party. The Quranic maxim of individual burden-bearing is a moral stance in its own right but is also directed against the Christian doctrine of vicarious atonement.

The strict Quranic view is mitigated by references to collective judgement of nations (Q4.41; 17.71; 45.28–9). Common sense dictates that as families and groups, we bear one another's burdens of pain, sorrow and guilt (though not sin) in this life. Furthermore, the Quran certainly rejects the Torah's notion of intergenerational justice whereby God can, up to the third and fourth generations, visit on the children the sins of the fathers (Deut. 5.9). In later Jewish thought, the clear injustice of this stance was mitigated by the view that the forefather's sins were justly correlated with the sins of the children who were also, in any case, wicked (Jer. 16.10–11). Indeed, Ezekiel even reaffirms strictly personal responsibility (18.20), a view already found in the Torah (Deut. 24.16) and identical to the Quran. Furthermore, the Hebrew Bible and the Quran both support the claim that the actions of the righteous can outlive them so that their offspring may enjoy the benefits of their parents' piety. God can visit on the children the virtues of the fathers (see Q18.82; Deut. 5.10, 7.9, Ex. 20.5–6, Ps. 103.17–18).

Finally, the extra-Quranic doctrine of *radd al-maẓālim* (restoration of wrongs) mitigates strict burden bearing. It states that we will be burdened with direct divine penalty for injustices we commit against others but surprisingly, in a Muslim setting, we must additionally bear some of the sins of others. Why? God relieves the burden of the actual perpetrators of these particular sins – but only as a compensation for wrongs committed against them by others. Several secure prophetic traditions support this stance of vicarious or transferred bearing of the burden of another's sins; some equivocal Quranic support is also available (see Q16.25).

XIV

Unlike the New Testament, the Quran contains no counsels of perfection, only counsels of prudence. A few of Jesus' injunctions set a standard of perfection for the spiritually elect (based on Matt. 19.21); these were supererogatory requirements that went beyond the commandments. The Quran, however, asks us only to do the best we can, to fear God as much as possible (Q64.16); the context here is the requirement to live out the faith's social obligations, independently of whether or not this discharge of legal duty secures the purity and integrity of associated inner attitudes and dispositions. That is a larger task.

God burdens no soul with more than it can bear (Q2.286; 7.42; 65.7). While the beginning of one long verse (Q2.286) reveals that God burdens no soul with more than it can bear, the same verse continues by counselling the believer to beg God not to burden him with more than he can bear. Earlier communities – Jews and Christians – were presumably burdened even more than the Muslim community founded by Islam's formidable prophet. The petition of this long verse further affirms our frailty while the opening pledge that God does not overburden us is a reminder that he is a just and merciful God. As a practical and practicable revelation, the Quran draws on the resources of human nature: 'It will be good for whoever obeys his own impulse to goodness' (Q2.184; see also Q2.158). We can do otherwise: a son of Adam chose to obey his soul's impulse to do evil – and murdered his brother (Q5.32).

A practicable religion must command us to make only those righteous choices that we have the strength to make. For our strength, unlike the divine strength, is of the kind that may fail us. The magnitude of the natural impulse to good should match the quality of piety demanded. The Quran promulgates realistic and practicable ideals that make allowances for the divinely created weakness in our nature. Muhammad saw Islam as a religion for governing the lives of all human beings, not an elite faith suited only for saints and idealists. Muslims generally regard Christianity as being suited only to a spiritual elite and some Muslims see that elite as behaving irresponsibly by neglecting their social and political duty to establish God's Kingdom on this side of the grave. This is not the place to adjudicate such a large controversy but there can be no doubt where I stand on this matter.

The Quran condemns sentimentality as an enemy of practical reason (Q11.42–7). Emotion immobilises practical reason and blurs the distinction between wrong conduct and right conduct. There are no innocent wrong acts. Natural disasters are tragic in their consequences but, in the human world, there are no tragedies. Indeed, neither the Quran nor the Arabic language even has a word for what we call tragedy. The Quran does not recognise it as a category of thought. In a tragedy, we have no right, no wrong – and no choice. That is not the Muslim condition.

The Quran rejects optimistic estimates of the unaided human potential for self-perfectibility through obedience to revelation. Muslims acknowledge a permanent discrepancy between the stringent demands of piety, on the one hand, and the ambiguous resources of human nature as created by God, on the other. Our divinely designed human nature is intrinsically incapable of being *fully* malleable to the divine will: human recalcitrance is not accidental. The capacity for frustrating our higher nature is a divinely intended and therefore irremovable feature of human nature. We shall therefore always need divine grace to become fully submissive to God.

Notes

1 In the Quran, this word has idiosyncratic additional meanings at Q12.45 and 15.79.

2 The late Yasser Arafat struggled to locate Kashmir on the map while Kashmiri Muslims, themselves often victims of Hindu hegemony, were donating their jewellery to support Palestinian resistance to Israeli occupation.

3 *Hudā* is a popular female name roughly corresponding to Sophia (wisdom). The Arabic for wisdom (*ḥikmah/ḥikmat*) is usually a male, not female name.

4 Sir William Muir (1819–1905), quoted by Edward Said, *Orientalism* (New Delhi: Penguin Books India, 2006), p. 151.

5 See E.P. Sanders, *Paul and Palestinian Judaism* (Philadelphia: Fortress, 1977), N.T. Wright, *Paul: In Fresh Perspective* (Minneapolis: Fortress, 2005), and J. Dunn, *The New Perspective on Paul* (Grand Rapids: Eerdmans, 2007).

6 Works of the law *(erga nomou)* can validly be understood as a covenant of works. Ethnic Israel failed to live up to its stringent demands. Christ has now fulfilled this covenant on behalf of Adam, Israel and all Adam's descendants. A covenant of works can nurture a law-observant righteousness in the individual believer, encouraging individual legalism. It is worth adding here that this dispensationalist view is interesting from an Islamic perspective. The law provides the basis for establishing God's Kingdom but Israel failed to establish it on that basis. The Quran would support both parts of this claim but cannot accept the rest of the dispensationalist doctrine which claims that, during the age of the church, the requirement of *erga nomou* has been suspended only to be re-established at Christ's second coming. The law is *postponed* as a way of salvation.

7 See the works cited in footnote 5 above.

8 It is found in 4QMMT (4Q398) 29. T Cf. *ma'asē torā* in 4QFlor (4Q174) 1.7 where *torā*, without the definite article, can be read to mean thanksgiving instead of law. This is a confirmed and certain reading, not subject to variant readings. The confirmed reading, with the definite article, is used in 4QMMT to refer to the infamous curses and blessings of Deut. 27–30. This usage clearly resembles Paul's idiom in Gal.3.8–14. For more, see J. Dunn, '4QMMT and Galatians'. *NTS*, 43, (1997), 147–53, esp. 148, 150.

9 See Sanders, *Paul and Palestinian Judaism, op. cit.*, p. 44. See also p. 117.

10 R. Bauckham, 'The Sonship of the Historical Jesus in Christology', *Scottish Journal of Theology*, 31, (1978), 245–60.

11 Comm. Gal. 5.6; *CNTC* (Calvin's New Testament Commentaries), 11.96.

9

EPILOGUE

Missionaries in reverse: learning from the rival

I

The study of Paul's letters fails to yield any uncontested views of the Apostle, even among Christian scholars. An outsider cannot be expected to offer any wholly new or implausibly controversial estimates of the man. Thus, for example, there are differences of opinion, often merely of emphasis, among considerably learned scholars, with regard to the continued role of the law in Christian life, the nature and consequences of sin, the precise status of redemption, the body of Christ and so on. Some of these differences are effectively canonised in the New Testament since that scripture can be read by non-Christians as simply the documentary record of a new faith movement that emerged within the full light of classical history. Indeed, that is how I intend to read that remarkable book in my forthcoming research.[1]

The Protestant reading of Paul, especially its Lutheran and evangelical interpretation, is one I have favoured in my commentary. I know that it is by no means the only Christian reading but I also believe that its status as normative Christian reading can be established. Paul continues to divide Christians no less than he divides Christians from Jews and Muslims. The Apostle of justification by faith alone is not the only Paul. This comes out in much recent Protestant-Catholic dialogue, heightened as it is in 2017, the 500th anniversary of the Reformation.

Paul's impact within Christianity is not a disputed thesis. His role in the formation of Christian-Muslim debate and polemic, however, is not a field that can claim much impartial scholarship and scrutiny. Engaging with Paul, beyond the Islamic paradigm of *taḥrīf*, the uniquely Islamic accusation that the Christian gospel has been humanly doctored and altered, will help to reframe Christian-Islamic debates and move us away from an ancient and stale deadlock.

While my book is a Muslim reading of Paul, it is open to Christian challenges that are beyond mere polemical point-scoring. My underlying hermeneutic differs in some respects from that of many practitioners of 'Scriptural Reasoning'. I recognise, indeed applaud, the inescapability of our commitments and therefore the impossibility of neutral readings that result from a mere juxtaposition of sacred texts. The participant-observer model is commonplace in anthropological and ethnographic fieldwork where many pretend to go native or be a communist for a few years. Writers often spend time among the natives, expressing fake sympathy, as they gather materials for their next book, in which they publish unflattering views of the innocent, hospitable natives. One has to defend one's explicit views and their insinuations. If one does not, it is intellectually dishonest. When offering a sympathetic view of an opposed opinion, one runs the risk of giving the impression that one actually believes permanently (rather than merely temporarily), what one is claiming to disown or refute in due course. It is important to announce a disclaimer, at the start, to distance oneself from the view under intellectual scrutiny.

This happens at a time when there is a larger shift in focus too as Christian theologians and secular and agnostic philosophers reclaim biblical texts as sites of insight, beyond the captivity of a sterile historical criticism that interests only specialists. Thus, for example, there are new philosophical readings of Paul's letters. Many non-Christians are now engaging with Paul in innovative ways that help to locate him in the broader contemporary intellectual culture of critical theory and indeed of liberal secular humanism.[2]

Nor do I wish to offer simplistic views and estimates of Jews and Judaism, especially of these realities in Paul's remarkably complex time. (Islamic origins are simpler, indeed simple.) Many Jewish writers are intelligently and sympathetically engaging Paul's thought and Christian theology. This is part of a larger trend among the writers, including some Christians, who read Paul (and the New Testament) in ways that resist, albeit in my view ineffectively, the long history of Christian triumphalism and supersessionism.[3]

II

I have intervened in the growing field of Christian-Muslim relations by offering a new model of engagement, one that is avowedly particular to Islam while being open to a Christian text and seminal thinker whose ideas challenged Judaism and later Islam. While I acknowledge the competing key doctrines and the accompanying rival colonial histories that have historically shaped the exchanges between these two powerful faiths, I do not assume that the legacy of this contentious history must be our only future. But first, some more history so that we can see how and why Muslim orthodoxy arrived at the view that virtue is not beyond but through the law.

A Muslim reader of Galatians might see the slogan of Christianity, with its offer of a gospel of free grace, as: 'Repent of the notion that even your good deeds can save you!' Reliance on works is seen as a subtle kind of idolatry, what Muslims call '*shirk*'. In this critical commentary on Paul's letter to the Galatians, I have also effectively reconstructed Paul's hypothetical stance on Islam and its view of the relationship between faith and works of the divine law. In doing so, we realised that Islam is a religion of orthopraxy, not orthodoxy. It replaces theology with what I call *ergatology*, the systematic study of works of the law. Islamic theology, insofar as it exists at all, collapses into hermeneutics and at times, as in much New Testament exegesis, reduces to a jejune and claustrophobic obsession with speculative philology. The ergatology strand is fundamental to Islam, a practical moral faith centred on the doing of good works, not on faith as such or on the mystery of God's character.

'Repent of your evil deeds' was the motto of many in early Islam when Muslims were consumed by continuous controversy over the status of the sinner's works. A protracted and fierce legal battle gradually led to the emergence of opinions that later ossified into Sunni juristic orthodoxy. The hidden impulse behind what might be called a 'gospel of works' was the enthusiastic desire to track heresies that could affect the integrity of the state in an age when every religious controversy, if we understand 'religion' in its narrow contemporary secular meaning, was a surrogate for some political disagreement that could threaten communal cohesion.

After the assassination of the third caliph, 'Uthman, there arose the earliest *theological* problem that could affect the unity, identity and integrity of the Muslim community. It might surprise Christians and Jews to learn that it was a problem identical to the one that arose in the origins of Christianity: the question of defining the believer's faith status in relation to his or her actions or works of the law. The larger concern was supplied by the irresolvable dilemmas of free will versus divine determinism. The crucial difference was that, unlike the case of Christian origins, the problem of the balance between faith and works was already (though implicitly) answered by the Quran, a document that had fully defined Islam and guided its potential legal and political implementation. The Hebrew Bible implicitly addressed the question of the right balance between faith and works for Jews – but the new puzzle certainly arose for Gentile followers of Jesus, a task that Paul tackles.

In the debate concerning how to determine the correct relationship between faith and works, there arose three factions: the Kharijites (seceders) who opposed the Murji'ites (postponers) and a third party, the Mu'tazilites (the separatists), who maintained their own intermediate stance. The Kharijites regarded works as an absolutely valid index of true faith: anyone who committed a major sin was *eo ipse* a disbeliever at least while he or she committed it. A person who commits a grave or heinous sin becomes, solely by virtue of that, an apostate. These were a group with the puritanical and uncompromising temperament of the modern Islamic State. They were, to award them a dubious honour, the first terrorists produced by Islam, though they did not aspire to the level of brutality practised by ISIS.

Their opponents were the faith-centred (fideist) opponents, the Murji'ites or the 'hope-postponed ones' who held that actions, good or bad, were both independent of one's faith. Even sinners who perpetrated moral atrocities remained nonetheless believers, the question of their ultimate status and that of their deeds being in God's hands. Even such reprobates had grounds for hope since their case was postponed – deferred to another world, awaiting God's grace and mercy. Since we never know the nature and moral weight of our sins, it was argued, the wise man deferred judgement to God.

The Mu'tazilite camp housed the 'separatists' who adopted a position between the Kharijites and their Murji'ite opponents: the one whose deeds did not bear out his or her profession of faith was, for the Mu'tazilites, neither a believer nor a disbeliever but occupied 'a stage between the two stages' (*al-manzila bayna al-manzilatayn*). The Mu'tazilites wanted to maintain the integrity of God's character, his justified reputation for moral justice and held, therefore, that all human actions are integral to faith (*īmān*). They suspended judgement only concerning the grave sinner's ultimate status in God's eyes. The Mu'tazilites were self-described as 'the people of justice and unity (of God)' while their opponents condemned them as divisive. Among non-Muslim scholars, they were to acquire a reputation for being Islam's first rationalists, possibly liberals. They were, however, no less zealously attached to their own position than the two warring parties whom they opposed.

Fortunately, the Kharijites eventually disappeared, as is the fate of overly zealous groups, while the Mu'tazilites and the Murji'ites agreed that one either has faith (the dual testimony of Islamic faith) or does not have it. The undue complexity of the debate arose from the accompanying qualifying views. Some asserted, defensibly enough, that true faith increases with virtuous deeds, a view not explicit in the Quran, although God is said to increase the believers' faith (Q9.124) and enlarge his grace towards them (Q24.38). The rationalists added, barely defensibly, that faith does not correspondingly decrease with commission of wicked deeds. Other groups, including the Murji'ites, held, more plausibly, that it increases through the doing of good deeds and diminishes with the performance of evil ones but never to the point of reaching zero – since the profession of faith safeguards even the worst sinner against that disastrous possibility. The Quran is silent on this audacious latter claim. But there is some equivocal support for it in the Prophet's sayings.

The Islamic scripture entertains varied views on the precise relationship between faith and righteous action. In the context of the first murder, when the sacrifice offered by one of Adam's sons is rejected, the other son replies: 'God accepts only from the righteous' (Q5.27). This verse implies the priority of faith to works since God will not accept even the righteous deeds of someone who is not righteous as to faith. Elsewhere, however, the Quran virtually identifies faith with righteous actions (Q3.110), an identification emphasised strongly in the Prophet's sayings. However, the Quran concedes that faith can coexist with varying degrees of hypocrisy and disbelief since many sinners mix their righteous deeds with wicked ones (Q9.102). This acceptance of nuance and compromise enabled communal cohesion in a politically conscious faith.

III

The French post-impressionist painter Paul Gauguin (1848–1903) searched for a perfect place, a virgin paradise, an Eden on earth – and eventually decided to travel to Tahiti. But he wanted to learn from the natives, not to teach them or preach to them. There were many Christian missionaries, often with the same Christian name as the painter, already in Tahiti, adrift in that unknown paradise of Oceania.[4] Armed with the imperial confidence of the late nineteenth century, most probably felt they had nothing to learn, only to teach. Gauguin became a missionary in reverse, perhaps a little like his namesake the Apostle Paul had become an anti-philosopher who challenged the received wisdom of the philosophers. Can cultures and faiths learn from each other when they are so entrenched so confidently in their own beliefs? Or can there be inter-doubt relations rooted in the humility of the spirit?

Can Muslims learn anything from reading Paul's letter? When communities lack political power, surviving in minority powerlessness and isolation, they are tempted to accentuate their legal piety in order to retain, maintain and sustain their religious identity. It is instructive for Muslims, Arab and non-Arab, to consider how and why Paul elected to move the new Christian faith away from the rituals and beliefs of its parent faith. Understanding Paul's concerns could help Muslims to make Islam a more self-consciously universal faith, finally removed from traces of its historically conditioned Arabolatry.

One God and his one people: that was Israel's self-understanding. Paul revised that self-image by rejecting Jewish assumptions about the superiority of historic ethnic Israel. Compare the transformation of Christianity, a Jewish sect which became an international religion dominated by Gentiles, with Islam which began as an Arab religion only to be overwhelmed by an influx of non-Arab converts, within a hundred years of Muhammad's death. Few modern Muslims live in the Arab heartland of this imperial faith. Its far eastern frontier is Indonesia while its most western outpost is Muslim-majority Morocco, meekly facing the proudly Christian Americas. In this profile, we deliberately exclude any Muslim immigrant minorities settled in culturally Western lands, whether these are in the geographic west or east.

No one enters a faith merely generically – simply and only as a human being, that is, independently of the particularities of language, ethnicity and gender. Believing and practising Christians and Muslims often have identities wholly defined by their faith. Unlike most believing Jews, most committed Muslims and Christians tend to define their humanity in wholly religious terms and therefore cannot, in given moral and legal contexts, simply divorce their humanity from their faith. Judaism, like Sikhism, combines an ethnic genealogical grounding with religious faith, the two strands often indistinguishable though always remaining in principle separable.

The point of these admittedly rather desultory observations above is that devout Muslims find it hard to see the point of 'human' rights for there are no human beings, only believers and disbelievers – only Christians, Jews, Hindus and so on. The attitudes towards the centrality of human rights often differ greatly among the Western monotheists. Muslims and, to a lesser extent, Christians entertain intensely religious anthropologies, based on their readings of the New Testament and Quran, which often prevent them from being enthusiastic about intrinsically human rights. (Of course, no one openly claims that disbelievers have no rights!) By contrast, Jews often warm to the notion of human rights as such.

Let me run this to earth by noting the implications of this for practical and lived realities. In the now defunct British race relations industry, we used to note that most Muslims do not see themselves as anything but Muslims. Some devout Muslims even denied, rhetorically, the very notion of race, asserting there is only one race, the human race (perhaps confusing race with species). Jews, by contrast, stood and continue to stand at the forefront of struggles for *racial* justice – especially for minorities settled in Western lands. Many are secular Jews, with enduring memories of Holocaust losses; they revere justice for all human beings as a supreme human value, not only or primarily as a revealed religious duty.

Let me put an end to these huge anxieties simply by concluding that all communities increasingly exist and even thrive as distinct solidarities, over against an indifferent or hostile world. Each needs a secure boundary, a central ideal or stance that serves as a final marker of identity, a stance not subject to compromise or negotiation. The cross of Christ, in the grace of divine love, suffices the Christian and decides his or her stance in any crisis of action or thought. Muslims are obedient to *Sharī'a* while the covenant-conscious Jews are possessive of their Torah. Abraham appears to be the common denominator of this trio of competitive pieties. Yet he unifies but also divides. The Abrahamic paradigm is automatically restrictive in religious studies for it excludes the eastern faiths. I am wary of it on other internal grounds too.[5]

IV

It is time now to take leave of the reader, as the early novelists such as Henry Fielding used to do in their long novels. Sadly, however, it is time for some hard statements. According to Muslims, including myself, Christianity offers guidance only in the life of faith and worship but does not guide the rest of life; it does not hallow the mundane. Christians would disagree strongly and retort, somewhat defensively, that the Incarnation does for Christians precisely what the law does for Jews and Muslims. I cannot decisively resolve this deadlock but hope that my commentary invites and offers a patient exploration of the terrain.

It is the radical inclusivity of law that makes juridical monotheism the most potent – some would say totalitarian and fascist – ideal in the history of ideas. It is the climax of goodness. It combines into a unique amalgam the revealed foundations of law with a human superstructure of legal ingenuity built on it – together securing society's true welfare. Muslims would see any lawless faith, including and especially Christianity, given its Jewish origins, as effectively a regress to an earlier and more primitive stage of religious evolution. Thus, for Muslims, tutored by the Quran and by their Prophet Muhammad, Christianity must finally emerge, after one has taken account of nuances and shades of scriptural meaning, as essentially a primitive faith, closer to a primordial paganism, a mystical pantheism infused with a vague notion of a human-divine interface whereby nature and the supernatural meet. The problem is that such a view offers no guidance on how to live well. Thus, for Muslims, the law is not a curse but a blessing, a reminder and a commandment from God, sent down for our collective benefit rather than to oppress us (see Q20.2–3). A robust moral virtue is not beyond the law but rather through the law.

The Christian would be desolated by this Islamic verdict on Christianity and no doubt dismiss it as a travesty of her faith and its noble moral ideals that go well beyond the merely legal and ritual realm and reach deep into the heart, the final citadel of sin, evil and also of true virtue. After this understandably angry first response, there will be a sense of despair: a law-centred Islam, in rejecting the salvation offer of the Gospel of grace, is not a scandal or an insult to Christianity but rather a tragic error. This view is condescending but no more so than the Muslim one which dismisses the Christian offer of salvation by grace as being the kind of regression described above.

Both Muslims and Christians typically refuse to take the rival seriously on its own terms. The deadlock between these two ideals of the life of monotheistic faith is permanent. The best position is to take the rival seriously on its own terms but conclude that it is simply in error. And that being in error in a matter of such ultimate moment is a tragedy, though not in the classical Greek sense. After all, no believer hesitates in proclaiming that total outsiders such as disbelievers are mistaken. Why be so cautious and diplomatic when dealing with the fate of rival religious family members?

In this essay, I have already raised the question of whether Paul, a Jew, continued to believe in one God. The final question here is: Can Paul qualify as a prophet of the one true God? This Muslim question has stimulated our inquiry although the reader had to wait until the end of our essay – and even then my answer is likely to be unsatisfying, hedged as it must be by complex qualifications and nuances. My considered guiding view, coloured by my own faith, is that Paul was a sincere preacher who got many things wrong. Sincerity is no bulwark against error. But, as a preacher, by definition, he got much right, since he was dealing with Jesus and the Jewish scriptures and a rich and authentic monotheistic tradition. (Some cynic might say that even a broken clock gets the time right twice per day.) Christians and Jews must give the same verdict regarding Muhammad – indeed must say that much if they are to be charitable but truthful. For if they say less, they do not give the man his due. If they say more, they do so at the risk of rejecting their own faith.

Granted that Paul was the last of the apostles of Christ, an apostle with honour in his native land, he was also a prophet *manqué,* the lost prophet who missed the mark, so to speak. But he was not simply a man of unfulfilled potential or misdirected energy. Where there are pretenders, there are even more pretences. But Paul was no false pretender. If he did pretend, he pretended, in the noblest sense, to the greatest things of the spirit. He broods in his theology as he attempts to make sense of his confused and unsettling experience of Jesus. Was he self-deceived? To outsiders, it must appear so. The comparison then is not to be with Jesus, a true prophet. Nor is the real analogy here with Muhammad – as if he were also in the wrong profession! Rather, it is with literary figures such as Charles Dickens who was not a novelist at heart but rather a novelist in the dramatic tradition of the master Shakespeare – but without knowing this truth. Like Milton, many men do not know which party they belong to until after they have reached the further side of experience.

If Muhammad was the last prophet, Paul was the lost prophet. That is the most charitable Islamic verdict on the man Muslims see as the founder of Christianity.

Notes

1 See my sequel to this volume, *An Islamic View of Christian Origins: The Nature of the New Testament*, forthcoming from Routledge.
2 For example, see the French thinker, Alain Badiou's pioneering *Saint Paul: The Foundation of Universalism* (Stanford: Stanford University Press, 2003).
3 In the bibliography, see the work of Peter Ochs who pioneered the Scriptural Reasoning movement.
4 Paul Gauguin's letter to the Danish painter J. F. Willumsen, sent in autumn 1890, is quoted in translation in H. W. Janson's magisterial survey of *History of Art* (Upper Saddle River, NJ: Simon & Schuster, 1995), 5th edition, p. 910.
5 See my *The Quran and the Secular Mind* (London: Routledge, 2007), pp. 27–28.

BIBLIOGRAPHY

No Muslim has written a commentary on any Pauline epistle. Islam's recorded authoritative sources – the Quran and the Prophet Muhammad's traditions – do not refer, in any clear or explicit way, to the Apostle Paul, his letters or his key ideas such as justification by faith alone. The Prophet's authentic traditions are collected in two canonical collections, those of Al-Bukhari and Al-Muslim.

S. Akhtar, 'Slaves of the Book', *The Times Higher Education Supplement*, October 1997.

S. Akhtar, 'Jerusalem, East and West', *The Times Higher Education Supplement*, February 2000.

S. Akhtar, *The Quran and the Secular Mind* (London: Routledge, 2007).

S. Akhtar, *Islam as Political Religion* (London: Routledge, 2010).

S. Akhtar, *An Islamic View of Christian Origins: The Nature of the New Testament* (London: Routledge).

I. Albayrak, 'The People of the Book in the Qur'an'. *Islamic Studies*, 47.3, (2008), 123–41.

T.D. Alexander, *Abraham in the Negev: A Source-Critical Investigation of Gen.20;1–22.19* (Carlisle: Paternoster, 1997).

C.F. Aling, *Egypt and Bible History* (Grand Rapids: Baker, 1981).

R. Alter, *Genesis* (New York: Norton, 1996).

C. Amos, 'Incomplete without the other: Isaac, Ishmael and a Hermeneutic of Diversity'. *Islam and Christian-Muslim Relations*, 20.3, (2009), 123–32.

E. Badawi and M.A.S. Haleem (eds.), *Arabic-English Dictionary of Qur'anic Usage* (Leiden: Brill, 2010).

R. Badenas, *Christ, the End of the Law: Romans 10:4 in Pauline Perspective* (Sheffield: JSOT Press, 1985).

A. Badiou, *Saint Paul: The Foundation of Universalism*, trans. R. Brassier (Stanford: Stanford University Press, 2003).

C. Bakhos, *Ishmael on the Border: Rabbinical Portrayals of the First Arab* (Albany: State University of New York Press, 2006).

C. Bakhos, 'Abraham Visits Ishmael: A Revisit'. *Journal for the Study of Judaism*, 38.4, (2007), 553–80.

C. Bakhos, *The Family of Abraham: Jewish, Christian, and Muslim Interpretations* (Cambridge, MA: Harvard University Press, 2014).
J.M.G. Barclay, *Obeying the Truth: A Study of Paul's Ethics in Galatians* (Minneapolis: Fortress Press, 1988).
W. Barclay, *New Testament Words* (London: SCM Press, 1964).
C.K. Barrett, *The Epistle to the Romans*, 2nd edition (Peabody: Hendrickson, 1991).
K. Barth, *The Epistle to the Romans*, trans. E. Hoskyns (London: Oxford University Press, 1993).
R. Bauckham, 'The Sonship of the Historical Jesus in Christology'. *Scottish Journal of Theology*, 31, (1978), 245–60.
R. Bauckham, *Jesus and the God of Israel* (Milton Keynes: Paternoster, 2008).
M. Al-Bukhari, *Sahih Al-Bukhari*, trans. and ed. Muhammad Muhsin Khan (Riyadh, Saudi Arabia: Darussalam Publishers, 1997).
H.D. Betz, *Galatians* (Hermeneia; Philadelphia, PA: Fortress, 1979).
P.M. Blowers, 'The Regula Fidei and the Narrative Character of Early Christian Faith'. *Pro Ecclesia*, 6.2, (1997), 32–45.
D. Boyarin, *A Radical Jew: Paul and the Politics of Identity* (Los Angeles: University of California Press, 1994).
D. Boyarin, 'The Gospel of the Memra: Jewish Binitarianism and the Prologue to John'. *Harvard Theological Review*, 94.3, (July 2001), 243–84.
D. Boyarin, *The Jewish Gospels: The Story of the Jewish Christ* (New York: The New Press, 2013).
G. Bristow, *Sharing Abraham?* (Istanbul: Doorlight Academic, 2017).
R. Brown, 'Explaining the Biblical Term 'Son(s) of God in Muslim Contexts'. *International Journal of Frontier Missiology*, 22.3, (2005), 91–6.
R.E. Brown, *An Introduction to the New Testament* (New Haven: Yale University Press, 2016).
F.F. Bruce, *The Acts of the Apostles* (Leicester: Inter-Varsity Press, 1990).
M. Casey, *From Jewish Prophet to Gentile God: The Origins and Development of New Testament Christology* (Cambridge: James Clarke, 1991).
J. and K. Court, *The New Testament World* (Englewood Cliffs, NJ: Prentice Hall, 1990).
K. Cragg, *Mosque Sermons: A Listener for the Preacher* (London: Melisende, 2008).
K. Cragg, *Iron in the Soul: Joseph and the Undoing of Violence* (London: Melisende, 2009).
J.G. Crossley, *Reading the New Testament: Contemporary Approaches* (London: Routledge, 2010).
A. De Botton, *Status Anxiety* (London: Hamish Hamilton, 2004).
T.L. Donaldson, *Paul and the Gentiles* (Minneapolis: Fortress Press, 1997).
M. Douglas, *Purity and Danger* (London: Routledge & Kegan Paul, 1966).
S.J. Duffy, *The Dynamics of Grace* (Collegeville: The Liturgical Press, 1993).
J.D.G. Dunn, *Jesus, Paul and the Law* (Louisville: Westminster John Knox Press, 1990).
J.D.G. Dunn, *The Epistle to the Galatians* (London: A&C Black, 1993).
J.D.G. Dunn, *Christology in the Making*, 2nd edition (London: SCM Press, 1996).
J.D.G. Dunn, '4QMMT and Galatians'. *NTS*, 43, (1997), 147–53.
J.D.G. Dunn, 'When was Jesus First Worshipped? In Dialogue with Larry Hurtado'. *Expository Times*, 116.6, (2005), 193–6.
J.D.G. Dunn, *The New Perspective on Paul* (Grand Rapids: Eerdmans, 2007).
J.D.G. Dunn, *Paul and the Gospels* (Grand Rapids: Eerdmans, 2011).
P. Eisenbaum, *Paul was Not a Christian* (New York: HarperOne, 2009).
C.J. Ellicott, *Commentaries, Critical and Grammatical* (Charleston: Nabu Press, 2011).
G. Fee, *Pauline Christology* (Peabody: Hendrickson, 2007).

R. Firestone, 'Ishmael', in *Encyclopedia of Islam*, 2nd edition, ed. P. Bearman et al. *(Leiden: Brill, 1980–2004).*

D. Ford and C.C. Pecknold (eds.), *The Promise of Scriptural Reasoning* (Oxford: Blackwell, 2006).

D.M. Freidenreich, 'Holiness and Impurity in the Torah and the Quran', *Comparative Islamic Studies*, 6.1, (2010), 5–22.

B. Freundel, *Contemporary Orthodox Judaism's Response to Modernity* (Jersey City: KTAV, 2004).

V.P. Furnish, *Jesus According to Paul* (Cambridge: Cambridge University Press, 1993).

I. Glaser, 'The Concept of Relationship as a Key to the Comparative Understanding of Christianity and Islam', in *Solid Ground: 25 Years of Evangelical Theology* (Leicester: Apollos), 247–55.

I. Glaser, 'Towards a Mutual Understanding of Christian and Islamic Concepts of Revelation', *Themelios*, 7.3, (April 1982), 16–22.

I. Glaser, 'Reading the Bible with Islam in Mind', *Anvil*, 31.1, (2015), 18–31.

K. Grieb, *The Story of Romans: A Narrative Defence of God's Righteousness* (Louisville: Westminster John Knox press, 2002).

S.H. Griffith, *The Bible in Arabic* (Princeton: Princeton University Press, 2013).

K.N. Gruneberg, *Abraham, Blessing and the Nations* (Berlin: Walter de Gruyter, 2003).

D. Guthrie, *Galatians* (London: Thomas Nelson, 1969).

G.W. Hansen, *Abraham in Galatians* (Sheffield: JSOT Press, 1989).

D. Harink, *Paul among the Postliberals* (Grand Rapids: Brazos press, 2003).

D. Harrington and J. Keenan, *Paul and Virtue Ethics* (Lanham: Rowman and Littlefield, 2010).

S. Harris, *The New Testament*, 2nd edition (Mountain View, CA: Mayfield, 1995).

L. Hurtado, 'The Origins of the Worship of Christ', in *Solid Ground: 25 Years of Evangelical Theology* (Leicester: Apollos, 2000), 69–83.

L. Hurtado, *Lord Jesus Christ: Devotion to Jesus in the Earliest Christianity* (Grand Rapids: Eerdmans, 2003).

M. Ibn-Ishaq, *The Life of Muhammad*, trans. Alfred Guillaume (Lahore: Oxford University Press, 1995).

H.W. Janson, *History of Art*, 5th edition (Upper Saddle River: Simon & Schuster, 1995).

J.G. Janzen, *Abraham and all the Families of the Earth* (Grand Rapids: Eerdmans, 1993).

S.E. Karesh and M.H. Hurvitz, *Encyclopedia of Judaism* (New York: Checkmark Books, 2006).

M.L. Klein, *The Fragment-Targums of the Pentateuch According to their Extant Sources* (Rome: Biblical Institute Press, 1980).

J. Klawans, *Impurity and Sin in Ancient Judaism* (Oxford: Oxford University Press, 2000).

H. Kassis, *A Concordance of the Qur'an* (Berkeley: University of California Press, 1983).

J. Kilgallen, 'The Strivings of the Flesh (Galatians 5:17)'. *Biblios*, 80, (1999), 113–4.

K.-Y. Kuschel, *Abraham: A Symbol of Hope for Jews, Christians and Muslims*, trans. J. Bowden (London: SCM Press, 1995).

C. Lamb, *A Policy of Hope: Kenneth Cragg and Islam* (London: Melisende, 2014).

J. Lambrecht, 'The Right Things You Want to Do: A Note on Galatians 5:17d'. *Biblica*, 79.4, (1998), 515–24.

M. Lodahl, *Claiming Abraham* (Grand Rapids: Brazos Press, 2010).

R. Lowell, *Selected Poems* (New York: Farrar, Straus and Giroux, 1976).

S.L. Lowin, 'Abraham in Islamic and Jewish Exegesis'. *Religion Compass*, 5.6, (2011), 224–35.

S.L. Lowin, *The Making of a Forefather: Abraham in Islamic and Jewish Exegetical Narratives* (Leiden: Brill, 2006).

M. Luther, *The Bondage of the Will*, eds. J.I. Packer and O.R. Johnson (Old Tapppan: Revell, 1957). Originally published in Latin as *De Servo Arbitrio*), Christmas, 1525.

M. Luther, *Luther's Works*, 55 vols. eds. H.T. Lehman and J. Pelikan (Philadelphia: Fortress, 2002).

T. Maalouf, *Arabs in the Shadow of Israel: The Unfolding of God's Prophetic Plan for Ishmael's Line* (Grand Rapids, MI: Kregel, 2003).

H. Maccoby, *The Mythmaker: Paul and the Invention of Christianity* (London: Weidenfeld and Nicolson, 1986).

H. Maccoby, *Paul and Hellenism* (London: SCM Press, 1991).

A. Marshall, *NASB-NIV Parallel New Testament in Greek and English, with Interlinear Translation* (Grand Rapids, MI: Zondervan-Regency Reference, 1986).

J.L. Martyn, *Galatians* (New York: Adam & Black, 1988).

H. Mazuz, 'Polemical Treatment of the Story of the Annunciation of Isaac's Birth in Islamic Sources'. *The Review of Rabbinic Judaism*, 17.2, (2014), 252–62.

B.M. Metzger, *The Canon of the New Testament* (Oxford: Clarendon Press, 1997).

B.M. Metzger, *A Textual Commentary on the Greek New Testament*, 4th edition (New York: United Bible Societies, 1994).

L. Morris, *Galatians: Paul's Charter of Christian Freedom* (Leicester: Inter-Varsity Press, 1996).

C. Moucarry, *The Search for Forgiveness* (Leicester: Inter-Varsity Press, 2004).

C. Moucarry, *Two Prayers for Today* (Tiruvalla: Christava Sahitya Samitha, 2007)

C.F.D. Moule, *The Origin of Christology* (Cambridge: Cambridge University Press, 1977).

C.F.D. Moule, *The Holy Spirit* (London, Oxford: Mowbrays, 1978).

C.F.D. Moule, *The Birth of the New Testament*, 3rd revised edition (London: Adam and Charles Black, 1981).

W. Mounce, *The Analytical Lexicon to the Greek New Testament* (Grand Rapids, MI: Zondervan/ HarperCollins, 1993).

A. Munzinger, *Discerning the Spirits: Theological and Ethical Hermeneutics in Paul* (Cambridge: Cambridge University Press, 2007).

M. Nanos (ed.), *The Galatians Debate* (Peabody: Hendrickson, 2002).

E. Nestle *et al.*, *Novum Testamentum Graece*, 27th edition (Stuttgart: Deutsche Bibelgesellschaft, 2004).

S. Nicholson, *Dynamic Oneness: The Significance and Flexibility of Paul's One-God Language* (Eugene: Pickwick Publications, 2010).

F. Nietzsche, *Beyond Good and Evil*, trans. M. Cowan (Chicago: Henry Regnery, 1955).

F. Nietzsche, *The Anti-Christ*, trans. R.J. Hollingdale (Harmondsworth: Penguin, 1968).

F. Nietzsche, *Ecce Homo*, trans. R.J. Hollingdale (Harmondsworth: Penguin, 1979).

P. Ochs, T*extual Reasonings* (London: Eerdmans, 2003).

K.S. Oliphint, *God with Us* (Wheaton: Crossway, 2012).

G.R. Osborne, *The Hermeneutical Spiral* (Downers Grove: IVP, 2006).

F.E. Peters (ed.), *Judaism, Christianity, and Islam: The Classical Texts and Their Interpretation* (Princeton, NJ: Princeton University Press, 1990), vol. 2.

S. Poole, 'Review of Alain de Botton's *Status Anxiety*', *The Guardian*, March 27, 2004.

M. Poorthuis, 'Hagar's Wanderings: Between Judaism and Islam'. *Der Islam*, 90.2, (1989), 220–44.

F. Rahman, *Revival and Reform in Islam*, ed. with intro by E. Moosa (Oxford: Oneworld, 2000).

E.J. Revell, 'Scribal Emendations', in D.N. Freedman ed. *The Anchor Yale Bible Dictionary* (New York: Doubleday, 1992).

R. Routledge, *Old Testament Theology* (Nottingham: Apollos, 2008).

C. Rowland, *Christian Origins*, 2nd edition (London: SPCK, 2002).
E.P. Sanders, *Paul and Palestinian Judaism* (Philadelphia: Fortress, 1977).
I. Scott, *Implicit Epistemology in the Letters of Paul* (Tubingen: Mohr Siebeck, 2006).
F.A. Spina, *The Faith of the Outsider: Exclusion and Inclusion in the Biblical Story* (Cambridge: Eerdmans, 2005).
K. Stendahl, *Paul among Jews and Gentiles* (Philadelphia: Fortress Press, 1976).
C. Tilling, 'The Deliverance of God, and of Paul?' *JSPL*, 1.1, (2011), 85–101.
C. Tilling, *Paul's Divine Christology* (Tubingen: Mohr Siebeck, 2012).
E. Tov, *Textual Criticism of the Hebrew Bible*, 3rd edition (Minneapolis: Fortress, 2012).
P. Trible and L. Russell (eds.), *Hagar, Sarah and Their Children* (Louisville, KY: Westminster John Knox Press, 2006).
B. Trick, 'Sons, Seed, and Children of Promise in Galatians: Discerning the Coherence in Paul's Model of Abrahamic Descent' (Duke Divinity School, 2010, unpublished doctoral thesis).
C. Trueman et al. (eds.), *Solid Ground: 25 Years of Evangelical Theology* (Leicester: Apollos/Inter-Varsity Press, 2000).
K.J. Vanhoozer, *Dictionary for Theological Interpretation of the Bible* (Grand Rapids: Baker Academic, 2005).
J.R. Vannoy *et al.*, *The NIV Study Bible*, 5th edition (Grand Rapids: Zondervan, 2011).
F. Watson, *Paul and the Hermeneutics of Faith* (London: T&T Clark, 2004).
G. Wenham, *Genesis 16–50, vol. 2, Word Biblical Commentary* (Dallas: Word Books, 1994).
D. Wenham, *Paul: Follower of Jesus or Founder of Christianity* (Grand Rapids, MI: Eerdmans, 1995).
N.T. Wright, *The Climax of the Covenant: Christ and the Law in Pauline Theology* (Edinburgh: T&T Clark, 1991).
N.T. Wright, *The Crown and the Fire: Meditations on the Cross and the Life of the Spirit* (London: SPCK, 1992).
N.T. Wright, *Jesus and the Victory of God*, (London: SPCK, 1996a), vol. 2.
N.T. Wright, 'Paul, Arabia and Elijah (Galatians 1:17)'. *Journal of Biblical Literature*, 115.4, (1996b), 683–92.
N.T. Wright, *What Saint Paul Really Said* (London: Lion, 1997).
N.T. Wright, *Paul: In Fresh Perspective* (Minneapolis: Fortress, 2005).
C.J.H. Wright, *The Mission of God's People* (Grand Rapids: Zondervan, 2010).
R. Yudkowsky, 'Chaos or Chiasm?: The Structure of Abraham's Life'. *Jewish Bible Quarterly*, 35.2, (2007), 109–14.
H.M. Zellentin, *The Qur'an's Legal Culture* (Tubingen: Mohr Siebeck, 2013).
J. Ziesler, *Paul's Letter to the Romans* (London: SCM Press, 1989).
S. Zwemer, *Arabia the Cradle of Islam* (New York: Fleming Revell, 1900).
S. Zwemer, *Islam: A Challenge to Faith* (New York: Laymen's, 1907).

INDEX